ETHNICITY AND SUBSTANCE ABUSE

ABOUT THE AUTHORS

Grace Xueqin Ma, Ph.D., CHES, is an associate professor of public and community health in the Department of Health Studies, principal investigator and director of the Center for Asian Tobacco Education, Cancer Awareness, and Research (ATECAR) at Temple University. She has many years of experiences in research, teaching, grants management, as well as collaboration with other academic research institutions, Asian community-based organizations, and governmental agencies in the U.S. and China. Dr. Ma is nationally and internationally recognized for her work in transcultural and behavioral health issues among ethnic minorities, especially health service delivery, community-based tobacco and cancer control, substance abuse prevention and intervention research and health program evaluation. She has directed and co-directed fourteen (14) health research projects funded by the National Institutes of Health and other Federal agencies. Dr. Ma is the author and co-author of more than 50 scientific journal articles, about 60 research monographs and health education curricula, and numerous seminal books, including *The Culture of Health: Asian Communities in the United States* (1999) and *Rethinking Ethnicity and Health Care: A Sociocultural Perspective* (1999).

George Henderson, Ph.D., is a professor of human relations, sociology and education at the University of Oklahoma, where he has been awarded four distinguished professorships. A civil rights scholar and lecturer, he has served as a consultant to numerous state, national and international organizations. Dr. Henderson's work has been nationally and internationally recognized in the areas of cross-cultural counseling, transcultural health care, and substance abuse issues of minority populations, among others. He is the author or co-author of 28 books and more than 50 articles. His books include *Cultural Diversity in the Workplace* (1994); *Social Work Interventions: Helping People of Color* (1994); *Migrants, Immigrants, and Slaves* (1995); *Understanding Indigenous and Foreign Cultures* (1996); *Human Relations Issues in Management* (1996); *Our Souls to Keep: Black/White Relations in America* (1999); and *Rethinking Ethnicity and Healthcare: A Sociocultural Perspective* (1999).

ETHNICITY AND SUBSTANCE ABUSE

Prevention and Intervention

By

GRACE XUEQIN MA, PH.D.

and

GEORGE HENDERSON, PH.D.

CHARLES C THOMAS • PUBLISHER, LTD.
Springfield • Illinois • U.S.A.

Published and Distributed Throughout the World by

CHARLES C THOMAS • PUBLISHER, LTD.
2600 South First Street
Springfield, Illinois 62704

ISBN 0-398-07330-9 (hard)
ISBN 0-398-07331-7 (paper)

Library of Congress Catalog Card Number: 2002020302

With THOMAS BOOKS *careful attention is given to all details of manufacturing
and design. It is the Publisher's desire to present books that are satisfactory as to their
physical qualities and artistic possibilities and appropriate for their particular use.*
THOMAS BOOKS *will be true to those laws of quality that assure a good name
and good will.*

*Printed in the United States of America
MM-R-3*

Library of Congress Cataloging-in-Publication Data

Ethnicity and substance abuse : prevention and intervention / [edited] by Grace
Xueqin Ma and George Henderson.
    p. cm.
  Includes bibliographical references and index.
  ISBN 0-398-07330-9 -- ISBN 0-398-07331-7 (pbk.)
    1. Minorities–Drug use–United States. 2. Ethnic groups–Drug use–United States.
3. Drug abuse–United States–Prevention. 4. Drug abuse–Treatment–United States.
5. Minorities–Services for–United States. 6. Ethnic groups–Services for–United
States. I. Ma, Grace Xueqin, 1962- II. Henderson, George, 1932-

HV5824.E85 E877 2002
262.29'1525'08900973–dc21
                                                  2002020302

CONTRIBUTORS

Jasjit S. Ahluwalia, M.D., M.P.H., is an associate professor of internal medicine and director of research in the Department of Community Health and Preventive Medicine at the Morehouse School of Medicine. Dr. Ahluwalia is also a Robert Wood Johnson Foundation Generalist Physician Faculty Scholar, whose research interests focus on smoking cessation, hypertension, health policies and services, outcomes research, and minority health access to health care.

Marné Castillo, M.Ed., is employed at the Philadelphia College of Osteopathic Medicine in the Clinical Learning and Assessment Center. She received her M.Ed. in psychoeducation. She is a Ph.D. candidate in public health in the Health Studies Department at Temple University where she is focusing her studies on health communication and Latino health care issues.

Anita Chisholm, M.Ed., is director of the American Indian Institute, College of Continuing Education, University of Oklahoma. Ms. Chisholm received her B.A. and M.Ed. from Northwestern Oklahoma State University. For twenty-five years she has administrated grant and contract programs funded by federal, state and foundation sources totaling over twenty million dollars. She has developed and directed numerous major national, regional and state programs in child substance abuse, HIV/AIDS and culturally competence research. Ms. Chisholm is also the editor or co-editor of more than 40 curricular of various topics.

Kenneth C. Chu, Ph.D. received his Ph.D. in physical organic chemistry from the University of California at Los Angeles, working with Dr. Donald J. Cram, the 1987 Nobel Laureate. He has been with the National Institutes of Health for 27 years, and 25 years with the National Cancer Institute. He has more than 240 scientific publications in the field of cancer. His current research interests include the study of health disparities in special populations. He is with the Center to Reduce Cancer Health Disparities headed by Dr. Harold Freeman at the National Cancer Institute. Dr. Chu is the program director of the Special Population Networks for Cancer Awareness, Training and Research.

Janette Cline, M.H.R., is a substance abuse prevention coordinator for the Southwest Center for the Application of Prevention Technologies at the University of Oklahoma. She has been working in the field of substance abuse prevention for approximately 11 years with a focus on program evaluation.

Dorie Klein D. Crim, Ph.D., is a senior research scientist at the Public Health Institute. Her research and writing have focused on substance abuse and criminal justice issues, particularly those affecting Native American women. Her recent projects with American Indian communities in California have included a needs assessment of pregnant and parenting substance-involved women, evaluations of youth mental health service planning and women's HIV prevention, and a statewide needs assessment and evaluation guide.

Douglas S. Goldsmith, Ph.D., is an anthropologist who has done extensive field research focusing on drug injecting low-income people, many of whom are homeless. He has worked at numerous agencies, including the National Development and Research Institutes.

Robert M. Goodman, Ph.D., M.P.H., is a professor in community health sciences at the Tulane University School of Public Health and Tropical Medicine. Dr. Goodman has written extensively on issues concerning community health development, and the institutionalization of health programs. He has been the principal investigator and evaluator for numerous projects funded by the Centers for Disease Control and Prevention, the National Cancer Institute, the Center for Substance Abuse Prevention, the Children's Legal Defense Fund, and several state health departments.

Kari Jo Harris, Ph.D., M. P.H., is a research assistant professor of behavioral science and public health at the Public Health Institute in Berkeley, California. Her areas of interest include community health and development, evaluation research, women's health, community-based interventions, smoking cessation, primary prevention of chronic diseases, adolescent pregnancy, and HIV/AIDS.

Kara Hawthorne, B.S., MPH (c) currently works at the Philadelphia Health Management Corporation as a health educator for African American substance abusers. Her training and research experiences have focused on community and public health education and addiction prevention.

Sue Holtby, M.P.H., is a senior research scientist at the Public Health Institute in Berkeley, California. She has conducted research focusing on patterns of substance use among women of reproductive age, including pregnant Native Americans.

Judith Martin, M.D., is a physician trained in family practice who has worked with the multiethnic populations of the San Francisco Bay Area since 1978, and in addiction medicine since 1986. She is the medical director of the 14th Street Clinic, an outpatient facility addressing treatment needs of addicted patients and their families. She is a member of the American Association of Addiction Medicine, and the California Society of Addiction Medicine.

Alberto G. Mata, Jr., Ph.D., is a professor of human relations at the University of Oklahoma. He has served as a consultant and researcher on various planning groups, grants and workgroups, including those sponsored by the Office of the Surgeon General, the Office of Minority Health, the Office of Substance Abuse Prevention, the Centers for Disease Control, the National Institute for Mental Health, Substance Abuse Mental Health Service Administration, the National Institute on Drug Abuse, and the Administration for Families, Youth and Children.

Gene A. McGrady, M.D., M.P.H., is an associate professor in the Department of Community Health and Preventive Medicine at the Morehouse School of Medicine. He has a strong interest in training primary care physicians, particularly minorities, for careers in medically underserved communities.

Thomas O'Hare, Ph.D., A.C.S.W., is an associate professor in the School of Social Work at Boston College. His research interests center on co-occurring mental health and substance abuse problems and evidence-based social work practice. He is the author of numerous articles published in various prestigious journals addressing the issues of alcohol and other drug abuse among youth and adults.

Linda Pederson, Ph.D., is employed in the Department of Community Health and Preventative Medicine at the Morehouse School of Medicine. She has extensive research and training experiences in smoking cessation among African Americans. And she is involved in activities that provide future primary care physicians with the skills they need to scientifically analyze the health and health care delivery problems of ethnic minority and other underserved communities.

Deborah Jones-Saumty, Ph.D., is a chief executive officer with American Indian Associates and a clinical assistant professor at the University of Oklahoma. Her research has focused on substance abuse issues and recently developed treatment programs.

Steven E. Shive, Ph.D., M.P.H., is an assistant professor in the Department of Health and Community Services at the California State University of Chico, California. He currently serves as a research associate with the Asian Tobacco and Cancer Education Research Center (ATECAR) at Temple University. His research and publications are in the areas of ethnic differences in substance use; tobacco use among adolescents and adults; sources of tobacco procurement by minors; and knowledge, attitudes and behaviors related to tobacco use among Asian Americans.

Trusandra Taylor, M.D., is an internist with expertise in the field of addiction medicine and managed health care. She is the medical director for Bowling Green Brandywine in Kennett Square, Pennsylvania. She has over 20 years experience in a variety of clinical settings involved in the treatment of substance-related disorders. She is a member of the American Society of Addiction Medicine and also serves on several boards and committees.

Jamil Toubbeh, Ph.D., is an adjunct professor and a senior research associate in the Asian Tobacco and Cancer Education Research Center (ATECAR), and he also serves on its advisory and research committees at Temple University. He is nationally and internationally renowned for his work on public policy that affects ethnic minorities in the U.S. as well as academic program development in a wide range of public health and allied health fields.

Thanh Van Tran, Ph.D., is a professor and chairperson of Ph.D. Program in the School of Social Work at Boston College. He has extensive knowledge of mental health problems and substance abuse, especially among ethnic minority populations such as Asian Americans.

Walter Tsou, M.D., M.P.H., is the health commissioner for Philadelphia, Pennsylvania. He has a distinguished career in public health and currently serves on the executive board of the American Public Health Association and the national board of physicians for a national health program. He is a contributing editor of *Physician's News Digest* and *Pennsylvania Medicine.* He was named as the Practitioner of the Year 2001 by the Philadelphia County Medical Society. Dr. Tsou received his M.D. from the University of Pennsylvania; M.P.H from Johns Hopkins School of Hygiene and Public Health; and an honorary doctorate in medical sciences from Drexel University.

Beverly Wright, Ph.D., is director of the Deep South Center for Environmental Justice at Xavier University in New Orleans. She has been an effective advocate for utilizing social ecology approaches for substance abuse issues.

Elaine Zahnd, Ph.D., is a sociologist and a senior research scientist at the Public Health Institute in Berkeley, California. Her research has focused on women's behavioral health, substance abuse, violence and welfare issues among ethnic minority and low-income groups.

This book is dedicated to health care professionals who make it possible for their clients or patients to achieve healthy and substance-free lifestyles.

PREFACE

Ample research findings support the notion that in order to be optimally effective treating patients or clients, health care practitioners must have an adequate understanding of cultures different from their own. Although this book focuses most of its attention on ethnic minority substance abusers, considerable mention is made of their White peers, too. Thus, we offer cultural points and counterpoints—all of them given to achieve three objectives: (1) to make care providers aware of cultural factors that affect substance abuse and cessation; (2) to review multidisciplinary research studies in order to ascertain helpful and unhelpful health care practices; and (3) to provide practical suggestions for improving community-wide substance prevention and intervention programs.

The areas of knowledge covered in this book range from theoretical issues to historical perspectives, from objective data to subjective interpretations of them, from traditional to iconoclastic approaches to health care. And we have opted to use a spiral method of content; that is, information discussed in Part One is revisited again in greater detail in other parts of the book. The risk in this strategy is that some readers will view it as data overload instead of repetition for a positive effect. In the end, we decided that if we were to err it would be on the side of presenting too much instead of too little information.

From the beginning, we have tried to answer three questions: What kind of treatment and services do most ethnic minority substance abusers receive in our nation's hospitals, clinics and other community rehabilitation facilities? How effective are those programs? What can be done, when necessary, to improve the quality of treatment and services? The triadic relationship between culture, ethnicity and substance use is evident in answers to those questions.

Implicit throughout this volume is our belief that *how* care is given to substance abusers is just as important as *what* kind of care they receive. We know that there are many culturally sensitive and organizationally effective practitioners scattered throughout the United States. Our concern is that there are too few of them. Therefore, it is also a goal of this book to be of value to college and university professors, substance abuse workshop presenters, and in-service consultants who prepare professional helpers and paraprofessionals to render quality services to substance abusers.

As we edited the final drafts of the manuscript, it became evident to us beyond all doubt that it is counterproductive to treat all substance users and abusers as though they are a homogeneous group. In terms of ethnic minorities, we offer data that show which substance abuse behaviors African American, Asian Americans, Hispanic Americans, and Native Americans have in common as well as others that they do not share. We believe that it is important to be aware of these cultural similarities and differences. It is also important that care is taken to avoid creating ethnic group stereotypes and generalizations that do not leave room for individual differences. Therefore, being culturally aware to the extent the contributors to this book recommend can be a daunting challenge, but it is not an impossible one.

More than anything else, it is our wish that this book will help care providers to skillfully improve the quality of help they give substance abusers. That is not much for them to do; it will be life-threatening to substance abusers if they refuse to do it. If one person at risk is helped because of someone reading this book, the effort was worthwhile.

GRACE X. MA
GEORGE HENDERSON

ACKNOWLEDGMENTS

We gratefully acknowledge all the contributors. Further, we thank Betty Leverich and Shirley Marshall for typing what must at times seemed like endless drafts of the book. Our thanks also go to publishers who granted us permissions for adapting the following materials, including: (1) Pederson, L., Ahlwailia, J., Harris, K.J., & McGrady, G. (2000). Smoking cessation among African Americans. *Preventive Medicine.* Vol 31, (1) 23-38. Used with kind permission from Academic Press; (2) O'Hare, T. & Tran, V.T. (1998). Substance abuse among Southeast Asians in the U.S.: Implications for practice and research. *Social Work Health Care.* Vol. 26(3), 69-80, used with kind permission from The Haworth Press, Inc.

CONTENTS

ETHNICITY AND SUBSTANCE ABUSE

PART I

ETHNICITY MATTERS

Chapter 1

CONCEPTS OF ADDICTION IN ETHNIC MINORITY POPULATIONS

GEORGE HENDERSON AND GRACE XUEQIN MA

Substance abuse is a significant public health problem for all racial and ethnic groups. And it is becoming increasingly important to understand its impact on the ethnic minority groups that comprise American society, especially because they now account for 29.4 percent of our nation's population: Hispanics (12.5%), Blacks (12.3%), Asians and Pacific Islanders (3.7%), and American Indians, Eskimos and Aleuts (0.9%). The U.S. 2000 census documents an Hispanic population increase of 61.2 percent (from 21.9 million to 35.3 million), the Black population increased 15.7 percent (from 30 million to 34.7 million), the Asian and Pacific Islander population increased 45.2 percent (from 7.3 million to 10.6 million, and the American Indian, Eskimo and Aleut population increased 25 percent (from 2 million to 2.5 million).

The White flight out of our nation's major urban centers, combined with a significant influx of Blacks and Hispanics in particular, has resulted in nearly half (48) of the nation's largest cities being occupied mainly by ethnic minorities. Along with those changes have come differences in community substance use and dependency patterns.

DEFINITIONS

The term *drug addiction* is synonymous with *substance dependence* or *substance abuse.* These terms imply a physiological increase of tolerance to a substance; that is, more and more of it is required to achieve the same effect. When a substance addiction develops, the dependent individual cannot wait too long

5

between doses before his or her craving for it and dependence on it results in physical withdrawal symptoms. However, the time it takes for a substance to become addictive varies according to the substance. For example, addiction usually occurs in a shorter period of time for heroin or cocaine users than it does for alcohol or marijuana users. Contrary to popular opinion, alcohol and marijuana can cause the progressive deterioration of an individual's resistance to other drugs. Thus the term *gateway drugs* refers to alcohol, marijuana, inhalants and certain prescription drugs—to mention a few substances that may cause individual users to experiment with illicit substances.

Drawing on the World Health Organization's definition of drug addiction, we offer the following modified definition. *Any form of substance use which goes beyond traditional and customary dietary uses or deviates from a medical regimen and results in uncontrolled compulsive intake of the substance is an addiction.* Within that context, substance abusers are people whose substance use results in a loss of control over its intake and that, in turn, interferes with their health, employment or relations with their significant other persons, but they continue using it.

PATTERNS OF DRUG OR CHEMICAL USE

One thing is evident in the literatures: substance use is a complex paradox. For example, people who use drugs may do so to fit in socially or to obtain feelings of pleasure or to get relief from emotional stress or physical pain. Some people are infrequent drug users; others use drugs continuously. Thus we have the paradox: most individuals can take drugs or leave them alone; a minority of people should not use certain drugs but they do and cannot stop. Simply stated, they are hooked or addicted.

While the debates continue regarding the extent of substance abuse and dependency, it is less problematic for law enforcement officials and medical personnel. They describe substance abuse and dependency as culminating into a national epidemic which is destroying too many of our citizens. Relevant scientific journal articles note that children who are substance abusers, when compared to their peers who are nonsubstance users, are more likely to: (1) have parents who smoke cigarettes, drink alcohol or use other substances excessively; (2) come from physically and/or emotionally broken homes; (3) believe themselves to be worthless, helpless, impulsive and unhappy; (4) have friends who use substances; and (5) participate less in academically enhancing school activities. These, then, are the progenitors of substance abuse parents and who themselves often become such parents. A few selected national statistics highlight the grim nature of substance use and abuse:

- More than 10 billion amphetamine tablets are produced each year. This is enough to provide every man, woman and child in the country with over 30 doses.
- Fifty percent of all traffic fatalities are alcohol related. The percentage is higher among persons ages 16 to 24. In this age group, six out of ten traffic fatalities are alcohol related.
- Almost half of American males ages 15 through 20, and a slightly lesser percent of the females in this age bracket, drink alcohol.
- One-third of the American children who smoke marijuana began in grade school.
- Every 30 minutes a child will die in a motor vehicle accident, and in most of these instances alcohol or some other substance is involved.

Upon close analysis, it is evident that some individuals partake of particular substances because they believe that, when taken in "appropriate" amounts, no harm will occur to them. Some individuals abstain from using those same substances because they believe that even a small amount of them is injurious to their health. Yet other individuals, most of whom are unable to stop, excessively use them.

It is debatable whether there is a medical crisis. Despite the fact that drug addiction is labeled a "disease" by the American College of Physicians, the American Medical Association, the American Psychiatric Association, the World Health Organization and other health care organizations, countless Americans believe that drug dependency is a moral weakness rather than a disease. Whether it is a disease or a moral weakness or both, substance dependency is 100 percent debilitating; nobody who is addicted is spared the consequences. Substance abuse has four characteristics: (1) it is primary; (2) it is progressive; (3) it is chronic; and (4) sometimes it is fatal. Ideally, treatment of addicts involves whole persons, which includes their physical, mental, psychological and spiritual domains. And there are four mood-altering stages of substance use: experimental, regular, daily and dependency. Upon close examination, it is evident that these stages encompass behavioral and attitudinal dimensions of substance use that can lead to abuse.

Experimental users of substances such as beer, wine, whiskey or marijuana most often are infrequent users who try to fit in or to be more sociable with their friends, acquaintances or even strangers. And some people try substances, mainly alcohol, to relax or to unwind after a hard day's work.

Regular substance users move toward dependency as a result of their weekly or monthly patterns of substance use. Relatedly, their behaviors include doing things such as lying about their substance use, being absent from their jobs or frequently making heretofore atypical caustic comments when questioned about their substance use. Like a bad play, lies build on lies and before long, regular users are trapped in a cycle of denial, remorse and increased substance use. If unchecked, their substance intake escalates to a *daily preoccupation.*

Individuals obsessed with getting "high" on a daily basis must also try to insure that they have a daily supply of their substance of choice. Eventually, it is "normal" for these persons to be high. This is the *preaddiction stage,* when substance use ceases to be a social activity. Instead, it becomes a means of psychological escape from daily tensions and inhibitions. Although initially these individuals are in reasonable control of their substance use, gradually they lose control. Typically, they believe they can stop the slide into substance abuse at any time they choose to. However, they almost always "choose" to keep using it. When this happens, they have become dependent on a substance.

The same substance can affect different people differently, and often it affects the same person differently at different times. There is no clear-cut evidence that moderate substance use has any lasting harmful effects on the mind or body. However, there is strong evidence that excessive substance use does have permanent harmful effects on the body. The progression through the preceding stages does not occur in a social vacuum. Family members, friends, coworkers and, sometimes, strangers are also affected.

STAGES OF SUBSTANCE ABUSE

The behaviors of most substance abusers are predictable: They will lie, cheat, steal or do anything else to get high. As noted earlier, the road to addiction begins when substance use is no longer social but a means of psychological escape. Initially, preaddicted substance users are in reasonable control of their substance intake. As their abuse of a substance gets progressively worse, most users' self-image also get progressively worse and their ego strength ebbs. Further, they are unable to consistently control their non-substance-related behaviors, thereby prompting altercations with their loved ones. The greater the alienation, the higher and more rigid the abusers' defense mechanisms become. Sadly, they become victims of their own defense mechanisms. Jellinek (1968) concluded that alcoholism results in five basic types of alcoholics: alpha, beta, gamma, delta and epsilon. We will use his classifications to describe substance abusers in general.

Alphas rely on a substance to boost their morale, bolster their self-confidence or relieve pain. Alphas could be regarded as social substance users except for the fact that they often use a substance too much, at the wrong times, and with the wrong people, thereby affronting their significant others. Alphas do not lose control and therefore they can abstain when they want to. In short, they are presubstance abusers.

Betas, similar to alphas, do not become addicted, and they suffer no withdrawal symptoms when forced to stop using a particular substance. But their nutritional habit of substituting a substance for necessary amount of proteins, minerals and vitamins leads to medical problems such as peripheral neuritis, cirrhosis and gastritis.

Gammas' psychological dependence on drugs also grows into physical dependence. They lose control of their substance intake and suffer withdrawal when they abstain. In the early and middle stages of this abuse, the users' tolerance for their substance of choice is quite strong. But it decreases abruptly and pushes the user into the next type. *Deltas* maintain a steady concentration of the abused substance in their bloodstream. Seldom visibly high, deltas suffer withdrawal symptoms during times of abstention from using substances.

Then there is the last type: epsilons. Despite the assertion that they can stop their substance intake, *epsilons* constantly look forward to and plan for their next high. They believe that they no longer have a choice; they must get a high (or a fix), albeit temporary. Getting a supply of drugs becomes the most prominent activity in these users' lives. They will spend their last money and, if necessary, sell themselves or steal from other people to get a fix. They hide their supplies so that, whenever possible, their substance is available to them. Epsilons are constantly fearful of people stealing their supplies. At first, their lies about drug use are preposterous to other people; after a while they are even ridiculous to the epsilons. These are the most difficult persons to rehabilitate.

Within all communities, the ubiquitous nature of substance abuse disrupts lives absolutely. Families, friendships and individual personhoods are casualties. A reminder of this fact is a well-known saying of alcoholics: "I used to live to drink. Now I drink to live." It is important to remember that people of color who are substance abusers are in many ways a microcosm of the larger society. They are reflections of incalculative unfilled human potentials that characterize substance abusers. That is the human and cultural aspect of substance abuse. Sadly, countless children believe that some type of substance use, mainly alcohol or cigarettes, is a mark of sophistication, as part of a coming-of-age rite. This belief is bolstered by commercial advertising and movies that depict drinking and smoking as signs of maturity.

SUBSTANCE CATEGORIES

It is worthwhile to briefly review the six categories of substances: depressants, cannabis, stimulants, hallucinogens, inhalants and narcotics.

Depressants are normally ingested through the mouth, but they can also be injected. For example, alcohol can be injected in a fruit and consumed unnoticed during family meals or in public places. The effects of alcohol will produce slurred speech, disorientation, erratic behavior, and drowsiness. Other depressants which are commonly abused are barbiturates such as Valium®, Librium® and Quaaludes®, and they have several nicknames: ludes, spoors, yellow jackets, reds, pink ladies, blue devils, and barbs. Concerned persons should be on the alert for multicolored pills in the suspected user's possession or property. And, of course, they should be careful not to leave barbiturates in places where young children can get them. No matter how well a medication is hidden, however, older children will probably find it. Barbiturates are taken either orally or injected into the vein to speed up their effect. Barbiturate users have some of the same symptoms as persons who drink: drowsiness, stupor, dullness, slurred speech, drunken appearance and vomiting.

The next category is *cannabis*, or marijuana, which has many pseudonyms such as pot, reefer, tea, weed, grass, Acapulco gold, hemp, Mary Jane, joint, and roach. Cannabis is taken orally in pill form, placed into food for consumption, and, more commonly, smoked like cigarettes. The effects of cannabis produce euphoria, relaxed inhibitions, an increase in heart and pulse rate, reddened eyes, enlarged eye pupils, increased appetite, sleepiness, wandering mind, lack of coordination, craving for sweets, and disoriented behavior. Marijuana emits a strong odor similar to burnt hemp rope, and the smell settles in clothes. Other signs are small seeds in pockets and purses, cigarette rolling papers, and discolored finger tips.

Another chemical category is *stimulants*. Nicotine, caffeine, cocaine and amphetamines are in this category. Cocaine has nicknames such as coke, snow and speedball (a mixture of cocaine and heroin). Amphetamines, pills of different colors, also have several slang names, including pep pills, bennies, whites, co-pilots, and white crosses. Cocaine is the more difficult of the two to detect. Signs of cocaine use include white powder wrapped in tinfoil or cellophane, hypodermic syringes and needles, used cotton balls, and burnt bottle caps or spoons. Both cocaine and amphetamines can be injested by sniffing the powder, injecting the powder when in liquid form, or orally swallowing it. The effects of stimulants include increased alertness, excitation, euphoria, increase in pulse rate and blood pressure, insomnia, loss of appetite, aggressive behavior, giggling, silliness, rapid speech, confused thinking, dry mouth, and uncontrollable shaking.

The fourth category of chemicals is *hallucinogens*. The most abused hallucinogen is lysergic acid diethylamid, commonly known as LSD, acid, cubes and sugar lump. This drug has a unique smell and sometimes looks like discolored sugar cubes. When using LSD a person may emit a strong body odor. It is taken orally and produces illusions and hallucinations, poor perception of time and distance, feelings of detachment, incoherent speech, cold hands and feet, vomiting, laughing and crying.

The fifth category is *inhalants*. Technically known as hydrocarbons, they are associated with paint thinner, glue, gasoline and aerosol propellants. Often, one can detect inhalant use by finding large amounts of glue, stained handkerchiefs, paper bags with glue smeared in or on them, rags soaked with gasoline, or paint thinner found in bags and aerosol cans without any evidence of how they were used. These drugs are consumed by inhaling. Their effects include feelings of euphoria, giddiness, loss of inhibitions, aggressiveness, delusions, and depression. Physical symptoms include drowsiness, headaches, and nausea. Severe and lasting brain damage or nerve damage is caused by prolonged use of inhalants.

The last category is *narcotics*. This is largely heroin, which is known as horse, smack, crack, H, junk, snow, and skag. Clues which suggest heroin use are similar to cocaine clues: used cotton balls, hypodermic syringes and needles, tourniquet, and burnt bottle caps or spoons. This drug can be inhaled as a powder, injected as a liquid, or smoked in a cigarette by removing some of the tobacco and sifting the substance through the remaining tobacco. Symptoms are drowsiness; needle marks on the arms, thighs and other parts of the body where blood veins are located; watery eyes; blood stains on shirt or blouse sleeves; runny nose; constricted pupils; and nausea.

ALCOHOLISM: A COMMON ADDICTION

In 1999, 40 percent of the current alcohol users in the general population also had used cigarettes in the past month, compared with 18 percent of current alcohol abstainers. Current alcohol users are about five times more likely than nonusers to report past month use of an illicit drug (11% vs. 2%) (National Household Survey on Drug Abuse, 2000). Eighty percent of alcoholics in treatment programs are dependent on at least one drug (Miller, 1991). According to the U.S. Department of Health and Human Services (USDHHS) (2000), at least 14.8 million persons consume illicit drugs monthly. And it is important to note that ethyl alcohol is a drug, even if society does not always view it as such. Also in 1999, about 6.7 percent of the population over the age of twelve had an illicit drug problem; an estimated 12.4 million were alcohol dependent; and 20.2 million were alcohol abusing (USDHHS, 2000). Ninety-five percent of the alcoholics were middle-class Americans.

In 1994, research conducted by the Institute of Medicine stated that approximately four percent of women had alcohol abuse or alcohol dependence problems. According to the Substance Abuse and Mental Health Service Administration (1997), heavy alcohol users are more numerous than individuals who report no alcohol use in the past year (8.0% vs. 4.4%) and heavy drinkers are more likely than abstainers to have skipped one or more days of work in the past month (11.3% vs. 5.1%). The National Institute on Alcohol Abuse and Alcoholism, in a research report published in 1999 cited 41 percent of all fatal automobile crashes involved alcohol. Nine percent of injury crashes and five percent of property damage crashes involved alcohol. The National Institute on Alcohol Abuse and Alcoholism also reported that nearly 53 percent of the adult population of the U.S. (98 million persons ages 18 or older) had a family history of alcoholism or problem drinking. Approximately seven million children under age 18 lived in households with at least one alcoholic parent. Almost 14 million U.S. adults met medical criteria for the diagnosis of alcohol abuse or alcoholism. Using a commonly accepted formula that one person's behavior affects four to six other people, then 93 to 139 million Americans are regularly affected by a substance abuser.

Of the more than 10 million victims of violent crime each year, almost one in four, or nearly three million, reported that the offender had been drinking alcohol prior to committing the crime (Greenfeld, 1998). Alcohol involvement in perpetrators of violence has been estimated to be 28 percent to 86 percent of homicide offenders, 24 percent to 37 percent of assault offenders, 13 percent to 60 percent of sexual offenders, and six percent to 57 percent of male domestic offenders (Roizen, 1997). Alcoholism and alcohol abuse are ranked second to depression and other affective disorders as major risk factors identified for suicide (Blumenthal, 1988): Because drugs are readily available in the workplace, a growing number of employers are instituting drug testing (Redel & Abbey, 1993).

All citizens absorb the costs created by the many physical and psychological repercussions of alcoholism. Over $50 million is spent each year for the care of alcoholics in state institutions. This figure does not include the cost to insurance companies. Some mental hospitals estimate that 80 percent to 90 percent of their first admissions are alcoholics. A conservative estimated annual loss sustained by industries because of alcoholic employees is $10.4 billion. In 1998, it was reported by the National Institute on Alcohol Abuse and Alcoholism that the estimated cost of alcohol disorders and their social consequences create a 39 percent burden on the U.S. population in the form of increased government budgets. Little has changed since Fox (1959) succinctly described the overall U.S. alcohol situation in the 1950s:

> If some new and terrible disease were suddenly to strike us here in America—a disease of unknown cause possibly due to a noxious gas or poison in our soil, air or water—it would be treated as a national emergency with our whole citizenry uniting as a man to fight it. Let us imagine this poison or disease to have the pecu-

liar property of so altering a person's judgment, so brainwashing him that he would be unable to see that he had become ill at all; actually so perverting and so distorting his view of life that he would wish with all his might to go on being ill. Such an emergency would unquestionably be classed as a countrywide disaster, and billions of dollars and thousands of scientists would be put to work to find the cause of the disease, to treat its victims and to prevent its spread. The dread disease envisioned above is actually here. It is alcoholism. (pp. 1–2)

The cost of alcohol abuse is shared by employees, employers and co-workers. The cost could be as high as one-fourth of the employees' income (Sell & Newman, 1992). In 1998, it was reported by the National Institute on Alcohol Abuse and Alcoholism that the estimated costs of alcohol disorders and their social consequences were $185 billion. Of this sum, direct treatment and health care costs account for 14 percent; reduced worker productivity for 47 percent; and lost productivity due to premature deaths for 20 percent. Costs associated with alcohol-related traffic crashes, a leading cause of death for Americans of all ages, account for about 10 percent, as do costs associated with criminal activity.

Who contracts this illness? What kind of persons become alcoholics? The answer seems to be that all kinds of people become alcoholics. No one knows why some drinkers continue to drink and never experience the symptoms of alcoholism, while others continuously experience difficulty and become alcoholics. Many experts believe that it is a combination of physical, psychological and sociological causes. There is enough empirical evidence to suggest that alcoholics show a cluster of personality traits once their drinking patterns have been established. Included in the cluster are low stress tolerance, physical dependency, perceptual dependence, negative self-image, and feelings of isolation, insecurity and depression. However, the problem of interpretation centers on whether such traits precede the alcoholic behavior or whether they are a consequence of the addiction.

There are different types of alcoholics and different kinds of alcoholism, so it is dangerous to generalize, but alcoholics are usually the last to accept their illness. Denial of a drinking problem appears to be an inherent trait of alcoholics. For example, if an alcoholic is asked for the definition of an alcoholic, he will give a definition that does not include himself. If he never drinks before noon, the definition of an alcoholic is an individual who drinks before noon. If he drinks only at home, the definition of an alcoholic will be one who drinks at bars. If he drinks at bars, then an alcoholic is someone who drinks at home. Truth is, they are everywhere and they drink in all places, at all hours. And for a wide variety of reasons, alcoholics and other substance abusers have unpleasant confrontations with substance abuse staff members.

COLOR THEM SUBSTANCE ABUSERS

Culture is a broad concept that both includes and influences all facets of daily life within a community, including medical beliefs and health care practices. It also includes norms that dictate health behaviors. Cultures are shaped by historical, geographic, economic, social and political elements. And socioeconomic characteristics are influential determinants of health and disease care, which vary among and between different racial and ethnic groups. Members of one's family, friends, media, religious and voluntary organizations determine what is normative in regard to an individual's knowledge, attitudes and behaviors. Furthermore, adapting to changing environmental stressors by using a variety of behaviors can lead to health or illness.

Behaviors that lead to health could be considered appropriate adaptive behaviors and those that result in ill health are inappropriate health behaviors. Peoples of all racial and ethnic groups engage in a multitude of inappropriate, unhealthy behaviors, some of them culminating in abuse. Human beings abuse many things, including the environment, animals, and other people, to name just a few. Substance abuse is but another form of self-destructive behavior among many noted in histories of human societies (Hanson & Venturelli, 1998, p. 10).

While minority groups typically use less drugs than Whites, the use of substances such as tobacco and alcohol are major causes of morbidity and mortality among ethnic minorities. And substance use is increasing in these groups. For example, while overall smoking rates among high school students increased by 33 percent from 1991 to 1997, tobacco use by minority adolescents increased in a greater rate than White adolescents. During this time period, smoking among African American teenagers rose by 80 percent (Centers for Disease Control and Prevention, 1998). In general, African Americans have the greatest health problems among the minority groups. From 1990 to 1995, there was a reduction in respiratory cancers among African American men but incidences of respiratory cancer leveled off for African American women and it increased for Native Americans.

Alcohol consumption is the most prevalent substance used by all peoples. But ethnic minorities are underrepresented in alcohol research in the United States. Even though alcohol is the most used and abused substance among all groups in America, there are differences in alcohol use within subpopulations of various ethnic and racial groups. The first national survey which emphasized alcohol use by Blacks and Hispanics was conducted in 1984. Attention was called to the importance of the stressors related to social adjustment to the dominant U.S. culture by minorities. These stressors include acculturative stress, socioeconomic stress (disempowerment due to inadequate financial resources), and minority identity stress. In addition, the alcohol survey highlighted the importance of the variability within each ethnic group in alcohol use and the causative factors of use and abuse (Caetano et al., 1998).

UNDESIRABLE CLIENTS, UNACCEPTING HELPERS

A significant factor hindering a cooperative relationship between some health care providers and their clients is the fact that many substance abusers view themselves as incapable of being helped and incapable of understanding the skills of agency professionals, whom they frequently describe as talking among themselves and using "big" words. They are convinced that physicians and other health care professionals needlessly withhold drugs from them. Embarrassed by their depravity and controlled by their addiction, most addicts do not cooperate with care providers.

Confrontations with patients or clients are distasteful for most practitioners. Only by coming to terms with the feelings that confrontational clients arouse in them will practitioners be able to appropriately handle such conflict. Even this insight may not be enough when dealing with undesirable or hateful clients. Because of the way they look, smell, talk or behave, some clients frustrate or irritate care providers. Individuals who do not fit the constantly shifting and highly subjective normative characteristics of "good" patients or clients are labeled "problems," "undesirable," and "hateful." When these persons get into trouble or become sick, some practitioners are not very empathetic or forgiving.

Undesirable substance abuse clients fit five categories: socially undesirable, attitudinally undesirable, physically undesirable, circumstantially undesirable, and incidentally undesirable (Papper, 1970). *Socially undesirable* clients include individuals who are members of ethnic minority groups, and those who are crude in behavior. *Attitudinally undesirable* clients are individuals who are ungrateful. *Physically undesirable clients* include individuals who have identifiable physical illnesses, especially chronic illnesses. Some are *circumstantially undesirable* because of situations totally apart from them and beyond their control. An example of circumstantially undesirable persons includes clients who are forced to attend rehabilitation programs. *Incidently undesirable* persons behave inappropriately and the behavior is a major incident for staff discussion.

Some clients behave like the persons Groves (1974) labeled "hateful." They fall into four classes: (1) dependent clingers, (2) entitled demanders, (3) manipulative help-rejecters, and (4) self-destructive deniers.

Clingers escalate from mild and appropriate requests for reassurance to repeated perfervid, incarcerating cries for explanation, affect, analgesics, sedatives and all forms of attention imaginative: . . . Demanders resemble clingers in the profundity of their neediness, but they differ in that–rather than flattery and unconscious seduction–they use intimidation, devaluation and guilt-induction to place the doctor in the role of the inexhaustible supply depot: . . . Help-rejecters, or "crocks," are familiar to every practicing physician. Like clingers and demanders, they appear to have a quenchless need for emotional supplies. Unlike clingers, they are not seductive and grateful: unlike demanders, they are not overtly hostile. They actually seem the opposite of entitled; they appear to feel that no regimen will help. . . . Self-destructive deniers display unconsciously self-murderous behaviors, such as continued drinking of a patient with esophageal varies and hepatic failure. (p. 305)

The helper-client relationship is also fractured by social class differences. The degree to which the qualities ideally defined as essential to the helping relationship, namely mutual trust, respect and cooperation, usually occur inversely with the amount of social distance. That is, the greater the social distance the less likely care providers and their clients will be cordial to each other in terms of their roles as professionals and clients, and more likely they will interact with each other as adversaries. A seminal study by Hollingshead and Redlich (1958) concluded that professional helpers tend to behave positively toward clients whose social class is comparable to or higher than their own, and negatively toward those from a lower class. Subsequent studies have corroborated this observation.

Relatedly, if caregivers are to be effective helping poor people, they must understand the meaning of poverty. Poverty is characterized by conditions of not enough–not enough money, food, clothes, adequate housing or hope. Poverty has a familiar smell–a smell of rotting garbage and sour foods. It is the smell of children's and old people's urine and unwashed bodies. Above all else, it is the smell of people wasting away–physically, socially and emotionally. Poverty does not respect race or ethnic background; no one is safe from it. Generally, when affluent people go without soap, hot water, lights, food or medicine, it is because they elect to do so. When poverty-stricken people go without those things, it is because they have little or no choice. Therein lies the major difference between the poor substance abusers and the affluent ones. The former are controlled by economic systems, and the latter control them.

Most of the poor are not substance abusers. Typical lower-class clients have less than a twelfth-grade education and, if employed, are employed as unskilled or service workers. They do not get their names in the news as outstanding representatives of their race or ethnic group; nor do they show up on welfare rolls or in the crime statistics. On the one hand, their children manage to keep out of trouble, and are not what might generally be conceived of as "uneducable." On the other hand, their children are likely to be overlooked when teachers want someone to pose for a picture, or to represent the school. The working poor seldom qualify for welfare because they earn a few dollars more than welfare program guidelines specify. Not all clients from lower-class families—welfare or nonwelfare—enter health care settings with a readiness to be combative or noncompliant. There is a general agreement among researchers that low-status substance abuse clients have lower chances of obtaining optimal care than the high-status patients. Several generalizations are offered for this condition, including the following: low-status clients give less attention to medical symptoms, they are less willing to sacrifice immediate gratification for future health gains, and they display less initiative when seeking treatment. When taken at their face value, these reasons stereotype low-status substance abusers as being shiftless and lazy. That is not our intention in this book. Social status is but one aspect of numerous factors cited in the next chapters that delve into socioeconomic and environmental conditions that may lead to substance use and abuse among ethnic minority populations.

REFERENCES

Battaglia, F.C., Howe, C.J. & Stratton, K.R. (1996). *Fetal Alcohol Syndrome: Diagnosis, Epidemiology, Prevention and Treatment.* Washington, DC: National Academy Press.

Blumental, S.J. (1998). Suicide: A guide to risk factors, assessments and treatment of suicidal patients. *Medical Clinics of North America, 72,* 937–971.

Caetano, R., Clark, C.L. & Tam, T. (1998). Alcohol consumption among racial/ethnic minorities. *Alcohol Health & Research World, 22,* 233–242.

Centers for Disease Control and Prevention. (1998). Tobacco use among U.S. racial/ethnic groups. *Morbidity & Mortality Weekly Reports, 47,* 1–16.

Fox, R. (1959). *What Can Be Done About Alcoholism.* New York: National Council on Alcoholism.

Grant, B.F. (1994). *Prevalence of DSM-IV Alcohol Abuse and Dependence.* Epidemiologic Bulletin No. 35. Washington, DC: Alcohol & Health Research World.

Greenfield, L.A. (1998). *Alcohol and Crime: Analysis of National Data on the Prevalence of Alcohol Involvement in Crime.* Washington, DC: U.S. Department of Justice.

Groves, J.E. (1974). Taking care of hateful patients. *New England Journal of Medicine, 291,* 300–306.

Hanson, G. & Venturelli, P.J. (1998). *Drugs and Society.* Sadbury, MA: Jones & Bartlett.

Hollingshead, R. & Redlich, F.C. (1958). *Social Class and Mental Illness.* New York: John Wiley & Sons.

Jellinek, E.M. (1968). *The Defense Concept of Alcoholism.* New Haven, CT: College University Press.

Miller, N.S. (1991). Special problems of alcohol and multiple-drug dependent: Clinical interactions and detoxification. In R.J. Francis & S.I. Miller (Eds.), *Clinical Textbook for Addictive Disorders* (pp. 194–218). New York: Guilford.

National House for Clearing Alcohol and Drugs (1998) *Drinking Over the Life Span. Office of Applied Studies.* Washington, DC: author.

National Household Survey on Drug Abuse. (2000). *Worker Drug Use and Workplace Policies and Program Results From 1994–1997.* Pevline Prevention Online.

National Institute on Alcohol Abuse and Alcoholism: (1999). *Report of a Subcommittee of the National Advisory Council on Alcohol Alcoholism on the Review of the Extramural Research Portfolio for Epidemiology.* Washington, DC: author.

National Institute on Alcohol Abuse and Alcoholism. (2000). *Strategic Plan 2001–2005: The National Investment in Alcohol Research.* Washington, DC: author.

Paper, S. (1970). The undesirable patient. *Journal of Chronic Diseases, 22,* 771–779.

Redel, C.L. & Abbey, A. (1993). The arbitration of drug use and testing in the workplace. *Arbitration Journal, 48,* 80–85.

Roizen, J. (1997). Epidemiological issues in alcohol-related violence. In M. Galanter (Ed.), *Recent Developments in Alcoholism* (pp. 7–40). New York: Plenum Press.

Sell, A.R. & Newman, R.G. (1992). Alcohol abuse in the workplace: A managerial dilemma. *Business Horizons, 35,* 64–71.

U.S. Department for Health and Human Services. (2000). *Youth Drug Use Continues Downward Trend; First-Time State by State Data Available.* Washington, DC: author.

Chapter 2

EFFECTIVE CROSS-CULTURAL COMMUNICATION IN DRUG ABUSE INTERVENTION AMONG ETHNIC MINORITY POPULATIONS

TRUSANDRA TAYLOR

When considering the combined prevalence and overall consequences of the use of alcohol, illicit drugs and tobacco, psychoactive substance use disorders can be viewed as the number one preventable public health problem in the United States. In fact, epidemiological research has established that the level of use of mood-altering psychoactive substances in the United States is higher than in any other industrialized nation. Collectively, the socioeconomic consequences of substance abuse problems are staggering when accounted for in terms of health care costs, premature mortality, workers' compensation claims, reduced workplace productivity, crime, costs for incarceration, suicide, domestic violence and child abuse.

Substance-related disorders are chronic diseases and multiple factors influence effective treatment outcome. Managed behavioral health care has forced substance abuse treatment delivery systems to examine factors related to effective treatment outcome. A closer look at outcome studies has raised the issue of culturally relevant substance abuse treatment. Changing demographic profiles in the United States population has fueled much of the recent interest and imperatives to approach the issue of culturally relevant treatment and services in health care in general and other associated human services in particular. Consensus is mixed regarding whether it is appropriate to provide culturally and ethnically matched substance abuse treatment between the service providers and the service recipients. Specific to substance abuse treatment and the issue of culturally relevant treatment, outcome data are at best presently limited. A review of the literature reveals primarily published articles and texts based on clinical experience and empirical practices. This is not to suggest that efforts have not been directed toward application of scientific principles, but rather to highlight that research specific to this topic is developing.

This chapter will focus on philosophical approaches, conceptual frameworks and guiding principles related to culturally relevant substance abuse treatment. The chapter is divided into three parts. Because concepts and terms related to culture, ethnicity and race are often unclear and confusing, Part I addresses definitional understanding and applicability of culture, ethnicity and race in general. Initially, it is essential to understand this lexicon of terminology prior to broaching the subject of substance-related disorders. Part II focuses upon organizational cultural competence and diversity in the service delivery system. Issues of cultural competence and diversity training have become hot topics in many social and political arenas. Part II addresses guiding principles and standards for the substance abuse provider delivery systems. Finally, in part three emphasis is placed on analysis of cross-cultural communication, interventions and other relevant approaches in substance abuse treatment.

CULTURE, ETHNICTITY AND RACE

The term "culture" is used in many different contexts and its meaning has become enormously broad. Some authors have suggested that the term as a concept is confusing and has lost its utility and meaning. Originally, the anthropological view of culture was developed to describe characteristics of small, isolated tribes that had maintained a stable set of social customs and behaviors over many generations. In the specific tribal context, culture defined specific traditional roles, relationships, ceremonies and activities related to stable communities. Since the original definitional concept of culture, the world has changed significantly. In fact, the world has evolved into an entity characterized by a global perspective dominated by social change and technological developments. During the past 50 years, many industrialized nations have sustained tremendous change in their social structures involving demography, lifestyles, lifespan potential and economic systems. Advances in technology have provided the foundation for innovation that readily facilitates virtual experiences, hemispheric exchange of information, and rapid transport of goods and services.

Krober and Kluckhohn (1952) discovered more than 100 different definitions of culture. Later, Lonner and Malpass (1994) through their investigation determined the existence of as many as 175 definitions of the term or concept of culture in the social science literature. They emphasized that the many definitions range from being complex and fancy to simple ones such as "culture is the programming of the mind" or "culture is the human-made part of the environment." Further, they noted, "culture is a term invented to characterize the many complex ways in which peoples of the world live, and which they tend to pass along to their offspring." White (1947) indicated that culture denotes all of a group's symbolic behavior, especially language that makes possible the transmission of wisdom and passing on of the techniques for coping with the environment from generation to generation.

In terms of a metaphoric concept, culture may be viewed as an iceberg (Fatiu & Fodgers, 1984). Generally, the vast proportion of an iceberg is mostly out of sight (below the water line). Just as nine-tenths of an iceberg is out of sight, so is nine-tenths of culture out of conscious awareness. The out of awareness part of culture has been named "deep culture" and it approaches infinity in terms of thoughts, ideas and understandings. Issues related to culture that may be viewed as primarily out of awareness are notions of modesty, ideals governing child raising, courtship practices, incentives to work, conception of justice, ordering of time, patterns of visual perception and patterns of handling emotions, just to highlight a few. Examples of factors related to culture that may be viewed as primarily in awareness are: dress, skin color, gender, language, fine arts, literature, religion, food, geography and music.

Despite the above shortcomings, the concept of culture is ingenious and remains an integral element of scientific and lay languages and literatures. Defining culture in a manner that is agreed upon by all persons within scientific communities is not possible. There are myriad points of view and disagreements about the specific meaning of culture. Otting and Donnermyer (1998) generalize that the various definitions of culture seem to agree on three points: (1) Culture is a body of knowledge, attitudes and skills for dealing with the physical and social environments that are passed on from one generation to the next; (2) cultures have continuity and stability because each generation attempts to pass its culture on intact; and (3) cultures also change over time as the physical, social and spiritual environments change. Culture therefore is continuous, cumulative and progressive, constantly changing over time.

Next, it is important to distinguish between the terms culture, race and ethnicity. "Race" is commonly defined as any of the different varieties or populations of Homo sapiens distinguished by physical traits such as hair, eyes, skin color, body shape, blood types, genetic code patterns, and all their inherited characteristics which are unique to their isolated breeding population. The strict biological definition related to complex physiological measurements is overtly relevant to the study of human genetics and physical anthropology and is only relevant when physical characteristics are used as the basis by which people perceive similarities and or differences among them. Sociologist Van den Berge (1967) stated that race refers to a group that is *socially* defined on the basis of *physical* criteria.

The most common and obvious physical characteristic for social classification is skin color. Thus, for example, people can be classified into "Black," "Yellow" and "White" groups according to their skin color. One may call to question how useful such a classification may be; particularly when considering what may be learned, for example, by comparing the use of psychoactive substances across people grouped according to their skin color or any other physical characteristic. Cheung (1993) pointed out the erroneous assumption by researchers who use racial categories assuming that different racial groups exhibit different cultural values and behaviors, so that racial variations reflect cultural variations. People in the same racial category may belong to different ethnic groups, and thereby exhibit different ethnic cultural values and behaviors. For example, "White" includes a large number of ethnic groups such as English, French, German, Italian, Swedish, etc.

"Black" is just a convenient term used to refer to people with dark skin color who, or their ancestors, came from various parts of Africa and Central America. "Hispanic" is more correctly a linguistic group than a racial one and refers to people as diverse as Puerto Ricans, Mexicans, Cubans, Dominicans, Chileans and others. "Asians" and "Indians" are also far from being homogeneous groups. People of Asian descent are represented by large numbers of societies, many of which have different social, cultural and structural systems. Indians in North America are divided into a large number of languages and cultures.

Matters related to race are complex and based upon social, economic and political forces that are dynamic. While race does not represent specific cultural patterns in American society, the phenomenon of race as it pertains to discrimination and oppression has become a disturbing and dividing force. Racially disenfranchised individuals face many adverse conditions and live under circumstances that make it difficult for them to achieve success in their society. Noncultural factors such as poverty, lack of education, poor health status and unemployment may produce stressful existence and thereby influence the development of behaviors that are socially unapproved and deviant. In fact, Herd (1991), in a review of the literature involving Black drinking, indicated that what had been published related to historical and contemporary patterns of Black drinking values, behaviors and problems is best understood in terms of many noncultural factors such as: (1) the disadvantaged socioeconomic and political conditions of many Blacks in American society; and (2) the demographic shifts in the Black population.

Physical characteristics do not imply ethnic cultural patterns and therefore race is not a useful concept in the study of psychoactive substance use if the focus is on specific cultural patterns of substance use. Cultural interpretations may be erroneous if information is based on racial variations in psychoactive substance use. It is, however, appropriate that the relationships between race and issues such as psychoactive substance use are related to the social and psychological consequences of minority or majority status.

Lastly, "ethnicity" is commonly defined as the allegiance to or association with a distinctive nation, language or religion–sharing common customs or belonging to an ethnic group that is a minority within a larger society. Place of origin, or that of one's parents or ancestors, is a popular indicator of ethnicity and usually refers to country of birth. Smith (1984) defined this as the natal approach to ethnicity or *natal ethnicity*. One may call to question how useful the place of origin may be as an indicator of ethnicity. If an individual is born and raised in the same country before emigrating to another, the place of origin in this case reflects cultural values and norms specific to the country that the individual brings with him or her to the host society. However, analysis of immigration patterns has revealed that many migrants spend different periods of time in more than one country before settling permanently in one of them. For example, a large number of South Asian Indians lived many years in the United Kingdom before they moved to North America. Thus, for those immigrants who lived in different geographical regions and cultural domains, country of birth does not imply the retention of a particular country's cultural values and norms, and hence country of origin is not necessarily an accurate indicator of their ethnicity.

Ethnic identification is a concept that refers to the manner in which an individual expresses his or her feelings of attachment to a group on the basis of cultural origin or heritage. It is also commonly described as "ethnic pride" and involves a psychological process of developing a positive image of one's ethnic group or heritage to which one voluntarily feels that one belongs to. This dimension of ethnicity is subjective and is based on attachment of ethnic symbols that foster warm feelings, positive self-esteem, psychological security and primordial ties. It is important to recognize the distinction between the subjective attachment of ethnic identification and the objective behavioral dimension of ethnicity–the retention and practice of the ethnic culture. Cheung (1993) pointed out that, more often than not, a positive relationship between ethnic identification and ethnic culture is conveniently assumed: a high degree of ethnic identification implies the retention and practice of a large amount of the ethnic culture. And a high degree of retention and practice of ethnic culture reflects a strong ethnic identity. However, there is no logical connection between the subjective and the objective aspects of ethnicity, and many research findings in the field of ethnic studies show a lack of a significant connection between the two (Cheung, 1993).

In summary, the preceding discussion offers an overview of basic definitional understanding of terminology related to the concepts of culture, race
and ethnicity. It is not intended to be exhaustive or comprehensive but rather
to highlight some inherent difficulties in the interpretation of information
related to the confluence of understanding cultural issues and the subject of
substance-related disorders. Now, we will discuss organizational dimensions
of cultural competence.

CULTURAL COMPETENCE

In terms of social phenomena within the United States, a movement
developed predominantly during the last decade of the twentieth century
whereby many types of organizations and institutions became involved with
the examination of their cultural competence. The entire spectrums of cultural competence, cultural sensitivity, cultural diversity, multiculturalism and
pluralism have fostered highly charged and emotionally laden discussions
and debates among those who establish and determine matters of public policy. Multiple forces and developments have led to this cultural imperative
and policy initiative, largely because of changing national population demographics and the shift to a global economy, a social integration and interaction paradigm shift, and change from the melting pot ideology of assimilation to an emphasis on biculturalism. Health care organizations in the
Western world have increasingly come to recognize the importance of cultural inclusion, not merely diversity. Because of their emphasis and association with social services and the rehabilitative aspects of health care, organizations involved with managed behavioral health care services in particular
have begun to respond to the need to ensure the provision of culturally competent services to the diverse populations that they serve.

HISTORICAL PERSPECTIVE

Historically, the cultural competency movement within the public sector
of managed behavioral health care delivery systems began in response to the
need to improve treatment and services for children and adolescents. A small
federal pilot program, Child and Adolescent Service System (CASSP), was
initially responsible for recognition of the needs of children, particularly children of color (Day & Roberts, 1991). This pilot project, which was organized
in ten states, launched the operation and promulgation of the now familiar
concepts and guidelines for systems care and cultural competence (Stroul &
Friedman, 1986). Pennsylvania public mental health authorities accepted the

CASSP model of care and subsequently a special division, the State Mental Health Representatives for Children and Youth, was created. This division is now known as the Children, Youth and Families Division. The cultural competence principles and system of care facilitated the state efforts to serve a diverse population of adult and child consumers along clinical, socioeconomic, cultural, geographic and racial dimensions. Therefore, the CASSP program was responsible for bringing the positive value of cultural competence to the mainstream of society and thereby legitimizing it as an issue of prime significance.

CULTURAL COMPETENCE OVERVIEW

Cultural competence is: (1) more than being sensitive to ethnic differences; (2) more than not being a bigot; and (3) more than the warm fuzzy feeling of loving and caring for your neighbor. Cross and Associates (1989) defined cultural competence as " a set of congruent practice skills, attitudes, policies and structures which come together in a system, agency or among professionals which enables that system or those professionals to work effectively in cross-cultural situations." Within the spectrum of cultural competency, the definition and scope of the term culture is expanded to include the integrated patterns of human behavior that include thoughts, communication methods, customs, beliefs, values and institutions of a racial, ethnic, religious or social group based on age, gender, social class or sexual orientation. The word "competence" is used because it implies the capacity to function effectively. This definition moves beyond the concept of cultural awareness (knowledge about a particular group primarily gained through reading or studies) or cultural sensitivity (knowledge and some level of experiential exposure to a minority group other than one's own) and it focuses on the fact that there are levels of and skills development mastery that must also occur. Cultural competence functions along a continuum that ranges from cultural destructiveness to cultural proficiency and the points along this continuum are as follows (Cross et al., 1989).

Cultural Destructiveness. Culturally destructive agencies support attitudes, policies and practices that are detrimental to a particular culture. Those agencies adopt policies, practices and attitudes that negate cultural relativity. A system that adheres to this assumes that one race or culture is superior and should be able to eradicate the lesser races or cultures. And this denigration is accomplished through the process of dehumanizing minority clients, and it often results in care providers being unable or unwilling to utilize the clients folklore and folkways as integral parts of the treatment process.

Cultural Incapacity. In this instance, the agency does not intend to be destructive to a minority culture but it simply does not have the ability to be responsive to it. When this happens, a paternalistic posture is assumed toward clients of a purportedly "lesser" culture. These agencies frequently disproportionately apply their resources, rewarding those clients of color "who know their place." Within these agencies, there is a resistance to even the concept of cultural competence. And these agency policymakers, administrators and practitioners are agents of oppression who condone racist policies while themselves maintaining racial stereotypes. Relatedly, there is discrimination in hiring practices and the delivery of services to people of color.

Cultural Blindness. An agency that functions at this point along the continuum is one that adopts an expressed philosophy of being "totally unbiased." Its philosophy is like that of well-intentioned liberals who believe that all people are the same. That is, the same as them. Variations in color or culture make no difference, they say. The basic belief held is that if the system worked as it should, all people regardless of their race or culture would be served with equal effectiveness. The consequences of such a belief is to make services so ethnocentric in terms of the dominant culture as to render them useless to all but the most assimilated people of color. This type of agency ignores cultural strengths and blames the victims for their health-related problems or weaknesses. The outcome of therapy in such an agency is usually measured by how closely the client and his family approximates a middle-class nonminority existence.

Cultural Precompetence. The culturally precompetent agencies recognize their ability to provide appropriate services to minority clients and attempt to improve some aspects of their services to a specific population. They realize their shortcoming in serving people of color and explore ways of reaching those clients in their service areas. These agencies initiate cultural sensitivity training for their staff. There is the *desire* to deliver quality services, even though the agencies lack the information needed to perform effectively. With support, culturally precompetent agencies can become culturally competent.

Cultural Proficiency. All of the concepts of cultural competency are incorporated in the policy, practices and staff attitudes of these agencies. They can be characterized as care providers who hold cultures of their clients in high esteem. Through their work, they are able to add to the knowledge base of culturally competent practices by conducting research and developing culture-specific therapeutic approaches. They also hire staff who are specialists in culturally competent practices.

According to Cross and associates (1989), most mental health and other human service organizations fall primarily within the "cultural blind" level on the continuum. This is related to their fundamental acceptance of the "melting pot" theory of social interaction, namely, that all Americans are essentially alike and have the same basic needs. Based this assumption, cultural differences are unimportant since everyone is expected to adopt mainstream American values and attitudes. Issacs and Benjamin (1991) argued that the melting pot paradigm does not accurately reflect the experiences of most ethnic groups of color that reside in the United States. Some writers argue that the melting pot theory hypothesized more than 30 years ago is a myth and has not come to existence and further there is no reason to believe that such blending of ethnic groups will take place (or is desired) to any significant degree in the foreseeable future.

Issacs and Benjamin (1991) concluded that given the inaccuracy of the melting pot theory, it is important that mental health and other service organizations address instead the significance of culture and ethnicity in service delivery.

ELEMENTS OF CULTURAL COMPETENCY

Cross and associates (1989) postulated five core elements that contribute to an organization, institution or system's ability to become culturally competent: (1) value diversity, (2) awareness of the "dynamics of differences," (3) ability to institutionalize cultural knowledge, (4) adaptation to diversity, and (5) cultural self-assessment.

Valuing Diversity. To value diversity is to see and respect its worth. A health care system is strengthened when it accepts the reality that the people it serves are from different backgrounds and will make different choices based on their cultures. While all people share common basic needs, there are significant differences in how people of various cultures go about meeting those needs. In health care systems, awareness and acceptance of differences in communication, life views and definitions of health and family are critical to the successful delivery of services.

The Dynamics of Diffferences. Interactions that occur during cross-cultural encounters bring into play their "dynamics." That is, each party interprets the other's response within the context of his or her cultural experiences. Responses are judged based learned expectations or underlying feelings about working with someone who is "different." This may result in stereotyping and misinterpretation of client responses. As one learns more about other cultures and becomes increasingly aware of the dynamics of differences, cross-cultural misunderstanding and misjudgment are less likely to occur and the ability to work effectively across cultures is enhanced.

INSTITUTIONALIZATION OF CULTURAL KNOWLEDGE

Health care systems must sanction and in some instances mandate the incorporation of cultural knowledge into their service delivery frameworks. This knowledge must be available at every level within a system. And it should include relevant information about a culture, including its people–behaviors, communication patterns, history and values. It is also extremely important to learn how cultural values are related to identity formulation, help-seeking behavior, and concepts of health and family.

Adaptation to Diversity. The systems approach to helping must be adapted to create a better fit between the needs of people of color and services that are available to them. Styles of management, definitions of who is included in "family," and service goals are but a few of the issues that can be changed to meet specific cultural needs.

Cultural Self-assessment. Each organization must be able to assess itself and have a sense of its own culture. Assessment of both the individual staff members' and the agency's ability to function in a cross-cultural context is essential. It should not be assumed that because staff members are also members of a particular minority group that they are automatically culturally competent. As noted earlier, people of color and those from the majority culture, all fall along a continuum ranging intercultural sensitivity to insensitivity. Each individual must be aware and understand where she or he falls along this continuum and, if necessary, strive for cultural competency.

MANAGING CULTURAL DIVERSITY IN ORGANIZATIONS

In the planning and development of cultural competency, organizations may adopt and follow prominent practice guidelines. In the areas of health care, social services and human resources, there are many reference materials and resources for organizations to adopt as guidelines or to apply as templates for their respective systems. Institutions involved in mental health and substance-related disorders treatment may draw from several sources of information, particularly the comprehensive monograph written by Jackson and Lopez (1999) that provide an itemized list of resources.

Additionally as a conceptual framework, the *Diagnostic and Statistical Manual of Disorders (DSM-IV)* of the American Psychiatric Association has incorporated some of the recommendations of the National Institute of Mental Health Work Group on Diagnosis, Culture, and Care for the implementation of cultural considerations in the process of care delivery (Lu, 1996). This outline for cultural formulation is intended to complement and supplement the multiaxial diagnostic assessments and to address difficulties that may be encountered in applying *DSM-IV* criteria in a multicultural environment. In the next pages, I discuss five culture-specific issues relevant to substance use disorders treatment.

Cultural Identity of the Client. Practitioners should note each client's ethnic or cultural reference group. For immigrants and ethnic minorities, they should note the degree of involvement with both the culture of origin and the host culture. Also, they should appraise the strengths of their clients' ethnic identities. Some individuals have strong ethnic identities and others do not. One should not make assumptions about a client's ethnic identity without assessing it. Also, it is important to note the client's language abilities and his or her language use and preference.

Cultural Explanations of Illness. The predominant idioms of distress through which symptoms or the need for intervention is communicated may be nerves, possessing spirits, somatic complaints, or inexplicable misfortune. Practitioners must understand the meaning and perceived severity of an individual's symptoms in relation to norms of his or her cultural reference group. Any local illness category used by the client's family and community to identify the condition (culture-bound syndrome) should be identified. It is important to recognize the perceived causes or explanatory models that clients and their reference groups use to explain their illnesses. Lastly, practitioners should gain an understanding of the client's current preferences for and past experiences with professional and alternative sources of care.

All of the above things may be stated in a useful and practical manner such as in the form of a series of questions adopted by the Boston City Hospital (1987) to elicit health beliefs. The style of questioning is a simple tool that is patient-centered. I have modified the tool to emphasize substance-related disorders:

1. What do you call your problem? What name does it have? Do you identify the problem or problems with alcohol other drug abuse? If not, then how do you see your problem?
2. What do you think caused your alcohol (or other drug) abuse problem?
3. Why and when do you think it started?
4. What does your alcohol (or other drug) abuse problem do to you?
5. How severe is your alcohol (or other drug) abuse problem? Will it have a short or long course?
6. What do you fear most about your alcohol (or other drug) abuse problem?
7. What chief problems have your alcohol (or other drug) abuse caused you?
8. What kind of treatment do you think you should receive? What are the most important results you hope to receive from the treatment?
9. What have you done so far to treat your alcohol (or other drug) abuse problem?

Cultural Factors Related to Psychosocial Environments and Levels of Functioning. Practitioners should note the clients' culturally relevant interpretations of social stressors, available social support systems and levels of functioning and disability. This includes stresses operant in the clients' local social environment and the role of religion and kin networks in providing emotional, instrumental and informational support. Stress can weaken the connection between individuals and their cultures. And inordinate stress can destroy it.

Cultural Elements of the Relationship Between the Client and the Clinician. It is important to be aware of differences in culture and social status between the client and the clinician and problems that these differences may cause in diagnosis and treatment. That is, it is imperative to conceptualize these differences in terms of substance-related problems. For example, the clinician may have difficulty in communicating in the clients' first language, in eliciting symptoms or understanding their cultural significance, in negotiating an appropriate relationship or level of intimacy, or in determining whether a behavior is normative or pathological. Practitioners must be aware of "cultural camouflage." That is, some clients may use their culture as an excuse or defense against other issues. Also, there are cultural elements that merit consideration because they are specific to the substance-related disorders treatment community.

Commonly, individuals who have become successful in "recovery" are employed as staff members to help in the treatment of substance-related disorders. This may or may not influence the clinician/client relationship in a positive manner in terms of negotiating an appropriate degree of understanding or level of intimacy needed to abate substance-related problems. It is often assumed that a clinician's personal experience in recovery from substance-related problems automatically facilitates a helpful relationship with clients suffering from similar substance-related problems. This is not necessarily true. A recovering staff member may overidentify with the client. At times, relevant factors other than the clinician's substance use may be more important, e.g., his or her age, gender, ethnic identification, professional status or socioeconomic level.

Overall Assessment for Diagnosis and Care. Practitioners should be cognizant of how cultural considerations specifically influence comprehensive diagnosis and care. Access to and the setting of health care for an individual with substance-related problems may influence the quality of care received. Access to care is a compelling problem for poor individuals and many ethnic minority populations. And this problem is further compounded for individuals suffering from substance abuse problems. For example, in many hospital clinics and emergency rooms, patients with substance-related problems become frustrated when they are shunted aside, seen last or incompletely examined. The personal and cultural experiences of clinicians can significantly influence patients' assessment and the treatment available to them as well as referral for further care.

The preceding brief overview delineated some of the core elements required to effectively treat culturally diverse individuals suffering from substance-related problems. A "one size fits all" approach is not effective as measured by numerous outcome studies (McGoldrick et al., 1996). Staff members in institutions that offer services for substance-related problems who become culturally proficient in managing diverse populations have many opportunities to increase access to care, enhance communication with clients, improve individual quality of life, increase consumer satisfaction, improve public health outcome measures related to morbidity and mortality, decrease health care costs, and indirectly impact the clients' community in a positive manner.

CROSS-CULTURAL COMMUNICATION, INTERVENTIONS AND OTHER APPROACHES

A review of the literature reveals that the state of the art of culturally-relevant substance abuse treatment is evolving. Various program models, treatment approaches and specific interventions have been described and published during the past 35 years. The precise number is difficult to ascertain and therefore it is not feasible to comprehensively describe in any text all of the different theories and methodologies related to this field of knowledge. As previously stated, opinions vary as to whether substance-related disorders treatment should be given through cultural or ethnic matching between treatment providers and treatment recipients. However, there is less disagreement and more of a consensus that there is disparity involving various cultural and ethnic minorities' access to health care, particularly their motivation to seek treatment, retention in treatment, adherence to treatment recommendations and treatment outcome for substance-related disorders (Institute of Medicine, 1989). In the remaining pages, I will review and describe a sampling of culturally-relevant substance abuse programs and services targeted for specific ethnic minority groups. The list is neither exhaustive nor representative of such programs, but rather it is presented to highlight some of the exemplary developments in the field of health care.

The Haight Ashbury Free Clinics (HAFC), Incorporated and the Glide Memorial Methodist Church of San Francisco, California, collaborated in 1992 in response to the growing urban drug abuse problem within their community (Smith et al., 1993). This collaborative church-clinic program combined all of the elements of an effective drug abuse treatment program. It addressed the spiritual as well as the medical and psychological aspects of the disease of addiction. The programs of the HAFC/Glide African-American Extended Family Program were designed to respond to the cultural needs of the African American community. Special emphasis was placed on specific points of resistance, including the issue of powerlessness inherent in the First Step of addiction recovery in the Alcoholics Anonymous 12-Step Program, and through the group process clients were empowered to take control of their lives by accepting the fact that they were powerless over their drug of choice. Counseling that occurred within the framework of a church program was culturally and politically meaningful to the clients because it related to the African American experience.

The key to this culturally specific program was adapting the 12-Step principles of recovery to an African American urban culture. The African American Extended Family Program was developed based on the premise that the church is a pivotal institution because it provides a point of cohesion and a center for both spiritual and community values, as well as a common ground for positive community activities. Simply stated, it is a model of community action and involvement, education, referral, treatment and community-based support for recovery and the reintegration of recovering drug users and dealers into the community. Careful culturally-based assessment of the target population was instrumental in the overall program design and revealed the following client problems: (1) low self-esteem, (2) late introduction into recovery, (3) short-term abstinence, (4) unique, often dysfunctional, family structures, (5) dialect, (6) institutionalized racism, and (7) internalized racism. Within this framework, culturally responsive activities were identified in order for staff members to appropriately intervene and help individuals to establish recovery regimen support groups, women's meetings, intervention meetings, fun days, African history classes, a generation of Glides AAEF, and generations of graduates of addicts in recover (for a more in-depth understanding of this extensive program, see Smith et al., 1993).

During the 1960s, the Black Muslims claimed remarkable success in the rehabilitation of African Americans suffering from narcotic addiction (Haley, 1965). The Nation of Islam's Black Muslim program revolved around the relationship between people of color and addiction, pointing out the higher prevalence of drug abusers living within African American ethnic urban areas, such as Harlem, during the1950s and 1960s. The program involved a six-point therapeutic process that concentrated using former drug abusers to "fish out" other addicts with whom they were associated during their drug abusing days. Since the 1960s, the Black Muslims and the Nation of Islam have continued culturally-specific involvement focused on rehabilitation of alcohol and other drug abusers. Fundamentally, their approach is centered on the teachings of the Prophet Muhammad. Currently, members of the

Islamic faith provide a 12-Step Muslim Program, entitled "Millati Islami," which attempts to recognize and address the devastation of drug addiction within their community. The weekly meetings are based on the fundamental teachings of the Islamic faith.

The American Indian and Alaska Native populations are also culturally diverse. The Indian Health Service (IHS) has identified drug and alcohol problems as the most significant health problems affecting American Indian and Alaska Native communities. In response to those problems, the IHS has initiated several programs that provide drug abuse treatment and prevention services. More then 300 IHS alcohol and other substance abuse treatment programs offer services to American Indians living on reservations and in urban communities, among them are primary residential treatment, halfway houses, outreach, and aftercare programs. Together, with other federal entities, tribal communities and their leadership, the IHS is developing effective and permanent alcoholism and other substance abuse intervention and prevention program.

American Indians and Alaska Natives have preserved and revitalized a number of traditional healing practices and they apply them to the treatment of alcohol-related problems (Abbott, 1998). These healing practices include the following: nativistic movements, sacred dances, sweat lodges, talking circles, four circles and cultural enhancement programs. Additionally, Western treatment approaches have been applied in the treatment of problems related to alcohol, such as medication for detoxification, disulfiram (Antabuse), Alcoholics Anonymous and behavioral interventions.

Similar to other minorities, Asian Americans are diverse and heterogeneous. There are more than 30 distinct Asian ethnic groups with different languages, customs and other behaviors. Thus, there is significant complexity and difficulty in understanding the full extent of alcohol and other substance abuse problems within Asian communities (Cheung, 1989). Regarding treatment, the diversity of the Asian population compounds the problem of establishing service models to respond to more than one Asian ethnic group. The establishment of treatment for Asians with substance-related disorders is further complicated by institutional and community barriers to treatment. Such barriers involve underdocumentation of need, lack of culturally-specific models of treatment, scarcity of resources and lack of community infrastructure (Davis & Aoki, 1993). Strong community advocacy and political efforts are required to overcome these barriers.

The cultural relationship involving Asian substance abusers and their families is especially critical as a variable in successful treatment. Davis and Aoki (1993) described in detail the dynamics, communication factors, and multiple cultural issues related to the Asian family and substance abuse treatment. Another critical risk factor includes problems attendant to immigration.

Asian families often become dysfunctional in the process of immigration because of inadequate housing, socioeconomic hardships, language difficulties, inadequate social survival and vocational skills, and loss of country of origin supportive networks (Takaki, 1990). The Asian American Residential Recovery Services (AARRS) opened in San Francisco in 1985 as a culture-specific treatment service (Davis & Aoki, 1993). Multiple variables were determined to be successful in the treatment of the Asian substance abusers: understanding motivation as a reason for treatment, establishing stability by providing a structured, designing concrete treatment paradigms, setting precise limits in order limit-setting to provide reinforcement to clients regarding the seriousness of the program, managing the fear and anxiety attached to the process substance abuse treatment, providing an atmosphere of positive support in handling confrontational counseling, and providing family counseling.

The U.S. Census Bureau predicts that by 2030 the Hispanic population will increase from 12.5 percent to 18 percent. As previously stated, the Hispanic population is multinational, consisting of several culturally distinct ethnic groups. Review of the clinical literature call to our attention the paucity of published research focused upon Hispanics alcohol and other drug abuse (Gilbert & Cervantes, 1987). Caetano (1993) critically reviewed alcohol treatment research among Hispanics and outlined priorities for improvement. The ideal program structure for the treatment of alcoholism and other drug abusers among Hispanics is not presently known. (Caetano, 1993; Gilbert & Cervantes, 1987). Crucial issues pertaining to Hispanic substance abuse include limited health coverage, inadequate access to care, lack of cultural sensitivity, program in treatment programs, and too few staff members who can communicate in Spanish with clients for whom English is a second language.

The Institute of Medicine (1990) has recognized that treatment programs for minorities should be heterogeneous. Based on a consensus gleaned from a review of the literature, I recommend the following fundamental imperatives that may be applied in order to design culturally-relevant services for all substance clients with related disorders:

1. Patterns of substance use, interpretation of symptoms, diagnosis and determination of appropriate treatment must be based on knowledge of normative behavior that is culture-specific.
2. Differentiation is needed to determine which program components and interventions should be culturally-specific versus those that need to be universal. Consideration must be given to program modifications in order to allow optimum opportunities for clients to express feelings and in ways most comfortable to them.
3. Multiple barriers to treatment must be addressed. Adequate health care

coverage and benefits, access to health care, communication barriers, staff cultural competency, and continuity of multiple service delivery networks are a few of the salient issues that require immediate attention.

4. More evaluation and measurement of the effectiveness of culture-specific program interventions and strategies are needed. Multidisciplinary research that focuses on staff performances and outcome of services is needed to address the cross-cultural client populations.

From a practical and simplistic approach, organizations providing services for different cultural groups must gain the knowledge, skills and tools needed to help the people of the cultures they assist. This involves actively observing culture groups, understanding them and then adapting treatment programs to make them relevant to the groups. A standardized cookbook approach for providing substance abuse treatment services for any population consisting of culturally diverse groups is of limited value. Meeting these challenges will help substance abuse treatment organizations in achieving cultural competency, and that would decrease morbidity and mortality involving substance-related disorders. Meeting these challenges will also allow organizations to accomplish the managed behavioral health care mandate of building efficient and cost-effective substance abuse services for the diverse populations they serve.

REFERENCES

Abbott, P. (1998). Traditional and Western healing practices for alcoholism in American Indians and Alaska Natives. *Substance Use & Misuse, 33* (13), 2605–46.

American Psychiatric Association. (1994). *Diagnostic and Statistical Manual of Mental Disorders*, 4th ed. Washington, DC: author

Boston City Hospital. (1987). The bilingual medical interview I and II: The geriatric I interview, *Medical Interviewing Across Language Barriers*, General Internal Medicine, Boston: author.

Caetano, R. (1993). Priorities for alcohol treatment research among U.S. Hispanics. *Journal of Psychoactive Drugs, 25* (1), 53–50.

Caetano, R. (1991). Broadening alcohol treatment in the U.S.: Comments on a recent IOM report. *British Journal of Addiction, 86*, 853–856.

Cheung, Y. (1993). Approaches to ethnicity: Clearing roadblocks in the study of ethnicity and substance use. *The International Journal of the Addictions, 28* (12), 1209–1226.

Cheung, Y. (1989). Making sense of ethnicity and drug use: A review and suggestions for future research. *Social Pharmacology, 3* (1–2), 55–68.

Cross, T. Bazron, B., Dennis, K. & Issacs, M. (1989). *Towards a Culturally Competent System of Care*. Washington, DC: CASSP Technical Assistance Center. Washington, DC: Georgetown University Child Development Center.

Day, C. & Roberts, M. (1991). Activities of the child and adolescent service system for program for improving mental health services for children and families. *Journal of Clinical Child Psychology, 20,* 340–350.

Fatiu, I. & Fodgers, I. (1984). A Workshop on cultural differences, *AFS Orientation Handbook Vol. IV,* Multicultural Training and Research Institute. Philadelphia: School of Social Administration. Philadelphia: Temple University.

Gilbert, M. & Cervantes, R. (1987). Alcohol services for Mexican-Americans: A review of utilization patterns, treatment considerations and prevention activities. In M. Gilbert and R. Cervantes (Eds.), *Mexican Americans and Alcohol.* Monograph 11. Los Angeles: University of California Spanish Speaking Mental Health Research Center.

Haley, A. (1965). *The Autobiography of Malcolm X.* New York: Ballantine Books.

Herd, D. (1991). The paradox of temperance: Blacks and the alcohol question in nineteenth century America. In A. Barrows and R. Room (Eds.), *Drinking: Behavior and Belief in Modern History.* Berkeley: University of California Press.

Institute of Medicine. (1990). *Broadening the Base of Treatment for Alcohol Problems.* Washington, DC: National Academy of Sciences.

Institute of Medicine. (1990). *Treating Drug Problems.* Washington, DC: National Academy of Sciences.

Institute of Medicine. (1989). *Prevention and Treatment of Alcohol Problems: Research Opportunities.* Washington, DC: National Academy of Sciences.

Issacs, M.R. & Benjamin, M.P. (1991). *Towards a Culturally Competent System of Care Volume II.* Washington, DC: CASSP Technical Assistance Center, Georgetown University Child Development Center.

Jackson, V.H. & Lopez, L. (Eds.). (1999). *Cultural Competency in Managed Behavioral Healthcare.* Providence, RI: Manisses Communications Group, Inc.

Krober, A.L. & Kluckhohn, C. (1952). *Culture: A Critical Review of Concepts and Definitions.* Cambridge, MA: The Museum.

Lonner, W.J. & Malpass, R. (Eds.) (1994). *Psychology and Culture.* Boston, MA: Allyn & Bacon.

Lu, F. (1996). Getting to cultural competence: guidelines and resources. *Behavioral Healthcare Tomorrow,* April, 49–51.

McGoldrick, M. & Giordano, J., and Pearce, J. (1996). *Ethnicity and Family Therapy* (2nd ed.). New York: The Guildford Press.

Oetting, E. R. & Donnermeyer, J. F. (1998). Primary socialization theory: The etiology of drug and deviance. Part I. *Substance Use & Misuse, 33* (4) 995–1026.

Smith, T.W. (1984). The subjectivity of ethnicity. In C.F. Turner and E. Martin (Eds.), *Surveying Subjective Phenomena,* Vol. 2. New York: Sage.

Stroul, B.A. & Friedman, R.M. (1986). *A System of Care for Children and Youth with Severely Emotional Disturbances.* Washington, DC: CASSP Technical Assistance Center, Georgetown University Child Development Center.

Substance Abuse and Mental Health Services Administration. *National Household Survey on Drug Abuse Advance Report.* (1998), Washington, DC: U.S. Government Printing Office.

Van den Berge, P. L. (1967). *Race and Racism.* New York: Wiley.

White, L.A. (1947). Culturological vs. psychological interpretations of human behavior. *American Sociological Review, 12,* 686–698.

Chapter 3

SOCIAL ECOLOGY AND
SUBSTANCE ABUSE PROGRAMS

Robert M. Goodman and Beverly Wright

No matter how the data were analyzed, we could find no strong relationship between the type of innovation adopted and the outcomes. Indeed, it became apparent that the same technology was implemented in very different ways in different institutional settings with very different results. Moreover, factors associated with how the project was implemented explained a relatively high proportion of the variance in outcomes. In other words, in the instance of educational innovations, implementation typically dominates the outcomes. Berman & McLaughlin, 1978, p. 418

The quote from Berman and McLaughlin (1978) illustrates the importance of developing strategies to assure effective implementation if program outcomes are to be assured. Implementation assessment is a relevant prerequisite, especially in light of the current emphasis among funding organizations on outcome-based program assessments. As Koepsell et al. (1992) remarked, "this focus on final outcomes may result in overlooking the need to characterize both the intervention itself and causal mechanisms by which it is supposed to work. Interventions then become ' black boxes' whose overall effects may be detectable, but whose contents are obscure" (p. 33). Where desired outcomes are not evident and the intervention mechanisms are unknown, the program is at risk of a Type III error; that is, little result due to faulty implementation (Steckler, 1989).

Contemporary community-based programs may be particularly susceptible to Type III errors as these programs often are quite complex with multiple program components. To illustrate, in the last 20 years several large-scale community trials for chronic diseases have had enormous influence in shaping community-based, health promotion programming. These studies, which include the Stanford Five Community, the Minnesota Heart Health, and the Pawtucket Heart Health Projects in the United States, as well as the North Karelia Project in Finland (Elder et al., 1986; Farquhar et al., 1985; Jacobs et al., 1986; Mittelmark et al., 1993; Puska, et al., 1985) all implemented numerous community activities both simultaneously and sequentially. For instance, the Minnesota Heart Health Project included risk factor screening, general and specific media messages, worksite physical activity, menu labeling at restaurants, grocery labeling, school programs, work with health practitioners, community-wide contests, community task forces, speakers bureaus, and others (Jacobs et al., 1986). Other community trials used similar approaches. For example, the U.S. Centers for Substance Abuse Prevention funded over 250 community initiatives for the prevention and reduction of alcohol, tobacco, and other drug abuse. These partnerships organized community coalitions with representatives from local businesses, schools, clergy, government, health providers, law enforcement, and community organizations to plan and implement multifaceted community programs to reduce substance abuse (Davis, 1991).

Although great expense and effort went into such initiatives, they often produced modest results that some have attributed to the inadequacies of community-based interventions; (Butterfoss et al., 1996; Fisher, 1995; Kreuter et al., 2000). A fundamental question that this paper addresses is how funding and implementing organizations can bridge the gap that currently exists between the desire to use community strategies for improving health and the strategic implementation of programs to better assure outcomes.

This chapter is divided into several sections. The first provides a brief overview of the evolution of health promotion programming from implementation strategies that focus primarily within organizations, to program strategies that are community based. Then, the implications for shifting program implementation models and related strategies from organizations to communities is discussed. A social ecology model is then offered as an appropriate guide to community-based interventions. Then, an illustration is offered of social ecology approaches pertaining to the reduction of alcohol, tobacco and other drugs (ATOD) misuse, and possible implications for ATOD interventions in minority communities. The chapter ends with recommendations for bridging the gap between strategies for modeling community programs and strategies for maximizing the effective implementation of such program models.

HISTORIC BACKGROUND: PROGRAM IMPLEMENTATION AS A PROCESS WITHIN FORMAL ORGANIZATIONS

A main premise of this chapter is that a shift in emphasis has occurred in program implementation from organizations to communities that requires a rethinking of program models and related strategies in order to maximize implementation effectiveness. A review of the literature prior to the early 1980s, indicates that formal organizations, and not communities, often were the dominant emphasis of program implementation models, and management strategies were the primary vehicle used to foster effective program implementation (e.g., Berman & McLaughlin, 1978; Beyer & Trice, 1978; Pressman & Wildavsky, 1973; Williams & Elmore, 1976). For instance, in studying how to optimize the implementation of mental health programs, Scheirer (1981) provides a program implementation model that divides organizations into the macro (or the policy) level, the intermediate (or the supervisory) level, and micro (or the staff) level. Scheirer uses the model to inform implementation strategies that emphasize adequate decision-making processes, resource acquisition, supervision, workers skills, and incentives within the implementing organization.

In a similar vein, Elmore (1978) articulates model and management strategies that are contingent upon the organizational approach taken when implementing a program. According to Elmore, the systems management approach is one in which implementation follows an ordered, rational process that is planned by management. In the bureaucratic approach, implementation is a question of identifying and altering standard routines. The organizational development approach requires consensus building among management and staff for implementation. The conflict and bargaining approach is one in which implementation results from a negotiated process among stakeholders who may hold different goals for the program and who must reconcile their difference constructively if the program is to chart a clear direction.

Roberts-Gray and Gray (1983) propose a third organizational model that also emphasizes management strategies to optimize program implementation. They divide the implementation stage into three substages and examine the accommodations that organizations make with the program at each substage including: orientation, during which organizations plan the program; initiation, during which the organization tries the program; and integration, during which the program becomes routine within the organization. To implement the program at each substage, the organization makes different adaptations in role structures, resource availability, and management procedures. In order to accommodate the program, the organization also increases organizational acceptance and control of the program by altering its rules and attitudes.

Leonard-Barton (1988) presents a fourth model that emphasizes management strategies and how they interact with the characteristics of the program. The model concentrates on three inherent program characteristics: transferability, or the program's perceived feasibility and how easily it is understood; complexity, or how many sections and members of the organization are involved in the program; and divisibility, or the degree to which the program can be segmented so that it may be implemented in stages or in parts. Depending on whether these program characteristics are high or low determines the management strategy that is optimum in fostering implementation.

The focus on strategies within formal organizations to improve implementation is further reflected in popular evaluation textbooks used in the health sciences. For instance, King, Morris and Fitzgibbon (1987) emphasize staff roles in the assessment of implementation. Similarly, Windsor et al. (1994) emphasize provider competence and program adequacy in implementation (or process) evaluation of health promotion programs. Provider competence consists of evaluating the practitioner's knowledge of the state of the art and technical skill; program adequacy consists of examining resources, facilities, equipment, adequate level of effort, and adequate documentation of progress.

This brief overview illustrates that implementation within organizations was the predominant focus of program models prior to the 1980s. The growth in the 1980s of community-wide health promotion interventions signaled a shift away from the emphasis placed mainly on formal organizations. The following section suggests that program implementation as a community-wide process requires an expansion of models and strategies beyond the implementing organization to assure adequate program development.

CONTEMPORARY APPROACH: PROGRAM IMPLEMENTATION AS A COMMUNITY-WIDE PROCESS

As noted previously, the movement toward comprehensive community-wide programming for health promotion was influenced by the Stanford, Pawtucket and Minnesota Heart Health Initiatives. The lessons taken directly from these community trials revealed the need to alter implementation strategies in a way that reflected the unique challenges of executing programs outside of organizational settings and in community settings. For instance, Green and McAlister (1984) assert that ". . . community or large-scale programs, even within large institutions, require a shift in perspective and the employment of the distinct set of analytic and programmatic tools from those used with patients, clients, or customers" (pp. 323–324). Flay (1986) writes of the unique impediments in implementing complex community programs, including reaching the planned targets at the correct time, with adequate intensity and desired effects. Altman (1986) recommends disaggregating program components to understand the multiple causal mechanisms within complex community interventions. Guba and Lincoln (1989) suggest that mini interventions in complex programs never occur quite the same way across communities. This concept, known as "mutual simultaneous shaping," requires flexibility in the temporal ordering of mini interventions. The emphasis on "teasing out" the elements of complex community programs is evident in the recent work of Scheirer (1994) who concludes that complex interventions require "micro-evaluation" because community programs are composed of many mini interventions, all of which require dose measures. Where programs are targeted at the community, the dose for any individual often is small, a reason cited for the modest results of community trials; when dose is accounted for, results may improve (Fisher, 1995).

Collectively, these observations reflect a shift in perspective in applying implementation strategies to maximize community-wide outcomes. The shift in emphasis from management strategies in formal organizations to strategies that focus on community context reflects two different metaphors for organizational systems. The first is characterized as a closed and rational approach in which formal organizations, in the main, function independently of outside forces or environmental considerations, and decisive management of the organization's internal operations is paramount in producing greater efficiency and productivity. The implementation approaches prior to the 1980s best reflect this metaphor. The second metaphor is considered open and naturalistic in which environmental and community factors are central considerations, and unanticipated and uncontrolled events often disrupt organizational plans and divert the attainment of preset goals. The key to success is for organizations and programs to adapt to uncertain community environments (Shortell & Kaluzny, 1988). This latter metaphor is best illustrated by the large-scale community trials and the CSAP coalitions, and requires new models and strategies to assure effective program implementation. As discussed in the following section, social ecology models and strategies have evolved in response to the early critiques of community-wide programming (Minkler, 1989).

SOCIAL ECOLOGY AS A CONTEMPORARY CONTEXT FOR UNDERSTANDING IMPLEMENTATION

The social ecology perspective holds that the potential to change individual behavior is considered within the social and cultural context in which it occurs. Interventions that are informed by this perspective are directed mainly at social factors, such as community norms and the structure of community services including their comprehensiveness, coordination, and linkages, in addition to individual motivations and attitudes (McLeroy et al., 1988). Stokols, Allen and Bellingham (1996) write that ecologically informed programs address the ". . . interdependencies between socioeconomic, cultural, political, environmental, organizational, psychological, and biological determinants of health and illness" (p. 247). They envision the shift to comprehensive ecological formulations as a needed transformation for program implementation because pockets of prevalence for ill health remain fixed in communities when interventions are limited in scope. Stokols and colleagues hold that such limited programs are the cause of high relapse and attrition rates. This recent emphasis on social ecology is reflected by its inclusion as a focal concept in a leading model for health promotion programming (Green & Krueter, 1999) that was previously informed by clinical practice (Green & Krueter, 1992). Also, program assessment approaches based on social ecology are beginning to appear in the evaluation literature (Shinn, 1996).

Stokols (1996) offers several guidelines based on social ecology principles for planning and implementing health promotion programs that include: examining the links between multiple facets of well-being and adverse conditions of the socio-physical environment, considering the joint influence of intra-personal and environmental conditions on individual and community well-being, developing health promotion programs that enhance the fit between people and their surroundings, focusing health promotion interventions on high-impact behavioral and organizational "leverage points," designing health promotion programs that address interdependencies between the physical and social environment and encompass multiple settings and life domains, integrating multidisciplinary perspectives in the design of health promotion programs, and using multiple methods to gauge the scientific and social validity of the interventions. Koepsell et al. (1992) recommend specifying theoretical models for the intervention. Similarly, Kumpfer et al. (1993) and Scheirer (1996) recommend the use of logic models which Kumpfer defines as ". . . a fancy term for what is merely a succinct, logical series of statements that link the problems your program is attempting to address, how it will address them, and what the expected result is" (pp. 7-8). Scheirer et al. (1995) add that collecting data as events occur permits accurate records of the "unfolding" of the program. The use of logic models is confluent with Altman's (1986) call for longitudinal assessments of community initiatives that are sensitive to detecting intermediate stages in reaching ultimate outcomes. Goodman et al. (1996) suggest that programs informed by social ecology models develop in stages and applying evalua-

tion measures that are specific and appropriate to each stage of development
can improve program implementation.

AN IMPLEMENTATION MODEL BASED
ON SOCIAL ECOLOGY PRINCIPLES

Figure 3.1 uses youth substance abuse as an illustrative attempt to demonstrate how many of these recommendations may be incorporated into a single model that is based on social ecology principles and directed at the strategic implementation of community-based programs. In Figure 3.1, program
components occur across five levels of the social ecology: individual, interpersonal, organizational, community, and macro-policy. At each level the
program elements are composed of mediating, modifying, and outcome conditions (Porras & Robertson, 1987). For instance, at the individual level, substance abuse among youth is a presenting concern, with substance abatement
as the desired outcome condition. Counseling and peer social support services are program elements, termed mediating conditions because they are
intended to intervene between the initial condition (i.e., youth substance
abuse) and the desired outcome (i.e., substance abatement).

The effectiveness of interventions such as counseling and peer social support may increase when family members are supportive and involved.
Hence, the presence of family support at the interpersonal level is a modifying condition that may influence the effectiveness of counseling and peer
support at the individual level (Figure 3.1). If families are ill prepared to
address substance abuse of their children, then this too becomes an initial
condition that requires a program intervention at the interpersonal level. In
Figure 3.1, family support training is the program component that mediates
between a lack of family preparedness as an initial condition and effective
parental involvement as the desired outcome condition. The availability in a
community of an adequate number of organizations that offer parent effectiveness training, youth counseling, and peer social support training is a modifying condition at the organizational level that influences the likelihood that
parenting and youth programs are implemented. The lack of such programs
becomes an initial condition at the organizational level that requires program
interventions aimed at developing anew or expanding existing services
(mediating condition). That is, parental involvement may increase when
local organizations such as churches, health agencies, and schools provide
family support services. So, the development of such services becomes an
intervention in its own right.

Such services may be more adequately funded and in sufficient number
when communities advocate on their behalf. Thus, advocacy becomes a

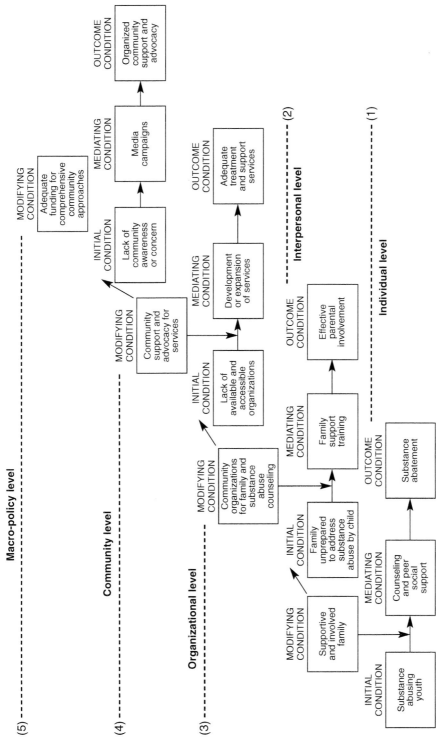

Figure 3.1. Intervention Strategies for Youth Substance Abuse Prevention Informed by Social Ecology Principles.

modifying condition at the community level that may enable the development of additional family and youth programs. Where adequate community awareness and concern for such services is lacking, then these too become initial conditions that suggest additional interventions, such as media campaigns (mediating condition) that are intended to influence community support and advocacy. At the macro-policy level, active community support may be contingent upon adequate governmental funding to communities that are directed at stimulating comprehensive community approaches.

In summary, when mediating and modifying conditions are implemented with sufficiency across all social levels, communities may recognize increased outcomes related to and including the abatement of youth substance abuse. The Figure 3.1 illustration is limited in that other program interventions may be necessary or superior depending on the presenting conditions in any community. Sufficiency may require multiple mediating and modifying conditions at each stratum. Simply put, the more program elements and supportive activities that are logically linked across strata, the more comprehensive the community approach. Also, because communities exist within dynamic environments, therefore, conditions within the social ecology are not static and may change over time. Consequently, the regular reexamination of ecological conditions may be important in continually refining and adjusting program strategies.

These limitations notwithstanding, the Figure 3.1 model is consistent with the ecological perspective. First, it is ecological in that the interventions occur at different social strata (i.e. individual, interpersonal, organizational, community, and macro-policy). Second, as Stokols (1996) and others suggest, the interventions are linked across levels in a "daisy chain" with each program element (mediating condition) logically connected to supportive activities (modifying conditions) at the next stratum. Third, Figure 3.1 can be a blueprint for constructing a logic model because the figure reflects the sequence of events that must occur for effective outcomes to result. Fourth, the Figure 3.1 model also fits the criteria for disaggregating program components at each level of the ecology for micro-evaluation as recommended by Altman (1986) and Scheirer (1994). Fifth, by focusing evaluation strategies on each mediating condition, implementation assessment may account for the dose, or degree of implementation. Sixth, by concentrating assessment strategies on each modifying condition, the evaluation strategies may take into account the degree of support within the community for each program element. Last, by taking repeated or longitudinal measures of dose and support, the assessment can account for their stage of development and fluctuations in implementation over time. Thus, dose and support measures become important indices of program implementation and for understanding why and to what degree the desired outcome was reached.

SOCIAL ECOLOGY APPROACHES IN ETHNIC MINORITY COMMUNITIES

As noted above, ecological interventions take cultural and social factors into account, and, in order to achieve cultural and social relevance, intervention pathways and mechanisms may operate differently across socioeconomic or racial/ethnic groups (House & Williams, 2000). Consequently, ecological interventions do more than connect logically across the individual, interpersonal, community, and policy levels. At each level, the interventions are constructed with cultural and social relevance in mind. Although the authors are not aware of ATOD interventions in minority communities that are linked comprehensively across all ecological levels; nevertheless, the literature does provide many examples of strategies that take social and cultural factors into account and link across at least two levels of the ecology. The following discussion refers to the interventions listed in Figure 3.1 to illustrate promising interventions that are ecologically informed and account for social and cultural factors.

For instance, at the individual level in Figure 3.1, counseling and peer social support services are suggested program interventions. In writing about such individual-level interventions, Watson (1992) underscores the significance that culture, racism and oppression may play among minority group members who are in recovery. Programs that account for such factors within the intervention may increase relevance and effectiveness. To illustrate, Wallerstein and Bernstein (1988) report on a culturally appropriate intervention among Hispanic and Native American youth that is informed by Freire's (1971) work on critical thinking and which emphasizes the sharing of life experiences, problem-posing, and constructive action. Wallerstein and Bernstein report that the approach promoted greater self-awareness of the consequences of ATOD use, more confidence in talking about difficult issues among their friends, and a spin-off of peer-led teaching groups.

At the interpersonal level in Figure 3.1, family involvement with and support of the member in counseling is viewed as important. Yet in some minority communities, a lack of treatment seeking may be reinforced by a lack of familiarity and a mistrust of mainstream health care, and/or a tradition of seeking aid from native healers or spiritual advisors. In such instances, programs have been successful where they involved family members or lay health advisors of similar backgrounds. For instance, the program reported by Wallerstein and Bernstein (1988) links the promotion of self-awareness with family discussions. McAlister et al. (1992) report on an effective smoking cessation program in Texas-Mexico Border Communities, Programa A Su Salud, in which community residents were trained as volunteers to provide materials and links to services for smoking cessation.

At the organizational level, Figure 3.1 incorporates the need for an adequate number of organizations that provide family support and youth counseling for youth that misuse ATOD. Frequently, such health services are less available in minority communities (House & Williams, 2000). Organized community responses may be required in support of more readily available services that are socially and culturally appropriate. Goodman and Steckler (1987–1988) report on a youth-oriented, drug prevention program in a low-income housing development that was predominantly African American. The program received national recognition for its effectiveness, but when it was terminated because funds were redistributed to other communities, a local community organizer with political connections at the state legislature was able to secure the resources necessary to continue aspects of the program. In a different type of example, Powers (1993) studied how four minority communities combated drug dealing, noting that the communities differed in the particular ways that they responded, but possessed traits in common. Interventions in each community ". . . were initiated by individuals or small groups determined to protect their building or neighborhood from predatory criminals in the face of what they considered an inadequate response by the police department" (p. 118). Citizen committees were formed to influence more proactive evictions and arrests for crack dealers. Thus, effective mobilization at the community level influenced organizational-level responses from policing and other governmental agencies. Additional evidence supports the effectiveness of linking citizen and policing interventions in minority communities to reduce drug dealing (Skogan, 1987; Smith & Davis, 1993). Other organizationally-based examples of ATOD interventions that have the potential to be linked across ecological strata include church-based smoking cessation initiatives, particularly in African-American communities (House & Williams, 2000). Also, strategies that emphasize coordination among service organizations to improve access to care have been employed for smoking reduction during pregnancy among high risk women (Emmons, 2000).

At the macro-policy level, Figure 3.1 focuses on assuring adequate governmental funding for community-based programming. But other aspects of policy are notable as they pertain to ATOD and minority communities. For instance, minority communities tend to have a higher density of billboards advertising alcohol and cigarettes, and a higher density of liquor outlets (Moore, et al. 1996). Law and policy also discriminate against minorities as evidenced by differential sentencing for crack as opposed to powder cocaine. Policy initiatives that influence equitable sentencing, program funding, and the content of advertisements can provide support by linking interventions at other levels. Such strategies also have been linked to interventions at the policy level. For example, Smith and Davis (1993) report that citizen associations have not only been successful in influencing neighborhood policing, but also have affected decisions of local liquor licensing boards to close ". . . noisy bars in which drugs are sold, fights occur regularly, firearms are conspicuously displayed, and street congregation are commonplace . . ." (pp. 126–127). McAlister et al., (1992) report that Programa A Su Salud not only used community volunteers, but also linked this intervention to a mass media campaign that presented real stories about local residents who stopped smoking, thus providing counter advertising to prevalent billboards.

BRIDGING THE GAP BETWEEN MODEL AND PRACTICE

The contemporary literature provides numerous recommendations for improving implementation of complex community programs. The following presentation concentrates on four recommended strategies that are informed by social ecology principles and suggested by the Figure 3.1 model. These recommendations should be considered merely as suggestive of the plethora of possible strategies that may warrant consideration in order to increase the effective implementation of complex community programs.

The first recommendation concerns developing logic models such as Figure 3.1 as a strategy for mapping out complex community-based interventions. As in Figure 3.1, the linking of mutually supportive interventions across social levels in a well-reasoned and culturally acceptable manner is a fundamental aspect of such models.

The second recommendation is an extension of the first. The model that is developed should be used strategically as a blueprint for assuring the fidelity of implementation as planned. Several methods for developing logic models and assessing implementation fidelity exist in the literature and are cited here for in-depth exploration that is not feasible in this short rendering (Goodman & Wandersman, 1994; Kumpfer et al., 1993; Scheirer, 1996).

The third recommendation concerns the staging of multiple interventions across multiple social strata that are reflected in the logic model. Staging is important for at least two reasons: (1) it may be difficult to focus the necessary attention simultaneously on multiple interventions, therefore, the implementation of program elements may need to be staged sequentially; and (2) each intervention may require its own staging so that it fully matures. For instance, several writers elaborate on the development of community coalitions that take into account the stages of coalition readiness including initial mobilization, establishing organizational structure, building capacity for action, implementing, refining and institutionalizing. They provide detailed strategies for training, technical assistance, and assessment to assure that coalitions evolve from one stage of development to the next. Some of these strategies include methods of citizen recruitment, formation of coalition structure and rules, and skill building (Butterfoss et al., 1993; Florin et al. 1993; Goodman et al., 1996).

The fourth recommendation concerns the deployment of strategies that foster the development of community capacities to implement multifaceted program interventions and to manage complex program exchanges. The literature on coalitions that was just cited and other recent work on implementing community initiatives emphasizes the assessment and development of a community's capacity to take effective action (Kretzman & McKnight, 1993). From this perspective, the challenge is to build the community's capacity to work as an open system across organizations as in a community coalition, or with community residents as in a unified social network. Goodman et al. (1998) identify ten dimensions of capacity that are fundamental to implementing community-based programs: active citizen participation, effective leadership, a broad complement of skills, access to resources, established social and interorganizational networks, strong sense of community, understanding of community history, ability to leverage community power, a clearly articulated set of community values, and the ability to critically reflect upon the approach taken so that it may be improved. The Aspen Institute (1996) and The Colorado Trust (Easterling et al., 1998) have developed similar dimensions for community capacity that underscore the direct relationship between community capacity and health. Wickizer and colleagues (1993) use a method termed "community activation" to characterize contemporary thinking on program implementation as a process involving community organization efforts for advancing health. They study the involvement and coordination of major community institutions to mobilize leadership and resources for health promotion. The goal of community activation is a greater degree of interconnectedness among community institutions measured by quantifying the characteristics of the resulting network. Network interconnectedness, such as in the development of community coalitions, is reflective of capacities that communities must generate in implementing complex health programs.

Goodman et al. (1998) provide a checklist of capacity indicators that they recommend be used in communities to assure that the needed capacities are addressed. Wagner et al. (1991), have developed ways to measure network connectedness in community health promotion programs that serves as a measure of community activation and connectedness. These indices of capacity and activation illustrate that such measures are feasible and desirable. Other types of community-level indicators can be found in the work of Cheadle et al. (1992), Gruenewald et al. (1997), and Coulton (1995).

CONCLUSIONS

The main thesis of this chapter entails the need to bridge the gap between the desire to implement community-based programs that address socially enmeshed health problems and the development of culturally appropriate models and related strategies that may increase the outcomes which are expected (e.g., the abatement of youth substance abuse–Figure 3.1). The need is underscored by the experiences of large-scale community trials and the modest results that they have produced. Social ecology principles can provide a coherent basis for rethinking and refining implementation approaches. The model presented in Figure 3.1 is a reflection of how these principles can operate in constructing, implementing, and assessing community health initiatives within an open systems context. Four strategic recommendations are offered and references are provided for developing logic models that are informed by social ecology principles, for using such models to assess the fidelity of implementation, for staging the adequate development of complex community programs, and for assessing a community's capacity to engage in the development and implementation of multifaceted programs. These recommendations should be grounded in the unique social and cultural experiences of the communities in which they operate.

Programs that are informed by social ecology are likely to be complex. They require multiple interventions that are implemented simultaneously and sequentially. The interventions require a fit that links them synergistically across social strata. Also, the interventions must be culturally and socially relevant, occur in adequate dose, and occur over a sufficient time frame to produce synergy and, consequently, the desired outcomes. Assessment of these implementation processes must be multifaceted and durable. To accomplish comprehensive program implementation, communities may have to generate capacity as a needed first step that may require substantial resources and political will.

The implementation requirements for complex community interventions may seem to be daunting, and one may reasonably ask whether it is worth it. But it is equally reasonable to ask what are the alternatives? The answer to these questions for public health agencies is critical. Complex health problems like substance abuse have no magic bullets and ameliorating them has as much to do with context as it does with behaviors that are shaped and influenced by the environment–physical, social, cultural, economic and political. Interventions that are informed by this perspective are directed largely at social factors, such as community norms and the structure of community services. Complex community models like Figure 3.1 require application and testing to affirm that they are appropriate constructs for socially enmeshed public health concerns. A major challenge in implementing public health solutions in the twenty-first century revolves around our vision, political will, and flexibility in bridging the gap between our desire to implement community approaches and our ability to construct, implement strategically, and evaluate relatively complex models to determine whether they generate the appropriate outcomes.

REFERENCES

Altman, D.C. (1986). A framework for evaluating community-based heart disease prevention programs. *Social Science & Medicine, 22,* 479–487.

Aspen Institute. (1996). *Measuring Community Capacity Building: A Workbook in Progress for Rural Communities.* Washington, DC: The Aspen Institute.

Berman, P., & McLaughlin, M.W. (1978). *Federal Programs Supporting Educational Change, Volume VIII: Implementing and Sustaining Innovations.* Santa Monica, CA: Rand Corporation.

Beyer, J. M. & Trice, H.M. (1978). *Implementing Change: Alcoholism Policies in Work Organizations.* New York: The Free Press.

Butterfoss, F.D., Goodman, R. M. & Wandersman, A. (1996). Community coalitions for prevention and health promotion: Factors predicting satisfaction, participation and planning. *Health Education Quarterly, 23,* 65–79.

Cheadle, A., Wagner, E.W., Koepsell, T. D., Kristal, A. & Patrick, D. (1992). Environmental indicators: A tool for evaluating community-based health-promotion programs. *American Journal of Preventive Medicine 8,* 345–350.

Coulton, C. J. (1995). Using community level indicators of children's well-being in comprehensive community initiatives. In J.P. Connell, A.C. Kubisch, L.B. Schorr & C. H. Weiss, *New Approaches to Evaluating Community Initiatives: Concepts, Methods and Contexts.* Washington, DC: The Aspen Institute, 173–199.

Davis, D.J. (1991). A systems approach to the prevention of alcohol and other drug problems. *Family Resource Coalition, 10,* 3.

Easterling, D., Gallagher, K., Drisko, J. & Johnson, T. (1998). *Promoting Health by Building Community Capacity.* Denver, CO: The Colorado Trust.

Elder, J., McGraw, S., Abrams, D., Ferreira, A., Lasater, T., Longpre, H., Peterson, G., Schwertfeger, R. & Carleton, R. (1986). Organizational and community approaches to community-wide prevention of heart disease: The first two years of the Pawtucket Heart Health Program. *Preventive Medicine, 15,* 107–117.

Elmore, R. F. (1978). Organizational models of social program implementation. In D. Mann (Ed.), *Making Change Happen.* New York: Teachers College Press.

Emmons, K. M. (2000). Health behaviors in a social context. In L. F. Berkman & I. Kawachi (Eds.), *Social Epidemiology.* New York: Oxford University Press, 242–266.

Farquhar, J., Fortmann, S., Maccoby, N., Haskell, W., Williams, P., Flora, J., Taylor, C., Brown, B., Solomon, D. & Hulley, S. (1985). The Stanford Five-City Project: Design and methods. *American Journal of Epidemiology, 122,* 323–334.

Fisher, E.B. (1995). Editorial: The results of the COMMIT trial. *American Journal of Public Health,* 85, 159–160.

Flay B.R. (1986). Efficacy and effectiveness trials (and other phases of research) in the development of health promotion programs. *Preventive Medicine, 15*, 451–474.

Florin, P., Mitchell, R. & Stevenson, J. (1993): Identifying technical assistance needs in community coalitions: A developmental approach, *Health Education Research, 8*, 417–432.

Freire, P. (1971). *Pedagogy of the Oppressed.* New York: Continuum.

Goodman, R.M., Speers, M.A., McLeroy, K., Fawcett, S., Kegler, M., Parker, E., Smith, S., Sterling, T. & Wallerstein, N. (1998). An attempt to identify and define the dimensions of community capacity to provide a basis for measurement. *Health Education & Behavior, 25*, 258–278.

Goodman, R.M. & Steckler, A. (1987–88). The life and death of a health promotion program: An institutionalization case study. *International Quarterly of Community Health Education, 8* 5–21.

Goodman, R.M., & Wandersman, A. (1994). FORECAST: A formative approach to evaluating community coalitions and community-based initiatives. In S. Kaftarian & W. Hansen (Eds.), Improving methodologies for evaluating community-based coalitions for preventing alcohol, tobacco, and other drug use. *Journal of Community Psychology*, CSAP special issue, 6–25.

Goodman, R.M., Wandersman, A., Chinman, M.J., Imm, P.S. & Morrissey, E. (1996). An ecological assessment of community coalitions: Approaches to measuring community-based interventions for prevention and health promotion. *American Journal of Community Psychology, 24*, 33–61.

Green, L.W. & McAlister, A.L. (1984). Macro-intervention to support health behavior: Some theoretical perspectives and practical reflections. *Health Education Quarterly 11*, 322–339.

Green, L.W. & Kreuter, M.W. (1999). *Health Promotion Planning: An Educational and Ecological Approach* (third edition). Mountain View, CA: Mayfield.

Green, L.W. & Kreuter, M.W. (1992). CDC's Planned Approach to Community Health as an application of PRECEED and an inspiration for PROCEED. *Journal of Health Education, 23*, 140–147.

Gruenewald, P.J., Treno, A.J., Taff, G. & Klitzner, M. (1997). *Measuring Community Indicators: A Systems Approach to Drug and Alcohol Problems.* Applied Social Research Methods Series, Vol. 45. Thousand Oaks, CA: Sage, 1997.

Guba, E.G. & Lincoln, Y.S. (1989). *Fourth Generation Evaluation.* Newbury Park, CA: Sage.

House, J.S. & Williams, D.R. (2000). Understanding and reducing socioeconomic and racial/ethnic disparities in health. In National Academy of Sciences. *Intervention Strategies from Social and Behavioral Research.* Washington, DC: The National Academy of Sciences, 81–124.

Jacobs, D., Luepker, R., Mittelmark, M., Folsom, A., Pirie, P., Mascioli, S., Hannan, P., Pechacek, T., Bracht, N., Carlaw, R., Kline, F. & Blackburn, H. (1986). Community-wide prevention strategies: Evaluation design of the Minnesota Heart Health Program. *Journal of Chronic Disease, 39*, 775–788.

Kaluzny, A.D., & Hernandez, S.R. (1988). Organizational change and innovation. In S. M. Shortell & A. D. Kaluzny (Eds.), *Health Care Management: A Text in*

Organization Theory and Behavior, 2nd edition (pp. 379–417). New York: John Wiley & Sons.

King, J.A., Morris, L.L. & Fitz-Gibbon, C.T. (1987). *How to Assess Program Implementation*. Newbury Park, CA: Sage.

Koepsell, T.D., Wagner, E.H., Cheadle, A.C., Patrick, D.L., Martin, D.C., Diehr, P.H. & Perrin, E.B. (1992). Selected methodological issues in evaluating community-based health promotion and disease prevention programs. *Annual Review of Public Health, 13*, 31–57.

Kretzmann, J. P., McKnight, J. L. (1993). *Building Communities from the Inside Out: A Path Toward Finding and Mobilizing a Community's Assets*. Chicago, IL: ACTA Publications.

Krueter, M. W., Lezin, N & Young, L.A.. (2000). Evaluating community-based collaborative mechanisms: Implications for practitioners. *Health Promotion Practice, 1*, 49–63.

Kumpfer, K.L., Shur, G.H., Ross, J.G., Bunnell, K.K., Librett, J.J. & Millward, A. R. (1993). *Measurements in Prevention: A Manual on Selecting and Using Instruments to Evaluate Prevention Programs*. Rockville, MD: USDHHS, CSAP Technical Report–8.

Leonard-Barton, D. (1988) Implementation characteristics of organizational innovations. *Communication Research, 15*, 603–631.

McAlister, A.L., Ramirez, A.G., Amezcua, C., Pulley L., Stern, M.P. & Mercado, S., (1992). Smoking cessation in Texas-Mexico border communities: A quasi-experimental panel study. *American Journal of Health Promotion, 6*, 274–279.

McLeroy, K.R., Bibeau, D., Steckler, A. & Glanz, K. (1988). An ecological perspective on health promotion programs. *Health Education Quarterly, 15*, 351–377.

Minkler, M (1989). Health education, health promotion and the open society: An historical perspective. *Health Education Quarterly, 16*, 17–30.

Mittelmark, M.B., Hunt, M.K., Heath, G.W. & Schmid, T.L. (1993). Realistic outcomes: Lessons from community-based research and demonstration programs for the prevention of cardiovascular diseases. *Journal of Public Health Policy, 14*, 437–462.

Moore, D.J., Williams, J.D. & Qualls, W.J. (1996). Target marketing of tobacco and alcohol-related products to ethnic minority groups in the United States. *Ethnicity & Disease, 6*, 83–98.

Porras, J.I. & Robertson, P.J. (1987). Organization development theory: A typology and evaluation. In R.W. Woodman & W. A. Pasmore (Eds.), *Research in Organization Change and Development*, Vol. 1. Greenwich, CT: JAI.

Powers, S. (1993). Community responses to drugs: Manhattan and Brooklyn case studies. In R. C. Davis, A.J. Lurigio & D.P. Rosenbaum (Eds.), *Drugs and the Community: Involving Community Residents in Combatting the Sale of Illegal Drugs*. Springfield, IL: Charles C Thomas.

Pressman, J.L. & Wildavsky, A.B. (1973). *Implementation*. Berkeley, CA: University of California Press.

Puska, P., Nissinen, A., Tuomilehto, J., Salonen, J.T., Koskela, K., McAlister, A., Kottke, T.E., Maccoby, N. & Farquhar, J.W. (1985). The community-based strategy to prevent coronary heart disease: Conclusions from the ten years of the North Karelia Project. *Annual Review of Public Health, 6,* 147–193.

Roberts-Gray, C. & Gray T. (1983). Implementing innovations. *Knowledge: Creation, Diffusion, Utilization, 5,* 213–232.

Scheirer, M.A. (1996). A user's guide to program templates: A new tool for evaluating program content. *New Directions for Evaluation,* no. 72.

Scheirer, M.A. (1994). Designing and using process evaluation. In J S. Wholey, H.P. Hatry & K.E. Newcomer (Eds.), *Handbook of Practical Program Evaluation.* San Francisco: Jossey-Bass, 40–68.

Scheirer, M.A. (1981). *Program Implementation.* Beverly Hills, CA: Sage Publications.

Scheirer, M.A., Shediac, M.C. & Cassady, C.E., (1995). Measuring the implementation of health promotion programs: The case of the Breast and Cervical Cancer Program in Maryland. *Health Education Research, 10,* 11–25.

Shinn, M. (Ed.). (1996). Special issue: Ecological assessment. *American Journal of Community Psychology, 24,* no. 1.

Shortell, S.M. & Kaluzny, A.D. (1988). Organization theory and health care management. In S. M. Shortell & A. D. Kaluzny (Eds.), *Health Care Management: A Text in Organization Theory and Behavior.* 2nd ed. New York, NY: John Wiley & Sons,.

Skogan, W.G. (1987). Community organizations and crime. In A.H. Reiss, Jr. & M. Tonry (Eds.). *Crime and Justice: A Review of Research.* Chicago: University of Chicago Press, 39–78.

Smith, B. E. & Davis, R. C. (1993). Successful community anticrime programs: What makes them work? In R.C. Davis, A.J. Lurigio, & D.P. Rosenbaum (eds.). *Drugs and the Community: Involving Community Residents in Combatting the Sale of Illegal Drugs.* Springfield, IL: Charles C Thomas, 123–137.

Steckler, A. (1989). The use of qualitative evaluation methods to test internal validity: An example in a work site health promotion program. *Evaluation & The Health Professions, 12,* 115–133.

Stokols, D. (1996). Translating social ecology theory into guidelines for community health promotion. *American Journal of Health Promotion, 10,* 282–298.

Stokols, D., Allen, J. & Bellingham, R.L. (1996). The social ecology of health promotion: Implications for research and practice. *American Journal of Health Promotion, 10,* 247–251.

Wagner, E.H., Koepsell, T.D., Anderman, C., Cheadle, A., Curry, S.G., Psaty, B.M., Von Korff, M., Wickizer, T.M., Beery, W.L., Diehr, P.K., Ehreth, J.L., Kehrer, B.H., Pearson, D.C. & Perrin, E.B. (1991). The evaluation of the Henry J. Kaiser Family Foundation's Community Health Promotion Grant: Design. *Journal of Clinical Epidemiology, 44,* 685–700.

Wallerstein, N. & Bernstein, E. (1988). Empowerment education: Freire's ideas adapted to health education. *Health Education Quarterly, 15,* 379–394.

Watson, D.W. (1992). Prevention, intervention, and treatment of chemical dependency in the black community. In R.L. Braithewaite & S.E. Taylor (Eds.), *Health Issues in the Black Community.* San Francisco: Jossey-Bass.

Wickizer, T.M., Von Korff, M., Cheadle, A., Maeser, J., Wagner, E. H., Pearson, D., Berry, W. & Psaty, B. M. (1993). Activating communities for health promotion: A process evaluation. *American Journal of Public Health, 83,* 561–567.

Williams, W., & Elmore, R.F. (Eds.). (1976). *Social Program Implementation.* NY: Academic Press

Windsor, R.A., Baranowski, T., Clark, N. & Cutter, G. (1994). *Evaluation of Health Promotion, Health Education, and Disease Prevention Programs.* Mountain View, CA: Mayfield.

PART II

AFRICAN AMERICANS

Chapter 4

AFRICAN AMERICAN SUBSTANCE USERS AND ABUSERS

GEORGE HENDERSON, GRACE XUEQIN MA, AND STEVEN E. SHIVE

S ubstance use and abuse are pernicious public health problems that involve all racial and ethnic groups in the United States. In 1997, for example, over 100 million Americans used alcohol monthly, 76 million were alcoholics, 61 million used tobacco, 10 million smoked marijuana, two million used cocaine, three million used psychotropic drugs, one million used hallucinogens, and one million used inhalants (Califona, 1998; Hanson & Venturelli, 1998). Substance use among African Americans has received considerable attention from the media, politicians, and the general public. However, literature pertaining to substance abuse in ethnic minority communities has focused almost extensively on African Americans who live in urban areas. And the data are disheartening. Compilations of data from several sources indicate that over 12 million African Americans drink alcohol, almost three million use marijuana, eight million use tobacco, 500,000 use cocaine (and 200, 000 use crack), 75,000 use inhalants, and 50,000 use heroin.

Fortunately, the development of broad conceptual ecological frameworks have allowed researchers to gain better understandings of the multiple factors underlying substance use and abuse among African Americans. Based on such research, it is evident that the maintenance of healthy people involves more than one factor. Instead, it requires knowledge of the physical, mental and social dimensions of each person in order to facilitate healthy individuals, family members and community residents. This is best done through appropriate attitudes and health care practices. A significant feature of this process is the interdependence and dynamic interaction between practitioners in multiple health care disciplines. That is because health behaviors are influenced by the interaction of multiple levels of the client's intrapersonal, interpersonal and intergroup interactions as well as the inter-disciplinary interventions that are applied in various agency settings. Careful understanding of these psychosocial variables can lead to increased under-standing of substance use and abuse among all peoples. The ultimate goal of substance prevention and intervention agencies is to develop strategies that result in positive health behaviors. In this chapter, we will review research data pertaining to substance use behaviors and associated psychosocial factors among African American adolescents and adults.

ADOLESCENTS

While trends of drug use among adolescent minorities have consistently documented that African American males and females as a whole report less alcohol, tobacco, marijuana and cocaine use than their White or Hispanic peers, prevalence of substance use continues to be a major health problem for African Americans (Bachman et al., 1998; Everett et al., 1998; Johnson et al., 1997). A seminal study of 1,179 urban inner-city students found that of the five chemicals tried by more than five percent of the sample, their order of preference were marijuana (40%), cocaine (12%), mescaline (11%), hashish (7%) and PCP (6%). Also, approximately 40 percent of the students reported alcohol use. For alcohol users, their first preference was beer, followed by wine and then hard liquor. More males than females preferred beer and hard liquor, while the females preferred wine (Penfield, 1990). Although data from the 1997 Youth Risk Behavior Survey showed that 68.4 percent of Black adolescents tried tobacco (Centers for Disease Control and Prevention, 1998), alcohol was the most prevalent substance used by African American adolescents. And trend analyses show a decline in alcohol use by all American adolescents between 1991 and 1997, but African Americans had the largest increase in cigarette smoking (Centers for Disease Control and Prevention, 1998).

Approximately 80 percent of all tobacco use initiation occurs among persons less than 18 years of age; the younger the age a child starts smoking, the more probable it is that he or she will never quit. Marijuana use also increased dramatically among adolescents from 1991 to 1997. Heroin use only increased slightly during that period of time, while inhalant use declined. Changes in reported cocaine use among African American adolescents varied slightly. The data collected through the National Household Surveys show a decline in cocaine use, while the Monitoring the Future Surveys show an increase in cocaine use and a slight increase in heroin use. Perhaps the differences reflect disparate groups. The National Household

Surveys sample individuals 12 to 17 years-of-age and the Monitoring the Future Survey samples twelfth graders.

Numerous factors have been identified to explain variant uses of substances among African Americans. Some of them are unique to African Americans; other factors are operant in other racial and ethnic groups. These factors can be subsumed into three areas: personal, familial and social. Personal factors include such variables as need fulfillment, perceptions of risks, motivation, academic performance and religiosity. Familial factors include family structure and bonding. Social factors include peer group norms and influence, racial discrimination, athletics, drug dealing and gang membership.

PERSONAL FACTORS

One of the reasons that there are so many over-the-counter medications for common aliments such as colds, headaches and upset stomachs is that adults in general shop around for remedies that they believe will abate their illnesses. Some self-determined remedies work, but most of them do not. Substance use by adolescents work in much the same manner. In addressing the use of substances by adolescents, legal or illegal, an important factor is their need to feel good. An analysis of a drug such as heroin serves as an example. It has three main characteristics. Heroin is an analgesic that kills pain. However, unlike novocain that totally numbs one to the point that a person loses all physical feeling, heroin allows for the normal sensation of touch. It not only alleviates physical pain, it also alleviates psychological and emotional manifestations of the pain of living in difficult and unbearable socioeconomic situations. For example, heroin is a sedative; it reduces anxiety and helps a person to sleep. Simply stated, heroin creates euphoria, the illusion of well-being.

In particular, illicit drugs relieves physical and emotional pain, relaxes the users, and makes them feel good, albeit for brief periods. Perhaps drugs serve the purpose of blunting certain ugly realities that accrue to ethnic minority status and poverty. When taken in sufficient quantities, drugs can induce states of euphoria or numbness to almost everything. Although reality does not change with the use of drugs, there is temporary relief. A person's drug of choice in this case meets his or her need to transcend ethnicity or poverty.

A survey of 823 suburban high school students in the Southeastern United States was conducted using a questionnaire that contained a scale focusing on need fulfillment and substance use of adolescents: the Children's Depression Inventory (Mainous et al., 1996). The findings indicate that the higher the adolescent is on the Need Scale, the more likely he or she will engage in substance use. Substances such as cigarette smoking, drinking alcohol and smoking marijuana are associated with significantly higher scores on the Need scale for both males and females. The findings of this study indicate that adolescents who have high wants and needs that are not satisfied in legitimate, socially approved ways will turn to substance use and become substance abusers. Some will become dependent on substances.

Another factor which appears to influence substance use among adolescents is their perception of risks in using a particular substance. A 1997 study which examined racial and ethnic differences in perception of risks was compiled through a National Household Survey. It revealed that there are differences in perceived risks for using particular drugs and the greater the perceived risk, the lower the prevalence rate of use (Bachman et al., 1998). Further, it has been determined that if high school seniors perceive great risk of harm or disapproval from significant others, they are unlikely to smoke marijuana. The perceptions of risk of harmfulness then is among the most important determinants of actual substance use or abstinence.

Motivation, which is integral in the developmental stages of human growth, is a factor that also influences substance use among adolescents. The desire to achieve self-identity is characteristic of adolescents. And the use of certain substances such as cigarettes are often considered to be rites of passage to adulthood. Portrayed in the media as being related to popularity, sex appeal, independence and sophistication, smoking cigarettes is often considered chic. Indeed, cigarette use may be an attractive way for adolescents to define their identities. There are significant differences between the attitudes that sixth, seventh and eighth grade students have of smoking. The older the student, the more positive his or her attitude toward smoking is likely to be (Centers for Disease Control and Prevention, 1998). At some point in school the shift toward a positive image of cigarette smoking is unrelated to whether or not one's friends smoke.

Because interventions that aim at reducing particular substance use may be more effective if researchers could determine during which stage a student will probably use it, more studies must be done to correlate particular developmental stages of substance use. For example, the Multi-Component Motivational Stage Model, based on the stages of behavior change found in a transtheoretical model, has been used to estimate an adolescent's drug use acquisition stage, particularly with regard to alcohol use. Werch and associates (1995) surveyed 254 sixth, seventh and eighth grade students in an urban school to determine the students' current stage of alcohol acquisition. The model proposes five developmental stages of drug use acquisition: precontemplation (not considering use), contemplation (seriously thinking of initiating use), preparation (intending to use in the near future), action (initiating actual use), and maintenance (continuing use).

The researchers concluded that most (86%) students were in the precontemplation stage of alcohol use, followed by the preparation stage (6%), and the action stage (5%). It was further determined that alcohol use, intentions to use alcohol, influenceability, and perceived severity of alcohol problems significantly contributed to predicting alcohol acquisition stage status. These predictor variables accounted for 56 percent of the variance in alcohol stage classification; and alcohol use was the strongest predictor, accounting for more than half the variance. The study sample consisted of primarily African American adolescents, most of whom were relatively low risk for alcohol and other drug use as indicated by their stages of acquisition.

Use of certain substances has also been correlated with students' levels of academic performance and eventual dropping out of high school. A longitudinal study conducted in California and Oregon surveyed a sample of 4,390 students in the seventh grade and again when they were in the twelfth grade. The researchers found that after controlling for demographics, family structure, academic orientation, early deviance and school environment, smoking cigarettes in the seventh grade was a strong predictor of dropping out of high school (Ellickson et al., 1998). The alarming fact was that from 1991 to 1995 the prevalence of smoking among African American male adolescents nearly doubled (Everett et al., 1998). In order to reduce or prevent initiation of tobacco use, interventions targeting African American youth should begin before they enter seventh grade.

Although the National Cancer Institute and the Centers for Disease Control and Prevention recommend that education to prevent tobacco use be provided to students in each grade, from kindergarten through twelfth grade, most school-based tobacco prevention programs target adolescents in grades seven through nine (Centers for Disease Control and Prevention, 1997; Lynch & Bonnie, 1994; Schooler et al., 1996).

In 1978, a twelfth grader was three times more likely to be a current marijuana user than a twelfth grader in 1992, with prevalence rates of 37 percent and 12 percent, respectively. Reasons why a particular drug is popular at a certain time requires more longitudinal analyses of lifestyle factors such as academic abilities, employment, religious beliefs and recreation choices. As an illustration, analyses of trends in substance use by seniors from 1976 to 1986 showed that students who had good grades in school, were seldom truant, were strongly committed to a religion, worked few or no hours at a part-time job, and spent few evenings out for fun or recreation were far less likely than other seniors to smoke marijuana (Bachman et al., 1988). In addition to these lifestyle factors, it was determined that changes in attitudes alone could account for changes in marijuana use. An interesting finding by Amey and associates (1996) is that religiosity of White adolescents resulted in them being less likely to use drugs, but that was not true for black adolescents.

A fairly recent analysis, using data obtained from Monitoring the Future Survey of 1976 to 1996 senior classes and 1991 to 1996 eighth and tenth grade classes, is worth noting (Bachman et al., 1998). Three sets of predictors that analyzed lifestyle factors–grades, truancy, religious commitment, evenings out for recreation, perceived risk of substained harmfulness and peer group disapproval–were compared with the national mean in marijuana use. The researchers concluded that while individual lifestyle factors correlated with marijuana and other drug use, they did not explain the historical changes in marijuana use. However, decreases in perceptions of risk and harm and the belief that there would be peer approval did account for substance use increases among all grades. Marijuana use among African Americans ages 12 to 17 increased 29 percent from 1991 to 1997.

As important as lifestyle factors were, they did not account for changes in marijuana use because most adolescents did not become more conservative or conventional in the 1990s. Reports of recent marijuana use increases suggest that the focus of research should be on finding out why students are less concerned about the health risks associated with marijuana and why they do not disapprove of it as strongly as most students did in the 1980s. Todays students are no more rebellious or delinquent than their predecessors. As with tobacco use prevention and early intervention programs designed to curtail marijuana use, we need more grounding in research and program assessment. If youths use tobacco for different reasons then substance use and abuse programs will have to be differentially developed to address those factors.

FAMILIAL FACTORS

Because the family is the basic unit of society, values inculcated in the family through its organization and structure significantly influence an individual's substance use, which can vary greatly within and between ethnic and racial groups. There is little doubt among researchers that the family is the linchpin in explanations of differential substance use and abuse. While some researchers have found that the absence of a parent can precipitate negative behaviors by adolescents, other studies do not support that observation (Black et al., 1994; Brooke et al., 1998, 1999). Indeed, a family's structure is often more complicated than whether it consists of two parents or one parent or whether it is a nuclear or an extended nuclear family. This is especially true for African American families.

Contrary to television and movie stereotypes, African American adolescents use less illegal substances than their White peers. A study that focused on racial differences in family structures and functions ascertained that African American youths were significantly less likely to initiate drug use than their Latino or White peers (Allen & Page, 1994). And African Americans were significantly more likely than either Hispanics or Whites to live in single-parent homes. In 1994, approximately 22 percent of African American families were headed by never married parents, compared to only six percent of Hispanics and 1.6 percent of White families. Families that consist of parents who have never married, who are currently married but one of the parents is not the biological parent, or of parents who were married but are now divorced have higher tobacco and marijuana use. But they do not have significantly higher alcohol use when compared with families that have both biological parents in the home. The quality or parent/child relationships and the amount of time family members spend together are better predictors of the children's use of tobacco, alcohol and marijuana. However, race or ethnic differences per se do not explain drug initiation.

In order to examine the differential influences of family structure and function on African American adolescents' drug use, Amey and Albrecht (1998) analyzed data compiled in the 1992 National Survey of Families and Households. The survey sample consisted of 1,389 adolescents between ages 10 and 17. Findings from the study indicate that there were no significant difference between racial and ethnic family structures in terms of their members' use of tobacco, alcohol or marijuana. It was determined that while socioeconomic and demographic characteristics explained drug use differences between Hispanics and non-Hispanic Whites, African American and White adolescent differences could not be explained by either structural or functional family differences. Simply put, those characteristics, although important in explaining drug use, did not explain differences in drug use between African American and White youths.

African Americans seem to be influenced by family structure differently than Whites and Hispanics. White and Hispanic youths who live with both biological parents are less likely than their African American peers to use drugs. Surprising to some observers, Amey and Allbrecht note, single-parent African American families often provide a greater protection against drug use than does the two biological parents family unit. Of course, there are research findings that counter Amey and Albrecht's conclusions. In any case, consideration needs to be given to situations where nonresident African American fathers continue to be involved in the lives of their children (see Carter, 2001). Much of the research done with single African American mothers as the head of their household assumed that nonresident fathers were completely absent from the lives of their children. In some instances, that was an unverified assumption.

A 1994 Michigan study sampled 679 ninth graders who were enrolled in four public high schools (Salem et al., 1998). The interviews were conducted by male and female African American and White interviewers to determine family structure effects for problem behaviors that approached significance. Only marijuana use differed across racial and ethnic groups. Adolescents who lived with their mothers and in extended family situations reported more marijuana use than those adolescents who lived with both biological parents. Further, the researchers found that marijuana use was greater among Black youths who lived with their mothers only. When age was controlled for statistical significance, the effect of family structure disappeared. Also, the presence of fathers seemed to have a differential influence on sons and daughters. A sizable number of fathers helped their sons avoid drug-related behavior problems and they prevented their daughters from experiencing prolonged nondrug-related psychological distress. Thus, it is likely that a Black father's significance and the time he spends with his children are inversely associated with male children's marijuana and cigarette use and juvenile delinquency. For female children, however, Black fathers tend to help them to relax rather than avoid drugs.

Alcohol-related beliefs are mediating factors in the initiation and maintenance of most adolescent alcohol consumption behaviors. Generally, African American and Hispanic family norms do not encourage or support adolescent alcohol consumption. Nor is alcohol experimentation and abuse consonant with traditional African American and Hispanic cultures. Within African American female-headed households there are few dominant male adult drinkers who consistently serve as role models. Abstinence, rather than consumption of alcohol, is the norm.

SOCIAL FACTORS

Social factors include perceived peer group norms, sources for getting substances, racial discrimination, and participation in drug dealing and gang membership activities. Without a doubt, peers serve as a significant influence on substance use behaviors. A national study, which surveyed 113,289 junior high and senior high school students ages 10 to 19, found that students who used specific drugs in the last 30 days usually had friends who also used those same drugs, and students whose closest friends did not use drugs were less likely to use drugs themselves. For example, 97.5 percent of marijuana users surveyed by Dinges and Oetting (1993) had friends who used marijuana, compared to 41.6 percent of nonusers who had friends who used it. Only 43 percent of the adolescents who used marijuana had friends who used uppers, compared to 91.8 percent of the marijuana and uppers users who had friends who also used uppers.

Peers interact within the social context of their communities and perceived peer group norms. A study conducted of 1,283 middle school and high school students and 930 college students further showed that for both groups social context and perceived norms were associated with drinking intensity (Thombs et al., 1997). Drinkers believed that their close friends drank more than they actually did. And it was the perceptions of drinking practices of their close friends, rather than those of socially distant persons, that most determined the respondents' own drinking behaviors. Generally, African Americans do not perceive the quantity of use in the same way as other ethnic and racial groups. There is some evidence to indicate that African American youths are more likely to overestimate peer drug use than are Whites. And overestimation can greatly influence an individual's decision to use drugs (U.S. Department of Health and Human Services, 1991).

Among high school students, a sizable number of them tend to report that their friends are important sources for getting tobacco products (Epstein et al., 1999). The 1995 Youth Risk Behavior Survey noted that 33 percent of the students surveyed reported that they usually borrowed from friends the cigarettes that they smoked. More African Americans (48%) than Hispanics (33%) and Whites (31%) reported borrowing cigarettes. Among students younger than 17 years-of-age, 38.7 percent reported that they usually bought cigarettes in a store, and 2.2 percent purchased them from vending machines. Approximately 33 percent reported that they usually borrowed cigarettes, 16 percent gave someone else money to purchase cigarettes for them, and 4.2 percent stole the cigarettes that they smoked. Hispanic and White students were more likely (41.3%) than non-Hispanic and Black students (27.2%) to purchase cigarettes in a store (Centers for Disease Control and Prevention, 1996).

While tobacco is readily available to all adolescents through commercial and social sources regardless of their race or ethnicity, there is evidence that access is easier for African Americans. A study by Landrine and Klonoff (1997) examined discrimination in minors' access to tobacco. The study included eight African American and eight White children who each attempted to purchase cigarettes 36 times in Black and White neighborhood stores. The African American children were significantly more likely to be sold cigarettes than the White children. The African Americans bought cigarettes from non-Black clerks, especially in all-Black neighborhoods. Unfortunately, Black adult customers who witnessed the purchases made no efforts to stop them. The youths also attempted to buy tobacco in 24 stores in White, Black and Hispanic neighborhoods. To the extent there was racial discrimination on the part of the non-Black store clerks who sold the African American children cigarettes and tobacco, and to the extent that indifference exists in the Black community when Black children buy these substances, community leaders should be concerned.

Another social factor in adolescent substance use is their participation in athletics. While participation in athletics has been used by countless community leaders to provide positive alternative activities to drug use, there is evidence that substance use is a ritualized activity among some athletes, especially college athletes. The results of one study indicate that male athletes have a higher incidence of marijuana use than female athletes (Ewing, 1998). The male athletes were more likely than male nonathletes to have tried marijuana in high school. The study also found that female athletes used less marijuana than female nonathletes. Among females, African Americans used marijuana significantly less than Whites. These findings suggest that more emphasis must be placed on educating male athletes about the negative aspects of marijuana use. While substances such as marijuana may be more prevalent among athletes, White athletes, moreso than Black athletes are prone to use chemical substances.

For youths in the inner cities, drug dealing is becoming an increasingly severe problem, but it receives relatively little attention. Estimates of the prevalence of drug dealing among urban teens range from 10 percent among the general population to 16 percent among African American youths. An even larger proportion of African American students are approached to sell drugs (Stanton & Galbraith, 1994). According to Li and Feigelman (1994), approximately 15 percent of Black youths ages 13 to 15 were drug dealers in the early 1990s. Stanton and Galbraith (1994) also found that although African Americans comprised 60 percent of the adolescent population in Baltimore, Maryland, in 1991, they accounted for 91 percent of all juvenile drug arrests. The White juveniles drug arrests from 1981 to 1991 remained the same but there was a dramatic increase in the arrests of African Americans (from 86 in 1981 to 1,304 in 1991). Currently, even though as a whole African American youths have lower rates of substance abuse than their White peers, in most inner-city communities they are twice as likely than White youths to have been approached to sell drugs.

Severe social problems associated with drug dealing include getting entrapped in the juvenile justice system, being involved in violence as either a perpetrator or victim or both, using and abusing alcohol and drugs, exhibiting difficulties in psychosocial adjustment, and earning low school grades. Between 1981 and 1991, arrests for drug dealing in the U.S increased, while arrests for drug use declined (Stanton & Galbraith, 1994). Simply put, among adolescents, drug dealing is associated with other negative behaviors, including school truancy, carrying weapons and fighting (Li & Feigelman, 1994). It is also linked to poor academic performance and exasperated family interactions (Black & Ricardo, 1994).

An obstacle to reducing drug dealing among adolescents is that most offenders do not equate selling drugs to being the same low-level behavior as using drugs. Some youthful dealers even think that selling drugs will protect them from drug use (Feigelman et al., 1993). Also, the money that most youths earn from drug dealing is considerably more than their peers or even older adults earn from legitimate employment, but it is seldom as high as the exaggerated claims. Earnings from selling drugs were reported in one study to range from $672 to $5,000 weekly (Centers & Weist, 1998). That is quite an inducement for lower-class children—and adults.

Gang membership is related to drug dealing. Data from a study conducted with a sample of 1,143 inner-city African American adolescent females in the ninth and eleventh grades indicate that gang members have a higher rate of drug use than nongang members (Harper & Robinson, 1999). Differences in drug use between gang members and nongang members have been reported in cigarette, alcohol and marijuana use. Linear regression analyses have shown in several studies that gang membership is predictive of drug use. A corollary and unanswered question is how to curtail gang memberships.

COLLEGE STUDENTS

According to the 1988 National Household Survey, African American youths use less hallucinogens and inhalants than their White peers. However, young African American adults are more likely than their White peers to use cocaine and heroin (Brook et al., 1998). But Black college students are less likely than Whites and Hispanics to use tobacco, marijuana and cocaine. Black male college students are more likely than Black females to use chemical substances (Centers for Disease Control and Prevention, 1998). Several factors have been identified which influence substance use and abuse among college students, and they too can be subsumed into three categories: personal, familial and social. Personal factors include self-esteem and self-image, religious affiliation, expectations, associated with use of a substance, educational status, and friends. Family factors include living arrangements. Social factors include peer pressure, internalized group norms and the student subculture.

Personal Reasons. There has been relatively little attention paid to racial differences in college students' drinking. Studies of the general population show that African Americans are more likely to be abstainers, begin drinking later, and drink less than Whites. Despite the lower consumption levels, African American men have higher rates of alcohol-related problems than White men (Prendergast et al., 1989). A comparative study was conducted of African American students who attended historically Black colleges and those students who attended historically White colleges (Debro, 1990). The researcher also included a comparison of Black students and White students who attended historically White colleges. Blacks who attended historically Black colleges had lower rates of alcohol and drug use than did Blacks and Whites who attended historically White colleges. The researcher speculated that African Americans who attended Black colleges were provided with a greater sense of self-esteem and self-worth, which in turn helped prevent alcohol and drug use. The lower level of drinking may also have been due in part to the religious beliefs of some of the students. Many religious denominations, Black and White, do not approve of alcohol use (Amey et al., 1996; Jackson, 1995; Washington & Mokley, 2001).

Patterns of alcohol use among and between various racial and ethnic groups appears to be similar in both high school and college. A study of 700 college freshman corroborated that observation (Leibsohn, 1994). The reason that they are similar may be because most college freshmen tend to make friends who are very much like those who were their high school friends. It is a matter of social comfort level.

Familial Reasons. The family typically exerts less influence on young adults when peers become the focal point of their children's daily activities. Of course, the family's ongoing influence will vary. College students' residence and educational status also influence substance use behaviors. A study conducted by Gfroerer and associates (1997) found that students educational status and living arrangements during college attendance were indeed significant predictors of substance use. After controlling for age, race and gender, it was determined that educational status was a significant predictor of marijuana, cocaine, cigarette and alcohol use, but not of heavy consumption of alcohol. Heavy alcohol consumption was more likely to be reported by students who did not live at home than those who did. In addition, students who did not live with their parents were significantly more likely than students who lived with their parents to use marijuana. Generally, Gfroerer and associates concluded, there is no difference between students who lived at home or away from home in terms of cocaine and cigarette use.

Social Reasons. Factors such as peer pressure, social norms and integration into the student subculture partially explain substance use behaviors among African American young adults who attend college. Peer pressure is an abundantly studied factor that influences student behaviors, especially alcohol use and abuse. A sample of 493 students from two universities in Alabama were surveyed by Lo and Globetti (1993). The purpose of the study was to ascertain the extent to which factors such as institutional type, fraternity or sorority affiliation, student living arrangements, parental and peer influences, and religious attitudes toward alcohol use affected alcohol use. Only friends' attitudes toward alcohol use and fraternity or sorority affiliation were significantly correlated with students' drinking behaviors. When they were not discouraged by friends from drinking or they belonged to a fraternity or sorority, college students were three times more likely to become drinkers than those who did not have the two influences. These findings were consistent across race, comparing Whites with African Americans, and across gender.

Peers use common strategies, especially at parties, to persuade their classmates to drink alcohol. Several persuasive tactics were studied using a sample of 132 freshman and sophomore undergraduates who enrolled in communication courses (Harrington, 1997). It was determined that the most common persuasive strategy was a simple offer (46.4%) followed by availability (17.3%), statement of benefits in drinking (14.7%), appeal to group norms (11.5%), minimization of harm (7.3%), and facilitation (2.8%). Minimization was a method in which the persuader reduced the amount of alcohol offered or downplayed the risks associated with drinking, urging individuals to drink "just one," "split one" or "one won't hurt you." Persuaders also used availability, which consisted of telling the targeted person what alcohol was available and how much. Facilitation included statements in which the persuader offered to assist the targeted person, such as to pour a drink or offer to drive him or her home.

A student's drinking behavior is also influenced by his or her perceived campus drinking norms. These norms are usually guessed at and promoted by students who reinforce the perceptions, whether real or not. A nationwide survey of 17,592 undergraduates in 140 colleges and universities measured students' perceptions of campus norms about alcohol use (Perkins & Wechsler, 1996). The local collegiate environment accounted for only a small portion of the variances in perceptions of campus drinking norms. After controlling for personal attitudes, the more persuasive the perception of drinking as a college norm, the more significant was the association with personal alcohol use. If students had a permissive attitude towards drinking, the belief that the college norm was high alcohol use was even more persuasive. In general, students' perceptions of what is normative concerning campus alcohol vary significantly. Reduction of problem drinking can occur when college administrators correct misperceptions of exaggerated alcohol consumption. The majority of students probably want to drink alcohol but they do not want to become excessive drinkers. After a review of a college's alcohol policy, a researcher concluded that most students support college policies that center on moderate drinking (Haspel, 1998). Relatedly, students are prone to support policies that eliminate behaviors that lead to alcohol-related problems.

A study was conducted among 136 undergraduate students, applying the theory of planned behavior to binge alcohol consumption (Norman et al.,

1998). There were two key correlates of the theory: positive control beliefs and perceived behavioral control. Binge drinking was a common activity of 46 percent of the sample, who engaged in the activity at least once a week. It was determined by the researchers that frequent binge drinkers were more likely to have a positive attitude towards binge drinking. They often imagined that there was irresistible social pressure to engage in binge drinking; they believed that binge drinking led to various positive consequences; and they needed facilitators to help them binge. The data in the study offers the perspective that for many young people, binge drinking is very much an approved social behavior.

Marijuana use is a perennial problem on college campuses. A study of 17,592 undergraduate students in 140 U.S. colleges found that 25 percent of students reported past year use of marijuana, with prevalence rates ranging from 0 percent to 54 percent (Bell et al., 1997). The researchers found similar factors related to marijuana and other substance use. Characteristics which were highly correlated with marijuana use included being single, White, spent lots of time at parties and socializing with friends, and spent less time studying. Marijuana use was higher among students who participated in other health risk behaviors such as binge drinking, multiple sex partners, and tobacco use. Further, students who thought parties were important and who defined themselves as not being religious were at greater risk than those who held polar views.

Factors similar to those in marijuana use have also been found in regards to cocaine use. Data collected from a longitudinal study called the "Coronary Artery Risk Development in Young Adults" allowed the researchers to conclude that while cocaine use declined among Whites from 1987 to 1992, the prevalence of use remained stable among African Americans (Braun et al., 1996). The study consisted of 3,848 participants: 47 percent were African American, and 53 percent were Whites. Variables that related to high incidences of cocaine use included being African American, ages 27 to 32, male, single, unemployed, and users of other drugs such as alcohol, marijuana or heroin. The magnitude and strength of the relationship between the variables remained constant over time, except for the year 1992, in which there was increased odds of cocaine use among the unemployed and African Americans.

Drug use by college students also appears to be determined by how well the students integrate into the school's student subculture. The results of a study in which 433 undergraduate students were surveyed indicate that integration into a student subculture is a better indicator of drug use initiation and frequency and than are social background factors (Thomas et al., 1975). Blacks enrolled in predominantly White schools are less integrated into mainstream campus subcultures and therefore at greater risk for drug use.

Use of substances has also been correlated with other high-risk behaviors, especially among minority groups. Intravenous drug use is significantly associated with sexual risk-taking, which in turn can lead to the acquisition of AIDS. Minority groups in inner or central cities have the highest risk of acquiring AIDS. A study conducted by Schoenbaum and associates (1989) found HIV in 39 percent of a methadone maintenance population in New York City. The sample included 49.1 percent Blacks, 41.8 percent Hispanics, and 9.1 percent non-Hispanic Whites. Another study examined a sample of 1,561 Black, White and Hispanic individuals at the Bellevue Hospital Center in New York (Kim et al., 1993). Of the respondents who reported having sexual relations with a member of the opposite sex, many of them had sex with intravenous drug users. And many of them had anal sex. The use of protective measures, such as condoms, with steady partners and unsteady partners was reported to be low.

SUBSTANCE ABUSE ISSUES AMONG AFRICAN AMERICANS

There are key issues pertaining to African American substance use that interact across the life-span, affecting all age groups and both genders. These issues include drinking alcohol while under the influence, tobacco use, prescription drug use, violence associated with drug use, drug use during pregnancy, and the differences between the perceptions and the reality of drug use and abuse.

Alcohol Use. As noted earlier, alcohol is the most abused substance among African Americans. Studies which have focused on racial and ethnic differences in patterns of alcohol consumption among adults show that alcohol use declined among most age groups of African Americans from 1984 to 1992. But unlike other racial groups whose amount of alcohol consumption declined with increasing age, African American consumption remained stable with increasing age. A major problem associated with alcohol consumption is driving while intoxicated. Approximately 50 percent of all motor vehicle accidents involve alcohol (Hanson & Venturelli, 1998). But it is unclear that Blacks are more prone to be involved in vehicular accidents.

Caetano and Clark (1999) conducted a study in which 1,582 Blacks, 1,585 Hispanics and 1,636 Whites in U.S. households were interviewed for one hour in the respondents' homes. The respondents reported rate of driving a car after consuming alcohol varied significantly between ethnic and racial groups, with the highest rates occurring among White men (22%) and Hispanic men (21%) compared to Blacks (14%). White men and Hispanic men also had the highest arrest rates for driving under the influence of alcohol (DUI). There were significant differences in rates of DUI arrest, with approximately 20 percent of Hispanic men, 10 percent of White men, and four percent of Black men being arrested within 12 months prior to the interview. Recent statistics pertaining to racial profiling by police suggest that the arrest rates of people of color may be significantly higher than those cited by Caetano and Clark.

Drinking patterns among African Americans have been explained in terms of social disorganization, i.e., family breakdown and psychological dysfunction (Herd, 1987). More recent explanations focus on social change as contributing to alcohol consumption among African Americans. For example, the move from the South to the North in the early twentieth century led to an increase in alcohol consumption. Data in the 1984 National Alcohol Survey show that rates of heavy alcohol consumption among African American were highest for men in their 40s and 50s, while among Whites the rates were highest for men in their 20s. The 1995 National Alcohol Survey show that patterns of drinking have changed, and both White and African American men show similar patterns of drinking until they reach age 49, with the rates being higher among Whites than among African Americans ages 50 to 59 (Caetano et al., 1998).

Tobacco use is another problem for African American adults. In African American communities, smoking cigarettes is the number one risk factor for cardiovascular diseases and cancer and that translates into thousands of tobacco-related deaths (Centers for Disease Control and Prevention, 1998). It is not helpful for there to be four to five times more billboards advertising tobacco in African American communities than in White communities. Actually, those billboards encouraging tobacco use are not helpful in any community.

Prescription Drug Use. There are differences between Whites and African Americans in the use of prescription drugs. A 1992 study conducted by Khandker and Simoni-Wastiler (1998) compared 487,922 Black and 341,274 White Georgia Medicaid enrollees and found that Blacks used fewer prescription drugs and spent less on drugs than did Whites. This was determined by examining drug claims. The differences were calculated after controlling for demographic and Medicaid eligibility variables. Black children used 2.7 fewer prescriptions than White children; Black adults used 4.9 fewer prescriptions than White adults; and elderly Black adults used 6.3 fewer prescriptions than Whites of the same age. Those differences may have been the result of disparate health care opportunities.

Substance Abuse and Violence. Alcohol and other drugs are found in individuals who commit more than half of all homicides in the United States, and they are used by perpetrators of an even larger number of nonfatal violent acts (Fagan, 1993). In many cases, both the victims and the offenders had been drinking prior to the violence. Other types of violent acts committed while under the influences of alcohol and other drugs include sexual assaults and physically abusive altercations between strangers. Heroin addicts, in particular, are frequently involved in assaults. Several causal links have been established between substance use and violence. Often violence is linked to economic necessity, such as when an addict becomes violent in order to obtain money for drugs. Further, violence is common during the trafficking of illegal drugs (Goldstein, 1985). Studies of individuals across cultures and at various locations suggest that social contexts significantly influence addiction/violence relationships. Social contexts also determine the choice of substances used and the behavior norms related to their use, including aggression in some situations (Fagan, 1993).

The homicide rates among Hispanics are almost as high as among African Americans in all gender groups. Young African American and Hispanic men are more likely than their White peers to die from homicide, with 75 percent of the annual deaths involving firearms. African Americans, Hispanics and Asians are more likely to be killed by a firearm. But there usually is no association between using cocaine and being killed by a firearm (Donzinger, 1996; Valdez et al., 1997). The prevalence rates of homicide by young African Americans and Hispanics are more likely to be related to selling drugs instead of using them. Many writers speculate that there are numerous reasons for African American males in particular to sell cocaine and other drugs: (1) they become alienated and discouraged by nonmainstream acceptance; (2) they have very limited educational and employment opportunities; (3) they are bombarded with antisocial diatribes, and (4) they are victims of racism—all of which interferes with their healthy social development. Obviously, most people who are subjected to the same conditions do not sell drugs. Thus, the retort by some social commentators is that the four reasons cited for violence are merely psychobable.

A cross-sectional study using a sample of 401 women who met at-risk criteria for violence during substance use were compared to 746 other women who were not at-risk for substance-related violence (Zahnd et al., 1997). Variables such as neighborhood substance-related problems, being born in the United States, and being a woman of color were associated with substance-related violence done to them by individuals known to them. Various types of stresses, including unemployment, income disparity between spouses, and low socioeconomic status, can lead to violence against women by males who try to maintain their dominant status in their family or interpersonal relationships. Substance use and wife beating are not unique to low-income minorities, however. Heavy alcohol consumption and spouse abuse, for example, are problems conterminous in White and Hispanic families too. After factoring out socioeconomic variables, most researchers conclude that there is no association between African American alcohol consumption and wife assaults.

Pregnancy and Substance Abuse. Despite racial stereotypes, more White women than African American or Hispanic women smoke cigarettes during their pregnancies. In 1990, for example, approximately five million women of childbearing age used drug substances, including alcohol, and between 90,000 and 250,000 infants a year were exposed to cocaine as fetuses (Waters et al., 1997). In some health care facilities, 43 percent of neonates tested positive for drugs. It was further estimated that hospital expenses were at least seven times higher for those infants than for the nonexposed infants. This resulted in nearly seven times more in medical costs for drug exposed infants.

When data of past month drug use are compared by race and gender, African American females rates are only slightly higher than those of White females. Although they make up only six percent of the U.S. population, African American women are ten times more likely than any other women to report illicit drug use. The prevalence rate of AIDS is 10 to 15 times higher for African American women than it is for White women, and more than half of all pediatric AIDS cases in the U.S. are attributed to the high prevalence rate for African Americans (Waters et al., 1997).

There are differences in subgroups of African American women who abuse crack cocaine. Cohen (1999) conducted a study in Philadelphia to examine African American crack users, and he found that there were five subgroups based on indicators such as clinical syndromes, psychological symptomatology, lifetime and recent drug and alcohol use, prior physical and sexual abuse, and social context factors such as parental addiction and sharing a residence with a drug user. This classification into subgroups may be helpful to agencies that provide substance prevention programs and adequate assessment of their interventions and treatment techniques (Cohen, 1999).

SUBSTANCE USE PERCEPTIONS AND REALITY

While drug use patterns have shown reductions across populations, these data may be misleading in terms of the extent of the problem among specific populations (Blanken et al., 1987). Specifically, there are many misperceptions in American society about substance use among African Americans, who are often erroneously portrayed in the media as our nation's largest illicit drug users. These "stories" label African Americans as "villains," "druggers" and "dopers." Watson and Jones (1989) asked 400 multiracial participants in the Washington, DC area to close their eyes, envision a drug user and a drug seller and to describe the persons. More than 95 percent of the participants, including African Americans, envisioned the persons as male or female African Americans. There are a number of things that explain those misperceptions.

One reason that African Americans are associated with a higher prevalence of substance use is that they live in poverty areas where the most blatant drug deals occur; they are more than twice as likely than Whites to be unemployed; and when employed, they earn less than their White peers (National Urban League, 1993). These are stressors that increase the risk of substance use (Adams & Gfroefer, 1988). If drug use is a behavior for coping with environmental stresses, then to the uninformed most substance users must be African Americans, given their socioeconomic conditions. The surprise is not how *many* African Americans use drugs but how *few*. Further, a disproportionate number of them are, according to sociologists, marginal people in our U.S. society (Farley 1990). Life in a marginal group implies incomplete socialization into the dominant society's prevailing norms. Individuals who live in such groups, this theory speculates, tend to display positive attitudes towards illegal activities. In support of this notion, Gary and Gretz (1984) found that most of the people who lived in the low-income Black community they studied held marginal status, especially young adult males, and they had more positive attitudes toward substance use than Blacks who were less marginalized. *Most of the residents did not use illegal drugs.*

As noted earlier, another reason for the misperception of African Americans as the overwhelming majority of drug users is the fact that most illicit drug sales in U.S. occur in African American communities. Missing from this picture are the Whites who are the primary buyers of illegal substances. African Americans are more likely than Whites to be stopped, detained or arraigned for illegal drug possession (Donzinger, 1996; Klein, 1996). Although approximately 80 percent of all persons arrested for drug trafficking during the last decade were White, the image of Black "druggies" and "pushers" persist (Donziger, 1996). African Americans are arrested for drug possession at a rate disproportionately higher than the rate for Whites. This also leads to the impression that the drug problem is primarily a Black problem.

The use of cocaine caught the national spotlight in the 1980s. The most notable crack cocaine scare occurred between 1986 and 1992. Crack is a form of cocaine that can be smoked and it is readily available in the inner cities. Portrayed by the media as producing immediate addiction, crack also linked to gang violence. The national solution for this "crisis" is the "war on drugs" (Donziger, 1996). The purpose of the war is to reduce illicit drug supplies. The result has been an increase in drug enforcement budgets and an increase in arrests of ethnic minority drug users, most of whom are labeled as immoral, aggressive and self-indulgent (Covington, 1998). The presumption that cocaine causes violent outbursts is questionable because most crack-related homicides are among drug dealers (Goldstein, 1985). The claim of immediate addiction to crack is often based on evidence that is derived from the most depraved addicts. Unfortunately, these scenarios are treated as though they are typical cases (Reinarman & Levine, 1997).

Except for crack cocaine and heroin, drug use among White females exceeds that of African American females. In reality, very few people ever try crack, so the claim of its use being an epidemic is suspect. The fact that crack use can be regulated by the user during the early stages rarely gets mentioned. It is unfortunate that African American and Hispanic drug users and abusers are commonly presented as the worst cases (Covington, 1998).

Effective educational initiatives and substance abuse program intervention may need to differentially target populations not only for various age groups but also for gender- and ethnic-specific groups. We have described how various studies have highlighted the differences in drug use among racial and ethnic groups and the crucial role that demographic factors play (Andreski & Breslau, 1993; Connors et al., 1988; Kandel, 1995). A major difficulty in analyzing these data is the inadequacy of the labeling clients, e.g,. Black, White, Hispanic, Asian and Indian. These labels are generic terms and do not clearly identify specific groups. Several authors have cogently discussed problem of labeling (Bhopal et al., 1987; Bhopal & Donaldson, 1998; O'Donnell, 1991).

SUBSTANCE USE PREVENTION

It should not be assumed that drug use and abuse among different subgroups are based on the same set of factors. While there are factors that all racial and ethnic groups share in common, there are some factors that are more pronounced in certain groups. Likewise, it should not be assumed that successful prevention and cessation programs will be the same for all ethnic and racial groups (Amey & Albrecht, 1988). Within social, cultural and political contexts, African American males moreso than White males receive biased, unfair treatment based on stereotypical beliefs that they are dangerous, dishonest and ignorant. Researchers who have studied drug use and addiction patterns among African American males often recommend that intervention strategies focus on identity building or sustaining positive self-identities to counteract negative societal forces and agencies should not promote racism (Dixon & Yaazibo 1998; Longshore, 1998).

People who believe that existing national and local drug policies are effective in curbing drug use will be comforted by the overall general decline in the use of alcohol, tobacco, marijuana and cocaine use among African

Americans. However, despite this improvement, patterns of drug use still remain high and are worsening for young adults in African American communities. This suggests that the war on drugs has not been won. Additional interventions designed to reduce substance use and abuse among all ethnic minorities merit our nation's attention, including increasing the prices of cigarettes, initiating more peer education and peer helping programs, offering more home intervention services to drug abusing women, changing peer norms and, of course, incorporating culturally relevant interventions into all programs.

Increases in Cigarette Price. Data gleaned from the National Health Interview Survey (NHIS) indicate that when the price of cigarettes increase, minorities and people with low income smoke less. A 50 percent increase could conceivably result in a 12.5 percent reduction in cigarettes consumed in the United States–60 billion fewer cigarettes purchased each year. After controlling for other factors such as income, education, and other nonprice variables, McFarrelly and Bray (1998) projected that Hispanic and African American smokers were more likely than White smokers to reduce or quit smoking in response to price increases. Based on research data, consistent across all age groups, African Americans and Hispanic smokers ages 18 to 21 are more price-responsive than smokers in the 40 and older age group. Perhaps the federal government could tax cigarettes out of most minority group homes.

Peer Education Programs. Peer education has become popular in the United States and other countries (Bauman & Ennett, 1994; Gartner, 1996; Rhodes, 1994). This kind of health initiative has been developed because research findings show that young people seldom go to substance abuse programs for assistance. Instead, they are more likely to discuss substance-related problems with their peers. Ward and associates (1997) evaluated a peer education program in Britain. They surveyed 72 individuals who had participated in the program. The researchers found that the adolescent respondents wanted to learn more about drugs, especially information that would help them with future employment and also be useful when counseling other young people. Peer educators who completed the program were involved as substance information resources for their family members. A few peer educators used an outreach approach by speaking about drugs to people previously unknown to them. Others used the knowledge they gained in the program to educate coworkers. The peer educators tended to be nonjudgmental and objective when presenting drug-related information. Relatedly, in a meta-analysis study of 120 adolescent in drug programs, Black and associates (1998) concluded that interactive peer interventions for middle school students were statistically superior to noninteractive didactic, lecture programs led by teachers or researchers.

Home Interventions for Drug-Abusing Women. A randomized, clinical trial of 60 drug-abusing pregnant women were recruited and randomized into an intervention group (n=31) and a comparison group (n=29) (Black et al., 1994). Most of the mothers were single, African American, had multiple children, and were high school drop-outs from low-income families. All of the respondents admitted to using cocaine or heroin, and 24 of them were HIV positive. The women in the home intervention program were marginally more likely to report that they were drug-free than the women in the control group. The mothers who received home visits from health care practitioners were marginally more compliant with their children's primary care appointments during the 18 months period of the study.

Changing Perceptions of Peer Norms. A study was conducted of 1,426 college students assigned to one of four groups: peer norms education (PN), values clarification (VC), combined PN and VC, and a control group (Hansen et al., 1991). The findings support the notion that dissonance between college students' drinking levels and their corrected perceptions of their reference group's drinking norms tend to lead to a reduction in the estimates. And, relatedly, students revise their own drinking norm downward. Therefore, intervention programs using peers can be helpful in reducing alcohol consumption.

Relevent Health Education. Successful substance abuse intervention and prevention programs provide culturally relevant health care information, promote positive cultural identity, support family and peer networks, facilitate adaptive coping skills, and strengthen social role-life missions (Yee, 1995). Culturally relevant health education consists of developing health interventions that allow specific ethnic groups to cease or avoid high-risk substance use behaviors. Positive self-concepts that come from pride in one's cultural heritage can lead to a reduction in high-risk substance use behaviors. Encouraging wholesome social support systems, especially family members, can also reduce substance use and abuse. And, of course, coping skills that promote antidrug use can lead to a reduction in substance use risk behaviors. Finally, positive social roles and life missions are requisites to healthy lives.

SUMMARY

Treatment and prevention programs that lack a firm grasp of tradition-oriented African American cultural norms will be relatively ineffective in curtailing substance use and abuse. That is, programs that do not provide viable links to the Black community will fail in their vacuums—cut off from their individual clients and the community at large. Lack of such sensitivity can result in the misleading diagnoses of factors that contribute to clients' substance use. We are not suggesting esoteric or intellectual cultural sensitivity training. Rather, we strongly encourage the design and implementation of such training to be based on the active participation of people of color. Nor should the issue of crimes of violence, insensitive criminal justice officials, and the sheer hazards inherent in ethnic minority status be dismissed as irrelevant.

Sometimes people use drugs or hurt other persons in order to make sense of their seemingly merger lives. Depression and hesitance-seeking treatment, for example, while symptomatic of many African American substance abusers must be kept in proper focus. In some communities people are "crazy" if they are not depressed. Researchers must find out more about African Americans who become overwhelmed with their lives–and also those who do not. From this perspective, substance abuse is a social behavior, not an incurable disease.

REFERENCES

Adams, E. H. & Groefer, J.C. (1988). Elevated risk of cocaine use in adults. *Psychiatric Annals, 18*(9), 523–527.

Allen, O. & Page, R.M. (1994). Variance in substance use between rural Black and White Mississippi high school students. *Adolescence, 29*, 401–404.

Amey, C.H., Albrechtt, S.L. & Miller, M.K. (1996). Racial differences in adolescent drug use: The impact of religion. *International Journal of Addictions, 31*(3), 1311–1332.

Amey, C.H. & Allbrecht. S.L. (1998). Race and ethnic differences in adolescent drug use: The impact of family structure and the quantity and quality of parental interaction. *Journal of Drug Issues, 28*(2), 283–298.

Amode, M. & Jones, L.K. (1997). Viewing alcohol and other drug use cross-culturally: A cultural framework for clinical practice. Families in Society, 78, 240–254.

Andreski, P. & Breslau, N. (1993). Smoking and nicotine dependence in young adults: Differences between Blacks and Whites. *Drug & Alcohol Dependence*, 32(2), 119–125.

Bachman, J.G., Johnston, L.D. & O'Malley, P.M. (1998). Explaining recent increases in students' marijuana use: Impacts of perceived risks and disapproval, 1976 through 1996. *American Journal of Public Health, 88*, 887–892.

Bachman, J.C., Johnston, L.D., O'Malley, P.M. & Humphrey, R.H. (1988). Explaining the recent decline in marijuana use: Differentiating the effects of perceived risks, disapproval, and general lifestyle factors. *Journal of Health & Social Behavior, 29*, 92–112.

Bauman, K.E. & Ennett, S.T. (1994). Peer influence on adolescent drug use. *American Psychologist, 49*, 1230–1238.

Bell, R., Wechsler, H. & Johnston, L.D. (1997). Correlates of college student marijuana use: Results of a U.S. national survey. *Addiction, 92*(5), 571–584.

Bhopal, R., &. Donaldson, L. (1998). White, European, Western, Caucasian, or what? Inappropriate labeling in research on race, ethnicity, and health. *American Journal of Public Health, 88*(9), 1303–1309.

Black, D.R., Tobler, N.S. & Sciacca, J.P. (1998). Peer helping/involvement: An efficacious way to meet the challenge of reducing alcohol, tobacco, and other drug use among youth? *Journal of School Health, 68*(3), 87–93.

Black, M. & Ricardo, I. (1994). Drug use, drug trafficking and weapon carrying among low-income African American early adolescent boys. *Pediatrics, 93,* 1065–1072.

Black, M.M., Nair, P., Kight, C., Wachtel, R., Roby, P. & Schuler, M. (1994). Parenting and early development among children of drug-abusing women: Effects of home intervention. *Pediatrics, 94,* 440–448.

Blanken, A.J., Adams, E.H. & Durell, J. (1987). Drug abuse. Implications and trends. *Psychiatric Medicine, 3*(3), 299–317.

Braun, B.L., Murray, D., Hannan, P., Sidney, S. & Le, C. (1996). Cocaine use and characteristics of young adult users from 1987 to 1992: The CARDIA study. *American Journal of Public Health, 86*(12), 1736–1741.

Brook, J.S., Brook, D.W., De La Rosa, M. et al. (1998). Pathways to marijuana use among adolescents: Cultural/ecological, family, peer, and personality influences. *Journal of the American Academy of Child & Adolescent Psychiatry, 37,* 759–766.

Brook, J.S., Brook, D.W., De La Rosa, M. et al., (1999). The role of parents in protecting Columbian adolescents from delinquency and marijuana use. Archives of *Pediatric Medicine, 153,* 457–464.

Caetano, R. (1997). Prevalence, incidence and stability of Whites, Blacks and Hispanics: 1984–1992. *Journal of Studies on Alcohol, 58*(6), 565–572.

Caetano, R., Clark, C.L. & Tam, T. (1998). Alcohol consumption among racial/ethnic minorities. *Alcohol Health & Research World, 22*(4), 233–242.

Caetano, R. & Clark, C.L. (1999). Hispanics, Blacks and Whites driving under the influence of alcohol: Results from the 1995 National Alcohol Survey. *Accident Analysis Prevention, 32,* 57–64.

Califano, J.A., Sr. (1998). Substance abuse and addiction: The need to know. *American Journal of Public Health, 88*(1), 9–11, 27–33, 93–96.

Carter, J. (2001). African American fathers: Factors that motivate their commitment to their children. Unpublished dissertation. Norman: University of Oklahoma.

Centers for Disease Control and Prevention. (1996). Tobacco use and usual source of cigarettes among high school students–United States, 1995. *Journal of School Health, 66,* 222–224.

Centers for Disease Control and Prevention. (1998). Tobacco use among U.S. racial/ethnic minority groups–African Americans, American Indians, Alaska Natives, Asian Americans and Pacific Islanders, Hispanics. A report of the surgeon general. Executive summary. *Morbidity & Mortality Weekly Report, 47,* 1–16, 224–233.

Centers, N.L. & Weist, M.D. (1998). Inner city youth and drug dealing: A review of the problem. *Journal of Youth & Adolescence, 27*(3), 395–411.

Cohen, E.D. (1999). An exploratory attempt to distinguish subgroups among crack-abusing African-American women. *Journal of Addictive Diseases, 18*(3), 41–54.

Connors, G.J., O'Farrell, T.J. & Pelcovits, M.A. (1988). Drinking outcome expectancies among male alcoholics during relapse situations. *British Journal of Addiction 83*(5), 561–566.

Covington, J. (1998). Crack in America: Demon drugs and social justice. *Contemporary Sociology, 27*, 310–312.

Debro, J. (1990). Drug use and abuse at historically Black colleges. In L. Harris (Ed.), Problems of Drug Dependence 1990: Proceedings of the 52nd annual scientific meeting of the committee on problems of drug dependence, Inc. *NIDA Research Monograph 105*, (pp. 460–461). Rockville, MD: National Institute on Drug Abuse.

Dixon, P. & ya Azibo, D.A. (1998). African self-consciousness, misorientation, and a self-destructive disorder: African American male crack cocaine users. *Journal of Black Psychology, 24*(2), 226–247.

Dinges, M.M. & Oetting, E.R. (1993). Similarity in drug use patterns between adolescents and their friends, *Adolescence, 28*, 253–266.

Donziger, S.R. (Ed.). (1996). *The Real War on Crime: The Report of the National Criminal Justice Commission.* New York: Harper Collins.

Ellickson, P. Bui, K. Bell, R. & McGuigan K.A. (1998). Does early drug use increase the risk of dropping out of high school? *Journal of Drug Issues, 28*(2), 357–380.

Ewing, B.T. (1998). High school athletes and marijuana use. *Journal of Drug Education, 28*(2), 147–157.

Fagan, J. (1993). Interactions among drugs, alcohol, and violence. *Health Affairs, 12*(4), 65–79.

Farley, R. (1990). Blacks, Hispanics and White ethnic groups: Are Blacks uniquely disadvantaged? *APA Papers and Proceedings,* 237–240.

Gartner, A. (1996). Converting peer pressure. *Social Policy, 27*, 47–49.

Gary, L. & Gretz, B. (1984). Some determinants of attitudes toward substance use in an urban ethnic community. *Psychological Reports, 54*, 549–561.

Gfroerer, J.C., Greenblatt, J.C. & Wright, D.A. (1997). Substance use in the U.S. college-age population: Differences according to educational status and living arrangement. *American Journal of Public Health, 87*(1), 62–65.

Goldstein, P.J. (1985). The drugs violence nexus: A tri-partite conceptual framework. *Journal of Drug Issues, 15*, 493–506.

Grob, C. & Dobkin de Rios, M. (1992). Adolescent drug use in cross-cultural perspective. *Journal of Drug Issues, 22*, 121–138.

Hansen, W.B., Graham, J., Wolkenstein, B.H., Lundy, B.Z. et al. (1991). Differential impact of three alcohol prevention curricula on hypothesized mediating variables. *Journal of Drug Education, 18*(2), 143–153.

Hanson, G. & Venturellis, R.J., (1998). *Drugs and Society.* Sudbury, MA: Jones & Bartlett.

Harper, G.W., & Robinson, W.L. (1999). Pathways to risk among inner-city African-American adolescent females: The influence of gang membership. *American Journal of Community Psychology, 27*(3), 383–402.

Harrington, N.G. (1997). Strategies used by college students to persuade peers to drink. *Southern Communication Journal 62*(3), 229–242.

Haspel, J. (1998). Social pressure, not peer pressure, leads students to drink. Brown University *Child & Adolescent Behavior Letter, 14*(9), 1–3.

Herd, D. 1987) Rethinking Black drinking. *British Journal of Addiction, 82*, 219–223.

Jackson, M.S. (1995). Afrocentric treatment of African American women and their children in a residential chemical dependency program. *Journal of Black Studies, 26*, 17–30.

Johnson, P.B. & Gallo-Treacy, C. (1993). Alcohol expectancies and ethnic drinking differences. *Journal of Alcohol & Drug Education, 38*(3), 80–88.

Johnson, P.B. & Johnson, H.L. (1999). Cultural and familial influences that maintain the negative meaning of alcohol. *Journal of Alcohol Studies, 13*, 79–83.

Johnston, L.D. Bachman, J.G. & O'Malley, P.M. (1997). *Monitoring the Future-1995; Questionnaire Responses from the Nation's High School Seniors.* Ann Arbor: MI: Institute for Survey Research.

Kandel, D. (1995). The impact of drug use on earnings: A lifespan perspective. *Social Forces, 74*, 243–270.

Kim, M.Y., Marmor, M. Dubin, N. & Wolfe, H. (1993). HIV risk-related sexual behaviors among heterosexuals in New York City: Associations with race, sex, and intravenous drug use. *AIDS, 7*, 409–414.

Klein, S., Petersilia, J. & Turner, S. (1990). Race and imprisonment decisions in California. *Science, 247*.

Kline, A. (1996). Pathways into drug user treatment: The influence of gender and racial/ethnic identity. *Substance Use & Misuse, 31*(3), 323–342.

Landrine, H. & Knoff, E.A. (1997). Racial discrimination in minors' access to tobacco. *Journal of Black Psychology, 23*(2), 135–148.

Leibsohn, J. (1994). The relationship between drug and alcohol use and peer group associations of college freshmen as they transition from high school. *Journal of Drug Education, 24*(3), 177–192.

Li, X., & Feigelman, S. (1994). Recent and intended drug trafficking among male and female urban African-American early adolescents. *Pediatrics, 93*(6), 1044–1049.

Lo, C.C. & Globetti, G. (1993). A partial analysis of the campus influence on drinking behavior: Students who enter college as nondrinkers. *Journal of Drug Issues, 23*(4), 715–725.

Longshore, D. (1998). Promoting recovery from drug abuse: An Afrocentric intervention. *Journal of Black Studies, 28*(3), 319–333.

Mainous, A.G., Martin, C.A., Oler, M.J., Richardson, E.T. & Haney, A.S. (1996). Substance use among adolescents: Fulfilling a need state. *Adolescence, 31*(124), 807–815.

McFarrelly, M.C., & Bray, J.W. (1998). Response to increases in cigarette prices by race/ethnicity, income, and age groups–United States, 1976–1993. *Journal of the American Medical Association, 280*(23), 1979.

National Urban League. (1993). *Quarterly Report on the African American Worker, 15*, Washington, DC: Author.

Norman, P., Bennett, P. & Lewis, H. (1998). Understanding binge drinking among young people: An application of the theory of planned behaviour. *Health Education Research, 13*(2), 163–169.

Penfield, D.A. (1990). Surveying urban inner-city high school students: An assessment of drug and alcohol abuse. *Educational Research Quarterly, 14*(4), 5–14.

Perkins, H.W. & Wechsler, H. (1996). Variation in perceived college drinking norms and its impact on alcohol abuse: A nationwide study. *Journal of Drug Issues, 26*(4), 961–974.

Prendergast, M.L., Austin, G.A., Maton, K.I. & Baker, R. (1989). *Substance Abuse Among Black Youth.* San Francisco, CA: Western Center for Drug-Free Schools Communities.

Reinarman, C. & Levine, H. (1997). *Crack in America: Demon Drugs and Social Justice.* Berkeley: University of California Press.

Rhodes, T. (1994). Outreach, peer education and community change: Development and dilemmas. *Health Education Journal, 53*, 92–99.

Rosenthal, M.S. (1989). The therapeutic community: Exploring the boundaries. *British Journal of Addiction, 84*, 141–150.

Salem, D.A., Zimmerman, M.A., & Notaro, P.C. (1998). Effects of family structure, family process, and father involvement on psychosocial outcomes among African American adolescents. *Family Relations, 47*, 331–341.

Schoenbaum, E.E., Hartel, D. & Selwyn, P.A. (1989). Risk factors for human immunodeficiency virus infection in intravenous drug users. *New England Journal of Medicine, 321*, 874–879.

Schooler, C., Feighery, E., & Flora, J. (1996). Seventh graders' self-reported exposure to cigarette marketing and its relationship to their smoking behavior. *American Journal of Public Health, 86*(9), 1216–1221.

U.S. Department of Health and Human Services. (1991). *Drug Abuse and Drug Abuse Research: The Third Triennial Report to Congress.* Washington, DC: U.S. Government Printing Office.

U.S. Department of Justice, F.B.I. (1990). *Crime in the United States.* Washington, DC U.S. Government Printing Office.

Valdez, A., Yin, Z., & Kaplan, C.D. (1997). A comparison of alcohol, drugs, and aggressive crime among Mexican-American, Black, and White male arrestees in Texas. *American Journal of Drug & Alcohol Abuse, 23*(2), 249–266.

Ward, J. Hunter, G. & Power, R. (1997). Peer education as a means of drug prevention and education among young people: An evaluation. *Health Education Journal, 56*, 251–263.

Washington, O.G.M. & Moxley, D.P. (2001). The use of prayer in group work with African American women recovering from chemical dependency. *Family Sociology, 82*(1), 49–59.

Waters, J. Roberts, A.R. & Morgen, K. (1997). High risk pregnancies: Teenagers, poverty, and drug abuse. *Journal of Drug Issues, 27*(3), 541–562.

Watson, B. & Jones, D. (1989). Drug use and African Americans. *Runtafax sheet of the National Urban League, 2.*

Werch, C.F., Anzalone, D., Castellon-Vogel, E., Carlson, J. et al. (1995). Factors associated with the stages of alcohol use among inner city school youth. *Journal of School Health, 65*(7), 255–259.

Yee, B.W.K., Castro, F.G., Hammond, W.R. et al. (1995). Panel IV: Risk-taking and abusive behaviors among ethnic minorities. *Health Psychology, 14*(7), 622–631.

Zahnd, E., Klein, D., & Needell, B. (1997). Substance use and issues of violence among low-income, pregnant women: The California prenatal needs assessment. *Journal of Drug Issues, 27*(3), 563–584.

Chapter 5

SMOKING CESSATION AMONG AFRICAN AMERICANS

Linda Pederson, Jasjit Ahluwailia, Kari Jo Harris, and Gene A. McGrady

Tobacco use is recognized as the chief preventable cause of disease and death in the United States, accounting for more than 430,000 deaths each year (Fiore et al., 1996; U.S. Department of Human and Health Services, 1998). Mortality attributed to smoking is higher than the combined mortality caused by crack, AIDS homicide, suicide, and alcohol use (Centers for Disease Control and Prevention, 1991b; U.S. Department of Health and Human Services, 1998). Smoking causes multiple forms of cancer, heart disease, stroke, and chronic obstructive pulmonary disease. Recent estimates indicate that 25 percent of adults or approximately 47 million Americans smoke (Centers for Disease Control and Prevention, 1997). This statistic is particularly alarming given the dangerous effects of smoking and the public's long-standing awareness of these dangers. Morever, smoking prevalence among youth appears to be increasing, with more than 3,000 children and adolescents becoming regular users of tobacco each day (U.S. Department of Health and Human Services, 1994).

Although the overall prevalence of cigarette smoking among African Americans decreased from 37.3 percent to 26.5 percent between 1980 and 1995, and that of smoking cessation increased from 26.8 percent to 35.4 percent during the same period, African Americans experience substantial excess mortality from cancer, cardiovascular disease, and infant death (U.S. Department of Health and Human Services, 1998). Fifty-five percent of all deaths among Blacks are caused by these smoking-related diseases (Ramirez & Ripling, 1998). The cancer death rate (for all sites) for Black men was 319/100,000 vs. 213/100,000 for White men. For 1992-1994, the rate of cerebrovascular death (i.e., stroke) was two times higher among African Ameri-

87

cans than among Whites (U.S. Department of Health and Human Services, 1998). Perhaps even more alarming is the recent reversal in the consistent decline in smoking prevalence among young African Americans seen in the 1970s and 1980s. The prevalence of daily cigarette smoking among African American high school seniors increased from 4.1 percent in 1993 to 7.0 percent in 1996 (U.S. Department of Health and Human Services, 1998). Moreover the prevalence of smoking among young Black males (high school students) doubled from 14.2 to 28.2 percent from 1991 to 1997. Among young Black females, the prevalence also increased from 11.3 percent to 17.4 percent during the same period (Centers for Disease Control and Prevention, 1998). Differences in the magnitude of disease risk between Blacks and Whites may be directly related to differences in patterns of smoking and metabolism of nicotine (Caraballo et al., 1998; Perez-Stable, 1998). These patterns are probably the result of complex interactions of multiple factors such as socioeconomic status, cultural characteristics, stress, genetic elements, targeted advertising, and absence or presence of tobacco control initiatives.

In general, African Americans tend to start smoking later in life and smoke fewer cigarettes per day than Caucasian Americans (Centers for Disease Control and Prevention, 1991a; Centers for Disease Control and Prevention, 1993; Escobed & Paddicord, 1996; McGrady et al., 1998). These lighter smokers (25 cigarettes/day) are more likely to smoke within 10 minutes of awakening. African Americans are more likely to smoke higher tar and nicotine brands than Caucasian Americans. Fifty-five percent of all African American smokers use one of three brands that come only in mentholated form (U.S. Department of Health and Human Services, 1998). They are more likely to want to quit smoking, express greater confidence that they can do so within one year, and are more likely to have quit for at least one day during the previous year than Caucasian Americans (U.S. Department of Health and Human Services, 1998). Unfortunately, they are significantly less likely than Caucasian Americans to remain abstinent for one year or more and the difference cannot be accounted for by socioeconomic factors. In addition, Black smokers have higher serum cotinine levels (Caraballo et al., 1998) and a 30 percent higher intake of nicotine per cigarette (Perez-Stable, 1998).

Many studies examining the effectiveness of smoking cessation interventions and the relationships between a variety of factors and self-quitting (quitting smoking without the aid of a formal program or techniques) have been conducted over the past 30 years, but few have focused on African Americans. Generalizability of the existing findings to African Americans may not be appropriate given the differences noted in smoking initiation and smoking behaviors. The purpose of this review is to examine smoking cessation in African Americans by reviewing studies that describe correlates of self-quitting and those that focus on cessation in the context of intervention trials, to make comparisons with findings from general population studies and to suggest directions for future research.

METHODOLOGY

To prepare the following literature review, articles published from 1988 to 1998 that specifically related to smoking cessation in African Americans were gathered from a variety of sources including Medline, other electronic databases, conference abstracts, personal files, and personal contact with researchers. Studies were included if they targeted African Americans. While we did not attempt to include all studies that have reported results separately by ethnic group, we have included some of the major studies to provide some indication of the patterns of results and comparisons with White smokers and quitters. The studies were divided into two main categories: evaluations of specific cessation interventions and examinations of self-quit behaviors and related factors.

Each article reviewed was entered into a table containing the following four categories: author/year, study design/sample size, variables/results, and comments. In the self-quit studies, a variety of designs are represented, including cohort studies and cross-section surveys. In some instances, information from intervention studies also provides evidence about factors related to cessation. The intervention studies were conducted in a variety of clinical and community settings, and the tables are presented with the studies grouped according to site. Intervention studies were characterized by their duration of follow-up, the maximal duration of abstinence observed along with the method of measuring abstinence from smoking, and the content of the intervention—advice/information, support/encouragement, behavior modification, pharmacological therapy, etc. In the variables/results column, we included all outcome (dependent) variables relevant to this review, and all independent variables reported, regardless of whether the association between variables was positive or negative and indicated whether the relationship was statistically significant. The Comments column contains information on response rates, sample size and power, and the specific definition of abstinence used indicating whether it is self-reported or validated.

It should be noted that there are several large smoking cessation initiatives targeting African Americans (e.g., "Legends," "For You and Your Family," and "Quit Today") currently under way (U.S. Department of Health and Human Services, 1998). However, in this review, we have included only studies for which there is evaluation information available.

RESULTS OF THE INTERVENTION STUDIES

The studies in this section will be presented in groups based on the setting in which the interventions were administered: churches, communities, clinics, or hospitals. Twelve intervention studies targeting Blacks or reporting results separately for African American involved were found in the literature.

Church-Based Interventions. Churches play an important role in African American communities (U.S. Department of Health and Human Services, 1989); a wide range of health-related interventions have been implemented and evaluated in this setting including diet and nutrition information, and screening protocols. Hence, the idea that smoking cessation treatment could be provided in this setting has some precedent. Two of the studies located used this setting. Both Schorling et al. (1997) and Voorhees et al. (1996) examined the effectiveness of a church setting in promoting smoking cessation messages, using somewhat different approaches. Schorling et al. (1997) used church coalitions to administer the interventions to church attendees in two counties. The treatment county residents were provided with one-on-one smoking cessation counseling and self-help quit materials. While the control county residents were given dietary and exercise counseling and general health/wellness materials (none of which addressed the issue of smoking). Voorhees et al. (1996) also compared the effect of two interventions, but in this case it was two differing levels of smoking cessation treatment. The intensive group (Heart, Body, and Soul) received sermons on smoking, smoking cessation counseling, and spiritual stop-smoking tapes and guides (Stillman, 1996; Stillman et al., 1993). The minimal group received a smoking cessation guide targeted to African Americans and both groups had access to baseline and follow-up health fairs.

There were no statistically significant treatment effects in either study, but in both there were trends toward the treatment of intensive intervention groups having higher rates of quitting than the control or minimal intervention groups. For Schorling et al. (1997), the self reported quit rates at 18 months were 9.4 percent vs. 5.9 percent (P=0.18). For Voorhees et al. (1996), comparable rates at one year were 27.1 percent and 21.5 percent (P>0.05). In the latter study, biochemical validation revealed some misrepresentation with recalculated rates of 19.59 percent and 15.05 percent respectively. In both studies, the treatment group was significantly more likely to make positive progress along the stages of change than the control group. Voorhees et al. (1996) found that both the intensive and the minimal intervention groups had significantly greater self-reported quit rates than a reference group from the same geographic area accessed through a random digit dialing survey (27.2 and 21.5% vs. 2.9%; P<0.05). In the Schorling et al. study (1997), `the effect of the interventions was measured at the population level only and fre-

Table 5.1
INTERVENTION-BASED SMOKING CESSATION ARTICLES TARGETING AFRICAN AMERICANS

Author/year	Study design/ sample size	Variables/results	Comments
Schorling et al. (1997) [15]	Clinical trial; rural Virginia; 18-month follow-up n = 304 African Americans (control: health education program not addressing smoking); n = 344 African Americans (treatment: smoking cessation program); both administered via church coalitions	Church based – No differences in smoking cessation between treatment & control, 9.4% vs 5.9% (P = 0.18) – Individuals attending church more likely to quit 10.6% vs 5.9%; treatment group more likely to have heard about cessation program 15.9% vs 9.4% – Treatment group made significantly more progress through stages of change those who quit smoked less at baseline 10 vs 14/day; more likely to be married, 75% vs 53% – Education, age, gender, & duration not related to quitting	– Regular attendees– at least once/ month – 70% follow-up rate – Higher baseline smoking prevalence for treatment group, 27.2% vs 24.4%; control group significantly less likely at attend church regularly, 42% vs 50% at baseline – Baseline distribution of stages of change similar for 2 groups – Power calculation – Only 2 communities – Self-reported quit rates – Continuous abstinence
Voorhees et al. (1996) [16]	Randomized clinical trial; East Baltimore; 1 year follow-up n = 10 African American churches (control: American Lung Association African American-specific smoking guide). n = 11 African American churches	– Both groups significantly higher quit rates than community population sample, 27.13% & 21.5% vs 2.87% – Biochemically validated, 19.59% vs 15.05% – No statistical difference noted in self-reported quit rates between 2 groups	– No difference in baseline stages of change between treatment & control – Point prevalence: duration of abstinence unspecified – Self-reported quit rates biochemically validated

Continued on next page

Table 5.1–*Continued*

INTERVENTION-BASED SMOKING CESSATION ARTICLES TARGETING AFRICAN AMERICANS

Author/year	Study design/ sample size	Variables/results	Comments
	(treatment: both organizational & individual/group interventions–spiritual counseling, sermons, guided cessation materials, CV risk with CO & cholesterol measures); both had access to health fairs	– Treatment significantly more likely to make positive progress along stages of change, OR = 1.68 P = 0.04 – Treatment group less likely than controls to regress through stages of change, 17% vs 25% – Smoking quit rates wree not associated with church denomination, age, gender, education	
Jason et al. (1988) [21]	Randomized clinical trial; low-income area of Chicago; post-test & 4-month follow-up; n = 87 (control: access to manual), 91% African American; n = 78 (intervention: 20-day program manual, phone calls), 96% African American; both groups had access to TV American Lung Association smoking cessation program	Community based – At 4 months more intervention participants had quit than controls (20% vs 9%, P = 0.06) – Significantly more continous abstainers among intervention (6%) than controls (0%) (P < 0.05) – Of those still smoking at post-test, intervention group smoked significantly fewer cigarettes (10.82 vs 14.43)	– At pre-test, intervention group significantly more motivated to quit smoking, but not related to success – Self-reported quit rates
Hymowitz et al. (1991) [25] (see Ockene et al.	MRFIT clinical trial–6-year period; 20 communities	– At 72 months SI group reported 48.9% cessation	– Objective validation of quit status performed – Quitter: abstinence

Table 5.1–*Continued*

INTERVENTION-BASED SMOKING CESSATION ARTICLES TARGETING AFRICAN AMERICANS

Author/year	Study design/ sample size	Variables/results	Comments
(111) [56])	across U.S. of varied composition; follow-up: evrey 4 months for intervention; every 12 months for control n = 3.722 (control: usual care (UC)); n = 3.755 (intervention: special medical care, counseling (SI)); % African Americans not reported	compared to 28.8% in the UC group – Cessation rate during first 12 months was 20.3% in intervention & 6.2% in control group – No difference in cessation rates found between Blacks & Whites in either group – Smoking cessation rate not related to marital status or Jenkins Activity Score – In both groups older, better educated, lighter smokers, had tried to quit were more likely to quit – Alcohol use related to relapse – Participants who had fewer friends who smoked were more likely to quit	at any one of six annual visits reported smoking 9 cigarettes/day & whose SCN ≤ 100 mμ
Hymowitz et al. (1996) [26]	Double-blind randomized Placebo control trial; New Jersey; 3-week & 12-month follow-up; All received self-help material & an instructional video & set a quit date n = 250 (control: placebo lozenge); n = 250 (interven-	– Silver acetate group 17% cessation, placebo group 11% cessation, n.s. – African Americans rated both lozenges significantly more aversive than Whites (silver acetate 7.07 vs 5.40, placebo 4.03 vs 2.45) – African Americans	– Participants recruited via electronic & print media – Sample size calculations done – Objective validation of quit stqatus performed – Point prevalence abstinence – Difficult to maintain blinding given the aversive taste of the acetate &

Continued on next page

Table 5.1–*Continued*
INTERVENTION-BASED SMOKING CESSATION ARTICLES TARGETING AFRICAN AMERICANS

Author/year	Study design/ sample size	Variables/results	Comments
	tion: silver acetate lozenge); 49% African American in each group	were significantly more successful in quitting smoking than Whites	smoking
Fisher et al. (1998) [24]	Quasi-experimental design 24-month intervention period treatment: 3 low-income African American communities in St. Louis, MO; community-based, neighborhood program; control: 3 comparable communities, Kansas City, MO	– Documented community meetings – Pre-post population telephone RDD surveys – Smoking prevalence–treatment group, 34 to 27% – Smoking prevalence 40 to 27% in treatment group who had heard of the agency – Smoking prevalence–control group, 34 to 33%	– Multivariate analyses controlled for intercommunity differences at baseline – No biochemical validation
Orleans et al. (1998) [22]	Randomized clinical trial 6- & 12-month (unplanned, opportunistic) follow-up; 14 communities–4 regional offices of the Cancer Information Service n = 689 African American smokers (control: standard counseling & guide. "Clearing the Air") n = 733 African American smokers (intervention: tailored counseling & guide, "Pathways to Freedome"); all	– At 6 months follow-up no difference in self-reported 1-week abstinence between intervention & control, 10.1% vs 9.1% (LTFs counted as failures) – At 12-month follow-up significantly higher quit rate among intervention than controls, 15% vs 8.8% (P = 0.034) (LTFs counted as failures) – At 6-month follow-up intervention significantly higher quit attempts & use	– At baseline control significantly more likely to be in preparation stage – Response rate at 6-month follow-up 63% control & 62% intervention – Self-reported abstinence

Table 5.1—*Continued*
INTERVENTION-BASED SMOKING CESSATION ARTICLES TARGETING AFRICAN AMERICANS

Author/year	Study design/ sample size	Variables/results	Comments
	participants responded to a radio-based media campaign	of prequitting strategies	
Boyd (1998) [23]	See Orleans et al. [22]	Further analysis of referenced study at 12 months, 7-day abstinence – Among those in preparation stage at baseline; 39% cessation using "Pathways to Freedom," 16% using standard guide	
Resnicow et al. (1997)	Randomized cluster design: Harlem, NY; smokers recruited from health care settings, churches, & public housing develop-ments; 6-month follow-up n = 641 African American (control: non-smoking-relat-ed health educa-tion materials) n = 703 African American (inter-vention: African American self-help guide & video, booster calls) 449/650 (interven-tion w/o call); 201/650 (interven-tion w/call) 93% follow-up rate 6	– Point prevalence quit rate interven-tion vs control, 11.2% vs 7.9% P = 0.06 – Follow-up absti-nence significantly higher in self-help group with call 16.4% – At follow-up, among those still smoking, a signifi-cantly greater per-centage of those with call attempted quitting in the past 6 months than without call (OR = 2.6) & control (OR = 2.3) – Quitting was not associated with gender, work & marital status, edu-	– Power calculations done – Point prevalence abstinence at 6 months – Intervention partic-ipants smoked more cigarettes/day at baseline – Only 31% of inter-vention would be contacted for booster call – Self-reported quit rates

Continued on next page

Table 5.1—*Continued*

INTERVENTION-BASED SMOKING CESSATION ARTICLES TARGETING AFRICAN AMERICANS

Author/year	Study design/ sample size	Variables/results	Comments
	months	cation, minutes to first cigarette upon waking, stages of change, & quitting efficacy – Smokers who were older (OR = 1.02), smoked fewer cigarettes/day (OR = 0.97), & who were recruited from church (OR = 1.2) were more likely to quit	
Windsor et al. (1993) [29]	Randomized clinical trial; Birmingham, AL; maternity clinics 3-component education intervention n = 414 pregnant smokers treated, 50% African American; n = 400 pregnant smokers control, 54% African American n = 100 historical comparison group followed at 4-8 weeks post baseline & 32 weeks postbaseline	Clinical setting – African American–E vs C quit rates at 32 weeks, 18.1% vs 10.7% – White E vs C quit rates at 32 weeks 10.0% vs 8.5% – Blacks had higher quit rates than Whites – Whites had higher reduction rates than Blacks	– Saliva cotinine validation self-reports – Compliance assessment – Losses to follow-up counted as smokers – Cost-benefit analysis – Sustained abstinence unknown
Ahluwalia et al. (1998) [30]	Randomized clinical trial double-blind, placebo controlled transdermal nicotine patch; Atlanta, GA; large innercity hospital 6-	– At 10 weeks quit rates were 22.5% in nicotine group & 13.7% in placebo group (P = 0.03) – At 6 months quit rates were 17.1% in	– Patients enrolled only if they expressed a desire to quit smoking – Smoking cessation defined as selfreported sustained abstinence (not

Table 5.1–*Continued*

INTERVENTION-BASED SMOKING CESSATION ARTICLES TARGETING AFRICAN AMERICANS

Author/year	Study design/ sample size	Variables/results	Comments
	month follow-up n = 205 African American (placebo patch) n = 205 African American (nicotine patch)	nicotine group & 11.7% in placebo group (P = 0.08) – Compliance with return visits decreased from 83% at week 1 to 31% at 6 months – At 6 months 63% of nicotine group & 44% of placebo group correctly identified patch they were on (P < 0.01)	even a puff) since last visit – At baseline, all 410 patients predicted they would be successful in quitting
Ahluwalia et al. (1998) [55]	Randomized clinical trial; Atlanta, GA; 45 house staff from large inner-city hosptial intervention period–smoking status stamp on patient charts (n = 1.229); control period–no stamp (n = 1.366)	– Exit interviews with patients – Intervention period: physicians more likely to "ask" 78.4% vs 45.6%, more like to "advise" 39.9% vs 26.9%, more likely to "arrange" follow-up 12.3% vs 6.2% – Intervention period: patients shifted toward a higher level of change	– Patient recall – No measure of cessation – No data on physician characteristics
Allen et al. (1998) [28]	Randomized clinical trial 3- & 12-month follow-up public hospital in Los Angeles, CA n = 571 control–user care; n = 515 intervention–brief physican-based smoking cessation message;	– 70% of intervention group reported doctor urged them to quit vs only 16% in control group – At 1-year follow-up biochemically validated smoking cessation rates ranged from 2.2–3.7% in	– Biochemical validation performed – High misrepresentation rate – Sample size calculations done, but estimated sample size was not met – Higher than expected loss to follow-up, 38 &

Continued on next page

Table 5.1–*Continued*
INTERVENTION-BASED SMOKING CESSATION ARTICLES TARGETING AFRICAN AMERICANS

Author/year	Study design/ sample size	Variables/results	Comments
	158 medical residents participated, 106 underwent a 2-hr graining program on cessation counseling, 92 counseled from 1 to 18 patients (all African American)	intervention to 2.8–4.6% in control group–no differences between groups were found – Significantly more light than heavy smokers reported quitting at 3 & 12 months – At both follow-up points no difference in quit rates between those who did & those who did not set target dates – Validated smoking cessation rates increased with increasing no. of clinic visits – Patients in intervention group smoked fewer cigarettes at 3 & 12 months & reported more quit attempts	40% at 3 & 12 months

quency of church attendance was used to measure exposure to the intervention. Quitting was significantly associated with smoking fewer cigarettes per day and being married; those who attended church were more likely to quit than those who did not (10.6% vs. 5.9%).

Community-based interventions have provided the setting for a number of large-scale evaluations. Both COMMITT (U.S. Department of Health and Human Services) and ASSIST (Manley et al., 1997) have implemented and evaluated community-wide tobacco control interventions. The overall goal for these community-wide interventions is to reduce the prevalence of smoking in the targeted communities, compared to similar communities that do not receive any specific interventions (Manley et al., 1997). The rationale is that the social environment, in which the individual exists, as well as the individual himself/herself, can be the target for change. African Americans have participated in these large-scale studies and treatment effectiveness has been examined (Boyd, 1998; Fisher et al., 1998; Hymowitz & Eckholdt, 1996a; Hymowitz et al., 1991; Jason et al., 1988; Orleans et al., 1998).

Of the community-based studies found in the literature, two studies focused specifically on African Americans and both used media-based strategies. Jason et al. (1988) evaluated a televised smoking cessation program based on knowledge of personal reasons and triggers for smoking and how to avoid them and behavioral and cognitive strategies to maintain abstinence. In addition to the manual, the participants in the intervention group also met three times and received supportive phone calls regarding the manual and televised program. Orleans et al. (1998) used a similar approach, combining a radio-based campaign with a tailored and a standard intervention in 14 communities. The tailored group received counseling and a guide tailored to the needs and barriers of African Americans (Pathways to Freedom), while the standard group received counseling and a generic guide.

Media programs appear to be effective in community-based settings, particularly when they are supplemented with additional strategies. Jason et al. (1988) found that at post-test and at the four-month follow up, self-reported cessation was higher for intervention participants than for controls, using measures of both point prevalence rate (20% vs. 9%. P=0.06) and continuous abstinence (6 and 0%, $P < 0.05$). Those who were still smoking reduced the number of cigarettes smoked. Orleans et al. (1998) found that the 12-month self-reported one-week abstinence rate was higher among the tailored group than among the standard group (15% vs. 8.8%, P=0.032, with nonrespondents categorized as failures.) At the six-month follow-up, intervention participants had made a significantly greater number of quit attempts. In addition, the intervention smoking cessation guide was rated as being more favorable than the control group guide. Additional analysis of the six-month data (Boyd, 1998) reveals that for among those individuals in the *preparation stage*, the one-week abstinence rates was 39 percent for the tailored group, compared to 16 percent for the other group, a statistically significant effect.

A community organization approach was employed by Fisher et al. (1998), incorporating community involvement in planning and implementation for a program promoting cessation. Neighbors for a Smoke-Free North Side emphasized community involvement as much as specific program activities; wellness councils in each neighborhood organized and directed activities that ran for 24 months and contained smoking cessation classes, advertising, door-to-door campaigns, and a "gospel fest." Three predominantly African American neighborhoods from St. Louis comprised the treatment group and were compared with similar communities from Kansas City, using a quasi-experimental design and data collected at the 24-month intervention point. Significant pre-post differences in smoking prevalence were found for the treatment communities (34% vs. 26%) and the reduction in prevalence was significantly different from the control communities (34% vs. 33%). It is not clear how many individuals actually quit smoking because of the programs; however, among those who had heard of the agency through which the program was implemented, the smoking rate decreased even more dramatically from 40 percent to 27 percent.

Hymowitz and colleagues reported findings from the Multiple Risk Factor Intervention Trial (MRFIT). This study enrolled men from 20 communities across the United States of varied racial/ethnic, socioeconomic, and occupational composition who were at above average risk for coronary heart disease (Hymowitz et al., 1991). The special intervention group, unlike the usual care group, was exposed to a smoking cessation program. Regular visits were scheduled every four months for the intervention group and annually for the control group. While this project does not precisely meet the criteria specified because the percentage of African Americans in both groups was not stated, the findings are of interest here because of the failure to note ethnic group differences. There was no difference in smoking cessation rates between African Americans and Whites in either group. In the first 12 months, a biochemically validated cessation rate of 20.3 percent was found in the intervention group compared to only 6.2 percent in the control group. The investigators noted that smokers who were better educated and had made previous quit attempts were more likely to quit.

Hymowitz et al. (1996a) examined the effectiveness of silver acetate lozenges in a double-blind placebo controlled study with 500 individuals. While this study can be considered to be a clinical trial, it has been categorized in this section because recruitment was done through community-based advertising and not through clinics, as is the case with the studies categorized in the Clinical Setting section below. (Silver acetate can be administered as a gum, lozenge, or spray. When used repeatedly, it interacts with smoking to produce a noxious metallic taste, which through aversive conditioning lessens the urge to smoke). Subjects were provided with self-help materials, shown a motivational video on the use of silver acetate lozenges, and then randomly assigned to a group. Lozenges were provided with instructions on usage and a quit date set. At 12 months, point prevalence biochemically validated quit rates were 17 percent for the silver acetate group and 11 percent for the placebo group, a nonsignificant difference. African Americans rated the lozenges as significantly more aversive and were significantly more successful in quitting than Whites. Those individuals, regardless of race, who rates the product as most aversive, who smoked the fewest number of cigarettes per day, and who used the greatest number of behavioral techniques to stop smoking were most likely to quit.

Resnicow et al. (1997) developed and tested a culturally sensitive smoking cessation intervention among low-socioeconomic status African Americans in Harlem, New York. Study participants were recruited from health care settings, public housing developments, and churches. Participants were exposed to a smoking cessation intervention, which consisted of a printed guide, video, and a telephone booster call, while the control group received health education materials not directly addressing tobacco use. At the six-month follow-up, the difference between the self-reported point prevalence rates of quitting for the two groups (11.2% treatment group vs. 7.9% for controls) was close to statistical significance (P=0.06). They found that those individuals recruited from the church setting were more likely to quit than those from the other two settings. Among the intervention group, however, those individuals who were able to be reached for the booster call were significantly more likely to be abstinent at the six-month follow-up (16.4%) than either those individuals in the intervention group could not be reached for the call (8.9%) or those participants in the control group (7.9%). In both this study and the MRFIT trial, quitting was not associated with martial status but was associated with being an older, lighter smoker.

The clinical setting provides a promising opportunity for smoking cessation interventions because over 70 percent of the population visits a physician at least once a year. The reasons for the visit may frequently be exacerbated by tobacco use and a majority of smokers say that they would quit smoking or at least make an attempt to do so, if they were advised to quit by their doctor (Fiora et al., 1996). However, it has been noted that physicians are less likely to advise their African American patients who smoke about quitting than they are their Caucasian American patients (Fiora et al., 1996).

Allen et al. (1998) examined the effectiveness of a brief smoking cessation message given by physicians. Over 100 physicians underwent smoking cessation training in which they learned about the health consequences of tobacco use, how to make individual assessments and the necessity of delivering brief cessation messages during medical care. The predominantly African American patients in the intervention group were asked to complete a baseline questionnaire, prior to receiving a three- to five-minutes counseling session focusing on the health risks related to smoking, discussing methods and barriers to cessation, and setting a quit date. In addition, they were given a self-help pamphlet to reinforce the physicians' message. The control patients were similar in ethnic background and were provided with usual care. At three and 12 months no significant difference in biochemically validated quit rates was found between the intervention and the control groups, with quit rates reported at 2.8 percent to 4.8 percent. However, patients in the intervention group smoked fewer cigarettes and reported more quit attempts at both three and 12 months.

The importance of the timing of the advice is clearly demonstrated in a study by Windsor et al. (1993), in which a three-component health education program was presented to randomly selected pregnant women. The program included cessation skills, clinic reinforcement, and social support using the buddy system. Compliance with the program was assessed and saliva cotinine was measured to objectively validated self-reported cessation. At 32 weeks, the quit rate among the treated group (N=400) was 14.75 percent, with the comparable rate among the control group being 8.5 percent. Interestingly, the Black E and C women had higher quit rates than White E and C women.

One study used the transdermal nicotine patch as an adjunct to physician advice to quit smoking. Ahluwalia et al. (1998a) compared the nicotine patch with a placebo patch in 410 patients from an inner-city hospital clinic. Groups were matched for physician attention with returns at one, two, six, and 10 weeks after the quit date, with a final visit at six months. At 10 weeks, the self-reported quit rate (complete abstinence for the last 30 days) was significantly higher for the nicotine patch group than for the placebo group (21.5% vs. 13.7%. P=0.03). At six months, however, the quit rates were still higher for the nicotine group (17.1% vs. 11.7%), although no longer significant (P=0.08). Compliance rates for return visits decreased dramatically; from 83 percent at week one to 31 percent at six months.

RESULTS OF THE SELF-QUIT STUDIES

Most people (over 80%) who successfully quit smoking do so on their own, without the help of specialized programs or formal treatments (Fiore et al., 1996). Thus, it is of interest to examine why and how people who quit successfully do so, and what factors are related to their success. In addition, since it has been documented that people who quit usually make two or three unsuccessful quit attempts before actually achieving abstinence (Pederson et al., 1996), factors related to cessation attempts should also be examined. Findings from studies will be grouped into the following categories: sociodemographic, smoking history and environment, psychological/psychosocial, and reasons for smoking and for quitting, based on categories that had been used in a review of self-quitters (Pederson et al., 1996).

As with research on interventions, very few studies have focused specifically on African American quitters.

Sociodemographic Variables. Variables in this category include gender, age, socioeconomic status, martial status, and employment status. Two variables that have been reported to be related to successful cessation are being male and being employed. Roye et al. (1995) reported these relationships in a study in a Harlem clinic that attempted to increase frequency of quitting through the use of physician advice. Orleans et al. (1989) found that ex-smokers tended to be older, married, employed, and in excellent health compared to current smokers. However, they were less highly educated than never smokers. These patterns have been noted in the general population (Pederson et al., 1996).

In secondary data analysis of African American men and women in the National Health and Retirement survey, Lockery and Standford (1995) found that there were some interesting differences between males and females with regard to factors related to successful quitting. For males, the gradients with education and income noted in other studies were replicated, while for females this gradient was not found and there appeared to be no consistent trend in cessation with either income or education. Royce et al. (1993), in cross-sectional analyses of eight of the 22 COMMIT sites, also noted that employment status was associated with successful quitting and found that a strong desire to quit smoking was associated with being older and a blue-collar worker. However, for females, the patterns were inconsistent. For example, the largest percentage of women who quit was found in the group who were divorced or separated (34.8%), while the largest percentage for males was in the married group (37.4%). Interestingly, results from some of the intervention studies described above mirror these patterns (Hymowitz & Eckholdt, 1995a; Hymowitz et al., 1991; Resnicow et al., 1997; Schorling et al. 1997). On the other hand, Royce et al. (1995) found that sociodemographic factors including employment were not a predictor of quit attempts.

Smoking History/Smoking Environment. Included in the category of smoking history are measures of nicotine dependency such as amount smoked. Fagerstrom score, years smoked, and type of cigarettes smoked. No studies could be located in which these factors were assessed in relation to successful cessation in African Americans. Wake-up smokers, smoking a lower nicotine brand, having a smoking-related illness, and trying to quit a

Table 5.2

SELF-QUIT SMOKING CESSATION ARTICLES TARGETING AFRICAN AMERICANS

Author/year	Study design/ sample size	Variables/results	Comments
Orleans et al. (1989) [33]	Cross-sectional survey; African American life insurance policyholders; 12 Souther, Midwestern, & mid-Atlantic states plus Washington, DC n = 1,163	36% current smokers, 14% ex-smokers – More than 2/3 ex-smokers cited health concerns as reason to quit & almost half cited setting a good example for children – Ex-smokers used fewer quit smoking aids/materials, relied on will power – Almost 80% of current smokers tried 1 or more times to quit, less than 5% tried a formal group or individual treatment – In the past year about 9/10 current smokers cut down & 1/3 received medical advice to quit – 2/3 current smokers thinking about quitting in next year, contemplation stage – Associations with strong desire to quit: female, LN cigarettes, smoking-related illness, medical advice to quit, more social support, greater no. of previous quit	– Self-reported smoking status – Low response rate (32%) – Data weighed but still could be biased – Not generalizable to general population: sample contained more females, older, higher education – Unclear definition of quit attempt

Table 5.2–*Continued*
SELF-QUIT SMOKING CESSATION ARTICLES TARGETING AFRICAN AMERICANS

Author/year	Study design/ sample size	Variables/results	Comments
		attempts & methods & beliefs in smoking harms & quitting benefits	
Hahn et al. (1990) [41]	Cross-sectional community survey; Minneapolis St. Paul, MN n = 1,052 Blacks n = 1,574 Whites	– Significantly more Blacks current smokers, BM 43%, WM 25%, BF 33%, WF 24% – Significantly more White men & women were former smokers, WM 44%, BM 30%, WF 29%, BF 18% – Among quitters, Whites more likely to be long-term (>1 year prior to study) quitters, WF 92%, BF 87%, WM 93%, BM 98% – Whites more likely to have reduced no. of cigarettes smoked in past year. WF 80%, BF 73%, WM 76%, BM 70% – Significantly higher percentage of White women (37%) than Black women (27%) tried LT/LN brands in past year – Significantly higher percentage of White men (63%) than black men (52%) tried to quit in past year &	– Two separate surveys: Whites from general population survey & Blacks from Black Twin Cities survey – Identical methodologies, similar response rates 68% vs 65% – Self-reported smoking status – Unclear definition of quitter

Continued on next page

Table 5.2–*Continued*
SELF-QUIT SMOKING CESSATION ARTICLES TARGETING AFRICAN AMERICANS

Author/year	Study design/ sample size	Variables/results	Comments
		planned to trying to quit *21% vs 14%)	
Manfredi et al. (1992) [42]	Cross-sectional survey women from metro Chicago n = 496 White general metro n = 246 Black public housing (PH) n = 117 (Other Black general metro (all smokers))	Between Black PH & other Blacks – Other Blacks have stronger desire to quit (90% vs 72%) & made greater no. of quit attempts (66% vs 56%) – Black PH significantly more likely to feel chance of getting lung cancer same among smokers & non-smokers (57% vs 46%) & unable to deal with stress if quit (35% vs 24%) – Black PH significantly less likely to report those closest to them want them to quit urgently (29% vs 57%), know where to get help to quit (38% vs 47%), want to quit to avoid future health problems (70% vs 84%) Between other Blacks & Whites – Other Blacks significantly more likely to have strong desire to quit (28% vs 17%), concerned about having withdrawal	– Educational level negatively associated with perceived difficulties in quitting & positively associated with perceived difficulties in quitting & positively associated with plans to quit & knowledge of where to go for help in quitting – Differences by race are most apparent among least educated – Data collection used both telephone & face-to-face interviews

Table 5.2–*Continued*
SELF-QUIT SMOKING CESSATION ARTICLES TARGETING AFRICAN AMERICANS

Author/year	Study design/ sample size	Variables/results	Comments
		symptoms (43% vs 30%) – Whites significantly more likely to report that they expect to get lung cancer (48% vs 33%), perceive strong effort necessary to quit (58% vs 39%), & know where to get help to quit (71% vs 47%)	
Royce et al. (1993) [35]	Cross-sectional 8/22 COMMIT sites (A) baseline survey n = 3,418 Black n = 8,550 Non-Hispanic White (all smokers) (B) attitude component/evaluation cohort n = 547 Blacks n = 1,888 non-Hispanic White (ex-non/current smokers)	– Significantly higher proportion of black smokers reported at least 1 serious quit attempt in past year, 43.3% vs 36.3% – Blacks significantly 1.5 times more likely to report strong desire to quit regardless of sociodemographic & smoking factors & have first cigarette within 10 minutes of awakening – Blacks significantly 1.8 times as likely to feel smoking serious problem, 1.7 times as likely to favor restrictions on vending machines, & 2.1 times as likely to prohibit smoking	– Smoking status self-reported – Unclear definition of quit attempt

Continued on next page

Table 5.2–*Continued*
SELF-QUIT SMOKING CESSATION ARTICLES TARGETING AFRICAN AMERICANS

Author/year	Study design/ sample size	Variables/results	Comments
		in car – Smokers who were older, blue collar workers, wake up smokers, or had made quit attempt in the past year were more likely to report a strong desire to quit	
Shervington (1994) [38]	Focus groups; New Orleans, LA n = 31 ever smokers n = 11 never smokers all African American women Topics explored: knowledge of health effect, attitudes about consequences, personal reaons for smoking, smoking practices, necessary components of cessation programs	– Current smokers have not yet personalized the distant threat of smoking because of the immediate consequences: decreased anxiety, tension, & depression – There are powerful barriers to cessation: no internal mechanisms for dealing with stress – Cessation programs need to deal with cognitive & behavioral dysfunction associated with smoking, mood elevation, social support – Smokers who had not been able to quit for at least 3 months had lowest education level & higher score on depression	– Generalizability of the findings in question because of possible selection bias
Hymovitz et al. (1995) [43]	Baseline telephone survey 10/22	– Blacks were significantly more likely	– Self-reported smoking status

Table 5.2–*Continued*

SELF-QUIT SMOKING CESSATION ARTICLES TARGETING AFRICAN AMERICANS

Author/year	Study design/ sample size	Variables/results	Comments
	COMMIT sites in CA, NJ, NM, NY, NC–sites with >20% minorities n = 3,322 non Hispanic blacks 11,128 Whites 537 Puerto Ricans 1,870 Mexicans	to smoke menthol cigarettes (OR = 5.27), smoke their first cigarette w/in 10 minutes of waking (OR = 1.96), increase the number of cigarettes smoked/day over the weekend by 15% or more (OR = 1.54), & to make 1 or more quit attempts in the past year (OR = 1.2) – Blacks were significantly less likely to smoke light or ultralight cigarettes (OR = 0.45) & be classified as heavy smokers (OR = 0.35) – Women were more likely to report quit attempts than m en in all ethnic groups	
Lockery and Standford (1995) [34]	Cross-sectional population survey data from the National Health & Retirement survey African Americans ages 50-61 years	– Married: 26.9% current smokers, 34.2% quitters – Increase in education, decrease in current smokers – Increase in income, decrease in current smokers – Greatest percentage of quitters in among currently divorced/separated females (37.5%) & married males	– Statistical significance not presented – Self-reported smoking status – Unclear definition of quitting

Continued on next page

Table 5.2–*Continued*
SELF-QUIT SMOKING CESSATION ARTICLES TARGETING AFRICAN AMERICANS

Author/year	Study design/ sample size	Variables/results	Comments
		(37.4%) – More females than males at every education level are never smokers; females are less likely to be quitters – More females than males with income <$10,000 are quitters – There does not appear to be a consistent relationship between smoking & physical activity	
Royce et al. (1995) [32]	Cohort (randomly selected from clinical trial–Harlem Health Connection) Harlem, NY 7-month follow-up n = 153 African Americans	– At follow-up, 21% reported they had stopped smoking – Significant predictors of quitting: employment, non-smoking partner, quit contract – Significant predictors of quit attempts: used materials, set a quit date – 27% of those smoking at follow-up did cut down no. of cigarettes – Physicians advice significantly influenced decrease in no. of cigarettes smoked by a least 50% – Those individuals receiving advice were significantly	– Cross-reference Table 1; Resnicow et al. [27] – Only 50% of healthcare providers attended intervention training sessions – Cessation defined as point prevalence – Self-reported quitting – 77% response rate at follow-up

Table 5.2–*Continued*

SELF-QUIT SMOKING CESSATION ARTICLES TARGETING AFRICAN AMERICANS

Author/year	Study design/ sample size	Variables/results	Comments
		more likely to use materials (65%) than those who did not receive advice (31%) – Physicians were significantly more likely to discuss smoking with those reporting strong desire to quit (71% vs 43%)	
Hymowitz et al. (1996) [37]	Cross-sectional (recruited via electronic & print media); New Jersey n = 114 White males n = 113 White females n = 78 African American males n = 168 African American females	– WM significantly more likely to have tried to quit smoking in the past year than BM (96% vs 88%) – Significantly greater percentage of WM reported that their doctor told them to quit than BM (80% vs 64%) – Whites significantly more likely to use NRT (WM 47%, BM 20%, WF 50%, BF 39%) & tried smoking cessation programs (WM 24%, BM 9%, WF 34%, BF 17%) – Whites, older smokers, & those with poorest health ratings were most likely to be advised by a physician to quit	– Self-reported smoking status – Unclear definition of quit attempt

Continued on next page

Table 5.2–*Continued*
SELF-QUIT SMOKING CESSATION ARTICLES TARGETING AFRICAN AMERICANS

Author/year	Study design/ sample size	Variables/results	Comments
Hymowitz et al. (1997) [36]	Cohort study n = 13,415 smokers COMMIT follow-up survey	– No difference in cessation for Blaks & White – 47% of smokers reported making at last one serious quite attempt – Reasons for quitting: health 91%; expense 60%; second-hand smoke 56%; example for others 55% – Statistically significant predictors of cessation: male, older age, higher income, less frequent alcohol intake, lower daily smoking, longer time to first cigarette, use of premium cigarettes, late initiation, prior quit attempts, strong desire to quit, no smokers in household	– Self-reported smoking status – Clear definition of cessation – Unclear definition of quit attempt
Manfredi et al. (1997) [51]	Focus groups with 54 women from Manfredi et al. (1992) [42] interviewed 3 years later	– Themes & images salient to participants – Low relevance of health risks, desptie knowledge – Smoking used to manage emotions, create time to be alone, to thin, to regroup	– Some consistency in the responses to surveys & focus groups – Survey tended to downplay the utility of smoking: coping with stress, pleasure – Inclusion of both methods addes to the quality of the information

Table 5.2–*Continued*
SELF-QUIT SMOKING CESSATION ARTICLES TARGETING AFRICAN AMERICANS

Author/year	Study design/ sample size	Variables/results	Comments
Ahluwalia et al. (1998) [39]	Cohort Study: Atlanta, GA n = 410 African American smokers (part of an RCT on transdermal nicotine patch) Relations of baseline variables to abstinence at 10 weeks & 6 months	– Total knowledge score & individual items not predictive of 10 weeks & 6 months cessation – Total attitude score & individual items were not predictive of 10 weeks & 6 months cessation – Overall knowledge was high: 84% questions re: risks & benefits of quitting answered correctly – 99% of patients wanted to quit to avoid smoking-related illness & feel better, 94% want to take greater control of their life, & 80% want to set good example for children – 62% said doctor advised them to quit	– Results generalizable for low-SES hospital population only – Cross-reference with Table 1 (Ahluwalia et al. [39])
Gibson et al. (1998) [40] (see Ahluwalia et al. (1998) [39])	Cross-sectional survey; Atlanta, GA; inner-city hospital clinic n = 883 African Americans n = 123 non Hispanic Whites	– African Americans smoked significantly fewer cigarettes/day, 11.8 v 18.9; significantly less likely to have regular source of care, 23$ vs 31$ – Non-Hispanic Whites significantly more like to be told by doctor to	– Self-reported smoking status

Continued on next page

Table 5.2–*Continued*
SELF-QUIT SMOKING CESSATION ARTICLES TARGETING AFRICAN AMERICANS

Author/year	Study design/ sample size	Variables/results	Comments
		quit, OR = 1.55 – African Americans significantly more likely to have tried to quit for at least 24 hr in past year, OR = 1.95; significantly more reported not knowing person/organization for quitting information, 44% vs 23% – African Americans significantly > likely to report using clergy or God to help quit, 17% vs 2%	

greater number of times were all found to be associated with a strong desire to quit (Hymowitz et al., 1996b; Hymowitz et al. 1997; Orleans et al., 1989; Royce et al., 1993), findings consistent with the general population (Pederson et al., 1996). With regard to smoking environment, not surprisingly, having a nonsmoking partner was a predictor of smoking cessation (Royce et al., 1995), but spousal smoking status was not a significant predictor of quit attempts.

Several variables have been examined that fall into this category; self-efficacy, perceived ease of quitting, motivation to quit, and adverse withdrawal symptoms. In general, having supportive spouses, family, or friends is related to achieving abstinence (Pederson et al., 1996). There were no studies found that examined variables in these categories directly as they related to self-quitting for African Americans. However, Orleans et al. (1989) found that greater social support was associated with a strong desire to quit. In a qualitative analysis of focus groups of African American women in New Orleans, Shervington (1994) noted that current smokers have not dealt with the distance threat of disease, when confronted with the immediate effects of continued smoking (i.e., decreased anxiety, tension, and depression that result from smoking).

Reasons for Smoking/Reasons for Quitting. Typically, concerns about health motivate smokers in the general population to quit (Pederson et al., 1996). However, Ahluwalia et al. (1998a) and Gibson and Ahluwalia (1998) found that neither reasons for smoking nor reasons for quitting were associated with self-quitting. Orleans et al. (1989) noted that a belief in the adverse health effects of smoking and the benefit of quitting was associated with a strong desire to quit. Because physicians and other health care providers often serve as the source of information about detrimental health effects, examination of the impact of this advice is useful. In Royce et al. (1995), physical advice results in a decrease in the number of cigarettes smoked by at least 50 percent. This study also found that those individuals who signed a quit contract with a physician were more likely to quit smoking.

DISCUSSION

One objective of this review was to reach conclusions, based on the data reported, about promising interventions. At least six of the studies that are described found significant intervention effects on smoking cessation outcomes. These included a televised smoking cessation intervention (Jason et al., 1988), interventions on the radio (Orleans et al., 1998), counseling in churches, (Voorhees et al., 1996), a clinic-based intervention for pregnant women (Windsor et al., 1993), the MRFIT project (Hymowitz et al., 1996) and a community-based intervention in Harlem (Rescincow et al., 1997). It is obvious then that there are some promising approaches that need to be pursued and disseminated.

In future studies, there are some methodological criteria that might be helpful to provide more stringent evidence about effectiveness. For example, one such criterion is that the outcome monitored be continuous abstinence from smoking lasting at least one year. For some, this criterion may be considered too stringent, but it seems appropriate given what is known about recidivism among "quitters." Of the intervention studies reviewed, those reported by Hymowitz et al. (1991), Schorling et al. (1997) and Ahluwalia et al. (1998a) tracked continuous abstinence. The first two studies (Hymowitz et al., 1991; Schorling et al., 1997) had follow-up periods equal to or exceeding one year. In these three studies distinct interventions were employed—counseling in a medical setting (1991), health education and support in a church environment (Schorling et al., 1997), and pharmacologic therapy in a medical setting (Ahluwalia et al., 1998a). Statistically significant differences were found between intervention and control subjects only in the Hymowitz et al. (1991) study.

Consideration should also be given to sample size so that statistical power will not be an issue (Schorling et al., 1997), to trying to ensure high follow-up rates to minimize bias that could result from low follow-up rates (Jason et al., 1998; Schorling et al., 1997), and to the inclusion of biochemical validation of verbal report (Ahluwalia et al., 1998d; Schorling et al., 1997; Stillman et al., 1993). In addition, attempts should be made to include process measures to document individual exposure when the intervention was implemented in churches or communities. There are reported differences in baseline characteristics that are presumably related to successful cessation (Jason et al., 1988). These are issues that are common in many intervention evaluations. However, there are some issues that appear to be unique to some groups of African Americans such as the lack of telephones in low-income communities (Jason et al., 1988) that precluded booster sessions and follow-up data collection and the inability to achieve required sample size (Allen et al., 1998). While misrepresentation may not be common in all of the studies, seemingly high rates of misrepresentation of smoking status in at least one of the reports (Allen et al., 1998) may be a cause for concern in interpreting the results of those studies in which biochemical validation was not used.

The major weakness in drawing any conclusions about African American self-quitters and comparing findings from the large body of information available from the general population (Pederson et al., 1996) is the dearth of information in the literature. Where information does exist, the patterns appear to be similar for African Americans and the general population. However, often the data available suffer from several limitations. For example, the studies that have been done have, for the most part, not been population based. Their response rates have been low (Hahn et al. 1990; Manfredi, 1992; Orleans et al., 1989). Other considerations in interpretation of findings include differences in sample procedures for Blacks and Whites (Hahn et al., 1990) differences in response rates in a mixed mode study (Manfredi et al., 1992), and denial/recall problems regarding patient report of clinician advice (Royce et al., 1995).

There are some things that are known about African Americans patterns of smoking and smoking cessation. Differences between Black and White smokers in the patterns of smoking and the type of cigarettes smoked have been well documented (Hymowitz et al., 1991; Hymowitz et al., 1995). We also know that intervention strategies that are culturally sensitive are more likely to have some impact at least on those who are ready to quit and that churches may provide a setting for such programming. It has been demonstrated that physician behavior can be modified so that more patients are being "asked, advised, assisted, and arranged" concerning smoking. In general, however, there is no information available to reduce the overall prevalence of smoking. There is not evidence of a theoretical formulation that incorporates the potential effect of race into the interventions and no consistent criteria for measuring outcome. The largest problem, however, is the paucity of findings, particularly with regard to the process and variables of self-quitting. As a result it is difficult to draw firm conclusions about treatment effects and factors related to achievement of abstinence. Hence the potential utility of the interventions available in terms of both outcome and cost is questionable.

Most people quit smoking on their own, without formal programs. With the increased availability of pharmacotherapies, an increasing percentage of smokers have tried some form of smoking cessation drug therapy (Ahluwalia, 1996). Therefore, it is essential to be able to describe and understand the natural history of cessation and the strategies leading to success, so that programs can be designed to facilitate the process. The kind of programs referred to may encompass educational materials and legislation, as well as specific cessation clinics and techniques. In this area, the minimal amount of existing knowledge does not provide a good basis from which to proceed. There is no information available on methods that have been used for cessation; there is also no evidence on precursors or on the natural history of cessation in Blacks. Again, there is no theoretical foundation suggested for research in this area. More studies are needed to be able to accumulate the type of data needed for accurate description and understanding of this process in African Americans and how the process may be similar to or different from that in other ethnic groups. There may be existing data that can be reanalyzed in an attempt to elucidate some of these relationships and there are some theoretical approaches that may provide guidance for these attempts (Pederson, 1996).

There are unique issues that need to be addressed in pursuing research on smoking cessation in African Americans, whether it be the development, implementation, or evaluation of intervention programs or research on the quitting process and factors related to the achievement of successful abstinence. It is essential that in future studies, we do not neglect to consider the complexities of the definition of race and the integration of the scientific findings with the sociocultural issues.

The cultural context and meaning of tobacco use for African Americans who smoke has not been documented. Nor is there much information available on the social norms for smoking or not smoking. There are differences among ethnic groups in knowledge of the health effects of smoking, both active and passive, and in knowledge about the process of quitting (Brownson et al., 1992; King, 1997; King et al., 1997; King et al., 1998; Martin et al., 1990). Interestingly, greater in-depth information is available on low-income African American women, including both quantitative documentation of the extent of knowledge, attitudes, and behavior (Ahlijevych & Wewers, 1993; King et al., 1997) and qualitative data from focus groups (Manfredi et al., 1992; Manfredi et al., 1997). Smoking apparently serves as a means of coping with stress, anxiety, and depression among low-socioeconomic-status women, and African Americans are disproportionately represented in this group. How prevalent these reasons are has not been quantified, nor have there been investigations into the relationship of social networks and smoking. Support for a potentially distinct function of tobacco comes from the pattern of initiation to tobacco, with Blacks demonstrating delayed initiation compared to Whites (McGrady et al., 1998). How and why this late initiation happens has not yet been investigated; however, it is not the same pattern that is observed in the general population in which initiation after age 20 is a rare event (McGrady et al., 1998).

In conclusion, one of the objectives for this review was to bring to light those areas of smoking cessation needing further research. The lack of studies of smoking cessation in the African American population coupled with the scattered focus and approach of studies that have been done suggests, in our opinion, that a useful approach might be to probe quitting behavior by way of established differences in smoking behavior. Thus, research might attempt to discover the effect (if any) of choice or brand on quitting behavior and on successful quitting, in the intervention setting as well as in observational studies. Such a research agenda bears on the third and final objective of the review; determination of how critical the construct of race might be in explaining patterns of cessation. This issue is not addressed in the studies reviewed, but has in fact received attention in other studies leading to the following conclusion: Race as a biologic or genetic classification does not appear to explain the differences in tobacco use that have been observed, but may serve as a surrogate for sociologic phenomena (Bhopal & Donaldson, 1998; Freeman, 1998; Fullilove, 1998; King, 1997; King et al., 1997; King et al., 1998; Martin et al., 1990). Thus, the variables leading to cessation and the interventions that will eventually be proven to be effective for specific racial and ethic groups may not be the same for all groups.

RECOMMENDATIONS

Upon close examination of the results, several areas of future research need to be pursued. More studies need to be conducted that explore the issue of nicotine dependence and the effectiveness of various over-the-counter nicotine products and prescription smoking cessation aids. In addition, researchers should further evaluate the role physicians play in delivering smoking cessation messages (Ahluwulia, 1998b). Specific attention needs to focus on delineating the factors that motivate health care providers to counsel certain patients to quit smoking so that interventions can be developed for providers as well as for patients. When developing and testing smoking cessation programs, attention needs to be given to issues of cultural sensitivity and to the appropriateness of the context of the intervention (e.g., churches).

All of the efforts aimed at developing appropriate interventions would be strengthened considerably by natural history data on initiation, maintenance, and self-quitting. There are numerous questions that need to be addressed. For example, why do African Americans begin and continue to smoke? Why do they smoke menthol cigarettes? Why do they begin smoking beyond adolescence? How do African Americans quit smoking on their own? Why do they quit smoking? These questions call for research specifically directed toward African Americans including population surveys, cohort studies, and case-control studies. In addition, qualitative research using in-depth interviews and focus groups is essential so that the quantitative information can be complemented by in-depth knowledge.

Attention should be paid to the uncritical use of racial categories and what the potential implications of these categories are. For example, if by their use, we are providing the background for the failure to examine the other factors that are related to initiation or continuation of smoking, then we may be ignoring the critical variables that could ultimately lead to a reduction in tobacco use and a consequent reduction in smoking-related diseases.

REFERENCES

Ahlijerych, K. & Wewers, M.E. (1993). Factors associated with nicotine dependence among African American women cigarette smokers. *Res. Nurs. Health, 16,* 283–292.

Ahluwalia, J.S. (1996). Smoking cessation in African-Americans. *American Journal of Health Behaviors, 20,* 312–318.

Ahluwalia, J.S., McNagny, S.E. & Clark, W.S. (1998a). Smoking cessation among inner city African Americans using the nicotine transdermal patch. *Journal of General Internal Medicine, 13,* 1–8.

Ahluwalia, J.S., Gibson, C.A. Kenney, R.E. et al. (1998b). Smoking status as a vital sign to change physician counseling patterns in an inner-city hospital, unpublished manuscript.

Ahluwalia, J.S., Resnicow, K. & Clark, W.S. (1998c). Knowledge about smoking, reason for smoking, and reasons for quitting in inner city African-Americans. *Ethnicity & Disease, 8*(3), 385–393.

Allen, B. Pederson, L.L. & Leonard, E.H. (1998). Effectiveness of physicians-in-training counseling for smoking cessation among adult African Americans. *Journal of the National Medical Association, 90*(10), 597–604.

Bhopal, R. & Donaldson, L. (1998). White, European, Western, Caucasian, or what: Inappropriate labeling on race, ethnicity and health. *American Journal of Public Health, 88,* 1297–1298.

Boyd, N.R. (1998). Personal communication.

Brownson, R.C., Jackson-Thompson, J., Wilkerson, J.C. et al. (1992). Demographic and socioeconomic differences in beliefs about the health effects of smoking. *American Journal of Public Health, 82,* 99–103.

Caraballo, R.S. Giovinno, G.A., Perchacek, T. F. et al. (1998). *JAMA, 280,* 135–139.

Centers for Disease Control and Prevention. (1991a). Differences in the age of smoking initiation between blacks and whites–United States. *WR Morbidity & Mortality Weekly Reports, 40,* 754–757.

Centers for Disease Control and Prevention. (1991b). Smoking attributable mortality and years of potential life lost–United States, 1988. *MMWR Morbitity & Mortality Weekly Reports, 40,* 62–71.

Centers for Disease Control and Prevention. (1997). Cigarette smoking among adults–United States, 1995. *MMWR Morbidity & Mortality Weekly Reports, 46*(51), 1217–1220.

Centers for Disease Control and Prevention. (1998). Tobacco use among high school students–United States, 1997. *MMWR Morbitity & Mortality Weekly Reports, 47*(12), 229–233.

Escobedo, L.G. & Peddicurd, J.P. (1996). Smoking prevalence in a U.S. birth cohort: The influence of gender and education. *American Journal of Public Health, 86,* 235–236.

Fiore, M.C., Bailey, W.C., Cohen, S.J. et al. (1996). *Smoking Cessation Clinic Guidelines No. 18.* Rockville, MD: U.S. Department of Health & Human Services.

Fisher, E.B., Auslander, W.F., Munro, J.F. et al. (1998). Neighbors for a smoke free north side: Evaluation of a community organization on approach to promoting smoking cessation in African Americans. *American Journal of Public Health, 88,* 1658–1663.

Freeman, H.P. (1998). *President's Cancer Panel: Report of the Chairman.* Bethesda, MD: National Institutes of Health.

Fullilove, M.T. (1998). Comment: abandoning "race" as a variable in public health research. An idea whose time has come. *American Journal of Public Health, 88,* 1297–1298.

Gibson, C.A. & Ahluwalia, J.S. (1998). *Characteristics of Quitting in African-American Smokers.* New Orleans: Society for Research on Nicotine and Tobacco.

Hahn, L.P., Folsom, A.R., Sparkfa, J.M. & Norsted, S.W. (1990). Cigarette smoking and cessation behaviors among urban Blacks and Whites. *Public Health Reports, 105*(3), 290–295.

Hymowitz, N., Sexton, M., Ockene, J. & Grandits, G. (1991). Baseline factors associated with smoking cessation. *Preventive Medicine, 20,* 590–601.

Hymowitz, N., Mouton, C. & Eckholdt, H. (1995). Menthol cigarettes smoking in African Americans and Whites. *Tobacco Control, 4,* 194–195.

Hymowitz, N. & Eckholdt, H. (1996d). Effects of a 25.5 mg silver acetate lozenge on initial and long-term smoking cessation. *Preventive Medicine, 25,* 537–546.

Hymowitz, N. Jackson, J., Carter, R. & Eckhol, H. (1996b). Past quit smoking assistance and doctors' advice for White and African-American smokers. *Journal of the National Medical Association, 88*(4), 249–252.

Hymowitz, N., Cumming, K.M., Hyland, A. et al. (1997) (Suppl 2). *Tobacco Control, 8,* 557–562.

Jason, L.A., Tait, E., Goodman, D. et al. (1988). Effects of a televised smoking cessation intervention among low-income and minority smokers. *American Journal of Community Psychology, 16*(6), 863–876.

King, G. (1997a). The "race" concept in smoking: A review of research on African Americans. *Social Science & Medicine, 45,* 1075–1087.

King, T.K., Borelli, B., Black, C. et al. (1997). Minority women and tobacco: Implications for smoking cessation interventions. *Annals of Behavioral Medicine, 19,* 310–313.

King, G., Bender, R., Delaronde, S.R. (1998). Social heterogeneity in smoking among African Americans. *American Journal of Public Health, 88,* 1086–1095.

Lockery, S.A. & Stanford, E.P. (1995). Physical acitivity and smoking: Gender comparisons among old African American adults. *Journal of Health Care for the Poor and Underserved, 7*(3), 232–251.

Manfredi, C., Lacey L., Warnecke, R. & Balch, G. (1997). Method effects in survey and focus group findings: Understand smoking cessation in low-SES African American women. *Health Education Behavior, 24*(6), 786–800.

Manley, M., Lynn, W. Epps, R.P. et al. (1997). The American stop smoking intervention study for cancer prevention: An overview. *Tobacco/Control,* (Suppl. 2), 55–511.

Martin, R.V., Cummings, S.R. & Coates, T.F. (1990). Ethnicity and smoking: Differences in White, Black, Hispanic and Asian medication patients who smoke.

American Journal of Preventive Medicine, 6, 194–199.

McGrady, G.A., Ahluwalia, J.S. & Pederson, L.L. (1998). Smoking initiation cessation in African Americans attending an inner-city walk-in clinic. *American Journal of Preventive Medicine, 14,* 130–137.

Ockene, J.K., Hymowitz, N., Lague, J. & Shafer, B.J. (1991). Comparison of smoking behavior for SI and UC study groups. *Preventive Medicine, 20,* 264–273.

Orleans, C.T., Schoenbach, V.J., Salmon, M.A. et al. (1989). A survey of smoking and quitting patterns among Black Americans. *American Journal of Public Health, 79*(2), 176–181.

Orleans, C.T., Boyd, N.R., Binger, R. et al. (1998). A self-help intervention for African American smokers: Tailoring cancer information services. Unpublished manuscript.

Pederson, L.L., Brock, J. & McDonald, J. (1996). *Self-Quitters and Those Who Continue to Smoke: A Review of the Literature.* No. 6. Ontario: The Ontario Tobacco Research Unit.

Perez-Stable, E.J., Herrera, B., Jacob, P. III & Benowitz, N.L. (1998). Nicotine metabolism and intake in Black and White smokers. *JAMA, 280,* 152–156.

Ramirez, A.G. & Kipling, G.J. (1993). Nicotine dependence among Blacks and Hispanics. In C.T. Orleans & J. Salde (Eds.), *Nicotine Addiction: Principles and Management* (pp. 350–364). New York: Oxford University Press.

Resnicow, K., Vaughan, R., Futterman, R. et al. (1997). A self-help smoking cessation program for African-Americans: Results from the Harlem health connection project. *Health Education Behaviors, 24*(2), 201–217.

Royce, J.M., Hymowitz, N., Corbett, K. et al. (1993). Smoking cessation factors among African-Americans and whites. *American Journal of Public Health, 83*(2), 220–226.

Royce, J.M., Ashford, A., Resnicow, K. et al. (1995). Physician- and nurse-assisted smoking cessation in Harlem. *Journal of the National Medical Association, 87*(4), 176–181.

Schorling, J.B., Roach, J., Siegal, M. et al. (1997). A trial of church-based smoking cessation in interventions for rural African Americans. *Preventive Medicine, 26,* 92–101.

Shervington, D.O. (1994). Attitudes and practices of African American women regarding cigarette smoking: Implications for interventions. *Journal of the National Medical Association, 86*(5), 337–343.

Stillman, F.A., Bone, L.R., Rand, C. et al. (1993). Heart, body and soul: A church-based smoking cessation program for urban African Americans. *Preventive Medicine, 22,* 335–349.

Stillman, F.A. (1996). Tobacco control and smoking cessastion efforts in an inner-city African American community. *Journal of Socially Distressed and Homeless, 5,* 55–66.

U.S. Department of Health and Human Services. (1989). *Churches as an Avenue to High Blood Pressure Control.* Washington, DC: U.S. Government Printing Office.

U.S. Department of Health and Human Services (1994). *Preventive Tobacco Use Among Young People: A Report to the Surgoen General.* Washington, DC: U.S. Government Printing Office.

U.S. Department of Health and Human Services. (1995). *Community-Based Interventions for Smokers: The COMMIT Field Experience.* Bethesda, MD: author.

U.S. Department of Health and Human Services. (1998). *Tobacco Use Among U.S. Racial/Ethnic Minority Groups–African Americans, American Indians and Alaska Natives, Asian Americans and Pacific Islanders.* Washington, DC: U.S. Government Printing Office.

Voorhees, C.C., Stillman, F.A., Swank, R.T. et al. (1996). Heart, body and soul: Impact of church-based smoking cessation interventions on readiness to quit *Preventive Medicine, 25*, 277–285.

Windsor, R.A., Lowe, J.B., Perkins, L.L. et al. (1993). Health education for pregnant smokers: Its behavioral impact and cost benefit. *American Journal of Public Health, 83*, 201–206.

Chapter 6

AFRICAN AMERICANS AND CRACK COCAINE

KARA HAWTHORNE AND GEORGE HENDERSON

The rapid increase of cocaine use in the United States during the last decade has been called a random epidemic that has far-reaching social as well as medical implications. Crack cocaine has been associated with increases in crime, admissions to drug treatment programs, and incidences of sexually transmitted diseases (Hudgins et al., 1995). Also, it has been closely linked to a myriad of other social problems, including crime and family dysfunctions. The association of crack use with increased crime rates is most evident in the big cities, where prevalence of its use is very high. Although crack use does not directly contribute to the transmission of HIV, many crack users exchange sex for their supply. In the process, they often engage in high-risk sexual behaviors (Hoffman et al., 1996). The recent spread of crack cocaine use in the inner cities has been accompanied by dramatic increases in juvenile delinquency and sexually transmitted diseases (STDs) among teenagers (Fulliolove et al., 1993).

AN URBAN CALAMITY

The seriousness of the cocaine epidemic that began in the 1980s is perhaps best reflected in statistics that chronicle cocaine-related deaths, which increased from 554 to 2,496 between 1985 and 1989 (Pena & Koss-Chino, 1992). Moreover, the high cost of cocaine abuse to society is evident in upwardly spiraling health care expenditures (Castro et al., 1987; National Institute on Drug Abuse (e), 2001). Although research data suggest a leveling off of cocaine use nationwide, rates of cocaine use will probably continue at endemic levels (Pena et al., 1992). National data indicate that during the 1980s cocaine was the most frequently mentioned substance in drug-related hospital emergency room visits. Of those visitors, 57 percent were African Americans and 67 percent were males. Several studies show that inner-city African American substance use rates are significantly higher (up to three times) than the rate for White substance use (Brunswick, 1988; National Institute on Drug Abuse (c), 2001).

Demographic profiles of cocaine abusers changed dramatically during the 1980s (Herridge & Gold, 1988). Once romantically associated with wealth and high social status, cocaine is now among the most maligned of the illegal substances. Along with the new image has come changes in cocaine distributors and consumers. Data gleaned from various National Household Survey on Drug Abuse (NHSDA) reports, the most comprehensive source of information on drug use demographics in the United States, show that frequent cocaine users are now more likely to be unemployed young males who live in large metropolitan areas—a significant change from the cocaine users who responded to the same survey in the 1980s. Simply put, cocaine abusers have become younger, less white and poorer. "Criminological literature suggests that cocaine use has become embedded in an urban deviance syndrome, the result of infrastructural decay, overcrowding, and the disintegration of social support networks" (Richard et al., 1995, p. 402).

In 1997, according to the National Household Survey on Drug Abuse, an estimated 1.5 million Americans were cocaine users. Based on additional data sources that take into account users underrepresented in the NHSDA reports, the Office of National Drug Control estimate the number of chronic cocaine users at 3.6 million (National Institute on Drug Abuse (a), 2001). Adults ages 18 to 25 have a higher rate of cocaine use than those in any other age group. Overall, men have a higher rate of cocaine use than women. Also, according to the NHSDA reports, rates of cocaine use are highest for African Americans, followed by Hispanics and then Caucasians.

The NHSDA estimated the number of crack users in 1997 to be approximately 604,000. The 1998 Monitoring the Future Survey, which annually surveys teenagers' attitudes and recent drug use across the country, reported that lifetime and past-year use of crack increased among eighth graders to its highest levels since 1991. The percentage of eighth graders reporting crack use at least once in their lives increased from 2.7 percent in 1997 to 3.2 percent in 1998 (National Institute on Drug Abuse (a), 2001).

Data from the Drug Abuse Warning Network (DAWN), gathered for the Substance Abuse and Mental Health Services Administration (SAMHSA), show that cocaine-related emergency room visits, after increasing 78 percent between 1990 and 1994, remained level between 1994 and 1996, with 152,433 cocaine-related episodes reported in 1996. In 1999, there were

554,932 drug-related emergency room visits. Alcohol, used in combination with other drugs is the most frequently mentioned drug at the time of hospital admission, followed in descending order by cocaine, marijuana and heroin/morphine (National Institute on Drug Abuse (c), 2001). According to DAWN, medical examiners list cocaine as the most frequently mentioned drug in drug abuse deaths. In cases where death is accidental or unexpected, heroin/morphine is the most frequently mentioned drug, followed by cocaine, and alcohol-in-combination. Among suicides, alcohol-in-combination with other drugs and cocaine are the most commonly mentioned drugs.

According to the Community Epidemiology Work Group, an increase in availability and use of cocaine has been reported in Denver, Detroit, New York, New Orleans, Philadelphia, Seattle and Los Angeles. The White House Committee on National Drug Control Policy conducted a study to determine how much money was spent on illegal drugs during the period of 1988 to 1995 that otherwise would have supported legitimate spending or savings. They concluded that Americans spent $57.4 billion on drugs, broken down as follows: $38 billion on cocaine, $9.6 billion on heroin, $7 billion on marijuana, and $2.7 billion on other illegal drugs and on the misuse of legal drugs (National Institute on Drug Abuse (e), 2001).

REASONS FOR USING CRACK COCAINE

In a study conducted by Boyd et al. (1998), a stress-diathesis conceptual framework was used to identify factors that may contribute to the initiation and maintenance of females' crack cocaine abuse. An important part of the diathesis conceptualization is that childhood vulnerability is often the result of childhood adversity, including inadequate parenting. For example, parental drug use could expose a child to risky interpersonal and unsafe situations more often than children in less stressful family environments. These types of adverse childhood experiences then lead to a diathesis, a fragility in psychological makeup, that is established through adverse childhood experiences" (p. 236). These experiences critically alter childhood and make people vulnerable to maladaptive behaviors in their adulthood.

It is not merely the vulnerability that creates behaviors such as crack cocaine use. The initiation to drug use is more likely to occur when adversarial demands of life exceed a person's adaptational capacity. Although vulnerability appears to increase the risk for initial substance abuse, other factors also influence the severity of the problem. It is suggested by researchers that the greater an individual's vulnerability during childhood, the more likely he or she will become a drug abuser. However, the onset or recurrence of adult drug abuse is also likely to be related to the occurrence of ongoing and/or episodic stressors that exceed a person's comfort threshold (Boyd et al., 1998).

By now it should be evident that multiple factors contribute to people becoming addicted to drugs. There is interplay among environmental, psychological and biological conditions that influence the initiation and maintenance of substance use. Parental substance abuse sets the stage for parenting that is characterized by inattentiveness and lack of parental protection of children. This parenting style, which leads to the psychological isolation of the child, has the effect of making girls in particular vulnerable to being victimized by males. Also, parental drug use creates an environment where drugs are readily available and where alcohol and other drug consuming behaviors are modeled.

A study was conducted by Boyd (1993) that consisted of 105 African American women who used crack cocaine, of whom 60 were in drug treatment and 45 were still using crack cocaine. Sixty-one percent of the respondents in this descriptive, exploratory study reported at least one sexual abuse experience, and 44 percent reported that it happened more than once. Sixty percent of those who were abused stated that the perpetrator was a male family member, and over 60 percent were abused before they reached the age of 17. Seventy percent of the women had three or more depressive symptoms for more than two weeks, and 17 respondents made at least one attempt to commit suicide. Thirty-one percent of the women reported depressive symptoms by the time they reached the age of 15. Most of the women began their illicit drug use around the age of 16, with 74 percent starting out with marijuana. Only seven respondents began their illegal drug use with crack cocaine. Eighty-seven percent of the women had used an illicit drug by the age of 20.

Boyd's study (1993) indicated that a significant number of women who used crack cocaine have a history of sexual abuse and depressive symptoms. Those who were victims of incest or rape had greater drug use and were younger than women without such sexual trauma. This was consistent with other studies in which regular crack was an outgrowth of stressful events such as the death of a parent or child or being a rape or incest victim. It appears that women, moreso than men, come to use substances as the result of family drug use, sexual trauma and depression. Because parental drug abuse and sexual trauma are assaults to the self that cause low self-esteem, depression and anxiety, drug use among females may function as a mechanism to mediate against the negative feelings, especially those that are extremely hurtful childhood experiences (Boyd, 1993).

African American women, similar to African American men, may use drugs in large part in response to the stresses they face in their adult lives, including conditions such as minority status and reduced economic, social and political expectations. Research further indicates that female substance abusers have fewer social support systems than males, and they have more family responsibilities than either nonaddicted women or addicted men. "Women are much less likely to use drugs for hedonistic reasons and more likely to use drugs as a coping mechanism for dealing with childhood life events, situational factors, and depression" (Boyd et al., 1998, p. 239).

According to Boyd, epidemiologists have noted that the majority of adults who have a drug problem also have a coexisting mental disorder. Compared with men, women substance abusers display significantly more affective disorders, lower self-esteem and greater anxiety and depression. Men are more likely to be diagnosed with antisocial personality disorders. Among all substance abusers, anxiety and depression usually preceded their addiction. Young adults who have a major depressive or anxiety disorder are twice as likely to develop a drug abuse problem than those without such a psychiatric history.

RISKS ASSOCIATED WITH CRACK COCAINE

A study of sexually active crack-using and nonusing Black adolescents in Oakland and San Francisco, conducted by Fullilove and associates (1993), reported that crack users initiated intercourse at an earlier age than nonusers. Also, noncrack users were more likely than users to have utilized a condom during sexual intercourse. The number of sexual partners reported for the last year was significantly higher among crack using boys than that reported by nonusing boys. Male crack users were almost four times more likely, and female crack users were three times more likely, than nonusers to report having had sex under the influence of drugs or alcohol. Relatedly, crack users were more likely to report an exchange of sexual favors for drugs or money. Specifically, male crack users were eight times more likely to report engaging in such exchanges than nonusers. Among the girls, one in four reported participation in such an exchange.

Approximately 63 percent of the participants in the study indicated that they had engaged in one or more of the following HIV or sexually transmitted disease risk behaviors: had more than five sexual partners per year, exchanged sexual favors for drugs or money, failed to use a condom in the last sexual encounter, and engaged in sexual relations while using either alcohol or other drugs. Boys who used crack were more likely to report at least one of those risk behaviors. Crack users were twice as likely to engage in such behaviors than nonusers. Also, crack use and having a relative who used drugs were significant predictors of who would engage in one or more of the HIV or sexually transmitted disease risk behaviors. Respondents who reported having relatives who used drugs were twice as likely to report one or more HIV or sexually transmitted risk behaviors. The majority of the participants had also used alcohol and marijuana. Thus crack use seemed to be part of a pattern of polydrug use, with all crack users having used at least one other drug. The use of drugs such as cocaine, hashish, phencyclinidine and heroin occurred most often among crack users, and daily use of any of those drugs was reported exclusively by crack users. All of the participants who reported intravenous drug use were also crack users.

Sexual degradation, violence and, sometimes, death become part of the crack life of female users. When compared to nondrug using women, their continuing drug and crime interactions place them at higher risk for rape, assault and death. Clearly, female crack abusers who trade sex-for-drugs place themselves at risk for sexual mistreatment and violence. In a study of 105 women in treatment for substance abuse, Boyd et al. (1998) reported that 59 percent were victims of physical assault as adults and 43 percent reported being victims of sexual violence as adults.

Numerous researchers conclude that the rise in HIV/AIDS rates among minority women is associated with the exchange of unprotected sex for drugs (Cohen et al., 1994). It is relatively common for female crack users to depend on bartering their bodies to support their drug use. During the course of sex-for-crack transactions, women typically engage in sexual relations with IV drug injectors or noninjecting bisexual men, some of whom carry HIV/AIDS. Most of these women get their drug highs in crack houses, copping areas and shooting galleries, and that places them in direct contact with an increasing number of HIV/AIDS carriers. Consequently, crack using women, particularly ethnic minorities, are especially at risk of acquiring HIV through such high-risk sexual behaviors. And because crack users have twice as many sexual partners as those who do not use crack, female crack users are six times more likely than nonusers to have had more than 20 sexual partners, 15 times more likely to sell their bodies sexual favors, and four times more likely to have syphilis or other genital diseases that facilitate the transmission of AIDS. Approximately 87 percent of the women in Cohen's study who were HIV positive were also crack users.

In the Cohen et al. (1994) study, most of the respondents were African American out-of-treatment women. The researchers found that over the three months prior to the interviews, 80 percent of the women had exchanged sex for crack, and 86 percent had exchanged sex for money to buy crack. Other studies report similar percentages. Cohen et al. further reported that 37 percent of the crack-smoking women reported having had more than 100 sexual partners. Condom use among this population is infrequent. And the infrequent use of condoms can be explained in part by the unequal power of women in relationships with men. "The degraded, vulnerable, and impoverished condition of the 'crack whore' precludes being able to insist on using condoms, or for that matter to refuse relations with IV drug-using men [who are likely transmitters of HIV to the women]" (Cohen et al., 1994, p. 238).

The paucity of condom use demonstrates the lack of power and low self-respect that characterize most women who survive in drug cultures. Sadly, most crack-abusing women have diminished concern for the medical and behavioral consequences of high-risk sexual intercourse activities. During such a desperate time in their lives, some of these women may actually be committing a less direct form of suicide. Over half of the crack-using women in the study had their children taken away from them by the Department of Human Services because of reported instances of child neglect or abuse. The main reason many crack using women in the study entered treatment was the desire to get their children back. And once such women do get them back, the desire to keep them causes some of the women to maintain their recovery efforts.

THE DESIRE TO BE HELPED

Longshore et al. (1997) stated that many African Americans with drug problems avoid formal sources of help such as drug use treatment programs; they prefer informal sources such as friends instead. The researchers found that problem recognition was the factor most related to desire to seek help. After a drug problem was acknowledged, the willingness of the respondents to seek help was higher among African American drug users, especially those who had internalized moral beliefs about the evils of drug abuse. In order words, they found a connection between their moral beliefs and the conventional societal belief that one's drug problem should be solved. Despite the ambivalence of African Americans towards drug-use treatment programs, the researchers found that the clients in their sample believed that they could be helped through formal treatment. For many African Americans, a favorable view of their own selves depends on them being actively engaged in the community through their spirituality, collective self-esteem, and assumption or resumption of conventional drug-free roles in their nuclear or extended families.

African Americans' traditional moral beliefs are often a very valuable but underutilized source of leverage in drug abuse programs. For example, many African American drug users are able to overcome their ambivalence about help-seeking and drug recovery more readily if health care providers focus on prosocial, including religious, reasons for drug abstinence instead of trying to force users to self-identify themselves as "addicts." Prosocial reasons can break down defense mechanisms and emphasize the negative aspects of continued drug use (Longshore et al., 1997). And it is important that prosocial reasons be expressed in culture-specific terms, e.g., entry or reentry into a moral community, renewed spirituality, collective as well as personal gains that result from abstinence, and the assumption or reassumption of wholesome roles in the family.

TREATMENT ISSUES

In 1995, there were nearly 1.9 million admissions to publicly funded substance abuse treatment programs. Men made up about 70 percent of the clients, and women 30 percent. Fifty-six percent were Caucasians, and 26 percent were Asian and Pacific Islanders. The largest number of illicit drug treatment admissions were for cocaine, 38.3 percent, followed by heroin, 25.5 percent, and marijuana, 19.1 percent (National Institute on Drug Abuse, 2001). Gawin and Kleber (1986) stated that individuals with mood disturbances are susceptible to cocaine addiction because of the drug's stimulant and euphoric effects. They found a 50 percent prevalence of affective disorders in cocaine abusers undergoing treatment. Weiss (1998) concluded that between the years 1992 and 1997 premorbid psychopathology became a less important factor for cocaine abuse. Earlier, Brunswick (1988) was emphatic that specific social environmental factors—dysfunctional families, lack of educational and employment opportunities, racist attitudes, and drug-filled environments—are better explanations of drug use than individual or personality problems such as depression. Since no pharmacologic treatment for cocaine dependence has been found that is consistently effective, psychosocial approaches must continue to be tested and refined. Efforts have been made to enhance the clinical efficacy of group therapies by including such elements as social skills training, relapse prevention, and social support systems.

Pena et al. (1992) described African Americans who lived in poverty as being powerless people trapped in high rates of unemployment, inadequate education, unemployability, delinquency and criminality. He traced the historical, economic and political factors that underlie those conditions. To such conditions must be added the complicating factor of drug use being both a cause and an outcome. Brunswick (1988) concluded that drug use explanations that only emphasize personality attributes are inadequate in the case of urban African American males. It is likely that in order for effective treatment to occur, a social situational modality must be utilized. That is, one that considers different norms and values, gender developmental needs, and community opportunities and constraints. Brunswick observed that drug use can spill over into occupational and recreational situations. For example, cocaine users are more likely to be employed than are heroin addicts, and that supports the hypothesis that cocaine abusers have less severe psychopathology than heroin abusers.

Ethnicity and Treatment Outcome in Cocaine Abuse. There is little consensus regarding the best treatment for cocaine abuse (Pena et al., 1992). It is important to note that various drug treatment modalities have been offered, ranging from pharmacological, cognitive-behavioral, individual psychotherapy, and psychodynamic forms of therapy. Some of them have had beneficial outcomes. Pena et al. noted the promising potential of supportive-expressive (SE) psychotherapy, which teaches clients to explore core conflicts in interpersonal relationships, while at the same time supporting the client's personality. So-called "here and now" behaviors are emphasized in order to help bring the cocaine abuse under the patient's control. Family therapy can also be beneficial (Spitz & Spitz, 1987).

Family therapy focuses on the family in dynamic equilibrium. Important factors include family boundaries, triangulation leading to dysfunction, scapegoating, overinvolvement, and detachment among family members. Indeed, family systems-derived techniques and treatments that focus on unpredictable symptoms associated with cocaine use can be especially helpful. Describing ways of adapting family therapy for African American families, Boyd-Franklin (1989) demonstrated the necessity of considering specific cultural values within the social and cultural contexts of family life. Further, she described African American families as "normal" households with routine family patterns that may include grandparents, aunts, cousins or stepparents. In fact, extended black families sometimes include neighbors and close friends–pseudokin folks, to be exact.

Boyd-Franklin (1989) postulated that while role flexibility is normal in African American families, it can sometimes lead to confusion and family dysfunction. She stated that it is important for care providers to consider their clients' religious and spiritual beliefs. And she suggested ways for the utilization of a multi-systems approach to therapy with African Americans. That is, it is important for care providers to tailor family therapy to the specific needs of African American families of cocaine abusers. Further, the type of family unit targeted for an intervention should reflect the clients' designation of the relatives with whom they are most closely bonded. "Family" members sometimes do not include blood relatives. The reality of countless African American families in the United States is that they often do not reside with or near their drug abusing relatives.

Pena et al. (1992) explored this issue in a sample population of African American males. They examined relationships that the respondents described as important to them during childhood and adolescence. For the majority of the respondents, both biological parents were important–mothers were more frequently mentioned than the father (99% and 89%, respectively). Stepfathers were mentioned more often than stepmothers (21% and 12%, respectively). More stepfathers than stepmothers replace a missing parent in the families of origin. In most cases, the biological father had left the family while the client was a child. That was true whether or not the respondents mentioned their biological father as being important and present during their childhood. Siblings, aunts and uncles were frequently mentioned as being important during childhood and adolescence. These data confirm many of the observations stated in the literatures focusing on African American child-rearing family patterns (Boyd-Franklin, 1989). In summary, for African Americans the definition of "current family" should not be limited to the nuclear family or to individuals who live in the same household. Instead, it should be defined to include any relatives or other individuals who are mentioned by clients as being important to them for financial or moral support.

Viable Treatment Models. Strategic family therapy assumes that individual family behaviors need to be understood from an interactive and interdependent standpoint (Pena et al., 1992). This implies that an individual's behavior is different when viewed in one-to-one situations as opposed to being viewed within a systems context. Family treatment should be problem focused; that is, the chief complaint, such as cocaine, is the context through which the family is engaged. And family therapy is time limited, with a generally recommended total of eight to 15 sessions. This model has several advantages that make it suitable for adaptation to African Americans, especially when there is an operationalized treatment guide and manual specifically developed for substance abuse treatment. The manual should include scales of conformity. Clearly, this treatment modality can be used with African Americans in a manner that reflects relevant sociocultural variables.

A study conducted by Hoffman et al. (1996) suggests that intervention programs incorporating a combination of approaches, along with client incentives, can be successful. In the study, a standard form of group therapy for cocaine abuse, in which clients attended group counseling sessions twice per week, was compared with a more intensive form of group therapy, in which clients attended group counseling five days per week. The latter model used a cognitive-behavioral approach, focusing on relapse prevention skills training. This type of intervention has been found to be superior to a more general clinical drug management approach. The impact of adding additional individual treatment services to both group therapy models was also examined. The study demonstrated that there can be a significant main effect for intensive versus standard group therapies. The clients who were assigned to intensive group therapy attended more sessions than those assigned to the standard group. And there was a significant main effect when using individual sessions and group therapy sessions. A Dungan's Multiple Range Test indicated that adding individual psychotherapy or individual psychotherapy and family therapy significantly increased the number of sessions the participants attended.

Upon admission into treatment, 84 percent of the clients were regular users of cocaine. At the time of the 12-month follow-up interview, only 23 percent of the clients reported regular drug use. Those who reported regular use of cocaine were more likely to have attended fewer treatment sessions than clients who did not report regular use of cocaine in the preceding year. Also, upon admission, 21 percent of the clients reported regular use of other drugs. During the follow-up interview, only seven percent of clients reported the continued use of other drugs. Clients reporting regular use of other drugs at follow-up sessions were more likely to have attended fewer treatment sessions overall than those who did not. Upon admission, 31 percent of the clients reported regular alcohol use. At the time of the follow-up interview, 16 percent reported regular alcohol use. Clients who reported regular use of alcohol at the follow-up interview attended fewer group sessions.

Upon admission, 31 percent of the clients reported engaging in illegal activities during the year before admission. At the time of the follow-up interview, 22 percent reported illegal activities. More clients who reported pre-study illegal behaviors reported such behaviors after treatment sessions than did clients who reported no such behaviors. Also, upon admission, 13 percent of the clients reported that they had participated in drug sales in the preceding 12 months. During the follow-up interview, nine percent reported involvement in drug sales. However, more clients who reported selling drugs during the year before treatment had done so after treatment than clients who reported no such pre-treatment behavior.

According to Richard et al. (1995), most crack cocaine treatment modalities are merely replications of existing powder cocaine treatment programs. Numerous clinicians contend that long-term outpatient treatment programs utilizing therapy modalities such as Rawsons' neurobehavioral therapy are the most effective means of treating powder and crack cocaine users. Specifically, these programs emphasize cognitive-behavioral techniques for countering specific environmental cues that trigger cocaine use. However, because cocaine users are particulary prone to relapse after months or even years of abstinence, short-term inpatient treatment such as the ones we described may be ineffective for most recovering crack users. "Studies suggest that after care treatment retention and post-treatment abstinence rates after intensive outpatient cocaine treatment compare favorable with those obtained after inpatient treatment and that cognitive-behavioral therapy is more effective than interpersonal therapy" (Richard et al., 1995 p. 402).

Rawson's neurobehavioral therapy is an example of a cognitive-behavioral technique that can be used in after care treatment to emphasize specific sequences or stages to recovery from cocaine abuse: withdrawal, honeymoon, the wall, adjustment and resolution. During each phase of treatment, clients are exposed to educational groups, stabilization groups, 12-step support group meetings, individual counseling sessions, urine tests and conjoint sessions with family members. Long-term therapies designed to alleviate the anxiety, depression, and other debilitating emotional effects associated with the initial period of abstinence in chronic cocaine users have been recommended as useful adjuncts to short-term cognitive-behavioral cocaine treatment. Three of the most popular adjunct therapies are acupuncture, anti-craving medications and brainwave therapy. In Richard et al.'s study, those therapies were combined with an intensive outpatient program employing a modified version of Rawson's neurobehavioral treatment model. Baseline, process and follow-up data were collected to determine whether any of the three adjunct therapies, when combined with neurobehavioral treatment, could improve long-term outcomes for indigent crack cocaine users as compared to neurobehavioral treatment alone.

On average, the participants who received adjunct therapy sessions stayed in treatment almost 60 days longer than the control group participants. These participants also attended at least 30 more neurobehavioral counseling sessions, than did those who received only neurobehavioral therapy. Therefore, adjunct therapies seem to be an efficacious means of improving overall program retention. The more adjunct therapy the participants received, the longer they stayed in treatment. "Adjunct therapy significantly improved retention in intensive outpatient neurobehavioral treatment for crack cocaine addiction independently of motivation for treatment at intake (p. 411). However, it was the neurobehavioral treatment itself and not adjunct therapies per se that was directly responsible for the drug use outcome effects reported in the study.

As noted earlier, there was an enormous increase in the number of people seeking treatment for cocaine addiction during the 1980s and 1990s. Treatment providers in most areas of the country reported that cocaine was the most commonly cited drug of abuse among their clients. The majority of individuals currently seeking treatment who smoke crack are likely to be users of more than one substance. The widespread abuse of cocaine has stimulated extensive efforts to develop treatment programs for this type of drug abuse. It is evident, however, that cocaine abuse and addiction are complex problems that involve biological changes in the brain as well as a myriad of social, familial and environmental changes. Therefore treatment of cocaine addiction must address a wide variety of problems. Like any good treatment plan, cocaine treatment strategies should assess the psychobiological, social and pharmacological aspects of the clients' drug abuse.

IMPROVING TREATMENT: ENTRY AND OUTCOME

Kirby and associates (1997) evaluated behavioral interventions for cocaine dependent, low-income African American inner-city clients who had multiple treatment needs. Like other populations of cocaine-addicted individuals, it was difficult to get addicts to enter treatment, to stay in treatment, and then have positive outcomes from the treatment. The researchers focused on three goals. The first goal was to gain better awareness of what types of problems the abusers encountered in their environment, and the best way to assess the clients' needs. The second goal was to determine how to increase the overall rates of treatment entry. Third, they wanted to see how they could improve treatment outcomes.

Cocaine-dependent individuals in urban environments are typically poor, uneducated, unemployed, lack both communication and vocational skills, estranged from their family and friends, and homeless (Kirby et al., 1997). At treatment entry, the clients are usually in acute distress, expressing feelings of hopelessness, dysphoria and agitation. However, such negative effects may be relatively short-lived, returning to baseline feelings within a few days or weeks. Therefore, self-report estimates of affect and anxiety during the entry stage of treatment are unreliable. However, psychometric evidence reveals a striking prevalence of Axis II disorders in this population, as well as a neuropsychological profile of cognitive deficits suggestive of a moderate frontal dyscontrol syndrome.

Approximately 20 percent of clients who begin outpatient therapy fail to continue after the first session. Between 37 percent and 45 percent of adult outpatients in urban mental health centers terminate psychotherapy before the third session. High attrition rates are common with cocaine-dependent individuals. They drop out of treatment 47 percent of the time between their initial clinic visit and their first counseling session. Cognizant of those data, Kirby et al. (1997) examined clients' records to identify factors that could predict attendance at the first counseling session. Individuals with low levels of anxiety and those that were depressed were predicted to attend the first session. Also, individuals who reported a history of Narcotics Anonymous (NA) involvement returned to treatment more often than those who did not. Clients who were not currently involved with the criminal justice system were more likely to return than those who were. Finally, clients who lived in the city where the treatment facility was located were more likely to return than those who lived in adjacent towns within the same county.

Even if care providers know what factors to look for in order to determine which individuals should be targeted for treatment retention strategies, that information is usually of little help in reducing the rates of attrition. Approximately half of the individuals Kirby and associates called to make intake appointments failed to show for their appointments. That was a cause for concern because many of the pre-intake dropouts were in dire need of treatment. Successful outreach methods for initiating contact and recruiting cocaine abusers into treatment have included providing treatment entry vouchers and training the clients' significant others to encourage treatment entry. Also, it is helpful to provide immediate access to treatment by offering same day appointments to cocaine users who call to schedule an intake appointment. These simple procedures may allow clinics to reach drug-addicted individuals who otherwise would procrastinate and not enter treatment.

Once clients have entered into treatment, issues of treatment retention and reduction of cocaine use should become the care providers' primary concerns. Consistent with the high attrition rates for first clinic appointments, high attrition throughout treatment seems to be common in substance abuse treatment settings. During their study, Kirby et al. had found that 76 percent of cocaine abusers stopped attending after the fifth session. Other cocaine treatment programs have reported 44 percent to 55 percent attrition from adult outpatient treatment by the fourth week of treatment. Behavioral treatments for cocaine abuse are among the few interventions that have gotten positive treatment outcomes in terms of client retention and documented cessation of cocaine use. Because cocaine use is one of many operant behaviors, each with associated consequences, problems arise when cocaine maintenance occupies a major portion of the client's behavior to the exclusion of other reinforcers (Kirby et al., 1997). The basic strategy is to rearrange the client's environment so that drug use and abstinence are readily detected, drug abstinence is reinforced, drug use is extinguished or results in a loss of positive reinforcement, and reinforcement from nondrug sources is increased.

Implementing a basic strategy should include provisions for getting frequent urine samples and immediate screening for benzoylecogonine, a cocaine metabolite. Cocaine-free urine samples can be immediately reinforced by providing the client with a voucher. These vouchers are, in turn, used to increase behavior modification through nondrug opportunities. Voucher exchanges can be negotiated with counselors and used to encourage prosocial activities that are in concert with the client's treatment plan and likely to have reinforcing consequences that will maintain the nondrug behavior after cocaine treatment has ended. Other aspects of these programs include helping clients to identify antecedents of cocaine use and devising plans to avoid them, or developing skills to respond positively to antecedents that are unavoidable, and contracting with the clients' significant others to participate in treatment.

Kirby et al. (1997) gave vouchers worth $30.00 to clients whose urine samples were cocaine-free. The schedule of reinforcement became more intermittent as the clients continued to provide cocaine-free urine samples. The maximum voucher value that could be earned over the 12-week period was $570. The clinical observations showed that clients who received vouchers achieved more cocaine abstinence than those who did not receive them. And the number of days in treatment was greater for clients in the no-voucher group, while the number of counseling sessions attended was higher for clients who received vouchers. A larger percentage of clients who received vouchers had more periods of sustained cocaine abstinence than nonvoucher clients. Also, the duration of continuous cocaine abstinence was as high in the voucher group. Although previous research had documented the importance of the voucher incentive component, Kirby et al.'s research was among the first to demonstrate that the *schedule of voucher delivery* may be critical in producing improved outcomes in the treatment of cocaine dependence.

PSYCHOTHERAPY FOR AFRICAN AMERICAN COCAINE USERS

Given the multiple sources of social and personal problems evident in the young African Americans who abuse cocaine, Pena and Koss-Chiono (1992) proposed that a psychotherapeutic intervention that deals with psychic processes which underlie conflictual interpersonal relationships has a high potential for empowering this population to control their drug abuse. Supportive-expressive psychotherapy (SE) is beneficial for certain types of people–those with narcissistic issues as well as those with personality disorders. It deals with the quality of the alliance between the care provider and the client. These factors are seldom dealt with in traditional drug counseling therapies. It is worth nothing that SE therapy can be effective treatment for low income, African American cocaine abusers.

Supportive-expressive psychotherapy has also been shown to be clinically significant for substance users with various levels of severity of psychopathology, even though low severity of psychopathology is typically found to be a statistically significant predictor of psychotherapy success (Brunswick, 1988). African American cocaine abusers are as likely to have problems with low self-esteem and narcissistic self-concepts as are other cocaine abusers (Boyd-Franklin, 1989). The origin of these difficulties can be seen in the way African American families become dysfunctional in response to societal constraints. Stranton and Todd (1982) stated that African American male substance abusers have negative family experiences that greatly influenced their cocaine use. Intrapsychic problems such as separation fears, overdependence, escapism and low self-esteem are relevant variables. From this perspective, supportive-expressive therapy has the capacity to help clients to develop awareness and solutions to their intrapersonal, interpersonal and intergroup problems. This can facilitate African American substance abusers to achieve their goal of being abstinent.

In order for therapeutic techniques to be successful with a particular ethnic group, attention must be given to the therapeutic alliance, which is a central factor in the success of psychotherapy. With regard to ethnic factors in the therapeutic alliance, most researchers report a lack of evidence that African American clients do better with African American therapists or counselors. There is almost no evidence that mandates similar therapist-client ethnicity for substance abuse treatment. Sue (1988) documented how this issue is sometimes confused with other factors such as therapist competence.

NEW DIRECTIONS

More treatment research and program assessment evaluations are needed to focus on the effects of various treatment modalities for urban, indigent populations for whom the consequences of crack cocaine addiction have been particularly painful. "It is suggested that future studies focus on the potency of anticraving medication as compared to nonpharmaceutical adjunct therapies, on psychological versus physiological effects of adjunct therapies, and on intervening psychosocial variables mediating the relationships between the adjunct therapies, client retention, drug use outcomes, and measures of short-term psychological and/or cognitive changes theoretically linked to adjunct therapies" (Richard et al., 1999, p. 412).

According to Cohen et al. (1994), there is a need to develop a treatment model for African American crack abusers that includes integration of intensive psychotherapeutic modalities, long-term psychosocial life skills training, assertiveness training, women empowerment workshops, and a comprehensive peer support system, perhaps utilizing a combination 12-Step self-help model/mentoring design. The utilization of spiritually-based treatment modalities, such as those found in 12-Step programs, could make the treatment experiences more attractive to ethnic minorities and women, particularly those who have a strong religious orientation. Most importantly, more tangible, essential resources for indigent clients, such as safe and stable housing, adequate child care and training for gainful employment, should be incorporated in any long-term substance abuse intervention program.

With the likelihood of depression and addiction co-existing in crack cocaine using persons, treatment centers must be prepared to employ a dual diagnostic model, concomitantly providing community support and treatment for addiction and depression. With so many clients reporting family members who abuse alcohol or other drugs, treatment personnel should, whenever possible, assess the families of their clients and offer family therapy. At the very least, clients involved in a treatment regimen should be given a chance to discuss the substance abusing environment in which they were reared and to which they may return. Further, strategies for coping with significant others who abuse alcohol and other drugs need to be incorporated into the treatment plan (Boyd, 1993).

In a study conducted by Rash et al. (2000) focusing on patterns of HIV risk and alcohol use among African American crack abusers, data on the first use of alcohol and crack and the association of alcohol and crack in sexual risk point to the need for care providers to carefully focus on and correctly time interventions that target substance abusers. This approach may help reduce the number of people who use and abuse crack cocaine. Also, it may help to reduce the HIV risks associated with substance use and other health problems associated with excessive substance use. An important approach to HIV risk reduction might begin by focusing on reducing alcohol use, especially among teenage African Americans.

In summary, African American cocaine users have been found to get positive results from various different types of treatments programs, ranging from behavioral therapy to family therapy. Whatever treatment is used, it must be culturally sensitive and culturally relevant. And, as we have stated earlier, effective treatment is impossible if drug abusers do not seek help. Considerably more research must be conducted in order to determine clear and comprehensive treatment modalities for African American cocaine abusers. In the interim, existing programs must be improved, amply financed, carefully staffed, and diligently marketed.

REFERENCES

Boyd, C.J. (1993). The antecedents of women's crack cocaine abuse: Family susbstance abuse, sexual abuse, depression, and illicit drug use. *Journal of Substance Abuse Treatment, 10*, 433–438.

Boyd, C.J., Hill, E., Holmes, C. & Purnell, R. (1998). Putting drug use in context: lifelines of African American women who smoke crack. *Journal of Substance Abuse Treatment, 15*(3), 235–249.

Boyd-Franklin, N. (1989). *Black families in therapy: A multisystems approach.* New York: Guilford.

Castro, F.G., Newcomb, M.D. & Cadish, K. (1987). Lifestyle differences between young adult cocaine users and their nonuser peers. *Journal of Drug Education, 17*, 89–111.

Cohen, E., Navaline, B.A., Metzger, D. (1994). High-risk behaviors for HIV: A comparison between crack-abusing and opioid-abusing African American women. *Journal of Psychoactive Drugs, 26*(3), 233–240.

Fullilove, M., Golden, E., Fullilove III, R.E., Lennon, R., Porterfield, D., Schwarcz, S. & Bolan, G. (1993). Crack cocaine use and high-risk behaviors among sexually active Black adolescents. *Journal of Adolescent Health, 14*, 295–300.

Gawin, F.H. & Kleber, H.D. (1986). Abstinence, symptomatology and psychiatric diagnosis in cocaine abusers: Clinical observations. *Archives of General Psychiatry, 43*, 107–113.

Herridge, P. & Gold, M.S. (1988). The new user of cocaine: Evidence from 800-COCAINE. *Psychiatric Annals, 18*(9), 521–522.

Hoffman, J.A., Cuadill, B.D., Koman, J.J., Luckey, J.W., Flynn, P.M. & Mayo, D.W. (1996). Psychosocial treatments for cocaine abuse: Twelve month treatment outcomes. *Journal of Substance Abuse Treatment, 13*(1), 3–11.

Hudgins, R., McCusker, J. & Stoddard, A. (1995). Cocaine use and risky injection and sexual behaviors. *Drug & Alcohol Dependence, 37*, 7–14.

Kirby, C.K., Marlowe, B.D., Lamb, J.R. & Platt, J.J. (1997). Behavioral treatment of cocaine addiction: Assessing patient needs and improving treatment entry and outcome. *Journal of Drug Issues, 27*(2), 417–429.

Longshore, D., Grills, C., Anglin, D.M. & Annon, K. (1997). Desire for help among African American drug users. *Journal of Drug Issues, 27*(4), 755–770.

National Institute on Drug Abuse, National Institutes of Health. (2001, February). *Nationwide Trends.* Bethesda, MD: Author. (a)

National Institute on Drug Abuse, National Institute of Health. (2001, January). *Cocaine Abuse and Addiction.* Bethesda, MD: Author. (b)

National Institute on Drug Abuse, National Institute of Health (2001, February). *Hospital Visits.* Bethesda, MD: Author. (c)

National Institute on Drug Abuse, National Institute of Health. (2001, January). *Treatment Trends.* Bethesda, MD: Author. (d)

National Institute on Drug Abuse, National Institute of Health. (2001, January). *Costs to Society.* Bethesda, MD: Author. (e)

Parham, T.A. & Helms, J.E. (1981). The influence of Black students' racial identity attitudes on preference for counselors race. *Journal of Counseling Psychology, 28*, 250–257.

Pena, J.M. & Koss-Chiono, J.D. (1992). Cultural sensitivity in drug treatment research with African American males. *Drugs Society Journal of Contemporary Issues, 6*, 157–179.

Rasch, R.E., Weisen, C.A., MacDonald, B., Wechsberg, W.M., Perritt, R. & Dennis, M.L. (2000). Patterns of HIV risk and alcohol use among African American crack abusers, *Drug & Alcohol Dependence, 58*, 259–266.

Richard, A.J. Montgoya, I.D., Nelson R. & Spence, R.T. (1995). Effectiveness of adjunct therapies in crack cocaine treatment. *Journal of Substance Abuse Treatment, 12*, (6), 401–413.

Stanton, M.D. & Todd, T.C. (1981). Engaging resistant families in treatment. *Family Process, 20*, 261–293.

Sue, S. (1988). Psychotherapeutic services for ethnic minorities. *American Psychology,*

43(4), 301–308.

Weiss, R.D. (1988). Psychotherapy in cocaine abusers: Changing trends. *Journal of Nervous & Mental Disease, 12,* 719–725.

PART III

ASIAN AMERICANS

Chapter 7

SUBSTANCE ABUSE AMONG SOUTHEAST ASIANS IN THE U.S.: IMPLICATIONS FOR PRACTICE AND RESEARCH

THOMAS O'HARA AND THANH VAN TRAN

Preliminary evidence suggests that Southeast Asian immigrants, refugees and their children in the U.S. are at increased risk for abusing alcohol and other drugs. The consequences of war trauma, leaving one's homeland and loved ones, and acculturation to American society may be contributing to stress-related mental disorders with co-occurring increases in substance abuse. Bernier (1992) has suggested four stress-related theories as a framework to account for problems among Southeast Asian refugees: stress related to *acculturation* in the new host country (e.g., struggling to learn a new language, encountering a new culture), *bereavement* (e.g., loss of status, physical possessions, loved ones), *change* (e.g., a new social environment, financial status), and *trauma* (e.g., war, famine, persecution, torture), the effects of which may endure for years.

Given the growing evidence that mental health and substance use problems frequently co-occur in both general population (Helzer & Pryzbeck, 1988) and clinical samples (O'Hare, 1995), the literature on psychological disturbances among Southeast Asians provides a cogent backdrop to a discussion of substance abuse disorders. In addition, the acculturation experiences of other Asian-American groups has apparently contributed to increases in substance abuse. The purpose of this chapter is to critically examine research findings relevant to Southeast Asian mental health and substance abuse problems in order to provide an empirical framework for preliminary practice guidelines and future research.

Having increased in numbers from 133,438 in 1975 to 1,204,900 in 1992 (U.S. Office of Refugee Resettlement), immigrants from Vietnam, Cambodia and Laos are a rapidly growing part of the Asian-American population in the United States. The vast majority of immigrants from these groups arrived as political refugees, and all have shown disproportionate signs of psychological strain when compared to U.S. population norms. Much of the distress found among Vietnamese immigrants and refugees has been associated with lower socioeconomic status, poor English language proficiency, less confidence in interacting with Americans and lack of other social supports (Nicassio, 1983; Tan & Wright, 1986), greater premigration stresses (Matsuoka, 1990), lower personal self-efficacy with subsequent depression (Tran, 1993), and a lack of adequate health care (Tran & Nguyen, 1994).

A recent study of a clinical sample of Southeast Asians in the Midwest showed that more than half had serious, often chronic, physical disorders which caused or exacerbated a mental health disturbance. Some of these conditions apparently were caused by preimmigration trauma, including torture (Ta et al., 1996). Suggesting that Cambodians experienced the worst trauma in recent Southeast Asian history, Carlson et al. (1991) conducted structured interviews with a small random community sample, and discovered that 86 percent of Cambodians met Post Traumatic Stress Disorder criteria (based on DSM-III-R criteria, r.85), 96 percent had high dissociative symptoms (Dissociative experiences Scale), and 80 percent appeared to be clinically depressed (Hopkins Symptom Checklist-25, r=.89). Almost all respondents reported a variety of traumatic experiences. Mollica et al. (1993), based on a refugee camp sample of 993, and Sack et al. (1994), surveying adolescents (n=209) and their parents (n=95), uncovered similar evidence in a sample of Cambodians who had survived the refugee experience, although the latter study may have suffered from a sample selection bias between the two sites. Even after ten years in the U.S., the Hmong community of Laos also showed higher rates of mental disturbances compared to American norms based on the analysis of 102 refugees who participated in structured interviews over 7 to 9 years (Westermeyer, to 1985). Lastly, Ying & Hu (1994) showed that over 1,700 Southeast Asian outpatient mental health clients experienced more anxiety disorders, had higher service utilization rates, and poorer outcomes overall perhaps due to their relatively recent and more traumatic migration to the U.S.

SOUTHEAST ASIAN SUBSTANCE USE PATTERNS AND ASSOCIATED PROBLEMS IN THE UNITED STATES

Although substance abuse data on Southeast Asians in the U.S. are only beginning to emerge, robust findings which include other Asian-American groups show changes in substance use patterns and consumption increases over recent generations apparently resulting from acculturation to American norms (Kitano, 1989; Sue et al., 1979). Data from the 1992 National Health Interview Survey (NHIS) found that 24.4 percent of Asian-American youth (12 to 21 years of age) consumed alcohol at least once within the past 30 days (vs. 43.8% whites). Regarding illicit substances, 15 percent of Asian-American youth used marijuana and 3.7 percent tried cocaine at least once in their life (vs. 28.5% and 6.4% for whites, respectively) (National Center for Health Statistics, 1995). Although there are no specific substance use data on "bi-cultural" Asian-Americans, one might suspect that they are at greater risk to drink excessively since they are more acculturated in general to American norms (Uba, 1994). One study demonstrated that a small proportion of Asian high school students who drank heavily actually consumed more than their heavy drinking non-Asian counterparts (Barnes & Welte, 1986). A survey at a large eastern university, a setting in which many Asian students are initiated to "American-style" drinking (Kitano et al., 1985), showed almost 15 percent of Asian students to be heavy-moderate to heavy drinkers (O'Hare, 1990). Indeed, heavy drinking for Chinese men (who often develop drinking problems after immigration as a result of easier accessibility of alcohol) seems related to drinking with friends and going to bars (Chi et al., 1998), increased family problems and social isolation (Chin et al., 1991). Heavy drinking among Japanese-American men and women is not uncommon (Kitano et al., 1988), and Japanese-American women appear to have a higher percentage of heavy drinkers than Chinese, Korean, and Filipino Asian-American females (Kitano & Chi, 1986/1987).

Although some have suggested that moderation in Asian-American drinking practices is, to some degree, physiologically mediated (Akutsu et al., 1989), the preponderance of evidence suggests that cultural factors have had a more powerful influence on substance use patterns (Li & Rosenblood, 1994; Sue, 1987). Kitano (1989) has asserted that the immigrant's traditional behavior will be modified over time. Variables which mediate this process may include length of time in the country, availability and cost of alcoholic beverages, and the amount and quality of interaction with the dominant culture. Acculturated Japanese and Chinese students, for example, drink more than do less acculturated Japanese and Chinese students, for example, drink more than do less acculturated counterparts (Sue et al., 1979). Although this process does not always occur uniformly among Asian-Americans (Kitano et al., 1992), alcohol abuse has increased overall, and the meaning, context and consequences of alcohol abuse have become more problematic.

Although no well-controlled longitudinal data are currently available, preliminary evidence suggests that pockets of trouble are beginning to emerge in Southeast Asian communities, and they appear to be directly related to a host of psychosocial stressors. Yee and Thu (1987) found in a study of

Vietnamese immigrants that almost 14 percent had trouble with other drugs "some of the time," over 40 percent reported using alcohol as a means of "coping with sorrows," and almost 12 percent reported using drugs for the same purpose. Structured interviews with a snowball sample of 120 Cambodian women on the East and West Coasts of the U.S. (D'Avanzo et al., 1994) revealed that almost seven percent reported a family member to have a drinking problem, about 15 percent of the East Coast group reported that a family member (usually an adolescent) was using street drugs, and 17 percent of the women reported using prescription drugs, in part, for their "street drug" effects.

Over 58 percent of the West Coast sample reported using medications for self-treatment of conditions other than that for which the drug was prescribed: coping with stress, forgetting troubles, and dealing with physical discomforts, including those associated with pregnancy. Based on longitudinal qualitative field research with nonrandom samples, Westermeyer (1985) reported Laotian alcohol consumption levels in the U.S. to be lower than premigration levels. However, drinking patterns appeared to be more problem-prone (particularly for young males) than the more narrowly prescribed ceremonial drinking which occurred in rural Southeast Asia. Although drinking has replaced opium for some in the U.S., opium use overall appears to be on the increase (Westermeyer et al., 1991). The same study which examined Hmong seeking treatment for opium addiction found that more than half experienced a range of co-occurring symptoms including: tolerance and withdrawals, occasional loss of control, guilt over opium use, nightmares, anxiety, panic, suicidal ideation, interpersonal and family distress, school and work-related problems, financial and legal difficulties. Rather than the pleasurable ceremonial or recreational activity it was generally regarded in their homeland where rates of opium use have been estimated at eight percent to 12 percent among farmers (Westermeyer et al., 1991), the use of alcohol or opiates has acquired very negative associations, and concerns about an expanding substance abuse problem are growing (Westermeyer, 1985).

Although most of the data are based on nonrepresentative samples, indications are that substance abuse is a growing concern for many Southeast Asian immigrants, once again challenging the myth of Asian-Americans as the "model minority" (Uba, 1994). Given these reports combined with evidence of disproportionate psychosocial stressors and the documented increases in substance abuse among other traditionally abstemious Asian-American groups, social workers should be vigilant to signs of substance abuse within the Southeast Asian community.

Implications for Practice and Research Clinic Assessment. Diagnosis of both substance abuse and mental health concerns should be conducted warily for SoutheastAsian clients. In particular, practitioners might consider employing a more heterogeneous perspective (Freeman, 1991) when making substance abuse assessments with these groups. A multivariate view emphasizes a continuum of abuse along which the causes, course and consequences are often intertwined with co-occurring health, mental health and other psychosocial problems. Such an assessment model may comport well with the problems of Southeast Asian clients who, for example, may not consume alcohol at levels of other American groups, but, nevertheless, suffer from a range of co-occurring psychosocial difficulties aggravated by the use of alcohol or other drugs. Practitioners also need to bring cultural context and meaning to the client's problems which often include grieving multiple losses and struggling with the stresses of acculturation and adaptation (Eisenbruch, 1991).

There is also a growing availability of assessment tools which can be employed in culturally sensitive practice research with Southeast Asian clients, or could be used to complement clinical interviewing. These include an acculturation scale which emphasizes language proficiency (Anderson et al., 1993), the Hopkins Symptom Checklist (HSCL-25) for measuring anxiety and depression among Vietnamese, Cambodians and Laotians (Mollica et al., 1987), and the Vietnamese Depression Scale (Kinzie & Mason, 1987), which measures various dimensions of the disorder.

Intervention. General guidelines recommended for social work practice with Southeast Asian clients include a focus on multiple losses, stress-related somatic concerns, and daily problems of adaptation. Recommended interventions include the use of psychoeducation, role modeling, and coping skills to bolster self-efficacy and to deal with stressful environmental challenges, and to strengthen support networks within the family and community (Land et al., 1988; McQuaid, 1989; Montero & Dieppa, 1982; Timberlake & Cook, 1984;). Psychoeducation is a direct way to impart knowledge about American culture (informal interpersonal styles, slang meanings, government bureaucracies, available goods, and services). Role playing new communication and coping skills can reduce anxiety and improve the client's confidence and effectiveness in obtaining resources and problem solving in a new and different culture.

With respect to problems related to substance abuse, practitioners are admonished to avoid insight-oriented therapies (Beohnlein et al., 1985; McQuaid, 1989; Timberlake & Cook, 1988) as well as approaches which pressure clients to admit "alcoholism," and engage in a recovery process based on Western views of spiritual redemption. This strategy may be particularly incongruent with Southeast Asian culture given the heavy emphasis on extensive self-examination and public confession. Evidence suggests, however, that cognitive-behavioral therapies (CBT) have been positively received by Asian-American clients and their practitioners (Mokuaua-

Matsushima et al., 1982), and offer much promise for work with substance abusing clients.

Effective interventions for substance abuse (Miller, 1992) typically emphasize learning new skills to reduce or eliminate consumption, prevent relapse, and reduce negative consequences in the community. CBT for persons who abuse substances typically include some combination of the following: (1) self-monitoring thoughts, feelings and situations which are likely to "trigger" an impulse to abuse alcohol or drugs; (2) teaching more effective social skills to deal with situations in which the client may be pressured to use drugs; and (3) teaching stress management skills to lower anxiety, deal with somatic complaints, and covertly rehearse new behavioral skills. These methods have been incorporated into individual, couples, family and community-based interventions (McCrady, 1991) and have a record of demonstrated effectiveness for a broad range of clients.

When adapting CBT approaches for Southeast Asian families, clinicians must be especially sensitive to the degree of guilt and shame, and skillfully enhance family communication skills while, at the same time, emphasizing respect for tradition, family hierarchy and the importance of indigenous community supports which may enhance the reduction or elimination of substance abuse (Ja & Aoki, 1993; Perez-Arce et al., 1993). CBT skills are also applicable to a range of problems such as depression and anxiety disorders which frequently co-occur with substance abuse. Future research efforts should examine the effectiveness of family-based CBT approaches with Southeast Asians who suffer from combined mental health and substance use disorders.

The evidence for the acceptability of CBT by Southeast Asian clients may be due, in part, to the complementarity between CBT principles and Asian cultural values including: (1) respect for the teaching modality inherent in psychoeducation and skill-based approaches; (2) the relative structure and emphasis on personal initiative and responsibility in treatment; (3) the ability to examine cognitive schemas relevant to the problem without being unnecessarily intrusive; (4) the use of stress management techniques based on Asian philosophies which clients may find familiar; and, (5) the ease of incorporating CBT methods into family and community-based interventions. Employing CBT interventions can also accommodate two ingredients crucial to engaging Asian-American clients: First, *credibility* (i.e., a client's perception that the clinician is both effective and trustworthy), and, secondly, a phenomenon known as giving, that is the client's experience that something of significant value has been received from the therapeutic encounter (Sue & Zane, 1987).

DIRECTIONS FOR FUTURE RESEARCH

Emphasis has recently been given in the addictions literature to avoiding broad ethnic and racial glosses to describe culturally disparate peoples (Cheung, 1991; Heath, 1991; Trimble, 1990). The same suggestions have been made specifically for Southeast Asian studies as well (Bromley, 1987; Fong & Mokuau, 1994). More specifically, Cheung (1991) has suggested that future research emphasize more accurate measures of ethnicity which address both the objective component of *culture retention* and the more subjective notion of *ethnic identification*. Other specific improvements to measuring ethnicity summarized by Trimble (1990) might include employing *natal measures* (i.e., birthplace of self, siblings, natural parents, grandparents and relatives), measuring *behavior* (i.e., language use, affiliative patterns with friends and acquaintances, media usage, participation in ethnic-specific activities such as cultural and religious events, music and food preferences, club membership); *subjective assessment of ethnicity* (e.g., self-identified ethnicity, assessment of aculturative status, real and aspired self-image, value preferences, role models and preferred reference groups, ego involvement in group, attitudes toward "out" groups), *hierarchical nesting procedures* (i.e., "layering" questions about place of birth, nation, ethnic composition of current neighborhood, preferences for acquaintances, colleagues, spouses, etc.), and accounting for the *variability in ethnic identity as a function of social context.*

Given the acculturation experiences of other Asian-Americans, co-occurring psychosocial risk factors and preliminary evidence of substance abuse problems among Southeast Asian-Americans, research is urgently needed to more completely measure the incidence and prevalence of substance use and abuse among these ethnic groups, and to examine the causes and extent of associated psychosocial dysfunction. Within the context of Bernier's (1992) framework, a multivariate model should, at a minimum, include: a thorough examination of *ethnic identity*, history of *trauma* and *losses* experienced by the respondent and their parents, measures or *assimilation* and *acculturation stresses*, *psychosocial* and *mental health* problem ratings, several *substance use* ratings (including premigration retrospective measures) to gauge consumption level and problem severity, and *alcohol and drug expectancies* (to measures can also be incorporated into research on culturally congruent treatment processes and outcomes, the need for which is clearly evident (Spencer et al., 1980; Sue & Zane, 1987).

REFERENCES

Akutsu, P.D., Sue, S., Zane, N. & Nakamura, C.Y. (1989). Ethnic differences in alcohol consumption among Asians and Caucasians in the United States: An investigation of cultural and physiological factors. *Journal of Studies on Alcohol, 50*, (3), 261–267.

Anderson, J., Moeschberger, M., Chen, M.S., Junn, P., Wewers, M.E. & Guthrie, R. (1993). An acculturation scale for Southeast Asians. *Social Psychiatry & Psychiatric Epidemiology, 28*, 134–141.

Barnes, G.M. & Welte, J.W. (1986). Patterns and predictors of alcohol use among 7–12 grade students in N.Y. State. *Journal of Studies on Alcohol, 47*, (1), 53–62.

Bernier, D. (1992). The Indochinese refugees: A perspective from various stress theories. *Journal of Multicultural Social Work, 2*, (1), 15–30.

Boehnlein, J.K., Kinzie, J.D., Ben, R. & Fleck, J. (1985). One-year follow-up study of Post-Traumatic Stress Disorder among survivors of Cambodian concentration camps. *American Journal of Psychiatry, 142*, (8), 956–959.

Bromley, M.A. (1987). New beginnings for Cambodian refugees–or further disruptions? *Social Work, 32*, 236–239.

Carlson, B.E. & Rosser-Hogan, R. (1991). Trauma experiences, stress, dissociation and depression in Cambodian refugees. *American Journal of Psychiatry, 148*, (11), 1548–1551.

Cheung, Y.W. (1991). Ethnicity and alcohol/drug use revisited: A framework for future research. *The International Journal of the Addictions, 25*, (5a & 6a), 581–608.

Chi, I., Kitano, H.H & Lubben, J.E. (1998). Male Chinese drinking behavior in Los Angeles. *Journal of Studies on Alcohol, 49*, (1), 21–25.

Chin, K., Lai, T. & Rouse, M. (1991). Social adjustment and alcoholism among Chinese immigrants in New York City. *The International Journal of the Addictions, 25* (5a & 6a), 709–730.

D'Avanzo, C.E., Frye, B. & Froman, R. (1994). Culture, stress, and substance use in Cambodian refugee women. *Journal of Studies on Alcohol, 55*, 420–426.

Eisenbruch, M. (1991). From post-traumatic stress disorder to cultural bereavement: Diagnosis of Southeast Asian refugees. *Social Science & Medicine, 33*, (6), 673–680.

Fong, R. & Mokuau, N. (1994). Not simply "Asian Americans": Periodical literature review on Asians and Pacific Islanders. *Social Work, 39*, (3) 298–305.

Freeman, E.M. (1991). Addictive behaviors: State of the art issues in social work Treatment (pp.1–9), in E.M. Freeman (Ed.), *The Addiction Process: Effective Social Work Approaches*. NY: Longman.

Heath, D.B. (1991). Uses and misuses of the concept of ethnicity in alcohol studies: An essay on deconstruction. *International Journal of the Addictions, 25* (5a & 6a), 607–628.

Helzer, J.E. & Pryzbeck, T.R. (1998). The co-occurrence of alcoholism and other psychiatric disorders in the general population and its impact on treatment. *Journal of Studies on Alcohol, 49*, (3), 219–224.

Ja, D.Y. & Aoki, B. (1993). Substance abuse treatment: Cultural barriers in the Asian-American community. *Journal of Psychoactive Drugs, 25*, (1), 61–71.

Kinzie, H.L. & Manson, S.M. (1987). The use of self-rating scales in cross-cultural psychiatry. *Hospital & Community Psychiatry, 38*, (2), 190–196.

Kitano, H.H. (1989). Alcohol and the Asian-American. In T.D. Watts and R. Wright (Eds.), *Alcoholism in Minority Populations* (pp. 143–156). Springfield, IL: Charles C Thomas.

Kitano, H.H. & Chi, I. (1986/1987). Asian-Americans and alcohol use. *Alcohol Health & Research World*, Winter, 42–47.

Kitano, H.H Chi. I., Rhee, S., Law, C.K. & Lubben, J. (1992). Norms and alcohol consumption: Japanese in Japan, Hawaii, and California. *Journal of Studies on Alcohol, 53*, 33–39.

Kitano, H.H., Hatanaka, H., Yeung, W.T. & Sue, S. (1985). Japanese-American drinking patterns, pp. 335–357. L.A. Bennett and G.M. Ames, (Eds.), *The American Experience with Alcohol: Contrasting Cultural Perspectives.* NY: Plenum Press.

Kitano, H.H., Lubben, J & Chi, I. (1988). Predicting Japanese American drinking behavior. *The International Journal of Addictions, 23*, (4), 417–428.

Land, G., Nishimoto, R. & Chau, K. (1988). Interventive and preventive services for Vietnamese Chinese refugees. *Social Service Review, 62*, (3), 468–484.

Li, H.Z. & Rosenblood, L. (1994). Exploring factors influencing alcohol consumption patterns among Chinese and Caucasians. *Journal of Studies on Alcohol, 55*, 427–433.

Lovell, M.L., Tran, T. & Nguyen, C.D. (1987). Refugee women: Lives in transition. *International Journal of Social Work, 30*, 317–325.

Matsuoka, J.K. (1990). Differential acculturation among Vietnamese refugees. *Social Work, 35*,4, 341–345.

McCrady, B.S. (1991). Promising but underutilized treatment approaches. *Alcohol Health & Research World, 15* (3), 215–218.

McQuaide, S. (1989). Working with Southeast Asian refugees. *Clinical Social Work Journal, 17* (2), 165–176).

Miller, W.R. (1992). Effectiveness of treatment for substance abuse. *Journal of Substance Abuse Treatment, 9*, 93–102.

Mokuau-Matsushima, N., Tashima, N. & Mursase, K. (1982). *Mental Health Treatment Modalities of Pacific Asian-American Practitioners.* CA: Pacific Asian-American Research Project.

Mollica, R.F., Donelan, K., Tor, S., Lavelle, J., Elais, C., Frankel, M. & Blendon, R.J. (1993). The effect of trauma and confinement on functional health and mental health status of Cambodians living in Thailand-Cambodian border camps. *JAMA, 270*, (5), 581–586.

Mollica, R.F., Wyshak, G., de Marneffe, D., Khuon, F. & Lavelle, J. (1987). Indochinese versions of the Hopkins Symptom Checklist–25: A screening instrument for the psychiatric care of the refugees. *American Journal of Psychiatry, 144*, (4), 497–500.

Montero, D & Dieppa, I. (1982). Resettling Vietnamese refugees: The service agency's role. *Social Work, 27*, 74–81.

National Center for Health Statistics (1995). *1992 National Health Interview Survey.* Hyattsville, MD: Centers for Disease Control and Prevention.

Nicassio, P.M. (1983). Psychosocial correlates of alienation: Study of a sample of Indochinese refugees. *Journal of Cross-Cultural Psychology, 14* (3), 337–351.

O'Hare, T. (1990). Drinking in college: Consumption patterns, problems, sex differences and legal drinking age. *Journal of Studies on Alcohol, 51* (6), 536–541.

O'Hare, T. (1995). Mental health problems and alcohol abuse: Co-occurrence and gender differences. *Health & Social Work, 20,* 207–214.

Perez-Arce, P.P., Carr, K.D. & Sorensen, J.L. (1993). Cultural issues in an outpatient program for stimulant abusers. *Journal of Psychoactive Drugs, 25* (1), 35–44

Sack, W.H., Mcsharry, S., Clarke, G.N., Kinney, R., Seeley, J. & Lewison, P. (1994). The Khmer adolescent project: Epidemiologic findings in two generations of Cambodian refugees. *The Journal of Nervous & Mental Disease, 182,* (7), 387–395.

Spencer, C.P., Heggenhougen, H.K. & Navaratnam, V. (1980). Traditional therapies and the treatment of drug dependence in Southeast Asia. *American Journal of Chinese Medicine, 8,* (3), 230–238.

Sue, D. (1987). Use and abuse of alcohol by Asian-Americans. *Journal of Psychoactive Drugs, 19* (1), 57–66.

Sue, S. & Zane, N. (1987). The role of culture and cultural techniques in psychotherapy: A critique and reformation. *American Psychologist, 42* (1), 37–45.

Sue, S., Zane, N. & Ito, J. (1979). Alcohol drinking patterns among Asian and Caucasian Americans. *Journal of Cross-Cultural Psychology, 10,* 41–56.

Ta, K., Westermeyer, J. & Neider, J. (1996). Physical disorders among Southeast Asian refugee outpatients with psychiatric disorders. *Psychiatric Services, 47,* 975–979.

Timberlake, E. & Cook, K.O. (1984). Social work and the Vietnamese refugee. *Social Work, 29,* 108–113.

Tran, V.T. (1993). Psychological traumas and depression in a sample of Vietnamese people in the United States. *Health & Social Work, 18* (3), 184–194.

Tran, V.T. & Nguyen, T.D. (1994). Gender and satisfaction with the host society among Indochinese refugees. *International Migration Review, 28* (2), 323–337.

Tran, V.T. & Wright, R., Jr. (1986). Social support and subjective well-being among Vietnamese refugees. *Social Service Review,* 448–459.

Trimble, J.E. (1990). Ethnic specification, validation prospects, and the future of drug use research. *The International Journal of the Addictions, 25* (2a), 149–170.

Uba, Laura (1994). *Asian Americans: Personality, Patterns, Identity and Mental Health.* NY: Guilford.

U.S. Office of Refugee Resettlement. (1992). *Annual Report.* Washington, DC: U.S. Government Printing Office.

Westermeyer, J.C. (1995). Hmong drinking practices in the United States: The influence of migration, (pp. 373–391). In G.M. Ames & L.A.Bennett (Eds.), *The American Experience with Alcohol: Contrasting Cultural Perspectives.* NY: Plenum Press.

Westermeyer, J.C., Lyfoung, T., Westermeyer, M. & Neider, J. (1991). Opium addiction among Indochinese refugees in the United States: Characteristics of addicts and their opium use. American *Journal of Drug & Alcohol Abuse, 17* (3), 267–277.

Yee, B.W.K & Thu, N.D. (1987). Correlates of drug use and abuse among

Indochinese refugees: Mental health implications. *Journal of Psychoactive Drugs,* 19 (1), 77–83.

Ying, Y. & Hu, L. (1994). Public out-patient mental health services: Use and outcome among Asian-Americans. *American Journal of Orthopsychiatry, 64,* (3), 448–455.

Chapter 8

TREATING SOUTHEAST ASIAN IMMIGRANTS: MIEN OPIUM USERS IN CALIFORNIA

JUDITH MARTIN

The 14th Street Clinic is an outpatient facility which has offered a wide spectrum of treatment to addicted patients and their families since 1979. It is located in the East Bay region of northern California, an area rich in ethnic diversity including a large and thriving Asian population. In 1991, the clinic staff was approached by mental health practitioners who serve the Asian community, seeking drug abuse treatment for a group of Mien opium smokers who did not speak English. Individual patients from this community had previously sought treatment at the clinic on their own, but this was an opportunity to work closely with professionals well versed in the cultural concerns pertaining to mental health in the Asian community. The clinic staff began the process of designing appropriate treatment strategies for this group.

In Laos, the Mien people live in rural mountainous areas where the opium poppy is cultivated. They have no written language. Opium is used, usually smoked, for a variety of symptoms at all ages. No stigma is attached to this use, and there is no word for addiction in the Mien language. The Mien became political war refugees and, to avoid genocide, they were transported to the United States in 1985. They were placed in various communities around the country. Community health workers estimate that there is a population of approximately 3,000 Mien in the Oakland area. Even though exposure to opium was high–estimated at around 80 percent–a much smaller number of Mien found themselves unable to stop their use of opium when faced with the criminal and legal problems associated with its use in the United States. Many of the factors described as contributing to the heightened vulnerability of the Hmong in Minnesota (Westermeyer, 1989) were

156

also present in Oakland: lack of support for health care, few occupational rehabilitation agencies, and difficult cultural readjustment.

The clinic personnel, including the administrative staff, physician and counselors, held several meetings with Asian mental health workers to discuss relevant Mien belief systems and healing practices, and to design appropriate treatment interventions. These discussions, although intensive in the first year of our effort, continue whenever needed, and treatment strategies are fine tuned and adjusted according to new needs and problems. This chapter describes some of the highlights and clinical insights we have gained during this experience.

CLINICAL ISSUES IN TREATING OPIATE ADDICTION: THE CLINIC'S EXPERTISE

Many of the shared techniques and models for treating addictions within the United States were not present in the Mien culture. For our clinic, this meant revising some of the standard approaches to fit the Mien patients. It also meant trying to bring the Asian mental health workers up to date on current research and treatment strategies pertaining to opiate addiction treatment so they could advocate for medically indicated interventions when Mien patients were confused or reluctant to engage in something new for them.

Current thinking about opioid addiction in the United States uses a chronic disease model (McLellan et al., 2000). This model views addiction as a chronic relapsing condition that has a spectrum of severity. The treatment, just as in other chronic medical conditions, is carried out in hopes of controlling the disease and preventing the long-term ravages and fatalities that results from uncontrolled illness. In more intractable cases, pharmacotherapy with methadone or LAAM may be indicated, and in some cases maintenance treatment with such agonist medications is very successfully used (American Society of Addiction Medicine, 1996; Dole, 1988). Early use of opioid agonists was controversial and seen as a simple substitution of one illicit opiate for a prescribed legal one. Later, research of endorphin and brain physiology confirmed that there is more to treatment with these long acting agonist medications than mere replacement. Their slower onset and longer duration of action allow normalization of endocrine and brain physiology, which can never be reached when the patient is using short bursts of rapidly metabolized opiates (Koob & Moal, 1997; Koob, Sanna & Bloom, 1998). This is mirrored in the patient's ability to take on normal life tasks, and in abstinence from illicit opiate abuse. At the right dose of medication, a steady state is reached where the patient is neither intoxicated nor in withdrawal, thus able to avoid compulsive drug seeking behavior (Payte & Khuri, 1993; Payte & Zweben, 1998).

From the clinician's point of view, the task was to identify the severity of the addiction—a concept itself foreign to Mien patients—and, in very severe cases, include these patients in the methadone maintenance services at the clinic. Methadone maintenance, although recognized in the field as the most effective of pharmacotherapies available (ASAM, 1991; NIH Consensus Statement, 1997), is fraught with regulatory constraints. The methadone treatment system, which takes place in the framework of a specially licensed Opioid Treatment Program (OTP), is not user-friendly in any language. Treatment options within the OTP in California are notorious for labyrinthine complexity and inflexibility. Assuming the intractable opiate abuser could be identified within the Mien cultural milieu, offering mainte-nance pharmacotherapy was seen as a difficult task.

Aside from pharmacotherapy, when indicated, psychosocial approaches to treatment of opioid addiction are used for all patients at The 14th Street Clinic. Using an integrative approach, and drawing on techniques from psy-chotherapy and drug recovery models, the counselors were specifically trained in supportive therapy, group therapy and relapse prevention, all techniques found useful in opioid addiction treatment (Obuchowsky & Zweben, 1987; Zweben, 1993; Zweben, 1998). The patient is assessed for readiness to change, and psychosocial interventions are matched to the patient's stage on this continuum, in a nonjudgmental supportive manner, emphasizing development of rapport (Miller, 1999; Miller & Rollnick, 1991). In the case of a patient who is not contemplating change, this would include giving information and remaining available. For a patient who has been abstinent, this might help to prevent relapse.

On-site acupuncture needles and alternative therapy in the ear is a wide-ly-used adjunct to detoxification in opiate addiction treatment (Brumbaugh, 1993; Konefal et al., 1994). In summary, the clinic brought together a willing staff trained in substance abuse treatment which has allowed them to use the options of pharmacotherapy, psychosocial intervention, and alternative approaches.

THE COMMUNITY MENTAL HEALTH WORKERS' EXPERTISE

As might be expected, the community mental health professionals had expertise in culturally-specific psychosocial approaches. In particular, through their experiences treating Asian war refugees, they learned that group therapy was a useful way to address post-traumatic stress disorder (PTSD) in patients who already had strong community bonds. Out of the experience with refugees, they predicted that Mien patients might be more reluctant than American patients to verbally state their feelings and emotions, and that they would condone the use of opium an appropriate response to a physical ailment. From the mental health professionals' point of view, our opium using patients needed detoxification so they could better participate in the treatment options. They specifically requested "non-methadone" detoxification and medical treatment based on their beliefs that methadone was not effective in the Mien patients. Even though individual Mien patients had received methadone treatment at the clinic since 1985 with some benefit, there was little support for this modality from among the mental health workers and community representatives who approached the clinic for help. Further exploration indicated that some of the difficulty might have been related to money: the clinic could not offer funded slots for treatment. One very valuable skill among the Asian mental health workers was their ability to serve as translators during psychosocial interventions.

DESIGNING THE INITIAL INTERVENTION

We speculated that many of the values and assumptions underlying addiction treatment in the United States were not present in the Mien culture. Also, we hypothesized that opium use has a positive value in Mien culture, which is a sharp contrast to American culture. Further, we speculated that Mien difficulties pertaining to opium use in the U.S. are directly related to their inability to achieve acculturation, not to any stigma for using it. Thus, we concluded that they would seek treatment because opium use is an expensive criminal lifestyle, that could result in the children's protective services removing their children from the home. Therefore we believed that the Mien would be ambivalent to abstinence-inducing programs. And the individuals identified for drug treatment would be those whose opium use was disruptive within the community. That is how we began our program design: believing that U.S. concepts such as recovery, relapse, and the need for substance abuse treatment would be foreign to Mien patients.

Because the Mien do not have a written language, substance abuse education has to be presented in verbal and audio-visual mediums. Also, just as opinions do not develop in isolation but instead in the community, so too would our outreach activities extend beyond the clinic. Thus, from the very beginning we decided to have community outreach staff members and to involve community leaders. The attitudes and the opinions of the community translators were deemed particularly important in our project. Community mental health workers arranged meetings of clinic personnel with Mien leaders, and recruited a group of eight patients for treatment, most of them were women. Health workers thought women, being emissaries from the community, but not leaders in it, would be more likely to risk a new treatment, and if the treatment failed there would be less loss of face or shame. A videotape showing a mock physical examination and blood and urine testing was prepared on the clinic premises to address the perceived strangeness of American procedures during opium abuse treatment. Block-time was prearranged so that patients could come to the clinic as a group for care.

Because opium is used for physical complaints in Mien culture, it was projected that medical problems, masked by opium, might surface during treatment. Accordingly, visits were arranged for the patients to meet with a primary care physician experienced in opiate addiction treatment. It was assumed that prompt treatment of medical conditions would be a key factor in preventing opium use relapse. It is important to note that Chinese medicine, including massage, liniment patches and acupuncture, is known and used in Mien communities. Time for acupuncture treatment at the clinic was set aside for this reason.

INITIAL EXPERIENCE: 1991-1992

Our experiences during the first two years of this endeavor was reported in the *Journal of Psychoactive Drugs* (Martin & Zweben, 1992). A structured intervention was carried out with eight patients. That is, a physical examination, including blood work, urinalysis, tuberculosis testing, pregnancy testing for women, and on-site urine screening for drugs was performed on the day of the intake. Because of the mental health staffs' "nonmethadone" request, symptomatic pharmacotherapy for withdrawal was administered with clonidine patches and antihistamines, when indicated. Clonidine is a centrally acting medication for high blood pressure that has been found to control some of the autonomic nervous system-related complaints associated with opiate withdrawal (Kasvikis et al., 1990). It is available in a long-acting patch designed to last a week. Clonidine patching was repeated in the second week of treatment.

Medical appointments were scheduled weekly in the first month, then they became monthly for a year. Acupuncture treatment was available daily and indefinitely if group support and counseling was concurrent and located at a familiar Asian mental health facility. Initially the group meetings were twice a week, individual meetings with an addiction counselor from the clinic were held once a week. Many of the patients were survivors of war, and it was postulated that PTSD was partly a reason for their drug abuse (Kroll et al., 1989; Mattson, 1993). Therefore, we believed that group therapy, which had worked with other Asian refugees with PTSD, would be a vital ingredient in the program. And if group therapy was successful, it would be continued indefinitely.

The mental health facility provided a translator. Even though he was not an actual family member of any of the patients, they all knew him and respected him outside the clinic. His ability to speak English and negotiate the American system conferred authority on him, and apparent therapeutic influence. His gender, family prominence, and older age were added status variables in the Mien culture, and that was taken into account during our initial planning. Informal conversations with the translator highlighted the need to educate him in available treatment options. He said that he had heard that methadone treatment was merely another addiction, no better than opium, and not really helpful. Realizing that this belief would close doors for patients who might need our maintenance treatment, additional time was invested in making him knowledgeable about all the treatments available for opiate addiction. He was very receptive to the information, and since receiving it, he works well with patients who need pharmacotherapy.

The initial eight patients who came for treatment, two men and six women, ranged in age from 39 to 64. Six of them participated in treatment from one to eight weeks, but they were not able to abstain from using opium for more than two weeks with their regimen. Reasons given for continued opium use included numerous physical symptoms, among them very prominently was a cough. The cough was described by the patients as "dangerous to my heart," "not letting me sleep," "hurting the chest," etc. It was speculated that this symptom was common because of the inhalation route of self-administration of the drug. Several of the patients had wheezing, and were given bronchodilators. The remaining two patients, a married couple whose cases are described below, remained abstinent from opium at the end of a year.

Contrary to our expectation, the Mien patients were actually quite familiar with the Western medical system, and had received medications and treatments for medical problems at their local county facilities. They knew what blood tests and urine samples were. They had been tested for drugs in refugee camps in Thailand before being transported to the United States, and our urine screen tests reminded them of that experience. All the patients insistently requested Western medications, although not by name. None requested prescriptions for narcotics or benzodiazepines.

CASE 1. A 39-year-old woman enrolled in our program to get her two-year-old daughter back from foster care. She had changed her method of opium ingestion from smoking it to drinking a dissolved form of it because, as she confided, it was less detectable by social service workers and her other children. She had a history of smoking opium for many years because of "tightness in the heart." During the year prior to entering this program, she had been treated with methadone 21-day-detoxification in another city, and was unable to maintain abstinence. From her point of view, methadone had failed to insure the return of her daughter, and she was quite despondent about its use. At this point, the translator said to the physician that he was quite surprised the physician would even consider methadone treatment.

Detoxification was carried out for the patient through clonidine. She was visibly depressed and tearful, so she was referred for antidepressant medication as well. Her weekly urine tests continued to be positive for morphine, and she was repeatedly encouraged by the physician to reconsider methadone maintenance treatment. She agreed to do this when a publicly funded slot for maintenance opened up at a nearby county clinic three months later. Throughout the year the patient was compliant with urine testing, kept her office appointments and attended counseling. Her urine tests became negative for illicit drugs after her admission into methadone maintenance. By the end of the year, she was given custody of her daughter for three months, and she was less depressed.

CASE 2. Married to the patient described above, this 50-year-old man entered the program for the express purpose of regaining custody of his two-year-old daughter. He wanted to show the authorities that he could stop smoking opium. His history of opium use was through intermittent smoking, and he claimed that he could stop using it at will. He also stated that he had been abstinent for two weeks prior to intake. He asked the physician whether he should get a divorce in order to get his daughter back. Divorce is a very serious step in the Mien culture. It is a sign of desperation. His urine test on admission was indeed negative. Clonidine treatment was unnecessary, but he continued to attend acupuncture treatments and kept his doctor visits, at which times he would discuss physical symptoms such as a cough. About nine months into treatment he described "needing to smoke" because his chest hurt. That was the only positive urine screen obtained in the year of treatment.

These two cases illustrate the primacy of family ties in seeking treatment, as well as the spectrum of severity of abuse within the culture. Case 1 easily fits DSM criteria for dependence, Case 2 does not. It also suggests that financial constraints are a major factor in the choice of treatment. The reasons given by several of the initial patients for dropping out of treatment were related to family obligations, such as taking care of grandchildren. There was no community-wide support for regular participation in counseling sessions, nor for the efforts needed to maintain abstinence.

CHANGES IN TREATMENT ENVIRONMENT

In 1996, Medicaid funding became more available for methadone maintenance in California. Before that time, including the time of our initial intervention from 1991 to 1992, there had been public funding limited to two-year periods at specific county facilities. For the first time, The 14th Street Clinic was able to offer methadone maintenance to patients who had Medicaid coverage. Since 1996, the clinic maintenance census, usually of around 350 patients, has included ten to 15 Mien patients at any given time. Some of the patients from the original group of eight are now doing well. The clinic has kept contact with them through Asian-specific health and mental health services professionals, including the translator, who is now very experienced in the addiction treatment modalities. And he continues to be involved in the treatment of the original patients. There are also Mien patients who do not need a translator, and who prefer not to meet in the group sessions. They are completely acculturated into the English speaking milieu.

SPECIFIC CHARACTERISTICS OF THE
MIEN MAINTENANCE PATIENTS

The Mien cultural group has several unusual features when it comes to methadone maintenance. As part of methadone maintenance, all patients are assigned a counselor. The clinic has eight to ten full-time counselors for methadone maintenance patients, and a counselor meets with them to discuss a broad range of issues, from housing to the dose level, and addiction-specific techniques are used in therapy. The clinic has designated a counselor to run a group for Mien clients. Those who want a translator in group counseling meet once a week in a group session. The patients often arrive together at the clinic, and they speak to each other in Mien in the waiting room. They remain an easily identifiable group, with distinct opium use patterns that differ from the usual use patterns of heroin-addicted patients. In general, they require lower doses of methadone to control symptoms: 30–40 mg, as opposed to 80–100 mg in most of the other clinic patients. When they continue to smoke opium, it is described as treatment of specific medical complaints, although they also describe usual withdrawal symptoms and obsessive thoughts of use associated with craving (Sullivan & Fleming, 1997). When they are not able to obtain opium, some patients have taken other illicit drugs such as cocaine, which create additional treatment problems. Although they do not have the severe needle-related morbidity of AIDS or Hepatitis C, several of the opium patients are quite ill with cancer, diabetes and chronic lung diseases.

CASE 3. A 69-year-old woman was unable to achieve abstinence on the original clonidine detoxification regimen in 1991, and she has been on methadone maintenance since 1996. She has been able to reduce, but not completely discontinue, her use of opium, which she smokes at night for "pain." She also receives prescriptions for codeine from her medical doctor. A methadone blood test drawn in 1997 at a dose of 15 mg showed a trough level of 95 ng/ml, well below the range of 400-600 ng/ml which is usually considered therapeutic in the United States. However, she did not want increases in her dose. In the past, she had tried doses approaching 30 mg and she experienced drowsiness in the daytime. In 1999, the urine screens for this patient began to show cocaine in addition to the usual morphine. She had begun to smoke crack cocaine when opium was scarce or unobtainable. Several months later she was arrested trying to buy cocaine from a narcotics officer, and has been on probation since then. She has not been able to discontinue her cocaine abuse. In group sessions, she expresses her resolve to stop using cocaine, and is told by other group members: "do it first, say it later," as an expression of their doubt of her ability to quit.

This case raises several questions, aside from highlighting the dangers of exposure to illicit drug sources. With the pattern of bedtime use of opium, described by other patients as well, daytime sedation is not tolerated. LAAM was considered for this patient, which is a less sedating maintenance medication, but the translator advised us that the patient does not keep track of the days of the week, and she would probably not be able to adhere to a Monday, Wednesday and Friday dosage schedule of LAAM. Perhaps if this patient had been able to earn take-home medication privileges–an area of treatment which is highly regulated, she would have chosen to take her methadone at bedtime, obviating the need for her nightly opium.

CASE 4. This 39-year-old woman was admitted to methadone maintenance treatment in 1995, after several attempts at 21-day-detoxification with methadone. She comes to the clinic by herself, and does not join the Mien support group. She has been able to control her opium use at a stable dose of 50 mg of methadone, and has achieved abstinence long enough to earn four methadone take-homes per week. She speaks English fairly well, has a job and pays her fees. She has repeatedly reported physical abuse by her brother, and on one occasion she lost consciousness due to head trauma. This has been addressed in the usual ways acceptable within United States professional practice, and repeated safe house referrals have been made by clinic staff over the years. In the Bay Area there are safe houses specifically for Asian women, and they are receptive to methadone treatment clients. However, the patient feels certain that if there are any Mien staff or translators at a safe house, she would not remain anonymous or safe. The patient has made plans, but has never made a move to leave home. She is dependent on her brother for shelter and status within the community. On one occasion, after a fight with her brother, she decided to purchase drugs, and did so from an undercover policeman. She spent several days in jail, and is currently on probation. With her permission, and in an attempt to explore other safeguards for Mien women who might be similarly abused, the translator offered to speak with the patient as a way of helping her. The patient agreed, but later reported that the translator had told her to adjust to the abusive situation and to stop complaining.

This case once again raises the dual nature of strong family and community bonds–at once supportive and enforcing. American professional ethics are strongly rooted in concepts of individual autonomy, and the patient's right to freely make choices, which in this situation may not be very helpful to a patient not accustomed to acting alone in her own behalf. She has difficulty imagining life alone outside the community, and this contributes to her ambivalence about her own safety. Nevertheless, the counselor is bound to use American professional mainstream approaches to the abusive situation.

CASE 5. A 47-year-old man has been on methadone maintenance since 1995. At that time he had a history of daily opium use for 24 years, and daily crack smoking for four years. Methadone maintenance, at a dose of 45 mg, has completely controlled his use of opium, but he continues to smoke crack three times a week. One day he told the group that he would have to get off methadone or his doctor at the Asian health clinic would no longer see him. This prompted a phone call to his physician after the appropriate releases were obtained. The physician was concerned about the patient's health. He had complained about several episodes of chest pain, but would not comply with follow-up visits or testing. He continued to smoke tobacco heavily and to abuse cocaine. The physician explained that she had tried to set limits with him, but she was in no way prohibiting him from using the agency's services. Since that phone call, the counselor has used the group sessions to remind and educate the patient about the need for continued health care surveillance, and to encourage him to keep his appointments with the primary care physician.

This case illustrates the broad role that an addiction clinic can play, including education about self care, and about utilizing other systems. It also emphasizes the need for coordination of efforts toward the patient's overall health. Just as the clinic counselor got incorrect information about what the doctor had requested from the patient, the primary care physician did not know that this patient's opium use was controlled.

CASE 6. This 60-year-old man was admitted to methadone maintenance in 1999, after four years of daily opium smoking, and several failed attempts at detoxification. He was at a stable dose of 32 mg, and continued to use opium and sometimes cocaine. The opium use is for "pain" and he smokes because he "likes it." The therapeutic effort has focused on encouraging his commitment to changing his addictive behavior. About 18 months into treatment, his dose was raised from 32 mg to 50 mg. He attempted to tell the dispensing nurse that this was not his dose, but when she checked, she could find no mistake. Four days later, with a translator present, he raised the issue at a group meeting. The error was corrected. The increased dose had been intended for a different Mien patient, who has the same last name and a very similar first name. The patient felt fine, but he was surprised that his name was not well known by clinic staff after nearly two years of attendance.

Correct patient identification is one of the built-in features of methadone dispensing. There are rules about stating one's name clearly at the window, removing dark glasses, and having photo identification whenever needed for a crosscheck. In the case of siblings, or twins, name alert markers are in the charts and on the dispensing computer screen. In spite of all this, the patient was incorrectly identified. There are two family names shared by most Mien: Saeturn and Saechao. There are minor variations in spelling, but in general the first three letters are the same when translated into English. The two men whose cases were transposed were about the same age and shared the last and one first name. They had a different middle name. The patient did not know enough English to explain this to the nurse, nor to read the original order and point out it was not his name.

Since that incident, the clinic has changed several procedures to ensure safety in prescribing medication. The clinic has computerized dispensing, and the usual way of finding a patient's file is to enter the first two letters of the first and last name. This does not work for obvious reasons with Mien names. To avoid confusion, the original orders for Mien patients are entered into the computer by patient identification number, with the name as a secondary identification check. In addition, when Mien patients check in, they are handed an identification card with their picture and name on it, which they present at the dispensing window. This system is not perfect, as patients resent being further marginalized with this procedure, and sometimes they don't look at the card they are given, which may have another person's picture on it. In a culture without written language, spelling is not the way to identify a person. Clinic executives continue to work on this issue. More Asian staff at the front desk and dispensing positions would be helpful.

SUMMARY

This chapter described the efforts of one clinic in Oakland, California to address the addiction treatment needs of Southeast Asian Mien opium smokers. The issues we examined include cooperation with Asian treatment agencies, assessment of addiction severity, use of a translator, the role of the community and extended family, and practical issues of treatment within a methadone maintenance program.

Our experiences confirm the need for careful evaluation of a Mien patient's level of addiction, as the very concept of "clinics" is foreign to the Mien culture. Patients may utilize a clinic for a variety of reasons related to opium use, but they may or may not be addicted. The usefulness of communication among social services and treatment facilities in planning interventions has also been highlighted through the illustrations presented in this chapter. Addiction professionals need information on culturally- relevant issues, and community representatives need education about addiction treatment options. Throughout this intervention, attention to choice and training of the translator is vital. The usefulness of group therapy for this population is supported by our experiences. although not all patients choose this modality. Clinic schedules must be flexible to accommodate patients arriving in groups and it is imperative to arrange for translators ahead of time. Clinic record keeping must have adequate provisions to carefully identify patients, especially those who share the same family names. The experience presented here suggests that lack of funds can be a significant barrier to treatment. It also raises questions about the rigidity of methadone in maintenance treatment regulations and whether more flexible dosing schedules might be appropriate for this ethnic group.

As the younger Mien generations grow up in the American educational system, I hope that more professionals from their culture will work in this field. So far there have been local reports of a Mien woman who is in social work training at a university, and of a young man enrolled in medical school. These are sparse beginnings. But they are important.

REFERENCES

American Society of Addiction Medicine. (1996). *Patient Placement Criteria for the Treatment of Substance-Related Disorders* (2nd ed.). Chevy Chase, MD: American Society of Addiction Medicine.

ASAM. (1991). *American Society of Addiction Medicine Policy Statement on Methadone Treatment.* Washington, DC: American Society of Addiction Medicine.

Brumbaugh, A.G. (1993). Acupuncture: New perspectives in chemical dependency treatment. *Journal of Substance Abuse Treatment, 10,* 35–43.

Dole, V. (1988). Implication of methadone maintenance for theories of narcotic addiction. *Journal of the American Medical Association, 260,* 3025–3029.

Kasvikis, Y., Bradley, B., Gossop, M., Griffiths, P. & Marks, I. (1990). Clonidine versus long and short-term methadone-aided withdrawal from opiates. An uncontrolled comparison. *International Journal of Addictions, 25*(10), 1169–1178.

Konefal, J., Duncan, R. & Clemence, C. (1994). The Impact of the addition of an acupuncture treatment program to an existing Metro-Dade County Outpatient substance abuse treatment facility. *Journal of Addictive Diseases, 13*(3), 71–99.

Koob, G.F., & Moal, M.L. (1997). Drug abuse: Hedonic homeostatic dysregulation. *Science, 278*, 52–58.

Koob, G.G., Sanna, P.P. & Bloom, F.E. (1998). Neuroscience of addiction. *Neuron, 21*, 467–476.

Kroll, J., Habenicht, M., Mackenzie, T., Yang, M., Chan, S., Vang, T., Nguyen, T., Ly, M., Phommasouvanh, B., Nguyen, H. et al. (1989). Depression and posttraumatic stress disorder in Southeast Asian refuges. *American Journal of Psychiatry, 146*(12), 1592–1597.

Martin, J. & Zweben, J.E. (1993). Addressing treatment needs of Southeast Asian Mien opium users in California. *Journal of Psychoactive Drugs, 25* (1), 73–76.

Mattson, S. (1993). Mental health of Southeast Asian refugee women: An overview. *Health Care for Women Internationally, 14*(2), 155–165.

McLellan, A.T., Lewis, D.C., O'Brien, C.P. & Kleber, H.D. (2000). Drug dependence, a chronic medical illness: Implications for treatment, insurance, and outcomes evaluation. *JAMA, 284*(13), 1689–1695.

Miller, W.R. (1999). *Enhancing Motivation for Change in Substance Abuse Treatment.* Vol. 35. Rockville, MD: U. S. Department of Health and Human Services.

Miller, W.R. & Rollnick, S. (1991). *Motivational Interviewing: Preparing People to Change Addictive Behavior*, New York: Guilford Press.

NIH Consensus Statement. (1997). *Effective Medical Treatment of Opiate Addiction* (pp. 1–38). Rockville, MD: National Institutes of Health.

Obuchowsky, M. & Zweben, J.E. (1987). Bridging the gap: The methadone patient in 12-step programs. *Journal of Psychoactive Drugs, 19*, 301–302.

Payte, J. & Khuri, E. (1993). Principles of methadone dose determination. In M. Parrino (Ed.), *Center for Substance Abuse Treatment.* Rockville, MD: U.S. Department of Health and Human Services.

Payte, J.T. & Zweben, J.E. (1998). Opioid maintenance therapies. In A.W. Graham & T.K. Schultz (Eds.), *Principles of Addiction Medicine.* Chevy Chase, MD: American Society of Addiction Medicine.

State Methadone Treatment Guidelines. Vol. 1. Rockville, MD: U.S. Department of Health and Human Services.

Sullivan, E. & Fleming, M. (1997). *A Guide to Substance Abuse Services for Primary Care Physicians.* Vol. 24. Rockville, MD: U.S. Department of Health and Human Services, Center for Substance Abuse Treatment.

Westermeyer, J. Lyfoung, T. & Neider, J. (1989). An epidemic of opium dependence among Asian refugees in Minnesota: Characteristics and causes. *British Journal of Addiction, 84*, 785–789.

Zweben, J.E. (1993). Recovery oriented psychotherapy: A model for addiction treatment. *Psychotherapy, 30*(2), 259–268.

Zweben, J.E. (1998). Integrating psychotherapy and pharmacotherapies in addiction treatment. In A.W. Graham & T.K. Schultz (Eds.), *Principles of Addiction Medicine.* Chevy Chase, MD: American Society of Addiction Medicine.

Chapter 9

SMOKING PREVENTION AND INTERVENTION IN ASIAN AMERICAN COMMUNITIES: A CASE STUDY

Grace Xueqin Ma, Kenneth C. Chu, and Walter Tsou

Cigarette smoking continues to be the most prevalent form of substance abuse as well as the leading preventable cause of death for all racial and ethnic groups in the U.S. today. Since 1964, when the Surgeon General's first report on Smoking and Health was released, and during a period of 30 years following issuance of the report, the U.S. witnessed a reduction in smoking prevalence rates from 42 percent to 26 percent (Centers for Disease Control and Prevention, 1996), a decline occurring mainly in the mainstream population, and notably among males (McGinnis et al., 1987). Smoking rates have remained either constant or have increased among some ethnic minority populations, especially among Asian Americans (AA).

Early references in the literature to AA populations singled them out as a "model minority" reflecting lower smoking-related mortality and morbidity rates than their counterparts in the population, namely Hispanics and African Americans. While this may have been the case when AA constituted a smaller subset of the U.S. population, the assumption that they represented a "model minority" in smoking habits no longer holds true.

This chapter describes the needs for tobacco control in AA communities and the barriers that have historically prevented the development and implementation of smoking prevention and intervention programs, and research activities on tobacco use in AA communities. We will discuss the influence of culture and economics on altering smoking behaviors, tobacco industry's strategies in targeting Asian communities, and the lack of resources not only to counter tobacco industry's marketing, but to initiate prevention and cessation programs in generally less affluent communities. Further, this chapter

169

will provide an overview of the Asian Tobacco Education, Cancer Awareness, and Research project (ATECAR) and present it as a case example of a long-term strategy to build tobacco and cancer control infrastructures, local and regional leadership and coalitions, prevention- and intervention-focused research, and training. ATECAR is a National Cancer Institute (NCI) funded project. Its current target population is the multi-ethnic Asian community residing in the Greater Delaware Valley region.

SMOKING AND ASIAN AMERICAN HEALTH

A national objective in *Healthy People 2010* is to increase to 40 percent the proportion of young people in grades 9 to 12, adolescents who have never smoked and to reduce the smoking rates of those who smoke from 36 percent to 21 percent (U.S. Department of Health and Human Services, 1998a); additionally, the 10-year goal is to ensure that every young tobacco user has access to appropriate and effective cessation interventions (Youth Tobacco Cessation Collaborative, 2000).

Asian American and Pacific Islanders (AAPI) constitute one of the fastest growing racial-ethnic groups in the U.S. Because they are the least studied among the country's racial-ethnic groups, AAPI members are also the least informed about the deleterious effects of tobacco on health. Recent studies have shown a high prevalence of smoking among all Asian youth. Data devised from *Monitoring the Future Survey*, a study on smoking among male high school seniors indicated that between 1989 and 1994, smoking rates among Asian students had increased from 16.8 percent to 20.6 percent (DHHS, 1998).

A study by Ma et al. (2001) examining 566 adolescents in an ethnically diverse part of the city of Philadelphia found that 18.2 percent of Whites, 9.0 percent of African Americans, and 14.1 percent of AA adolescents smoked daily. The results of ATECAR comprehensive needs assessment showed that 32 percent of Asian (Korean, Chinese, Vietnamese, and Cambodian) youth ever smoked, while 23 percent were current smokers. Among current smokers, 82 percent had tried to quit but were unsuccessful (Ma, Shive, Tan & Toubbeh, 2001).

Smoking rates among AA males also vary by ethnic subgroups: Vietnamese, 35 percent–56 percent (Jenkins, 1996), and Koreans, 33 percent, Laotians, 71 percent, Cambodians, 71 percent and Chinese, 55 percent (Han et al., 1989). A more current national study conducted in Vietnamese and Korean languages revealed the 34 percent of Vietnamese American men and 31 percent of Korean Americans men were *current* smokers (National Asian Women's Health Organization, 1998). Collectively, these findings indicate significantly higher smoking rates among Southeast Asian males than among other racial-ethnic groups studied to date (U.S. Department of Health and Human Services, 1998b; Thridandam et al., 1998; Jenkins et al., 1995; CDC 1992a, 1992b, 1992c; Jenkins et al., 1995; Moeschberger et al., 1997; Wiecha, 1996; Wiecha et al., 1998).

ATECAR needs assessment study showed that approximately 40 percent of AA *ever* used tobacco, while 30 percent reported *current* tobacco use. The *ever* smoking rates varied among AA by ethnic groups: Chinese 33 percent; Korean 43 percent; Vietnamese 47 percent; and Cambodian 50 percent. The *current* smoking rates reflected similar trends. Although the *ever* smoking rate among Asian males was 59 percent, the study indicated a variation of *ever* smoking rates among Asian males by ethnicity ranging from 46 percent to 71 percent as follows: Chinese men 46 percent; Vietnamese men 61 percent; Cambodian men 68 percent; and Korean men, 71 percent, the highest (Ma et al., 2001).

THE SOCIAL AND CULTURAL ROLE IN SMOKING

Tobacco has had a devastating effect on the health of Asian communities in the U.S. and abroad, partly because of the social and cultural role smoking plays in these communities, and also because of the industry's marketing strategies that use this role as a medium to promote its product.

The U.S. Asian population is culturally and ethnically diverse. Asian immigrants, past and current, comprise more than 30 different nationalities and ethnic groups; these differ in language and dialects, cultures, socioeconomic statuses, and patterns of immigration. The pattern of immigration is an important factor in program planning: two-thirds of AA (e.g., Chinese, Koreans, Vietnamese, Indians and Cambodians) are recent immigrants. As recent arrivals to the U.S., they tend to hold on to their native cultures, and their social fabrics continue to shape their values, beliefs, and customs. This presents a range of challenges to providers of care that encompass, among other, recent arrivals' culturally-laden health behaviors and lifestyle choices, as well as health care decision-making processes.

As a rule, traditional Asian cultures encourage smoking among adult males; nonetheless, smoking among this group is not only condoned but has become an essential social activity, and the activity itself has assumed, among adolescent and adult smokers, a role of "social medium." The concept of "social medium" justifies initiation of smoking at a young age. Most studies on this phenomenon show that the risk of smoking initiation among Asian adolescents increased through middle and late adolescence and continued to increase throughout early adulthood (Chen & Unger, 1999). The

ATECAR needs assessment study revealed similar trends: it found that Chinese, Korean and Vietnamese American youth are especially at risk of smoking initiation later in adolescence. The average age for initiation was 18 years (Ma et al., 2001). Studies focusing on Chinese and Vietnamese nationals in their respective countries also showed similar findings. In China, 50.7 percent of males reported initiating smoking at between 20 and 24 years of age, and 29 percent at between 25 and 29 years of age (Gong et al., 1995), while in Vietnam, the mean age of smoking initiation was 19 years (Jenkins et al., 1997).

Cigarette smoking is so common in Asian countries, it is considered a social lubricant. At social events in Chinese homes, for example, male guests are routinely offered cigarettes. Among certain male groups in China, having a cigarette after a meal is "having a life superior to that of God" (Chen et al., 1999). Smoking and the exchange of cigarettes are also common at major social events as weddings, funerals, and parties. The culture of smoking permeates other Asian societies, especially Vietnam. In recent years, smoking has become an integral part of Asian governmental meetings and commercial negotiations. Cigarette cartons or packs are often offered as gifts to higher authorities in exchange for favors (Jenkins et al., 1997). In Cambodia, smoke from cigarettes is believed to shield smokers against insects (Ma, 2000).

Today, there is wide social acceptability of smoking among AA, especially among new immigrants, and among the poor and the educationally disadvantaged. Traditional cultures perpetuate smoking behavior in new environments, where smoking continues to be a social lubricant or a medium for socialization. Many Cambodian Americans who practice Buddhism, for example, are offered cigarettes during religious ceremonies at Buddhist temples. Cambodians believe that every monk attains manhood through smoking. Cambodians who spent time in refugee labor camps feel that cigarettes offered them respite from difficult and traumatizing experiences, and from the memories of these experiences; to many, cigarettes also decreased hunger pangs, pain, stress and loneliness (Ma, 2000).

While Asian cultural norms do not condone smoking, and while these norms are routinely violated by adult and adolescent males, there has long been a dominant social norm not to allow Asian women to smoke. The behavior is considered unbefitting the female character and role, is unattractive to the opposite sex, and is a sign of loose morals in the context of Chinese, Vietnamese, and Korean cultures. This norm, however, is violated by older women who are permitted to smoke, as a sign of respect for their maturity.

Notwithstanding, smoking remains a rare phenomenon among women younger than 45 years, but the prevalence rates increases moderately post 45 years, peaking in the age group 35 and older (Jenkins, 1997; Ma et al., 2001). Among Asians, only young women are permitted to offer cigarettes in social gatherings. The ECAR study revealed that young Asian women often buy cigarettes for husbands, fathers or uncles, and offer cigarettes as a sign of respect to husbands, fathers or uncles.

In addition to social attitudes, individual's own perception of tobacco and tobacco use play important role in smoking behavior. Asians, those who smoke or do not, associate smoking with positive images of power, sociability, maleness, masculinity, alertness and relaxation. Some Asians believe that smoking helps to keep the body strong. These positive perceptions mask Asians' perceptions of smoking as a culprit of fatal disease and other chronic con-ditions.

Asian immigrants, whether recent arrivals in U.S. tend to preserve their respective sociocul-tural values and attitudes, as well as smoking-related practices. Strong cultural, linguistic and physical ties among AA communities tend to perpetuate these attitudes.

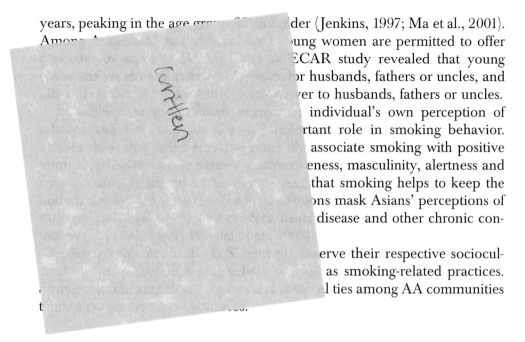

ECONOMIC ISSUES IN TOBACCO CONTROL

Cigarette retailing is a profitable business that attracts Asians, particularly new arrivals in the U.S. In cities with large populations of AA, or in China towns, convenient stores are easily accessed by Asian male smokers who are often enticed, through advertising and special incentives, to purchase ciga-rettes in large quantities at cut rates. Because cigarettes offer a wide range of profit at minimal outlay, restaurant owners participate in the distribution of tobacco products in Asian communities. Many convenience stores and restaurants are not smoke-free, attracting and encouraging smokers to seek shelter from smoke-free environments. Asian stores and restaurants are also often located in, or proximal to low-income housing or high concentration of recent immigrants. Their owners, patently ignorant of the effects of smoking on health, advertise their tobacco products heavily, using tobacco industry strategies to attract a range of age groups. In instances where owners are aware of the deleterious effects of smoking, the profit motive and the popu-larity of the product override considerations of potential injury to communi-ty members. A complicating factor is a shared belief between owner and cus-tomer about the value of smoking, where the owner provides a product needed by the customer, and the customer getting a product at a reasonable rate from a trusted community member. This symbiotic relationship between seller and buyer reflects the astuteness of the tobacco industry's retail strate-gies as observed by the authors.

TOBACCO INDUSTRY

The tobacco industry has long targeted ethnic minorities, especially Asians, in the U.S. Having lost a segment of its market in the U.S. as a result of anti-tobacco campaigns, the industry has extended and strengthened its marketing of tobacco products abroad. China, with its burgeoning population, has become the largest consumer of U.S. industry's product. Second only to China, Cambodia and Vietnam have attracted U.S. tobacco manufacturers mainly because of the high prevalence of smoking in these countries. The industry's marketing strategies have focused on Asian sociocultural norms as well as the educational levels of the target population, in particular, new arrivals who are well exposed to tobacco and those who are in blue-collar professions. To these populations, the industry has paired such buzzwords as health, wealth, freedom, glamour, sophistication and westernization with smoking to conceal any negative advertising against the product in AA communities. Importing successful marketing strategies from abroad, the industry has repacked its brand names and sold them under new names that include "Nutritional Cigarette," Natural Cigarette," "Herbal Cigarette," or "Long Life Cigarette." While these repackaged brand names do not appear often in U.S. mainstream markets, they are available to those who seek them.

Much of the marketing strategies used in the past in the U.S. are common today in Asian countries. The industry uses as its media sports and social and cultural events and, less often, health promotion and prevention events through direct sponsorship of these events. Other strategies include advertising in Asian magazines and on radio and television, and the distribution of cosmetics and home products with the sole aim of recruiting new Asian smokers, especially women and young girls. The combination of aggressive and subtle marketing used by the industry has had its deleterious effects on the Asian population as it did, and still does today, on the U.S. population. Asians and AA have a long way to catch up with their counterparts in the U.S. in their fight against the tobacco industry and its profitable and highly addictive products (Navarro, 1998).

There is an urgent need to counter tobacco industry's marketing of tobacco products in AA communities and to promote the health and well being of this underserved and economically disadvantaged population. A creative, culturally relevant program of education and training that includes well-tested approaches to cessation and prevention is a logical first step in this effort. In line with current research findings that multiple strategies provide the best results, implementing comprehensive tobacco education programs in AA will require consideration of cultural and linguistic variability in these populations, their economic statuses, and the communities' perceptions of tobacco use in their respective daily lives. Because many members of these communities are in poor health and lack health insurance coverage, state and federal intervention may be needed to support any cessation or interventional activity initiated at local levels. Coalition building, training of local providers in provision of services, and research are essential components of this comprehension strategy.

Recognizing the need to build cancer control capacity in ethic, racial and rural communities, the NCI recently funded 18 Special Population Network research programs in the U.S. among which, two targeting AA. The first project, the Asian American Network for Cancer Awareness, Research and Training (AANCART) project, with Moon Chen, principal investigator, is located at Ohio State University in Dublin, Ohio. The second project, Asian Tobacco Education, Cancer Awareness and Research (ATECAR), with Grace Ma, principal investigator, is located in Philadelphia, Pennsylvania. We will now present a detailed description of ATECAR as a case study of a successful, community- and research-based project that employs a variety of successful and comprehensive strategies for establishing a sustainable public health infrastructure and building partnership capacity that foster comprehensive community-based tobacco and cancer research, prevention, intervention, and training, leadership development and research dissemination and utilization in the Asian communities of the greater Delaware Valley region.

THE ATECAR PROGRAM FOR ASIAN AMERICANS: A CASE STUDY

The goals of the ATECAR project are to: (1) reduce the incidence and risk behaviors of cancer among AA; (2) stimulate participation in AA community tobacco control and other cancer prevention programs; (3) reduce barriers and improve access to tobacco and cancer resources in AA populations; (4) increase diagnoses of cancers among AA at earlier stages; and (5) increase research and training opportunities for AA in comprehensive tobacco and cancer control programs. Project outcomes include increase in knowledge, change in attitudes, and improvement in skills culminating, eventually, in an overall change in the health behaviors of AA regarding tobacco use and control, as well as an increase in awareness of tobacco-related cancers through community mobilization and participation in promoting, developing, and evaluating culturally appropriate tobacco and cancer control programs for AA.

To achieve their goals, ATECAR identifies the following principal objectives: (1) the building of an Asian Community Cancer Coalition (ACCC); (2)

the establishment of partnerships between Temple University and other entities; (3) the conduct of comprehensive needs assessment research on smoking and cancer awareness; (4) the provision of a variety of community-based tobacco education and cancer awareness, prevention and intervention programs; (5) the conduct of evaluation research on the impact of cancer awareness, prevention and intervention programs; (6) the use of various multimedia to increase the number of calls to the Cancer Information Services; (7) the enhancement of training opportunities for AA in cancer awareness and control; (8) the training and assistance to AA professionals in the preparation and submissions of research grant applications; (9) the enhancement of accrual of AA clients in clinical intervention trials; (10) the development of culturally appropriate smoking cessation strategies through pilot studies; and (11) the dissemination and the sharing of research findings, experiences and cancer awareness activities, regionally and nationally.

Target Population. Currently, ATECAR's target populations are Vietnamese, Chinese, Cambodians, Koreans and other Asian ethnic groups residing in the grater Delaware Valley region of Pennsylvania and New Jersey. These communities comprise the fastest growing ethnic groups in the region. The Asian population of the Delaware Valley region increased by 75 percent during the period 1990 and 2000, from 96,032 to 168,331. The large majority of Asian ethnic groups residing in this region showed substantial increases in populations with the exception of the Japanese who showed a 6 percent decrease for the same period; a drop of 262 from a high of 4199. Respective increases for other ethnic groups were: Filipino, 22 percent, from 11,234 to 13,686; Asian Indians 113 percent from 20,099 to 42,742; and Koreans 21 percent from 21, 739 to 26, 289. Most prominent increases were observed in the Chinese, Vietnamese, Cambodians, Thai, Laotians and Hmong communities. The Chinese and Vietnamese populations nearly doubled between 1990 and 2000, from 21, 902 and 10,139 to 38,271 and 21,612 respectively. Other Asian ethnic groups showed even more significant increases. Cambodians, Thai, Laotians, and Hmong, for example, increase nearly 300 percent during the same 10-year period, from 6,720 to 21,794. Distribution of various ethnic groups in the Asian population during the year 2000 was as follows: Chinese, 23 percent of the total Asian population of the region; Korean, 16 percent; Vietnamese, 13 percent; Filipino, 8 percent and other Asians, 13 percent (U.S. Census Bureau, 2001).

The estimated population growth in Pennsylvania during the period 1990 through 2000 was 62 percent from 135,784 to 219,813. During the same period, the Asian Indian population increased by 102 percent, from 28,396 to 57,241; Vietnamese by 89 percent, from 15,887 to 30,l037; and other Asian groups by 76 percent, from 16,379 to 28,783; Chinese by 71 percent, from 29,562 to 50,650; Filipino by 19 percent, from 12,160 to 14,506; Korean by

18 percent from 26,787 to 31,612; and Japanese by 6 percent from 6,613 to 6,984 (U.S. Census Bureau, 2001).

In New Jersey, the AA population increased by 77 percent from 270,839 to 480,276 between 1990 and 2000. Asian Indians showed an increase of 113 percent from 79,440 to 169,180, the highest reported. The second highest, 107 percent was that of Vietnamese, from 7,330 to 15,180, other Asian ethnic groups 89 percent from 16,046 to 30,295, Chinese and Koreans 70 percent from 59,084 to 100,355 and 38,540 to 65,349, respectively, and Filipinos 60 percent from 53,146 to 85,245 (U.S. Census Bureau, 2001).

ATECAR Model. An essential component of ATECAR is the model that has guided all ATECAR activities since project initiation. Promulgated as the ATECAR Model, the model has had wide acceptance among AA communities locally, regionally and nationally. It has been reviewed by the NCI and found to be a useful and effective practice model. In this model, ATECAR goals and objectives serve to guide and organize ATECAR program planning. The project design consists of three phases, each contributing to achievement of identified objectives.

In Phase I, the project accomplished the following: (1) established a regional network center, a sustainable public health infrastructure capacity, and strategic partnerships between academic research institutions, Asian community organizations, clinics, cancer center, Cancer Information Service, and government agencies; (2) it formed a Steering Committee, an Asian Community Cancer Coalition (ACCC), a Scientific Research Committee, and a community Consultant Group; (3) it conduced a comprehensive baseline needs assessment study and identified and prioritized Asian tobacco and cancer issues; (4) the ATECAR collaborative team developed joint plans, initiated the selection, development, and field-testing of tobacco-related cancer prevention and intervention programs, and initiated community-based participatory research projects; and (5) it developed and implemented process and impact evaluation mechanisms.

In Phase II, four components of project activities, based on community needs, were carried out: (1) development and implementation of community cancer awareness, prevention and intervention programs; (2) development and conduct of community-based participatory intervention pilot research projects; (3) provided professional training, mentorship and research opportunities for Asian junior researchers and special population investigators; and (4) initiated a research dissemination and utilization program through publications, presentations, medial campaigns and materials distribution.

Phase II, of the project focused primarily on development of pilot research projects in which junior researchers participated and encouraged to develop the pilot projects into full scale grant applications in cancer control prevention and intervention. During this phase, the ATECAR network continued to disseminate and share its research findings, experiences and cancer awareness activities with interested parties through various media formats.

All ATECAR activities are subject to track and evaluation throughout the three phases to ensure desired effects and ultimate success.

Formation of a Steering Committee. The ATECAR Steering Committee was established immediately upon initiation of the project. The committee represents a diversity of expertise that includes internal medicine, oncology, public health, epidemiology, community health education, health communication, media and health information systems, and experience in working with Asian communities. The committee also included NCI's Special Population Network Program Directors, representatives from Fox Chase Cancer Center, Cancer Information Service, City Department of Public Health, and Asian community organizations. One of its earliest responsibilities was to review the ATECAR proposal and provide comments to the principal investigator and her staff.

Since its establishment, the steering committee has played a key role in many facets of the project's activities, and has been engaged in face-to-face meetings with ATECAR staff. The committee has provided consultative, guidance and support services to ATECAR staff on a continuing basis via conference calls and other means. It has been especially helpful in strategic joint plan development, especially those that relate to Asian communities, as well as in review of pilot research projects.

Formation of the Asian Community Cancer Coalition (ACCC) and Partnership Network. In 2000, ATECAR established the first Asian Community Cancer Coalition (ACCC) in the Delaware Valley region. The ACCC was comprised to 20 official agency members, considered community partners. They represented Asian community-based clinics, community agencies, children and family services, and faith-based organizations in the four Asian language communities served by the project (Chinese, Korean, Vietnamese, and Cambodian Americans). ACCC members meet regularly to communicate community concerns and needs, and discuss ideas and joint plans on tobacco and cancer issues in Asian communities. The first three meetings focused on developing an operational working relationship and determining how the planning and implementation of the project should proceed.

The purpose of the ACCC was to mobilize the Asian community, increase cancer awareness of tobacco use, prevention and intervention, and to change knowledge, attitudes, skills, and behaviors regarding tobacco use and cancer awareness among AA. ACCC members play an important role in identifying community needs and risk factors, as well as in planning and implementing ATECAR program activities, initiating research projects, and providing community inputs and linkages to cancer prevention resources to Asian communities. The coalition provides a platform for its members and ATECAR staff to exchange views on tobacco control and cancer prevention issues, and has the capacity to serve as a forum for sharing resources and funding opportunities for future projects.

Based on our experience with Asian community partners, flexibility and willingness to work nights and weekend hours were essential. This flexibility allowed the ATECAR staff to reach out to the community and to become frequent guests at community events and activities, and putting into practice the concept of "equal partnership" in the life of Asian communities. A similar collaborative partnership was developed between ATECAR and a number of academic research institutions, Fox Chase Cancer Center, Cancer Information Service, American Lung Association, and local and state health agencies.

Comprehensive Needs Assessment Study. During Phase I of the project, ATECAR conducted the first comprehensive baseline needs assessment survey on smoking behaviors and cancer awareness among AA in the greater Delaware region. The purpose of the survey was to identify cancer-related concerns in the communities, determine rates of smoking among age groups, identify second-hand smoking issues among women and children, and assess the relative impact of tobacco advertising on the community. Additionally, the survey gathered information on community awareness of tobacco and cancer prevention resources and programs, knowledge and attitudes about tobacco use, risk factors for cancers, and cancer research among the AA populations in the region. The 77-item questionnaire, based on the theoretical models *Stages of Change and Social Learning Theory*, covered a range of variables that included: demographics, acculturation, tobacco use frequency, sources of cigarettes, social influences, smoking cessation, smoke exposure in the home, work place and dining facilities, and knowledge of cancer risks associated with tobacco use or exposure, availability of information related to cancer and clinical trials, and attitudes toward tobacco use. Reliability and validity of the instrument was established through the conduct of pilot tests. A panel of experts and ACCC members provided feedback and input for content validity. Participants had the option of completing the questionnaire in English, Chinese, Korean, and Cambodian or Vietnamese. One thousand three hundred seventy-four were recruited through 26 randomly selected organizations. A total of 1,141 (83%) completed the survey. The *ever* smoking rate of the target groups was 40 percent while the *current* smoking rate, 32 percent. The survey has generated a series of publications, a number of which will contribute to the development of culturally appropriate tobacco and cancer control programs for Asian communities.

COMMUNITY-BASED PREVENTION
AND INTERVENTION PROGRAMS

Research-based Tobacco and Cancer Prevention Skill Training in Asian Communities. The purpose of the Community Tobacco Prevention Education is to increase public awareness and knowledge about the health and health-related risks associated with tobacco use among AA. It is a research-based activity. Two training curricula were developed, one aimed at professionals, adults and youth, focusing primarily on generic tobacco use information and, another, focused on health risks associated with second-hand smoke. The curricula underwent minefield-testing workshops prior to finalization. To date, more than 30 training workshops have been conducted in cooperation with Asian community organizations, providing services to more than 6,000 multiethnic Asians.

Collaborative Intervention Projects with Asian Community Partners. To encourage ACCC members' participation in tobacco and cancer educational activities, empower Asian community members' creativity and awareness of tobacco control issues, build up community-based partnership organization's capacity on tobacco and cancer control, and strengthen ties between ATECAR and community needs, ATECAR provides a mini-grant program for ACCC members. Criteria for mini-grants are: (1) involvement with AA adults or youth; (2) one activity focused on tobacco prevention and education; (3) involvement of at least 20 people in the program activity; and (4) sending a tobacco prevention message to the AA community, among others. Examples follow.

In collaboration with ATECAR, (1) Cambodian Association of Greater Philadelphia conducted an "Anti-Tobacco Youth Theater Play" in which 50 Cambodian teens were involved. The play drew an audience of 800, predominantly Cambodians; and (2) the Korean Community Services Center participates in poster contest titled "Youth Anti-Tobacco Poster Contest" that attracted 50 Korean participants.

Media Campaign in Tobacco and Cancer Prevention. A media campaign in tobacco and cancer prevention and intervention was designed and implemented targeting the AA through local and regional Asian newspapers, program advertisements, an ATECAR Link column, ATECAR website, and TV and radio broadcasts. Community events brochures provided viable avenues for ATECAR advertisements. The ATECAR Link, a column in a local newspaper provides information on cessation strategies, statistics on smoking among AA and Cancer Information Service and NCI resources on tobacco and cancer prevention and intervention.

ATECAR website–*www.temple.edu/atecar*–was created solely to provide updated information on ATECAR functions, experiences, accomplishments and progress. The site also provides information on the ATECAR program, mission, goals, objectives and community activities. The site has become an important educational tool on a range of topics that include tobacco use and control, cancer prevention issues, and tobacco control dissemination information.

Asian Youth Smoking Intervention and Cessation Program. ATECAR and its partners provide culturally appropriate research-based smoking intervention and cessation services to Asian youth who are interested in knowing more about the risks of tobacco and who need help in quitting or reducing cigarette use.

Asian Adult Smoking Intervention and Cessation Program. ATECAR and its network collaborators provide culturally appropriate research-based smoking intervention and cessation services to Asian adults who are interested in knowing more about the risks of tobacco and who also need help in quitting or reducing cigarette use. Intervention is provided in English as well as Asian languages.

Community Outreach Activities. A series of Asian-adapted tobacco and cancer control prevention and intervention promotional materials have been made available to Asian communities particularly during large community events. These include: ATECAR brochures, key chains, T-shirts, ATECAR pens and a large banner. Additionally, ATECAR has provided information on its project, the funding agency-NCI, the slogan of "Building Tobacco Free Community," and CIS 1-800-4 Cancer. An ATECAR logo is used as an advertising visual tool to underscore ATECAR's community focus.

Community-Based and Culturally-Tailored Intervention Research Projects. ATECAR also conducts a variety of community-based and culturally-tailored tobacco education, prevention and intervention programs, as well as research counseling programs on second-hand smoking to AA youth, adults and professionals in the Delaware Valley region. Other research projects under development include smoking-related cancer education and intervention to increase cancer awareness and diagnoses at earlier stages, improving access and reducing barriers to the use of NCICIS cancer prevention resources, and increasing participation in cancer clinical trials in this population.

Asian Youth Smoking Intervention with Cultural Adaptation. The purpose of this ongoing study is to determine the effectiveness of a culturally appropriate smoking intervention and cessation program for AA youth. The research design includes two stages: in the first stage, the standard N-O-T (Not on Tobacco) program, developed by the American Lung Association, will be field tested on Asian youth. During this stage, culturally relevant factors will be identified to improve the efficacy of the standardized N-O-T curriculum. In the second stage, a random intervention trial will be conducted, and participants will be randomly assigned to three groups: standard (experimental intervention 1), modified (experimental intervention 2), and control. The three groups will be compared on their responses on: tobacco consumption, cessation, and attempts to quit. A pilot test involving 15 Asian youth from Holy Redeemer Chinese School and Chinatown Pediatric Clinic. A focus group was used to facilitate identification of cultural factors.

Theory-Based Asian Adults Smoking Cessation Intervention Trial. This study is a collaborative effort between Temple University, Fox Chase Cancer Center and Asian Community Cancer Coalition partners. Planning meetings preceded implementation. This is a comparative research design, adopting the Cognitive-Social Health Information Processing Model. Its aims are to: (1) evaluate whether a theory-driven, enhanced smoking cessation intervention, that is culturally adapted to the needs based on the findings of ATECAR's needs assessment survey, will result in increased rates of smoking cessation, compared to a time-attention-, and format-matched control condition; and (2) examine the process variables (e.g., cancer risk perceptions; health-related values) that mediate smoking cessation among AA populations.

Secondhand Smoke Prevention and Parent Counseling for Asian Families. Exposure to secondhand smoke is associated with a variety of adverse health effects especially in children. Children's ETS exposure is also associated with increased medical costs. Residential exposure is the major source of ETS among children. WHO estimates that about 700M, or 50 percent of the world's population of children, are exposed to ETS, mostly in homes. Smoking remains a major public health issue in AA communities. Studies suggest that Asian children have more prolonged exposure to secondhand smoke in the home than other children (NCHS, 1994). The purpose of this study is to develop and implement a culturally relevant, parent counseling program focusing on secondhand smoke exposure for Asian families.

Cancer Intervention Pilot Studies Under Development. In response to the needs identified by the ATECAR needs assessment study, ATECAR is conducting a series of pilot studies aimed at developing various clinical and community-based cancer prevention and intervention programs and assessing the feasibility and effectiveness of these programs. Results of these studies will help to initiate larger clinical or community culturally appropriate intervention research programs.

Launching Global Tobacco and Cancer Control Efforts. Tobacco use is a global issue. Responding to international concerns, ATECAR has begun to examine its role in the international community and has identified potential collaborators in Korea and China who are willing to cooperate on a variety of topics related to tobacco and cancer.

EVALUATION RESEARCH

Evaluation is an integral component of the ATECAR model. All ATE-CAR activities are subject to tracking and evaluation to ensure desired effect and ultimate success. Effectiveness and impact are also subject to process, impact and outcome evaluation research.

Process evaluation allows early detection of problems associated with implementation so that proper adjustments can be made early in the performance of an activity. Five ATECAR process evaluation tools have been developed and implemented. These include: (1) Major Events Tracking Log, (2) Biweekly Log, (3) Junior Researcher Training Tracking Log, (4) Materials Distribution Tracking Log, and (5) CIS 1-800-4-Cancer call tracking. This dynamic monitoring ensures implementation of program objectives and program responsiveness to target population needs.

Impact evaluation determines the effects of program on knowledge and/or attitudes, skills and behaviors of program participants or target populations.

Evaluation of Tobacco and Cancer Prevention Skill Training. The objective of this training was to increase knowledge and change attitudes regarding tobacco use and cancer prevention. The training curriculum is research-based with nine field-tested Asian cohorts. The evaluation research design includes pre- and post-tests and 3-month follow-up of participants. Process evaluation is also conducted by documenting observations about the workshops for program improvement.

Evaluation of ACCC. In order to improve coalition function and accomplishments, a cross-section research survey is conducted annually among ACCC members. The core measures focus on the ACCC members' perceptions of "coalition-related factors" including member influence, communication, leadership, coalition culture, benefits and costs of participation, and coalition's "self-efficacy: and the "coalition-effectiveness measures" as member satisfaction, and member participation (Kegler et al., 1998).

In collaboration with ACCC members and other community organizations, ATECAR has conducted a variety of community-based tobacco and cancer prevention/intervention activities such as tobacco prevention and cancer awareness training/education, mini-grant programs, and tobacco and cancer media campaign.

Monitoring and evaluating collaborative efforts include: (1) evaluation of the collaboration process; and (2) measuring the impact of the program. This evaluative research assesses the relative role and importance of ACCC in providing guidance for future community-based research on how to work with the Asian community and/or organizations.

PROFESSIONAL TRAINING AND EDUCATION

Training Asian junior researchers is a goal of ATECAR. ATECAR accomplishes this goal through partnership agreements with a number of academic institutions that have a sustainable base of graduate students, interns, and pre- and post-doctoral fellows in a variety of disciplines. The ATECAR program is considered a model training program for junior researchers because of its successful community-based research activities and its focus on public health, cancer research and associated disciplines. Training opportunities are available through internships, research assistantships, academic mentorships, scholarships, postdoctoral fellowships and volunteer involvement. These may include participation in pilot study research design, research instrument development, training curriculum design and development, community training workshops, survey administration, IRB training, smoking cessation training programs, community cancer awareness activities design, planning, implementation, literature searches, among others.

Training in cancer control research is also available to community health practitioners and partners. ATECAR community partners are encouraged to participate in the organization and administration of surveys, tobacco-related cancer control training academy, ACCC (coalition) joint planning, and community cancer awareness proposal writing. Special skill training workshops on cancer prevention are also provided to ACCC members in cooperation with Cancer Information Service. This partnership that incorporates elements of cooperative research efforts is considered a catalyst in mobilizing community interest and involvement in tobacco and cancer control.

RESEARCH DISSEMINATION AND UTILIZATION

Dissemination and the sharing of research findings and overall experience in program development, administration, and evaluation is another major goal of ATECAR. A series of articles for publication in peer review journals is either in preparation or have already been submitted for publication. Topics include: prevalence and predictors of tobacco use; awareness of smoking cessation and cancer information service; and perceived risks of certain types of cancer and heart disease among AA in the Delaware Valley region, among others.

Materials for dissemination include low literacy, easy to read newsletter articles, a column titled "ATECAR Link," published quarterly in local newspapers in English and four Asian languages. ATECAR also created its own website and updated it continuously as a function of ATECAR experiences, endeavors and progress. The website provides information on the ATECAR project, its missions, goals, objectives, research and community activities and accomplishments. ATECAR website has been playing and will play a more important role in the education of AA on tobacco and cancer control issues.

ATECAR staff has provided 40 professional presentations at regional, national, and international conferences and conducted more than 30 training workshops/seminars at Asian community agencies. More than 5,000 tobacco and cancer prevention educational materials were distributed at these and other gatherings. Currently, ATECAR is exploring the establishment of an Asian Tobacco and Cancer Resource Center.

SUMMARY AND IMPLICATIONS

A new model for community-based research is in the process of development at the National Cancer Institute. The model's underlying purpose is to address the future of community-based research, by educating the community, training its researchers and supporting the funding of its research activities. A prime example of the model's creative and successful implementation is the ATECAR whose own model, consistent with NCI's, is described in the preceding segments of this chapter.

ATECAR is part of a national effort, identified by the NCI as the Special Population Networks for Cancer Awareness, Research and Training (NCI-SPN). The NCI-SPN funds community-based participatory research that involves university researchers working with communities to aid in their cancer related concerns. It involves a three-pronged approach. The first is the development of community and university infrastructure to promote cancer awareness in special communities. ATECAR's Asian Community Cancer Coalition and ATECAR's working relationship with the Cancer Information Service are examples of this strategy. A unique component of the ATECAR program is the incorporation of needs assessment and evaluation, programmatic elements that broaden the scope of NCI's SPN cancer awareness through focusing and impact evaluation.

The second approach is to develop a training program for minority and underserved students so that they will pursue cancer research careers. The involvement of students in the ATECAR projects is an example of research career-building concept that becomes a living, learning laboratory bringing to life the theories of health education to their real world applications in the community.

The third approach is the development of research grants involving a partnership of researchers and the target community so that there will be development of community-based participatory research. This is a challenging task. To facilitate it, the NCI-SPN supports the development of research pilot projects which can lead junior researchers to development of research grants. Junior researchers are thus given the opportunity to explore research ideas, conduct research and obtain firsthand experience in the grant funding process. The community-based intervention research projects of ATECAR represent the application and implementation of this notion.

ATECAR's pioneering work redefined our understanding of smoking habits of Asian Americans and the important role of smoking especially in newly immigrant communities. Surveys conducted by native speaking Asians associated with ATECAR showed a far higher prevalence of smoking than previously reported in English, in particular among males. Many Asian American merchants ignore the health implications of tobacco and freely promote and sell cigarettes, perpetuating common practices in the immigrants' respective countries of origin. In most Asian countries, the stigma associated with smoking does not prevail; indeed, smoking is an integral part of the social fabric of Asian cultures. Habits learned in one's native country are transported to the new environment, the Asian American community.

Traditional interventions created and tested in American born populations do not translate well for Asian populations. Language and cultural competence are new areas of research for tobacco control for Asian American communities. Creating new models of tobacco prevention and cessation constitute new interventions which are important for health educators both locally and nationally.

The story behind creating the ATECAR research, according to one author of this chapter, is particularly gratifying in Philadelphia: "The city, like many others has a threadbare Asian public health infrastructure, divided by country of origin and neighborhoods. The creation and conduct of simple surveys, and the testing of intervention models, brought disparate ethnic and language groups into the city's first health infrastructure for Asia–a product of a successful merging of NCI-SPN concepts with those of ATECAR.

Notwithstanding the success of this collaborative effort, in particular, the building of a viable infrastructure that would ensure sustainability of current and future efforts in tobacco control and use, ATECAR,* the Asian Community Cancer Coalition, the Asian American communities and local, State and Federal officials will continue to face the challenge of tobacco industry's creative, aggressive and other subtle advertising campaigns directed especially at vulnerable communities.

Asian American communities, like other communities that attract new

*We are grateful to Frank Jackson, Program Director of the NCI Special Population Networks for his vision and support for ATECAR program and to members of the Asian Community Cancer Coalition for their contributions. The funding for this program is supported by the National Cancer Institute.

immigrants, are subject to change as a function of acculturation; as such, they present challenges to researchers and health providers. Education of these communities in tobacco use and cessation is a long-term process that requires close monitoring as well as resiliency in the application of prevention, intervention and cessation strategies. Education does not end with a good beginning.

REFERENCES

Centers for Disease Control and Prevention. (1996). Cigarette smoking among adults–United States. *MMWR Morb Mortal Wkly Rep. 45*, 588–590.

Centers for Disease Control and Prevention. (1992a). Behavioral risk factor survey of Vietnamese–California, 1991. *MMWR Morb Mortal Wkly Rep. 41*(16):69–72.

Centers for Disease Control and Prevention. (1992b). Behavioral risk factor survey of Chinese–California, 1989. *MMWR Morb Mortal Wkly Rep. 41*(16): 266–70.

Centers for Disease Control and Prevention. (1992c). Cigarette smoking among Chinese, Vietnamese, and Hispanics–California, 1989–1991. *MMWR Morb Mortal Wkly Rep. 41*(20): 362–7.

Chen, X, Unger, J.B.& Johnson, C.A. (1999). Is acculturation a risk factor for early smoking initiation among Chinese American minors? A comparative perspective. *Tobacco Control 8*, 402–10.

Gong, Y.L., Koplan, J.P., Feng, W., Feng, W., Chen, C.H., Zheng, P. & Harris, J.R. (1995). Cigarette smoking in China. *Journal of the American Medical Association, 274* (15), 1232–1234.

Jenkins, C.N.H., Dai, P.X., Ngoc, D.H., et al. (1997). Tobacco use in Vietnam: Prevalence, predictors, and the role of the transnational tobacco corporation. *Journal of the American Medical Association, 277* (21), 1726–1731.

Ma, G.X., Shive, S., Tan, Y. & Toubbeh, J. (in press, 2001). Prevalence and predictors of tobacco use among Asian Americans in the greater Philadelphia region, *American Journal of Public Health.*

Ma, G.X., Tan, Y., Feeley, R. & Thomas, P. (in press). Perceived risks of certain types of cancer and heart disease among Asian American smokers and non-smokers. *Journal of Community Health.*

Ma, G.X. (2000). Personal Interview Communication with Siek Kim Iem, President of Cambodian American Seniors, Philadelphia, PA.

Navarro, A.M. (1998). Smoking status by proxy and self-report: Rate of agreement in different ethnic groups. *Tobacco Control, 8* (Summer), 182–185.

Han, F.F., Kim, S.H., Lee, M.S., Miller, J.S., Rhee, S. & Song, H. (1989). *Korean Health Survey: A Preliminary Report.* Los Angeles, CA: Korean Health Educational Information and Referral Center.

Jenkins, C.N. (1996). Response. *Journal of National Cancer Institute, 88* (12), 841.

Jenkins, C.N., McPhee, S.J., Ha, N., Nam, T.V. & Chen, A. (1995). Cigarette smoking among Vietnamese immigrants in California. *American Journal of Health*

Promotion, 9(4), 254–6.

McGinnis, J.M. Shopland, D., & Brown, C. (1987). Tobacco and health: Trends in smoking and smokeless tobacco consumption in the United States. *Annual Review of Public Health, 8*, 441–67.

Moeschberger, M.L., Anderson, J., Kuo, Y., Chen, M.S., Wewers, M. & Guthrie, R. (1997). Multivariate profile of smoking in Southeast Asian men: A biochemically verified analysis. *Preventive Medicine, 216*, 53–8.

National Asian Women's Health Organization (1998). *Smoking among Asian Americans: A National Tobacco Survey.* San Francisco: National Asian Women's Association.

National Center for Health Statistics. (1994). *National Center for Health Statistics, Public Use Data Tapes, 1991–1993.* Hyattsville, MD: U.S. Department of Health and Human Services, Public Health Service. National Center for Health Statistics.

Thridandam, M., Fong, W., Jang, M., Louie, L. & Forst, M. (1998). A tobacco and alcohol use profile of San Francisco's Chinese community. *Journal of Drug Education, 28*(4), 377–93.

U.S. Department of Health and Human Services. (1998a). *Healthy People 2010 Objectives: Draft for Public Comment.* Washington, DC: Office of Public Health Service.

U.S. Department of Health and Human Services. (1998b). *Tobacco Use Among U.S. Racial/Ethnic Minority Groups:African Americans, American Indians and Alaska Natives, Asian Americans and Pacific Islanders, and Hispanics: A Report of the Surgeon General,* Atlanta, GA: U.S. Department of Health and Human Services, Centers for Disease Control and Prevention, National Center for Chronic Disease Prevention and Health Promotion, Office of Smoking and Health.

Wiecha, J.M. (1996). Differences in patterns of tobacco use in Vietnamese, African American, Hispanic, and Caucasian adolescents in Worcester, Massachusetts. *American Journal of Preventive Medicine, 12*(1), 29–37.

Wiecha, J.M., Lee, V. & Hodgkins, J. (1998). Patterns of smoking, risk factor for smoking, and smoking cessation among Vietnamese men in Massachusetts (United States). *Tobacco Control, 7*, 27–34.

Youth Tobacco Cessation Collaborative. (2000). *National Blueprint for Action: Youth and Young Adult Tobacco-use Cessation.* Washington, DC: Center for the Advancement of Health.

U.S. Census Bureau. (2001). Census 2000. Available online at: *http://factfinder.census. gov/servlet/BasicFactsServlet.*

PART IV

HISPANIC AMERICANS

Chapter 10

HISPANIC SUBSTANCE ABUSERS IN THE UNITED STATES

Marné Castillo and George Henderson

There is a paucity of research that focuses on the various ethnic peoples who are broadly identified through the generic terms "Spanish," "Hispanics" or "Latinos." Perhaps the difficulty that has blocked comprehensive studies resides to some extent in the fact that these peoples have social histories and geographical countries of origin that are far more diverse than most researchers are prepared to deal with.

OUT OF MANY PEOPLES DOES NOT COME ONE

Predominately Spanish-speaking peoples' phenotypes reflect centuries of intermarriage, resulting in physical characteristics of so-called "Whites," "Blacks" and "Browns." Further, there are distinct dialects within the various Spanish-speaking groups and that somewhat impedes the ease of Hispanics communicating with each other. The heterogeneous nature of Hispanics is evident in their bloodlines, which include Latin Americans, Indians, Europeans and Africans (Gratton & Gutman, 2000). And each subgroup has its own unique set of cultural beliefs, values and behaviors as well as those that they share with other groups. The term "Hispanic" was used in the 1980 U.S. census to designate peoples whose country of origin was Mexico, Puerto Rico, Cuba, Central America, and other Latin American countries. To differentiate these peoples from Spaniards and Brazilians, in particular, the U.S. Census Bureau coined the terms "Non-Hispanic Whites" and "Non-Hispanic Blacks."

Several researchers have denounced the term Hispanic as being nondescript. Also, within some communities, the terms "Latino" or *la raza* (the race) are preferred. As for those people of Mexican descent, some individuals identify themselves as "Mexicanos"; others prefer to be called "Mexican Americans." And the debate goes on and on. In spite of a lack of consensus regarding the most appropriate label, most service providers, prompted by the U.S. census designation, use the term Hispanic.

Country of origin often determines the composition of Hispanic enclaves in the United States. For example, most persons of Mexican origin, the majority of U.S. Hispanics, are concentrated primarily in the Southwestern and Western states; Puerto Ricans are mostly located in the Northeast; Cubans are found mainly in the Southeast; Dominicans live largely in Northeast Atlantic states; and persons from Guatemala, El Salvador and Paraguay, Nicaragua, to mention a few of the other Hispanic peoples, are largely scattered throughout the different regions. Accurate census counts are unavailable because of the sizable number of Hispanics living in this country illegally. Further compounding this situation is the fact that whether they are legal or illegal U.S. residents, there are great educational disparities among and between Hispanic groups.

TRENDS IN SUBSTANCE USERS AND RESEARCH

Most substance use research that involves Hispanic respondents are in two categories: (1) those that identify Hispanic substance users by their country of origin and (2) those that identify substance abusers by specific substances (e.g., Puerto Ricans as being heroin and cocaine abusers; Mexican Americans as being inhalant abusers). Despite their diversity, there are more similarities than differences within and between Hispanic groups. Therefore, as repeated throughout this book, carefully thought-through generalizations can be helpful to substance abuse agency personnel but their treatment plans or strategies must be designed for specific individuals, not ethnic groups.

Also as noted throughout this book, substance dependency and addiction do not discriminate based on social class, race, ethnicity or age. A multitude of researchers and health care providers are trying to discover the conditions under which individuals become dependent on alcohol and other drugs. The answers will allow them to develop effective treatment programs and prevention strategies. Historically, the focus of this pursuit has been primarily on White males. As an example, although nationwide household alcohol surveys have been conducted since 1964, the first one with an emphasis on Blacks and Hispanics was not implemented until 1984 (Caetano et al., 1998). Therefore it is not surprising that until recently Whites were the almost exclusive client groups in treatment facilities, including those operating to assist U.S. military veterans. However, the changing demographics of the United States gradually brought to the forefront the need to diversify research and broaden the base of substance abuse clients in order to address the unmet needs of different populations.

As noted in Chapter 1, Hispanics are now the nation's largest ethnic minority group, surpassing Blacks in the latest general population census. And this new largest minority group has a multitude of unique characteristics that deserve attention in the areas of public health research and substance abuse services. The purpose of this chapter is to describe several of the factors contributing to the presence of addiction in the Hispanic population and to identify a few successful efforts to abate them.

One of every 100 Hispanics is 15 years old or younger, compared to 30 years old or younger for African Americans and 37 years old or younger for Whites. Also worth noting is the fact that Hispanics have a higher percentage of persons living in poverty than African Americans or Whites (Nielson, 2000), and they have the lowest percentage rate of persons who have health care coverage. As a whole, Hispanics have less access to health care than either Whites or African Americans (Epstein et al., 1999). According to U.S. Substance Abuse and Mental Health Administration data, although substance abuse patterns differ greatly between racial and ethnic groups, alcohol is the predominant substance used and abused by all groups. Based on countries of origin, for example, the use of illicit drugs varies within Hispanic subgroups: opiates are the most commonly used illicit drug among Mexicans (25% for men and 30% for women) and Puerto Ricans (49% for both men and women). For Hispanics of Cuban descent, cocaine is the most commonly used illicit substance.

Researchers have found that Mexican Americans and Puerto Ricans are more likely than Cuban Americans to have ever used marijuana, cocaine, inhalants or sedatives (Finch, 2001). Much of these subgroup substance use variations are explained by differences in age, income, education and place of residence. The data also indicate that substance use is generally lower for Hispanics than non-Hispanic Whites, but this difference may be attributable to the fact that the number of substance users are disproportionately low for Hispanic women. Regardless of gender, the preponderance of research data is reflective of the fact that alcohol dependence is the most prominent addiction among Hispanics.

Indeed, the need for more research focusing on alcohol consumption among Hispanics is not surprising because they consume almost one-fourth of all alcohol drank in the United States, and that results in higher rates of alcohol-related diseases and deaths than for non-Hispanics (Epstein et al., 1999; Nielsen, 2000; Randolph et al., 1998; Saitz et al., 1999). Numerous studies indicate that when compared to Whites, Hispanics have disproportionately more alcohol-related problems. But, they are underrepresented in alcohol treatment programs even though, relative to Whites, Hispanic men are more likely to be alcohol abusers and dependent on alcohol (Nielsen, 2000). However, the opposite is true for Hispanic women, who are less dependent on alcohol than White women, but there are indications that the gap is narrowing (Caetano et al., 1998). These patterns reflect the broader U.S. population in which males generally consume more alcohol than females (Treno et al., 1999). Among adolescents, Hispanic youth consume a larger amount of alcohol than their African American, Asian American or American Indian counterparts (Epstein et al., 1999; Ma, 2000).

Gender Gap. Analyzing data compiled for a 1993 national survey, Nielsen (2000) identified differences among Hispanic groups in terms of alcohol consumption. She convincingly dispelled the myth of Hispanic substance use homogeneity. Despite the fact that she coded the respondents into only four groups (Cubans, Mexican American, Puerto Rican and other Hispanics), her research provides valuable insight to Hispanic drinking patterns. Mexican American and Puerto Rican respondents in her study engaged in more frequent heavy drinking than other Hispanic groups. A more dramatic finding was the gap between alcohol consumption among male and female Hispanics, which was so great that it is now common for researchers to acknowledge it. In fact, this disproportion exists for licit and illicit substances. The comparatively low substance use by females is due to multiple factors, foremost among them are traditional distinctions between male and female roles that contribute to or curtail substance use (Caetano, 1988; Canino et al., 1992).

The concept of female *marianismo* places women in the center of family life, and it demands of them chastity, purity and abstention from alcohol and other drugs (Caetano, 1994). Within this context, opportunities for females to freely drink alcoholic beverages will be present in very few social settings. Family economics also play a role in determining if female members of a household will have disposable income available for them to purchase alcohol. Simply put, cultural norms, religious injunctions and non-consenting male partners conspire to effectively limit Hispanic female alcohol consumption. But as more Hispanic women—and other ethnic minority women—begin to adopt "liberated" gender roles, the gap between male and female alcohol consumption is narrowing.

Machismo is the male counterpart to the traditional marianismo role (Caetano et al., 1998; Epstein et al., 1999). Machismo, which is difficult to define, implies that Hispanic men must strive to be strong and masculine. Therefore, the ability to consume large amounts of alcohol is seen as proof of one's masculinity. Although the concept of machismo in relation to alcohol dependence has been presented in most literatures as a uniquely

Hispanic characteristic, it is relevant to males of all ethnic groups. If asked to respond to the statement "A real man can hold his liquor," a large number of all American adult male respondents would probably say it is true.

Another commonality among all male subgroups is that single men tend to drink more than married men. Treno et al. (1999) found that young and single Hispanic males were among the highest alcohol consumers and binge drinkers, and Hispanic men who were separated or divorced showed an increase in drinking. It is possible that once the responsibility for protecting one's wife is removed, so too are the drinking restrictions. But that explanation is too simplistic. The issue of familial influence on male drinking patterns may not be as relevant as other lifestyle stressors, such as unemployment, underemployment or racism, which may lead to increased alcohol consumption and domestic violence. As stated by Jasinski et al. (1997), "Rates of domestic violence, including wife assault, are higher in Hispanic families than in Anglo families. Research on wife abuse has suggested that structural inequalities such as poverty and unemployment increase the risk of physical violence against wives and are associated with other violence promoting factors such as alcohol abuse" (p. 814).

OTHER SELECTED STUDIES

A study conducted by Brooks et al. (1998) of 1,687 Columbian adolescents in South America found that drug use among those youths did not differ from U.S. White, Black and Puerto Rican youths. Further, the researchers concluded that violence plays a larger role for Columbian youth because drugs are more available and Columbian peers exert greater influence on substance use than their Hispanic peers in the United States. Relatedly, Columbian family members and religious leaders are more likely than U.S. family members and religious leaders to protect children who use drugs. Another cross-sectional study by Brook et al. (1998, 1999) sampled 2, 837 Columbian adolescents, ages 12 to 17. The purpose of the study was to identify the influence of factors such as culture, ecology, peer groups, family members and personality as they pertain to marijuana use. The adolescents were interviewed in their homes and the findings indicated that tolerance of deviance and sensation seeking were positively related to both marijuana use and delinquency. It was further determined that when violence is endemic to a population and illegal drugs are available, a strong parent-child bond can lead to less substance use and fewer delinquent behaviors (Brook et al., 1997).

When compared with non-Hispanic Whites, Mexican American adolescents in a study conducted by Chavez and Swaim (1992) had higher rates of use of various substances. Their study of 8,157 eighth and twelfth grade Mexican American and White non-Hispanic students found that the Mexican Americans reported significantly higher rates of marijuana, cocaine or crack, heroin, steroids and cigarette use than their White non-Hispanic peers. Also, the Mexican Americans reported higher usage of alcohol, stay awake pills, diet pills and smokeless tobacco. They also reported higher rates of high-risk drug use behaviors than White non-Hispanics in such things as sharing needles and polydrug use.

One explanation for the high rates of tobacco use among Hispanics is that they are exposed to more tobacco advertising than other ethnic groups. In a study conducted by Schooler and associates, (1995), the Hispanic responders reported more exposure to magazine cigarette advertising than African Americans, Whites or Asians. Thus, they are more likely than other ethnic groups to experiment in the use of tobacco as students.

Polydrug use is a problem for most ethnic groups. A longitudinal study conducted by Galaif and Newcomb (1999) examined a sample of 529 White, Black, Hispanic and Asian American adults. The independent variables included social conformity, psychological distress, family composition, and support/bonding. Adult polydrug use was the dependent variable. Teenage polydrug use was a significant predictor of adult polydrug use for Whites, Blacks and Hispanics. This was not true for Asian Americans, however. There were differences between the diverse ethnic groups regarding the predictors of polydrug use. Parental support/bonding led to a reduction in adult polydrug use among Whites. General social conformity and high family approval resulted in decreased cigarette use among adult Hispanics. It is suggested then that culturally-related variables may be able to explain the differences between adolescents' substance use and the progression from adolescent use to adult use. This speculation is based on the belief that prevention programs should include culturally-related factors.

Different ethnic groups have differential rates of problems associated with substance use, including aggressive crimes and health-risk behaviors. For example, Valdez et al. (1997) found that there are differences between Mexicans, Blacks and Whites in reported types of aggressive or violent acts while under the influence of alcohol or other drugs. The researchers examined aggressive crime rates growing out of substance use among a sample 2,364 males. Ethnicity was significantly related to aggressive crime. Mexican-American arrestees were more likely to be arrested for aggressive crimes than were Blacks or Whites. And Whites tend to participate in drug social settings that are less conducive to violent behavior than do Blacks or Mexican Americans.

Kim et al. (1993) found that intravenous drug use among a sample of 1,561 heterosexual Black, White and Hispanic patients at Bellevue Hospital Center in New York City was significantly associated with sexual risk-taking that can lead to the acquisition of AIDS. Generally, minority groups in cities have the highest chances of acquiring AIDS. Another study found HIV in 39 percent of a methadone maintenance population in New York City which included 49.1 percent Blacks, 41.8 percent Hispanics, and 17.2 percent non-Hispanic Whites (Schoenbaum et al., 1989).

ACCULTURATION

Aside from the risk factors associated with poverty, racism or personality characteristics, the degree of an individual's acculturation is a primary influence on Hispanics in terms of their use of alcohol and other drugs (Gutmann, 1999; Larkey et al., 2001; Miranda et al., 2000). This conclusion is heavily supported in the literature, which increasingly points to the importance of the psychosocial aspects of family, peers and ecology as phenomena that influence substance use and abuse patterns among Hispanics (Botvin et al., 1999; Carvajal, 1997; Finch, 2001; Fraugenglass et al., 1997; Harachi, 1997; Nielsen & Scarpitti, 1997; Wagner-Echeagaray et al., 1994).

Some of the most significant data on Hispanic substance abusers are found in the 1984 Hispanic Health and Nutrition Examination Survey (Hhanes) report, which cited two major findings: (1) substance abuse among female Hispanics was significantly lower than for males and (2) acculturation was a risk factor for substance abuse (Finch, 2001). Recent immigrants have a lower prevalence of drug use than non-Hispanic Whites or Hispanics born in the U.S. who are highly acculturated in the "dominant" White society. During the immigrants' acculturation in a new environment, new cultural knowledge and behavioral adaptation processes can be potentially stressful and that in turn can lead to substance use (DeLeon & Mendez, 1996).

Acculturation is an amorphous concept that is broadly defined. Although, multiple definitions are used that vary between research studies, there are similarities across these definitions. The important things to consider in acculturation is that it is a process by which the collective culture of one group is changed through direct contact with another culture. And the degree to which members of an ethnic group have immersed themselves in the dominant culture is indicative of their propensity to use drugs (Huerta & Macario, 1999). This process is different from *assimilation*, which assumes a complete rejection of one's native culture and the adoption of the perceived dominant one. Some researchers refer to assimilation as a stage of high acculturation. In the United States, the term "Americanization" is often used interchangeably with assimilation, which for Hispanics would mean becoming "American" in their behaviors and belief systems.

Another extreme state of cultural adjustment is *marginalization*, which in reality is a very low amount of acculturation. Because marginalized individuals do not have ample opportunities to adopt the dominant culture, they tend to maintain their native language and socialize primarily with individuals from their country of origin. This is different from being *bicultural*, another stage that sometimes linked with the acculturation process (Nielsen & Scarpitti, 1997). Bicultural individuals maintain their native culture, especially the language or languages, while at the same time they adopt elements of the dominant culture without overly integrating the two (Miranda et al., 2000). All of these processes are potentially harmful and complicated for Hispanics, but biculturality results in the least harm to them. Incorporating successful biculturality promotes good mental health by combining or retaining the supportive ego-reinforcing aspects of one's traditional culture and learning the host society's major associational elements. Studies have found that bicultural Hispanics achieve higher indices of quality of life and have greater psychological adjustment when compared with Hispanics who have achieved low or high acculturation (Miranda et al., 2000). In other words, a moderate amount of acculturation in which some of the best of both cultures are maintained is more healthy than no acculturation or complete assimilation.

Much of what has been documented about acculturation among Hispanics is based on anecdotal information that links acculturative stress to a diminishing support network of family members, who in turn are the most protective factor against external stressors (Fraugenglass et al., 1997; Huerta & Macario, 1999; Johnson & Johnson, 1999). The concept of *familismo*, feelings of loyalty, reciprocity and solidarity with members of one's family, as well as the notion of the family being an extension of oneself, explains how the Hispanic family provides ego protection (Miranda et al., 2000). Although entire families may enter the Anglo culture at the same time, in most instances different family members experience different levels of acculturation at varying times. And disruption of the family can be linked to differential acculturation, as in the case of children who tend to seek assimilation while their parents prefer acculturation, leaving the adults in a low level of Anglo culture adjustment or as marginalized people. In other words, generational status impacts the acculturation process and can ultimately cause conflict that may lead family members to separate from each other.

Family interactional theorists identify three major influences on the child, with the first being the impact of parental behavioral modeling (Fraugenglass et al., 1997; Harachi, 1997). The second major influence is the promotion of a strong mutual attachment between parents and their children, and the third influence is parental control techniques. As the primary manager and promoter of a child's mental health, it is critical for health care providers to find ways to use parents in the assessment and treatment of Hispanic children. Generational status is certainly an important factor in acculturation. For example, second generation Puerto Rican adolescents, or those born in the United States to migrant parents, show higher rates of substance abuse than those born on the island of Puerto Rico (Brook et al., 1997). This correlates the relationship between the decrease in family influence and an increase in drug abuse. In short, the evaluation of the level at which a family structure protects its members from stressors or exacerbates them can be directly linked to their potential for substance abuse.

The connection between stress-related substance abuse and spouse abuse has been amply documented for Hispanic males, but not much has been done with women. Many Hispanic male professional workers who migrate to the U.S. from other countries work in menial labor jobs once they arrive in the U.S. because of their inadequate English speaking abilities or outright discrimination. The necessity to support their family causes these men to take demeaning pay jobs that do not allow them to fully utilize their education or job skills. Typically, their wives become low-status, low-paying workers too. And that is yet another assault on their husband's self-esteem as it becomes evident to him that he is incapable of supporting his family. This type of role reversal makes the man a high risk for substance abuse. Also, this situation increases the potential for domestic violence in the home. Jasinski et al. (1997) suggest that structural inequalities such as poverty and unemployment or underemployment increase the risk of physical violence against wives of all groups and this is also associated with substance initiation or abuse.

There is convincing evidence that Hispanics use alcohol rather than community service agencies to deal with life stressors. Overall, economic marginality, as evidenced by lower family incomes, increased high school dropout rates and English language barriers are phenomena commonly linked with the risk for becoming a substance abuser. This is especially well documented in cases of alcohol abuse (Finch 2001; Polednak, 1997).

TREATMENT AND PREVENTION

Four things must occur before Hispanics, or any person who abuses substances, can be helped: (1) they must recognize that something is wrong which they cannot correct without help; (2) they must be willing to tell someone about the problem who can help them; (3) they must give that person permission to help them; and (4) they must be willing and able to change in some way.

A 1984 through 1986 study of Northeastern region substance abuse programs conducted by DeLeon and Mendez (1996) found that the overall 30-day retention rate was 67.2 percent and the rates varied between racial/ethnic groups: the Hispanic rate was 60.3 percent, the Black rate was 69.2 percent, and the White rate was 70.6 percent. The overall one-year retention rate for the sample of 519 Blacks, 229 Hispanics, and 177 Whites who comprised the study sample was 27.8 percent: the Hispanic rate was 22.7 percent, the Black rate was 30.1 percent, and the White rate was 27.7 percent.

Caetano and associates (1998) found a paucity of research pertaining substance abuse treatment programs for Hispanics. Two words summarize the number of Hispanic-related studies that have been reported in the literatures: very few. We could speculate as to why there are so few Hispanics treated in these programs: limited access because of the location of most treatment facilities, inability to pay for treatment, and inhospitable, or outright racist, staff members. Often, Hispanics do not seek substance abuse treatment outside their family or other community support networks. Nor do those same persons always acknowledge substance addiction as a disease within their own cultural context.

Alcohol, tobacco and other substance abuse interaction activities are more likely to succeed when families, friends and well-trained agency personnel engage in productive processes that empower substance abusers and help them to alter or abandon personal, familial, organizational or community situations that place them at risk. Although the designs and effectiveness of programs that have Hispanic clients vary greatly, most care providers agree that their clients' families have a considerable impact on substance use, abuse and cessation.

Families First. There is an increasing body of evidence that supports the belief that Hispanic families play an important role in terms of causing, abating or preventing substance abuse. Identifying risk factors is a key element in effective substance abuse prevention, especially when interpersonal relationships erode. For instance, studies of the family members of drug abusers generally corroborate a high rate of family pathology, including parental histories of substance abuse. In fact, dysfunctional familial behaviors carried to an extreme place children at risk for substance abuse. In addition to substance abuse, dysfunctional behaviors include child abuse and neglect, and inadequate child supervision.

Equally important, the quality of family interaction is critical to the inception and deterrence of adolescent drug abuse (Johnson & Johnson, 1999). Factors such as the degree of parental nurturance and support, the type of parent-child communication, and the quality of the parents' interpersonal relationship with their children yield correlations in terms of substance usage and nonusage among adolescents. Further, a growing number of studies document that family effective and relational variables such as cohesion, discipline and open communication between parents and their children are important predictors of adolescent substance use. Conversely, studies suggest that the erosion of family bonding sets the stage for the likelihood of children associating with delinquent peers.

Hispanic family members tend to be more numerous than White family members. Over one-fourth of Hispanic families consist of five or more members, compared to less than 10 percent for White families. Equally important, approximately one-half of Hispanic families are made up of four or more family members. These statistics document an important characteristic of traditional Hispanic families. Too few agencies have the awareness, resources or skills to handle such large families. Similar to African Americans, Hispanics not only claim immediate blood relatives, they also value extended networks such as lifelong friends, cousins, uncles, aunts, and so forth. Thus a Hispanic family member can be anyone who has a prolonged and significant interaction in one's life. In inner-city communities, such extended kinship networks are often useful and necessary for survival.

A disturbing trend involves Hispanic females, particularly adolescents ages 12 to 17. Data gleaned from the National Household Survey on Drug Use indicate that for some substances (e.g., stimulants and tranquilizers) this age group is more likely than their male peers to report lifetime use, and the trends across Hispanic age groups suggest that the traditional prohibition against substance use by Hispanic females is becoming less effective.

It is estimated that by the year 2021, only 53 percent of the U.S. population will identify themselves as Whites of European descent (Huerta & Macario, 1999). As noted earlier, until the 1990s, almost all of the substance abuse programs were geared for White male clients. Fortunately, there is a new trend toward efforts to implement programmatic concepts that are relevant to different genders and cultural populations. Research has shown that many treatment modalities, such as support groups, inpatient or outpatient therapies, have not been equally effective for all groups. For example, support groups such as Alcoholic Anonymous may not be an effective treatment strategy for Hispanics because of a cultural norm that deems it improper to disclose personal information to a group of strangers. Also, if these groups include females, it may hinder Hispanic males from participating due to their embarrassment; or females may feel threatened by the presence of males.

Baseline Information. Gathering information relevant to a targeted Hispanic community involves becoming familiar with specific aspects of the community. More specifically, service providers should know the country of origins of their clients. They should also know how persons from diverse Hispanic subgroups differ; how they are the same; and their cultural histories. Equally important, they must know whether their clients came to the United States voluntarily or involuntarily. If recent immigrants comprise a significant portion of the targeted Hispanic clients, care providers must surmise what is the likelihood that their clients are in the country illegally. Also, are the clients staunchly traditional in cultural norms, somewhat acculturated to mainstream U.S. culture or highly acculturated? These data are foundations of knowledge upon which can be built effective treatment plans.

Research Instruments. Researchers are developing instruments and scales to assess potential health risk factors of Hispanics (Canino et al., 1999). Also, research is being conducted on the validity and reliability of established instruments translated into Spanish, such as the following CAGE questions utilized by physicians to check for problem drinking patterns (Saitz et al., 1999):

- Have you ever needed to *cut* back on your drinking?
- Have you ever felt *angry* at someone who said you drank too much?
- Have you ever felt *guilty* about drinking?
- Have you ever needed an *"eye-opener"* in the morning?

This simple set of questions may be an effective initial screening tool for health care professionals. On a more comprehensive scale, research findings associated with acculturation have resulted in complex assessment tools that incorporate culturally sensitive items appropriate for use with Hispanic substance abusers. According to DeLeon and Mendez (1996), the Cultural Life Style Inventory, the Ethnic Loyalty Scale, and the Acculturation Rating Scale for Mexican-Americans are the most useful assessment instruments currently available. Common to these scales is the attempt to acknowledge the unique characteristics of Hispanics in order to predict their potential for participating in at-risk substance abuse behaviors by assessing their status in the acculturation process. Selected variables include language preference, cultural pride and affiliation, cultural identification and preference, and social behavior orientation. Furthermore, assessment instruments and agency materials must be carefully written in English and Spanish (Ramirez & Baraona, 2000; Santiago-Rivera, 1995).

Considering the prevalence of research that connects level of acculturation to substance abuse, instruments such as the ones we have cited need to become widely distributed and utilized. Successful methods of health communication, assessment, treatment and intervention must consider the presence of core Hispanic values and family infrastructures. Some of these values include cultural pride, familialism, collectivism (the importance of friends and extended family), and the need to maintain respect in order to "save face" (Huerta & Macario, 1999; Larkey et al., 2001). For example, substance use prevention programs for adolescents could promote pride in the Hispanic culture, utilize beliefs and attitudes culture-specific when designing interventions, and involve carefully selected people from the local community as mentors and role models. And, of course, programs that encourage participation from multiple family members and other community residents merit further research. Nor should peer influence be ignored (Chappin & Brook, 2001; Strait, 1999).

Additionally, cessation and prevention assessment instruments that target Hispanic populations must be especially sensitive to the gender-specific aspects that grow out of the acculturation process (Huerta & Macario, 1999; Polednak, 1997). It is of utmost importance for researchers and practitioners to utilize instruments that have Hispanic-wide generalizability. Any assessment instrument will be fatally flawed if it is not carefully designed, thoroughly evaluated, and appropriately revised. On an even more basic level, research is needed to ascertain substance risk factors for people of all racial/ethnic groups who do not have access to adequate jobs, top quality education, ample health care or other community services. And researchers must put to rest the debate about the need for Spanish language proficient agency personnel. The authors of this chapter believe that it is a nonissue. The importance of the linguistically-competent "trusted messenger" who is well versed in the culture of the clients needs no additional study.

CONCLUSION

There is little doubt that researchers who study substance use and dependency in the United States must utilize culturally inclusive foci. The United States has yet to become a "melting pot" for all of its people, especially not for people of color. Nor should researchers or practitioners disregard the potential for dysfunction inherent in the acculturation processes endured by too many ethnic minorities. Although substance abuse is found in all U.S. populations, and it is predominant among White Americans, ethnic minorities need culturally-relevant prevention and treatment programs. Although the development of programs to treat Hispanic substance abusers is of paramount importance, they must not themselves incorporate risk factors such as dysfunctional staff members who trigger clients' substance abuse.

Identification and acknowledgment of stages of acculturation may further enhance assessment, prevention and treatment. Assisting Hispanics as they progress through the stages of acculturation can reduce their stress. Contrary to the popular belief that complete assimilation into mainstream U.S. culture is best for all Hispanics, research has found that individuals who are able to maintain pride in their native cultures are better adjusted than those who do not. If the melting pot substance abuse prevention agency is to be a cultural gumbo, then it will not be a homogeneous mixture. Instead, it will, in the case of Hispanics, African Americans, Indians and other minorities be comprised of many peoples. This, of course, is easier said than done within the context of language wherein "Speak English Only" is the mandate in a sizable number of health care agencies.

From a national perspective, the importance of properly addressing the issue of substance abuse among Hispanics has great implications for the general public and the health status of the United States. Any programs that decrease Hispanic domestic violence, illiteracy, poverty, and unemployment will also decrease substance abuse. The movement to invest in research focusing on Hispanic substance abusers as heterogeneous groups and attempts to include more Hispanics as care providers give hope to those of us who have internalized the belief that for too long Hispanics have been accorded second-class status in health care.

REFERENCES

Botvin, G.J., Baker, E., Diaz, T. & Epstein, J.A. (1999). Impact of social influences and problem behavior on alchol use among inner city Hispanic and Black adolescents. *Journal of Studies in Alcohol, 60*, (5), 595–664.

Brook, J.S., Whiteman, M., Balka, E.B. & Win, P.T. (1997). African-American and Puerto Rican drug use: A longitudinal study. *Journal of the American Academy of Child & Adolescent Psychiatry, 36*, 1260–1268.

Brook, J.S., Brook, D.W., De La Rosa M., Duque, L.F., Rodriquez, E., Montoya, I.D. & Whiteman, M. (1998). Pathways to marijuana use among adolescents: Cultural/ecological, family, peer, and personality influences. *Journal of the American Academy of Child and Adolescent Psychiatry, 37*(7), 759–766.

Brook, J.S., Brook, D.W., De La Rosa, M., Whiteman, M. & Montoya, L.D. (1999). The role of parents in protecting Columbian adolescents from delinquency and marijuana use. *Archives of Pediatric Medicine, 153*, 457–464.

Caetano, R. (1988). Alcohol use among Hispanic groups in the United States. *American Journal of Drug & Alcohol Abuse, 14*(3), 292–308.

Caetano, R., Clark, C.L. & Tam, T. (1998). Alcohol consumption among racial/ethnic minorities. *Alcohol & Research World, 22*, 233–241.

Canino, G., Burham, A. & Caetano, R. (1992). The prevalence of alcohol abuse and/or dependence in two Hispanic communities. In J. Heizer & G. Canino (Eds.), *Alcoholism in North America, Europe, and Asia* (pp. 131–154). New York: Oxford University Press.

Canino, G., Bravo, M., Ramirez, R., Febo, V., Rubio-Stipec, M., Fernandez, R.L. & Hasin, D. (1999). The Spanish alcohol use disorder and associated disabilities interview schedule (AUDADIS): Reliability and concordance with clinical diagnoses in the Hispanic population. *Journal of Studies on Alcohol, 60*, 79–799.

Carvajal, S.C. (1997). Relating a social influence model to the role of acculturation in substance use among Latino adolescents. *Journal of Applied Social Psychology, 7*,

1617–1628.

Chappin, S.R. & Brook, J.S. (2001). The influence of generational status and psychosocial variables on marijuana use among Black and Puerto Rican adolescents. *Hispanic Journal of Behavioral Sciences, 23*, 22–36.

Chavez, E. & Swaim, R.C. (1992). Mexican-American and White non-Hispanic 8th and 12th grade students' substance use. *American Journal of Public Health, 82*(3), 445–447.

Cherpitel, C.J. (1998). Differences in performance of screening instruments for problem drinking among Blacks, Whites, and Hispanics in an emergency room population. *Journal of Studies on Alcohol, 59*, 420–426.

DeLeon, B. & Mendez, S. (1996. Factorial structure of a measure of acculturation in a Puerto Rican population. *Educational & Psychological Measurement, 56*, 155–162.

Epstein, J.A., Botvin, G.J. & Diaz, T. (1999). Etiology of alcohol use among Hispanic adolescents: Sex-specific effects of social influences to drink and problem behaviors. *Archives of Pediatrics & Adolescent Medicine, 153*, 1077–1084.

Finch, B.K. (2001). Nation of origin, gender, and neighborhood differences in past-year substance use among Hispanics and non-Hispanic Whites. *Hispanic Journal of Behavioral Sciences, 23*, 88–101.

Fraugenglass, S., Routh, D.K., Pantin, H.M. & Mason, C.A. (1997). Family support decreases influences of deviant peers on Hispanic adolescents' substance use. *Journal of Clinical & Child Psychology, 26*(1), 15–23.

Galaif, E.R. & Newcomb, M.D. (1999). Predictors of polydrug use among four ethnic groups: A 12-year longitudinal study. *Addictive Behaviors, 24*(5), 607–631.

Gratton, B. & Gutman, M.P. (2000). Hispanics in the United States, 1850–1990. *Historical Methods, 33*, 137–154.

Gutmann, M.C. (1999). Ethnicity, alcohol and acculturation. *Social Science & Medicine, 486*(2), 173–184.

Harachi, T.W. (1997). Effective recruitment for parenting programs within ethnic minority communities. *Child & Adolescent Social Work Journal, 14*, 23–39.

Huerta, E.E. & Macario, E. (1999). Communicating health risk to ethnic groups: Reaching Hispanics as a case study. *Journal of the National Cancer Institute, 25*, 23–28.

Jasinski, J.L., Asdigian, N.L. & Kantor, G.K. (1997). Ethnic adaptations to occupational strain: Work-related stress, drinking, and wife assault among Anglo and Hispanic husbands. *Journal of Interpersonal Violence, 12*, 814–831.

Johnson, P.B. & Johnson, H.L. (1999). Cultural and familial influences that maintain the negative meaning of alcohol. *Journal of Alcohol Studies, 13*, 79–83.

Kim, M.Y., Marmor, M., Dubin, N. & Wolfe, H. (1993). HIV risk-related sexual behaviors among heterosexuals in New York City: Associations with race, sex, and intravenous drug use. *AIDS, 7*, 409–414.

Larkey, L.K., Hecht, M.L., Miller, K. & Alatorre, C. (2001). Hispanic cultural norms for health-seeking behaviors in the face of symptoms. *Health Education & Behavior, 28*, 65–80.

Ma, G.X. & Shive, S. (2000). A comparative analysis of perceived risks and substance abuse among ethnic groups. *Addictive Behaviors, 25*, 361–371.

Miranda, A.O., Estrada, D. & Firpo-Jimenez, M. (2000). Differences in family cohesion, adaptability and environment among Latino families in dissimilar stages of acculturation. *Family Journal, 8,* 341–350.

Nielsen, A.L. & Scarpitti, F.R. (1997). Changing the behavior of substance abusers: Factors influencing the effectiveness of therapeutic communities. *Journal of Drug Issues, 27,* 279–298.

Nielsen, A.L. (2000). Examining drinking patterns and problems among Hispanic groups: Results from a national survey. *Journal of Studies on Alcohol, 61,* 301–310.

Polednak, A.P. (1997). Gender and acculturation in relation to alcohol use among Hispanic (Latino) adults in two areas of the Northeastern United States. *Substance Use & Misuse, 32,* 1513–1524.

Ramirez, A.G. & Baraona, M. (2000). *Developing Effective Messages and Materials for Hispanic/Latino Audiences.* Washington, DC: Substance Abuse and Mental Health Services Administration.

Randolph, W.M., Stroup-Benham, C., Black, S.A. & Markides, K. (1998). Alcohol use among Cuban-Americans, Mexican-Americans and Puerto Ricans. *Alcohol & Research World, 22,* 265–269.

Saitz, R., Lepore, M.F., Sullivan, L.M., Amaro, H. & Samet, J.H. (1999). Alcohol abuse and dependence in Latinos living in the United States: Validation of the CAGE (4M) questions. *Archives of Internal Medicine, 159,* 718–824.

Santiago-Rivera, A.L. (1995). Developing a culturally sensitive treatment modality for bilingual Spanish-speaking clients. *Journal of Counseling & Development, 74,* 12–18.

Schoenbaum, E.E., Hartel, D. & Selwyn, P.A. (1989). Risk factors for human immunodeficiency virus infection in intravenous drug users. *New England Journal of Medicine, 32,* 874–879.

Schooler, C., Feighery, E. & Flora, J. (1996). Seventh graders' self-reported exposure to cigarette marketing and its relationship to their smoking behavior. *American Journal of Public Health, 86*(9), 1216–1221.

Strait, S.C. (1999). Drug use among Hispanic youth: Examining common and unique contributing factors. *Hispanic Journal of Behavioral Science, 21*(1), 88–103.

Treno, A.J., Alaniz, M.L. & Gruenewald, P.J. (1999). Drinking among U.S. Hispanics: A multivariate analysis of alcohol consumption patterns. *Hispanic Journal of Behavioral Sciences, 21,* 405–420.

Valdez, A., Yin, Z. & Kaplan, C.D. (1997). A comparison of alcohol, drugs, and aggressive crime among Mexican-American, Black and White male arrestees in Texas. *American Journal of Drug & Alcohol Abuse, 23*(2), 249–266.

Wagner-Echeagaray, F.A., Schutz, C.G., Chilcoat, H. & Anthony, J.C. (1994). Degree of acculturation and the risk of crack cocaine smoking among Hispanic Americans. *American Journal of Public Health, 84*(1), 1825–1827.

Chapter 11

HISPANIC HEROIN ABUSERS: UP CLOSE AND PERSONAL

DOUGLAS S. GOLDSMITH

"Neither a borrower, nor a lender be," the sensible advice Shakespeare has a parent tell a child about to leave home, sounds just as apt today. Unfortunately, it does not match the situation one finds oneself in if involved in an urban drug scene. The necessities of the street often mandate a kind of reciprocity amidst repeated stances of self-reliance. Efforts to obtain a continuous supply of needed heroin leaves people dependent upon each other. The heroin user with a regulated habit, a steady supplier and a reliable source of income is an ideal that does not seem readily maintainable in the current law enforcement climate. The image of a "stand-up cat," as described by Finestone (1964) in the 1960s, still has resonance as the ideal presentation of self in the street drug scene. But the stand-up cat must be prepared to deal with any eventuality, especially "hustling" and avoiding "being hustled." Preble noted this when a drug user, who had been cheated, told him: "He beat me today, I'll beat him tomorrow" (Preble & Casey, 1969, p. 8). On the street, one hears that "you have to watch your back" and "you have to put shade on to hide your business." While a drug user relies on other users in one instance, they rely on him or her at another time.

It is easiest to paint the extreme picture of addicts completely dependent on the actions of others in order to obtain their needed drugs. Expressions of contempt, such as "taste face," and of ridicule, such as "hope fiend," describe the abject reliance on others by hangers-on at drug markets and injecting places. A "taste face" gets a "taste" (a small portion of drugs) for rendering a low-status service such as "steering" a buyer to a seller or "touting" a particular brand or bag of drugs or as, Preble noted, "one who supports his habit by renting out works selling oneself" (p. 14). A "hope fiend" is a term for the more righteous dope fiend with hopes that even without money he will get lucky somehow and get his or her next fix.

In 1969, Preble and Casey noted that "heroin users commonly say, "I have no friends, only associates" (p. 8). A dozen years later, when Preble introduced me to the street research scene, I heard drug users insist that "there are no friends, only acquaintances" in street drug lifestyles. In 1993, I heard a young (26-year-old) woman make an assessment of her local drug scene, saying, "Any one that's doing [using heroin] doesn't give a shit if it f____s up your whole life, they just want to see if they can get some of yours or if you can get them some." Another woman (a 34-year-old) made a similar assessment to me in 1990, saying this about the "crowd" that "crashed" (stayed) at her boyfriend's apartment: "They shot up there–when they had it sometimes they shared. Every one there got high if they had the stuff. It wasn't a gallery [drug den], just a place to stay. It wasn't like a family. Sometimes they tried to act like they were united but there's no such friendship out here. They'd say they're friends to see what the other had. They'd hang together but it wasn't friendship in the sense that I know it."

If you hang around and watch the flow of activities and relationships in an urban street drug location, what is most evident is the extensive reliance of people on each other.

THE NOT-SO SUNNY SIDE OF THE STREET

Through direct street observation, open-ended interviews, and group discussions conducted from 1989 through 1990, I became acquainted with about 150 homeless drug injectors and prostitutes in several social networks in New York City. Most often, we met at a drop-in drug rehabilitation center located in the South Side of Williamsburg, in Brooklyn, New York. The staff promoted HIV-risk reduction efforts and outreach to the surrounding neighborhoods, and they offered referral assistance for drug treatment, HIV treatment, and many other social services. Frequently, they also offered hot food and donated clothing to clients. The drop-in center was run by ADAPT (The Association for Drug Abuse Prevention and Treatment). Financial and human resources support was received from the National Drug Rehabilitation Institute through the project I worked for.

Many members of the drop-in center's staff had personal experiences with injecting drugs and drug user lifestyles. And they responded to their clients with patience, firmness, familiarity and compassion in spite of the many demands placed upon them. In creating this island of concern and education for the people of the South Side, ADAPT also created an atmosphere of trust that was vital to my research. The friendly relationships I had with the staff of ADAPT flowed from my prior efforts to help ADAPT reorganize and secure funding for their advocacy work with drug users, and my several years of work as a volunteer with ADAPT's AIDS outreach and "buddy" (companion) programs. I believe the street people trusted and confided in me because of my association with the drop-in center[1] (for a fuller description of this research, see Goldsmith & Friedman, 1991).

Mutual assistance was widespread among male drug dealers, "working women," and other participants in the street survival networks. The street "hustles" of the men ranged from selling heroin and crack cocaine, to prostitution, to "cons" and petty theft, and to collecting redeemable cans. The women were primarily "hustling" as prostitutes or selling crack. Without access to the more lucrative indoor "call girl" trade, they typically offered their bodies through streetwalking or "hawked" (sold) small quantities of drugs on particular street corners. People "looked out for" partners during drug and sex sales, and guarded each other's few belongings if they slept in doorways, rooftops, shacks, abandoned buildings or city-run shelters. Friendships, kinships and persistent partnerships marked these street-based social spheres. Some of the relationships were long-standing—a sibling or a cousin or a neighborhood "homegirl" or "homebro"—and some stemmed from recent mutual experiences such as imprisonment or inpatient drug treatment. My perceptions of those relationships have been reinforced by my research beginning in 1980 among drug users in the New York City Area.

"The street" is central and vital for local street drug connections and consumption, and for prostitution contacts and consummation. Off the street locations—"shooting galleries," "crack houses," brothels and the like—can be considered an extension of the street. And street activities can be thought of as including other "outlaw" behaviors, regardless of location. This broad usage overrides the sometimes unclear distinction between *outside* and *inside* in the often very makeshift arrangements used to shield illicit activities from public view. People could readily be seen smoking crack in doorways. I saw them injecting in public areas, and also injecting themselves behind scrawny bushes and in the rubble of a razed building. Several women described "turning tricks" (sexual activities) in abandoned cars. Another woman selected the shadow of a large dumpster on a quiet street as a place where she felt she could have unobserved sex in a "date's" car.

I have seen structures, called "shacks," used as "shooting galleries" for injecting heroin that were made merely of propped-up mattresses and assorted objects found nearby. The shacks were tucked behind park buildings or concealed by bushes alongside highways. At least three such shacks were used for six months to a year before they were destroyed by fires that reportedly were set by local police officers. One or two men also slept in each of these makeshift shacks and were acknowledged by neighborhood injectors as the "proprietors" of their galleries. The path to a five feet high, eight feet square shack that I visited was through a large hole ripped in a wire fence. The nearby area was strewn with garbage, including many used needles and a complete drug set (a syringe and a needle with a small orange plastic cone that protected the tip).

A "working woman prostitute," as she referred to herself, told me what it was like injecting herself in that shack. She called it "dirty and disgusting" and she recounted having jokingly disparaged an offer by the two shack "owners" to "spend the night." AIDS outreach workers frequently left needle cleaning Safety Kits with the shack proprietors. The kits, and sometimes jugs of bleach, were frequently available because the proprietors constantly changed on short notice as a result of addicts reporting the owners to police officers, who gave them informant fees. One of several galleries was set up in an abandoned factory building and another was in an overturned, decommissioned armored delivery truck.[2]

Street life, which occurs around-the-clock ("24/7"), also involves homeless persons seeking shelter for themselves or storage for their belongings. A street corner, a park, a pier or an abandoned building may be a meeting place for some people, but for others it is the place where they live. Most street people participate in multiple social spheres from which they draw support and to which they contribute. For many of the homeless street people, their family relationships have been truncated or broken, and street locations and street people relationships became central to their lives.

About half of the women and most of the men I met while conducting research in 1989 and 1990 were homeless. They lived on the street, sometimes they showered at the public baths, and occasionally they spent a night in a public shelter. Only a small number of the women and even fewer of the men seemed to be living amicably at home with their families. The meager jobs that the addicts who worked held did not allow them to contribute much to their family's household. Perhaps one-third of the women and a few of the men lived at home some of the time, usually when their drug use was relatively under control. They stayed in the streets at other times, especially when "binging" on drugs for several days. During a cocaine "run" or a crack "mission," they might spend the night doing drugs in a gallery or a cheap hotel room, or they might "break night" (stay awake) on the "stroll" (walking) or otherwise hang out and return home exhausted, dirty and penniless after a few such days.

The primary stroll area where the prostitutes I met stretched along six blocks, crossing under a bridge. They also worked at another stroll of several blocks along the waterfront, where some individuals preferred to stand alone several blocks away on separate corners. Drug use was extensive among them. Despite their many difficulties, they established some measure of social solidarity and kept watch over each other when one was in the car of a "customer," or when buying or selling drugs, or when asleep in hallways or abandoned buildings.

The starkness of the dangers facing the women and men I met was always evident, and the resources they had to counter these threats hardly seemed adequate. One day in 1990, I was standing with a young woman who described to me the dangers of the stroll. A second woman arrived and she was furious. The first woman, who the second was "looking out for," had left in a customer's car but the second woman claimed that the first one had not returned to meet her and be her "lookout" at a designated doorway. The first woman protested that she had returned and saw the prearranged meeting "signal" (a rolled-up ball of paper stuffed into the chain-link fence), but when she had looked in the doorway all she saw was a bundle of old clothes. The second woman admitted that she had fallen asleep under some coats in the doorway, but she was still angry and threw the first woman's handbag, which she had guarded, on the ground. Her frustration was evidence of her feeling vulnerable to the whims of others as much as it was a lack of gratitude. These women were very vulnerable to abusive language and assaults from customers, area residents, and even police officers.

Many of the women I met who engaged in prostitution told me they preferred to be called "working women." Most of them spent the money they earned to support their drug habits, and often they had little or no money left over for other expenses, although a few of them maintained apartments and some of them made important purchases, such as a computer game for a child at Christmas. From discussions about prices, I learned the expected rates of payment (current in 1990 at that location). They said a "date" (customer) typically paid $10 for a "hand job" (manual stimulation), $15 for a "blow job" (fellatio), $20 for "sex" (intercourse). Final prices were subject to negotiation. And there were "boyfriends," usually much older men intent on rescuing them, who provided the prostitutes with money and sometimes drugs. During discussions about the street prices of drugs, I learned that in the 1980s, and continuing into the 1990s, the basic drug units purchased were $10 bags of heroin (of low, approximately 1% to 20% purity), $10 and $20 bags of cocaine (of higher, perhaps 50% to 70% purity), and $5 bags of crack, and $2, $3 and $5 vials (two or three "rocks") of crack to smoke.

The two dozen square blocks of the New York City community that I observed in 1989 and 1990 were pockmarked with places where people purchased and used drugs. Even a three-month-long police "drug sweep" (repeated arrests) during the winters of 1989 and 1990, which had a dramatic dampening effect on the amounts of visible daytime drug sales, had seemingly little effect on the number of drug users or the amount of drugs they used. The drug sweeps and supply demands merely moved the open dealing to an adjacent neighborhood. But the drug dealing continued.

Before the drug sweeps, heroin dealing was an open-air event at a dozen corners, in several abandoned and some occupied apartment buildings, and also in some stores. Crack was sold in nearly as many comparable locations. Four brands of crack (such as "Green Top," "Clear Top," "Black Top" and "Yellow Top") were sold by young men and women standing next to each other on street corners, and four bags of heroin (such as "Obsession," "No Name," "48 Hours," and "Midnight Express") were sold in buildings a few blocks apart.

The marketing of drugs has retained an informal pattern of interchangeable and replaceable suppliers, sellers and buyers. A young woman, who was selling both heroin and crack in New York City in 1993, described her selling arrangements: When dealing heroin, "If I get 10 bags, I have to give back $80." When dealing crack in $5 vials, "I get 20 to sell. I keep $25 and give back $75." She sold for several different dealers who knew her from the neighborhood. She had a good reputation and did not owe anyone nor did she have to sell drugs for a particular dealer. Her situation was rare. More often, I heard of less advantageous arrangements for sellers: $10 or one bag kept when selling ten for $10 or $20; or two bags kept when selling a bundle of twelve for $120. I also heard of many ways people who got into trouble, even killed, for not adhering to the arrangements, usually for not giving dealers money owed to them for a consignment of drugs.

A DIRECT OBSERVATION OF A HEROIN "FIX"

As I became better known and as more people understood my research role, I became privy to more and more personal confidences. Some individuals kept me up to date on their drug use, others told me about their attempts to avoid drugs. Some individuals made it a point to tell me their side when it involved an event such as an argument, a fight, an accusation or a dangerous escapade. Two of the confidants gave me a glimpse into their shadow world. The eventful day took place on March 15, 1990 at the Williamsburg drop-in center. I will describe an interaction between two addicts, whom I call "Tara" and "Solo," and mention other persons largely in terms of their relationships to Tara or Solo. I first met Tara on the morning of this episode. I was introduced to her by Solo, whom I had known for about five months. I had known Solo's former girlfriend, "Claudia," and one of his friends, "Joseph," for about six months.

Solo was a 24-year-old man, about 5'10" tall and usually soft-spoken and mild-mannered. He grew up on the South Side, then a predominantly Puerto Rican area that still had remnants of its former Italian, Polish and Jewish residents. All these groups, and smatterings of many other ethnic groups, especially African Americans, were represented in the local street drug and prostitution scenes. Solo told me that his parents were Puerto Rican and Italian. Tara was 21-years-old, about 5'7" tall and thin but muscular. She seemed vivacious and quick-witted. She characterized the suburban neighborhood on Long Island where she grew up as "all white." (Solo later told me that he thought her parents were Italian). She said that her fluency in Spanish was achieved in high school. Joseph was about 22 years of age, and Claudia was 24. Both of them grew up in the neighborhood. Joseph said that his parents were born in the neighborhood to Puerto Rican-born parents. Claudia said she was brought up by her father's Puerto Rican family after her Jewish mother abandoned her and returned to drug use and prostitution.

Similar to the ambiguity between inside and outside when describing street activities, there was ambiguity between the housed and the homeless people I encountered on the South Side during the course of this research. Both Claudia and Tara were homeless during the time I knew them. Tara seemed to rely on new contacts, particularly new boyfriends who grew up in the neighborhood, some of whom provided her shelter and others provided physical protection. She and Claudia both spoke of being "good" at what they did, referring to mastering the skills of survival as well as getting a "fair" price for sex.

Claudia was well known in the area, often greeting the men and women she met as "cousin." She had an apartment about four years before I met her. She left it when her teenage marriage to an older man broke up. Claudia learned to use her wits to obtain shelter and to keep her possessions (clothes, diaries, eyeglasses and makeup) while waiting for her "steady boyfriend" to be paroled from prison. She showered in a public bathhouse and often slept in hallways, sometimes with a girlfriend or two who also shared with her a "wake-up" bag of heroin in the mornings.

Solo and Joseph were homeless part of the time I knew them. But they also spent time at their respective parents' apartments, most often when they had money to give their parents. Solo's younger sister rarely stayed at home and sometimes he strolled with her. Joseph and Solo complained about catching cold after spending the night on a rooftop, while "looking out" for her. Joseph described how Solo and his sister would slip into their father's apartment during afternoons to inject heroin and cocaine. She had a heavier heroin habit than both of them (she was stabbed to death in 1991, apparently after dispute about money from drug sales).

On the morning of my enlightenment, Joseph had center stage at the drop-in center. He was being videotaped by a Spanish-language TV station. His appearance was disguised because he was a witness to a homicide of a woman in the neighborhood. Tara sat at the table in front of the drop-in center with Solo. I sat down at the table and was introduced to Tara by Solo, who explained to her who I was and what I did. I further emphasized to Tara my interest in HIV-risk reduction behaviors and I gave my promise to keep her identity confidential. Then she told their story.

Describing the day before she met me, Tara said that she "broke night" (stayed out all night) and came into the storefront feeling "dope-sick." I asked whether she had already gotten any of the heroin she needed "to get straight" and feel well. She replied "Nada, I'm disgusted. It serves me right to be dope-sick. Serves me right to have to contemplate being sick. I did it to myself." She then outlined for me the steps she had to go through to "get straight": "Go out. Pick up a date. Get the money. Cope with the risk of being caught by the police. Get a bag of heroin. Get a needle, a cooker and water. Make that clean water I don't make a draw from a 'puddle.' Then go find a cool place to get off. Get the vein up, which is a hassle and a half for me." She looked at Solo's right forearm, pushing his sleeve up, and said to him, "Just give me one [a vein]!" He found a vein. "And then," she added, "you have to hit and pray the dope is decent."

Tara said that the heroin she injected the night before "was kicking." She said it was called "Chinatown," and she got it near the drop-in center from a guy who had brought it over from an adjacent neighborhood. She said that he had "busted out" (taken the heroin he was supposed to sell there, and sold it on his own on the South Side in an attempt to keep all the proceeds but avoid repercussions from the distributor). When Tara and Solo returned for more heroin, he was gone.

Tara said that she had her first heroin injection at age 16 on Long Island, when a boyfriend brought back some "dope" from Manhattan. After a year of occasional heroin use she stopped, but she resumed using it regularly about a year ago. She said that she was just back from a short visit in New Jersey where she "chilled" (took it easy) and reduced her "habit." (I later learned that she left the South Side for New Jersey after the shooting gallery apartment where she had been crashing [staying] with Solo was raided by the police).

Tara got anxious as the TV camera turned away from Joseph and towards the reporter in the direction we were seated. She called to Solo, "Lets get out of here! I'm going to get straight!" A staff member cautioned her to "take a bleach kit." As she was leaving, Tara kissed the staff member on the cheek and she called back to him so that he would notice that she took a Safety Kit from the basket on the front table. They left at noon and returned about 45 minutes later. Tara told me she had gotten the money she needed to get high. She had $20, presumably from giving a customer a blow job. She later said she didn't go to the regular stroll to "turn the trick" because some police officers who were there knew her and would have arrested her up in that area.

"Just that morning," she frowned, "a homeboy, a white cop, told me to get away. I hate white men—no offense (Tara laughs)." While turning the trick, Solo had "watched her back" (guarded her as closely as possible). Tara then asked if I wanted to see how she and Solo got straight. I nodded my head and followed them.

Tara assumed the lead, walking fast and purposefully, taking the shortest route around cars and across the street, saying "I'm in a hurry to get off." Solo and I trailed behind her. She walked past a cluster of about half a dozen young Latino men in their twenties, who are standing quietly by a stoop. Before Solo and I could catch up with her, she stopped in front of a young, very skinny Latino man, half astride a bicycle on the side walk. "Hello," Tara said to the young man but he just leaned back, silently staring at us. Tara leaned forward, spoke softly and handed him $20. He put two small folded paper packets into the palm of her right hand. She turned quickly and walked past him to the street side of the parked cars and called to Solo impatiently, "I've got it, where to?"

I was surprised that she did not plan this beforehand, even though I knew that she was homeless and reliant on Solo's knowledge of the neighborhood. We walked a few blocks, following Solo's lead. Tara told me that Claudia's boyfriend told them earlier that morning that good heroin was sold at the stoop location, but that he didn't know the brand name. Nor did Tara ask her dealer the name of the heroin she purchased.

We stopped at a six-story apartment building, where Solo told me a relative of his lived. Tara asked Solo if he had a key to the apartment security door. When he said "No," Tara, upset and agitated, responded, "We'll have to wait, then." A minute later Tara saw a resident entering the building. "Let's go," she said. We followed the apartment resident through the security door just before it closed. The woman stopped at her vestibule mailbox and looked suspiciously at the three of us. When we get to the elevator, Tara was annoyed that our destination was not the main floor. We took the elevator to the top floor, and then we walked out a fire escape door, across an open-air passageway, through another door and up a short flight of stairs into a wide landing that contained the door to the roof. Tara stopped at the door as I get to the top of the stairs. Solo, walking more slowly, paused at the bottom of the last flight of stairs.

Tara sat on the step in front of the door, leaned forward over her pocketbook, and took out a disposable syringe and a plastic bottle with a small amount of clear liquid. I sat on the floor opposite Tara and started writing. She held up her syringe which, she explained to me, had already been used twice. Tara called to Solo, "You've got a new set, right?" He grunted yes as he climbed the last flight of stairs. She broke the point of her needle against the water pipe on the wall and tossed the syringe into the stairwell. She told me that old needles hurt, and Solo always provided her new ones.

When Solo got to the landing by the door, he uncapped an opening in one of the large horizontal water pipes (part of the fire protection sprinkler system), took a disposable syringe out of one of the pipes and handed it to Tara. She drew some liquid from her small bottle (which she later realized was actually baby oil rather than water) and was annoyed when it did not squirt out in an even stream. She scolded Solo, saying, "Oh damn, these are clogged. You've got to clean them right away." She asked Solo, "Do you have another set?" He retrieved what he said was "Joseph's set" from behind the grill work above the stairwell (all three sets appeared to be identical disposable types with clear plastic syringes marked with lines for quantity, with white plastic plungers and thin needles about an inch long). (Solo later told me that while the needle and syringe that Tara broke had been used only by her, he had previously shared with somebody else the one they eventually used.) Tara drew some of the same liquid using Joseph's needle and she was again annoyed that the "water" did not squirt out in an even stream. Solo, who had been smirking as Tara suffered through the moments, asked, "What's that smell? It smells like baby oil!"

Tara asked out loud, "Why did I break my needle?" She seemed very nervous. Solo was preparing to "cook up" the heroin and he handed Tara a bottle cap that would serve as a "cooker" (container) in which to liquify the heroin powder through heating it. He had extracted the cap from the empty door knob opening (and so probably he had used it the previous time he was there and he shot up). He took the small bottle out of Tara's hands and smelled it, feeling some of the liquid around the opening, and said, "This is baby oil." Tara, who had placed the plunger end of the syringe in her mouth so that it dangled from her lips, had taken out the two folded packets of heroin. She stopped before she poured them into the cooker and, looking bewildered, she took the syringe out of her mouth with one hand and asked Solo, "How'd I get baby oil? How am I going to clean it out?" Solo said, "Use the water in the bag" (i.e., the Safety Kit contained a two ounce bottle of bleach, a two ounce bottle of water, a metal bottle cap cooker, a piece of cotton and an instruction leaflet).

Tara put down the packets of heroin and the cooker. She put the syringe back in her mouth, took a Safety Kit out of her pocketbook, and took out a bottle of water. She drew water from the bottle and squirted it out in a now clear stream. She repeated the process three times and was visibly relaxed as the needle squirted out a clear stream of the water. Then she dangled Solo's syringe from her mouth and picked up Joseph's syringe. She drew water from the bottle and squirted it out in a clear stream rather than the jerky stream produced by the baby oil. Playfully, she repeated drawing the water up into Joseph's syringe two more times, waving the syringe back and forth in her hand as it squirted out the water. She put the syringe on a ledge and picked up the two packets of heroin.

I asked Tara and Solo, "Are you going to use the bleach?" Solo half turned towards me and hesitantly shook his head no but he made an "Uuhh" sound that seemed to indicate ambivalence. Tara took the syringe from her mouth and said, "If he [Solo] wasn't my boyfriend and we hadn't shot together numerous times. . . . What's the point? If one of us has it [HIV], both of us have it." I asked, "Would you object if the other person wanted to use bleach?" Solo and Tara both said "No" quickly and quietly. Softly, Tara said, "I wouldn't mind but he'd better not be f_____g around with anyone else!" "She gave Solo a playful shove to his shoulder as he grinned. Then Tara shouted out angrily at Solo "you f____d Claudia, damn it. You could have gotten us both infected [with HIV]!" Solo stopped grinning.

Tara put the syringe back in her mouth and opened the two packets. She poured the white powder into the old bottle cap. The volume of powder in each packet was about the size of a penny. She dropped the empty paper packets onto the floor, took Solo's syringe from her mouth and drew water from the bottle, checking to see the level to which she was filling the syringe. She smiled and whispered, "Let's do this in 20, baby" (telling Solo how much water she had drawn. Tara continued, "You're supposed to do it in 40, but since we don't know how good this is. . . ." Then she squirted the water into the bottle cap.

Tara handed the filled bottle cap to Solo who turned away from me in a crouch, faced the door, and used the step as a table surface. He heated up a mixture of the contents in the two bags with the water in the bottle cap, using a plastic butane lighter. Tara drew up some heroin from the cooker and squirted some back into it. "I draw it all up and shoot half back in," she explained to me. Tara then asked Solo impatiently for "the tie." He handed her the drawstring which he pulled out of this sweatshirt hood. Tara slipped the tie up around her right biceps but the preset noose did not close tightly. (It was probably the size of Solo's arm when he last used it.) She told Solo the tie was "wrong." He took it, adjusted the knot, and handed it back to her. Tara tied up her right biceps by pulling the draw string tight. She located a vein in the crook of her elbow by tapping a spot where there was a "track" of cellulitis about 1/8 inch wide and 1/2 inch long. She inserted the needle into the center of the track, which seemed to be her accustomed place. She succeeded on her first try. She made the insertion with the needle as parallel as possible to her vein and arm. It was inserted at about a 15- to 20-degree angle. After she pushed in the plunger and drew out some blood, she left the needle and syringe dangling from her arm for about two minutes.

While the needle was dangling from her arm, Tara told me, "From the head down I feel my body relaxing. You're dope-sick one minute and all of a sudden your head feels good and then the rest (of the body)." She mentioned about half a dozen parts of the body, in descending order, that felt good. "And your nose stops running." She then talked about the times she had been dope-sick. Solo handed her a piece of cotton, which he had ripped in half. She touched the puncture site with the cotton and pushed the plunger as she withdrew the needle so that the syringe was empty of visible blood when she handed it to Solo. Then she blew her nose loudly into a tissue and Solo laughed. I believe she put the used cotton in that tissue.

Taking the same needle that Tara had just injected with, Solo turned his back to me, faced the door in a crouch, and mostly obscured my view of him, drew the contents up from the cooker, tied his arm, and injected the heroin. I told Tara that Solo had never discussed his heroin use with me. She replied, "Solo has been very private about injecting." I made no attempt to see what he was shielding from my view. Tara responded to this quiet moment by telling me how important it is that some "other people know exactly what you are doing." She said, "The first few months I was out here nobody knew my last name. If I caught an overdose what would happen? Who would tell my family?" She called to Solo, somewhat jokingly and perhaps as punishment for him being secretive, "I'm not going to tell you if it's [the heroin is] good!" When Solo wasn't looking, she showed me a "thumbs up" sign, and mouthed the words, "it's good!"

Tara then asked Solo, "What are you doing there? You f____d up the shot!" She turned to me, "He's squirting it back in the cooker." Solo chuckled softly and I couldn't tell whether he was worried or just being mischievous. Tara noticed that Solo has drawn up more than she had. She leaned over toward him and said, "You've got 20 there." Then she speculated, "Maybe there was 22 to start with" (So that Solo had more than 10 left to draw). She asked him, "How did you do that?" and guessed to me, "Maybe he mixed in some more water [in the cooker]."

Solo didn't say anything in response to Tara's questioning about the amount in the syringe. He had shielded his actions from Tara's view almost as completely as from mine. I'm not sure this would have been the case had I not been present. I was unclear about the significance of Solo's efforts to hide his actions from Tara as well as from me. The only thing Solo said about his injection was "It feels numb," after he pressed the plunger. He took the other half of cotton in his hand before he drew out the needle, and presumably used it then, rather than earlier when drawing up the cooked mixture in order to filter out any large impurities. (It is possible that Solo added something to his shot when he shielded his actions. This is generally called "cheating," and it is a common concern between partners. Perhaps Solo added some cocaine, since heroin is not normally cut with additives that make the injection site feel numb. Even good quality cocaine can be numbing and poor quality cocaine may be cut with numbing additives such as procaine. In the following weeks I learned that Solo liked to mix equal amounts of cocaine and heroin in a "speedball." I also learned that he and Joseph observed that, unlike heroin, cocaine did not require heating, but rather dissolved when shaken in water.)

Tara put the Safety Kit back in her pocket book, but made no effort to pick up the things she has dropped, including the paper that had contained the heroin and the syringe she had broken. She scowled, "F–k the super" [superintendent, janitor] here. I hate him." Solo carefully picked up every scrap they have dropped and placed the two intact syringes back in their former hiding places. The extra bottle cap was placed back in the open doorknob space, and the used bottle cap, with its dregs of cooked-up dope, was placed high up on a concrete window ledge. As we left the stairwell, Tara grabbed Solo and they kissed amorously. I walked ahead, and they joined me by the elevator a few moments later. Soon after we left the building, we saw the dealer riding by on his bicycle. Tara called out to him, "The dope was dynamite." He seemed quite surprised and taken aback at her loud announcement.

On the walk back to the storefront Tara asked, "What [else] are you interested in?" I reiterated that I was also interested in observing how people practice HIV-risk reduction, and how they encouraged others to do that. Tara said, "Whoops, I didn't use bleach." I told Tara that it was very important for me to observe exactly what she normally did. She said, "Most people around here do not use bleach [to clean their syringes] no matter what they say [to researchers or treatment staff]. Maybe five people I know will use bleach!" I then asked, "What about condoms?" Tara replied, "Condoms I use 100 percent of the time. I'm not going to risk being the one in a million who gets sick [with AIDS]!" She was not aware of the obvious parallel between the risks from unsafe needle injections and the risks from unprotected sexual intercourse.

PERCEPTIONS OF INJECTION RISKS

The injection episode cannot by itself be said to be "typical" or "representative" as much as it was revealing of an extreme case—one in which knowledge of risk reduction techniques does not insure the use of available materials. The episode of observed injecting was instructive on several levels. First, a comparison can be made between self report about drug use and risk practices and observed instances of such behaviors. The behaviors can be interpreted independently of the accounts given by informant statements by others. Second, the interaction occurred in a microenvironment where the participants could interact naturally and intimately and be closely observed. Third, rationales for making decisions on needle use, bleach use, and condom use were expressed, and some of the faulty reasoning may have caused Solo and Tara to reconsider their behaviors.

Several things should be noted when interpreting my account of the needle sharing by Tara and Solo. First, there are implications for risk reduction. Tara did not use her own previously used needle but shared one she thought was new (or newer and therefore sharper) with Solo. She did not take the bleach bottle out of the Safety Kit but used the bottle of clean water from that kit. She also did not take the new metal bottle cap out of the Safety Kit, but used the old bottle cap that Solo gave her. Previously used needles and bottle caps are routinely retrieved from unguarded places that others, such as Joseph, knew about and strangers could discover present unknown health risks.

Things were said that may not be logical to non-injectors or to other drug injectors, but they accurately reflected the statements and behaviors of specific injectors and made sense to them. An example of this was Tara's explanations to me that she used half the normal dilution to make the mixture twice as potent. She said that she did not know the purity and wanted to insure a potent fix. If her primary concern was to avoid an overdose, one would expect her to do the opposite and further dilute the mixture, injecting only part of it initially to reduce the potency. In any case, if all of it is injected, the overall potency, as determined by the amount of heroin entering the body, remains the same, regardless of dilution. Other differences might be in the ways cotton and other paraphernalia are utilized, which presumably reflect local practices, and also relate to the cut and purity of locally available drugs.

I consider the observed episode as opportunity for analysis of perhaps a worst case scenario. It was a case example of the clear need for strong advocacy for public health measures. More is needed than providing information, however cogent and accurate. Self-empowering control strategies to curb drug usage, such as needle exchange programs and harm reduction (to the users) and harm minimization (to the community) activities have shown to be effective in The Netherlands (Hartgers et al., 1989), Great Britain (Stimson et al., 1988), Sweden (Ljungberg et al., 1991), Australia (Wolk et al., 1990), and the United States (Joseph & Des Jarlais, 1989). Dozens of injectors from the South Side participated in the New York City Department of Health's needle Exchange Program in 1989 and 1990, before the experiment was cancelled, and many injectors are still in the drug treatment programs to which they received referrals from the Needle Exchange Program staff. Initially, most injectors in Williamsburg got new syringes from underground sources. Hence, illicit needle exchanges were sponsored by people who kept regular but noncoventional, and thus more attractive, office hours (evenings and weekends). Fortunately, needle exchanges became legal in 1992. And by 1993, several organizations had expanded their hours to be client-friendly.

Client-empowering strategies are called for in light of the above case where one of the individuals, who had previously assisted in the assembly of bleach kits and who had sat through but not spoken up during group discussions about HIV-risk reduction, did not utilize bleach from a kit that was given to him even though his partner flushed the syringe with water from the kit in order to clear out baby oil. They had a new needle but chose not to use it even while under the scrutiny of a researcher who had stated his role as wanting to "understand how people encourage risky and risk-behaviors."

I cannot overemphasize the importance of safer injection practices, so that the episode where some injection practices are unsafe and attitudes toward safer practices are ambivalent is placed in a broader context. Page, writing in 1990, noted that for the injectors he interviewed "the drawbacks of self injection were known to [injectors] in varying degrees . . . [and strategies] for avoiding these unpleasant experiences have existed in the folklore of [injectors] for at least four decades," (Page & Smith, 1990, p. 303). Page and colleagues then observed the specific needle practices at "get-high places" in Miami, Florida (Page et al., 1990).

Gamella (1994), writing about drug injecting in a neighborhood of Madrid, Spain from 1979 to 1990, noted that "since 1987, when the consequences of AIDS become visible at the local level . . . [i]n the dozen of drug use episodes I observed . . . people avoided sharing syringes or needles and disposed of them more carefully. Often they blunted or wrapped needles before throwing them away. In several instances, however, people shared syringes and needles, against my advice. It is largely the inconvenience of waiting and obtaining new syringes that makes people share them" (p. 148). Grund et al., in their 1991 analysis of needle sharing in The Netherlands, presented several example of shared use of needles but found that "needle sharing as a planned or stereotyped sequence in which two or more people share, one after the other, the only available syringe was never observed" (Grund et al., 1991, p. 1603). They noted that "[r]isk behaviors such as needle sharing are . . . the end result of complicated interaction patterns in drug user networks, which have their specific rules and rituals, and larger social structures and official drug policy" (p. 1602).

In my research, direct observations and discussions revealed some dilemmas in the consistent practice of HIV-risk reduction through the use of condoms and the use of unshared, or cleaned, injecting paraphernalia. Drug injectors face many challenges when they attempt to practice consistent HIV-risk reduction. In the course of my many conversations and observations of life on the streets and HIV-risk reduction programs, a consensus of concerns emerged. Simply stated, it is difficult to avoid HIV exposure while engaging in improper behaviors associated with life on inner-city streets.

Despite the competing and sometimes contradictory demands of staying healthy, sheltered, and alive while remaining targeted for criminal justice punishment or death and not becoming "drug sick," many of the individuals I encountered who engaged in street drug activities and prostitution attempted to practice consistent HIV-risk reduction. A long life of harrowing tales of personal degradation and the cruelty of uncaring and abusive dealers, pimps, johns and rapists are additional concerns that often overshadow using condoms and not sharing needles. But the loneliness of the street is tempered by repeated generosity of peers. However, because most peers of drug users, drug sellers and prostitutes have their own demons to fight, generosity is intermittent and it is often unavailable.

The overall level of interest in HIV-risk reduction information among the injectors I met was high. They were especially interested in the facts pertaining to HIV transmission. This was one issue where the people I observed were quick to argue points and vehemently correct each other, usually without much rancor. Correcting someone who voiced misinformation was viewed as helping, even protecting them. Condoms were requested and taken consistently from the outreach staff of the drop-in center. Safety kits, containing bottles of bleach for use in disinfecting drug paraphernalia, were also requested and taken regularly, and they were often assembled voluntarily by groups of heroin injectors. Although high self-reported uses of the condoms and Safety Kits are found in numerous studies, the reports of consistent use are countered by frank accounts of sexual intercourse occurring without condoms, or drugs injected with borrowed, unclean needles.

Despite a high level of national concern, inadequate knowledge, destructive self-protective behaviors and inappropriate outreach efforts persist. And HIV continues to spread throughout communities of drug injectors. Perhaps the lapses in self-protection that some researchers describe in their studies are sufficient reason for the spread of the AIDS virus. Knowing which lapses in preventing HIV-transmission actually occur during drug use encounters, which ones are perceived as hard to avoid, and which ones go unrecognized as potentially dangerous are crucial to an adequate public health response. As Page and his colleagues (1990) pointed out, "Intervention to prevent the subtler gateways of contagion needs to be based on detailed understanding . . . [because [i]ntercommunity variations in self-injection practices are potentially infinite, and each [presents] . . . different kinds of risk of HIV injection" (p. 69).

CONCLUSION

Drug users' street life is replete with experiences of losses, such as loss of home, loss of welcome at alternative shelters, loss of health and even of limbs, loss of social status and self-esteem, and the recurrent loss of acquaintances from support networks. Losses of family members, schoolmates, running buddies, and homebros and homegirls, were common even before the emergence of HIV. Repeated losses might be caused by deaths from overdoses, car accidents, stabbings or shootings, arrests and imprisonments, flight from enemies or the police or creditors, evictions or hospitalizations, or entry into a drug treatment program. HIV, bringing with it the reality of lingering death, has only heightened these losses. A new personification of death arose with HIV. But long before it was given a name, it had been lurking on the streets and stalking drug injectors.

To mediate such losses, the drug users I met seemed to depend on a network of interpersonal relationships. Other people seemed to be one of the few resources that could be mobilized to cope with various unexpected or unwanted situations. Thus, loss of friends was devastating in part because there are so few friends available to start with. Yet time and again I saw people turn hopefully to other persons in an effort to create and maintain fragile support networks. In the most direct sense, whenever a dealer disappears, drug users, however sorry or inconvenienced they are, find another supplier. Rather than solitary loners, it seems that drug users coalesce in order to obtain survival information and to get to a supply of drugs. Through these fragile alliances, social connections are made. This kind of active lifestyle of drug users was noted in the 1960s by Preble and Casey (1969), and again in the 1970s by Agar (1973). Although HIV has created new problems, drug users continue to utilize their social networks to seek solutions to them. Professional service providers who want to be helpful can do so by becoming involved in the street social networks, and by making themselves available as problems arise.

Shakespeare's words "Neither a borrower, nor a lender be; for loan oft loses both itself and friend, and borrowing dulleth edge of husbandry" speak hauntingly to the AIDS dilemma, where self and friends may both be lost. Expressions of intimacy and trust are often entwined with the vector of HIV transmission–sex without protection and common use of drug paraphernalia. While borrowing needles and any reuse of them certainly dulls the needles, borrowing in varied forms is central to the husbandry and the hustle that characterizes drug users.

This chapter is a revision of a presentation at the session "Street Stuff: The Social and Political Contexts of inner City Drug Use," organized by Merrill

C. Singer at the 1993 annual meeting of the American Anthropological Association in Washington, DC. Further, portions of this chapter were a revised manuscript presented at the session "Taking it From The Streets: Risk perception and the Ethnography of AIDS among Drug Users," organized by Michael C. Clatts and Douglas S. Goldsmith, at the 1990 annual meeting of the American Anthropological Association, in New Orleans, Louisiana.

I would like to thank all my colleagues at NDRI, particularly Don Des Jarlais and Sam Friedman. At ADAPT, I particularly thank Yolanda Serrano, who encouraged my work. Those individuals were supportive of my efforts to get to know the people in that special community. My fieldwork was supported by grant R18 DA05283 from the National Institute on Drug Abuse to NDRI. But my serendipitous data collection opportunities and analysis and conclusions are my own and do not imply their approval. I would also like to acknowledge the inspiration I received from reading Bryan Page's account of direct observation of drug injecting, which emboldened me to accept "Tara's" offer. I will not acknowledge Tara, Solo and the others by name, but I thank them for confiding in me and patiently explaining the ways of their world. And I very much appreciate Terry Furst, Deborah Hillman, Stephaine Kane and Jo Sotheran, who made helpful comments on the initial write-up of the injection episode. My academic mentors, Bert Pelto and Steve Schensul, have shown me the way to be both an observer and an advocate, and have always shown interest in my efforts as both (George Henderson provided extensive copyediting of this version of the chapter).

NOTES

1. After 1990, my formal research in the South Side ended. Initially, I maintained contact with the staff of the drop-in center and with the "regulars" during my return visits, especially the Thanksgiving dinners in 1991 and 1992. In 1993, the drop-in center was relocated within the neighborhood and at a 1994 visit I saw only one familiar face.

2. Rick Curtis, an anthropologist at NDRI, had already been studying drug use in Williamsburg and showed me some of his injecting locations. I went to other injecting spots with AIDS outreach workers from ADAPT. I received visits from two anthropologists, Jean-Francois Werner in 1989 and Nancy Sawan in 1990, and showed them local drug and prostitution spots.

REFERENCES

Agar, M. (1973). *Ripping and running: A Formal Ethnography of Urban Heroin Addiction.* New York: Seminar Press.

Fiestone, H. (1964). Cats, kicks and color. In H. Becker (Ed.), *The Other Side.* New York: Free Press.

Gamella, J. F. (1994). The spread of intravenous drug use and AIDS in a neighborhood in Spain. *Medical Anthropology Quarterly, 8*(2), 131-160.

Goldsmith, D.S. & Friedman, S.R. (1991). Landrogue, Le sexe, le SIDA et survive dans la rve: Les voix des cing femmes. *Anthropologie et Societes, 15*(2), 13-35.

Grund, Jean-Paul C., Kaplan, C.D & Adriaans, N.F.P. (1991). Needle sharing in the Netherlands: An ethnographic analysis. *American Journal of Public Health, 81*, 1602-1607.

Hartgers, C., Buning, E.C., Van Santen, G.W., Vester, G.W. & Coutinho, R.A. (1989). The impact of the needle and syringe-exchange program in Amsterdam on injecting risk behavior. *AIDS, 3*, 571-576.

Joseph, S.G. & Des Jarlais, D.C. Needle and syringe exchange as a method of AIDS epidemic control. *AIDS Updates, 2* (5), 1-8.

Ljungberg, Bengt, Christensson, K.T., Andersson, B., Landrall, B., Lundberg, M. & Zall-Friberg, A.C. (1991). HIV Prevention among injecting drug users: Three years of experiences from a syringe exchange program in Sweden. *Journal of Acquired Immune Deficiency Syndromes, 4*, 890-895.

Page, J.B., Chitwood, D.D., Smith, P.C., Kane, N. & McBride, D.C. (1990). Intravenous drug use and HIV infection in Miami. *Medical Anthropology Quarterly, 4*,56-71.

Preble, E. & Casey, Jr., J.J. (1969). Taking care of business; The heroin user's life on the street. *International Journal of the Addictions, 4* (1), 1-24.

Shakespeare, W. Cited in W.L. Cross and T. Brook (Eds.), (1993). *The Yale Shakespeare.* New York: Bobbs-Merrill.

Stimson, G.V., Alldritt, L.J., Dolan, K. & Donoghoe, G. (1988). Syringe-exchange schemes for drug users in England and Scotland. *British Medical Journal. 296*, 1717-1719.

Wolk, J., Wodak, A., Guinan, J.L., Marcaskill, P. & Simpson, J.M. (1990). The effect of a needle and syringe exchange on a methadone maintenance unit. *British Journal of Addiction, 85*, 1445-1450.

Chapter 12

INHALANT USE AND ABUSE
AMONG HISPANICS

Alberto G. Mata, Jr.

This chapter focuses on inhalants and other volatile substances used and abused by American adolescents and young adults, including Hispanics. Problems inherent in inhaling volatile substances are longstanding throughout American society (Bass, 1984), and they generally are treated as lesser drug experiences than other substance abuse problems (Sharp et al., 1992). What was initially considered to be a problem of youthful experimentation with paint, gasoline and glue (Ackerly & Gibson, 1964), later became treated as a temporary youth drug experimentation phase (Cohen, 1973), and it is currently viewed as "the silent epidemic" (Barnes, 1979). Because of the young ages of most inhalant users (Lui & Maxwell, 1994), special attention is paid to potentially dangerous and toxic substances that youths inhale (Chadwick & Anderson, 1989; Fischman & Oster, 1979); Goetz, 1985; Taher et al., 1974). The evolving and expanding nature of inhalants as illicit drugs (Lockhart & Lennox, 1983; Parker, 1989) and the ephemeral societal reactions to those substances is becoming a major concern for state and local policymakers as well as social services practitioners (Schwartz, 1989) and behavioral sciences researchers (Schultz et al., 1994; Swadi, 1996).

BACKGROUND AND CONTEXT

The various modes of inhalant use, their wide variety (Linden, 1990; Ron, 1986; Streicher et al., 1981), availability, low cost, and their pervasive and extensive natures make it difficult for researchers to arrive at a consensus as to a succinct definition of inhalants (Beauvais & Oetting, 1987; Sharp &

Rosenberg, 1996). While popular and professional interests in inhalants have been noted for nearly sixty years or more, it is only during the past twenty years that a sizeable number of researchers have focused on policies and practitioner issues pertaining to inhalant etiology and incidents (Compton et al., 1994; Dinwidde, 1987; Fejer & Smart, 1973) and the prevalence and consequences of inhalant abuse among adolescents (Bryan et al., 1991; Cunningham et al., 1987). Even so, the research is uneven, intermittent and fragmented. Nonetheless, while the exact effects and long-term consequences of inhalant use are difficult to assess, there are serious toxic (Rosenberg, 1990; Rosenberg et al., 1992) and even legal consequences of inhalant use for regular and chronic users (Anderson et al., 1985; Bass, 1970; Garriotti, 1990; O'Brien et al., 1971).

Patterns. Societal attention to inhalant abuse is selective, episodic and gives way too quickly to other substance abuses. Thus, the predominant public agendas pertaining to inhalants are operationally fragmented actions and policies (Maxwell & Lin, 1997). Generally, it is recognized that inhalants are gateway drug experiences that often lead its users to becoming chronic users of other substances. Although inhalants are used experimentally, most experimenters quit or switch to other drugs. But whatever the use pattern, inhalant abuse has serious direct and indirect effects such as intoxication or stupor stages where users may asphyxiate or choke, become involved in near fatal to fatal accidents and injuries, or succumb to the sudden "sniffing death syndrome." Such consequences as these have resulted in calls for more community action from health care practitioners and others (Anderson et al., 1985; Getz, 1985; Pryor et al., 1978; Watson, 1979).

In many communities, illicit drug use venues have emerged and become permanent places, but inhalant abuse venues are less populous. Although inhalant abuse among youths and young adults is increasing or spreading, its exact parameters are not easily established. As new solvents such as gas, nitrate or aerosol become available, they attract a relatively small local network of users. And that adds to the number of people who experiment with inhalants and, as noted earlier, some of them become regular users or chronically dependent on illicit drugs. Although it is a pattern where only a few go on to become actual chronic users, social tragedies are not best gauged by numbers, especially if a member of one's own family is the abuser. Fortunately, inhalant use and abuse has not escaped the attention of national drug monitoring systems and reports like the Community Epidemiology Work Group (CEWG), Monitoring the Future (MTF), and staff members of the Substance Abuse and Mental Health Services Administration (SAMHSA), which conducts the National Household Survey (NHS).

Users. In 1997 and 1998, White non-Hispanics reported the most use of inhalants, followed by Hispanics, then African-Americans. Non-Hispanics reported the least recent use. Also, Whites and White non-Hispanics between 18 and 25 years of age reported higher levels of inhalant use than those 12- to 17-year-olds. Unlike the MFT survey, the NHSDA data suggest that female inhalant use is increasing. Young females between the ages 12 and 17 reported using more inhalants than their male peers. As their age increased, the inhalant gap also decreased. Also, NHSDA data indicate that females use inhalants at a very early age (National Institute on Drug Abuse, 1996, 1999a).

Youths who resided in small metropolitan areas are more likely than those who live in large metropolitan areas and nonurban areas to report inhalant use in the past year. Respondents in the NHSDA 18- to 25-year-old cohort from small urban areas were the only group to show a significantly higher reported usage. The NHSDA survey shows the Western areas of the United States to have more inhalant users than any other region, followed by the North Central region and then the Northeast region. Young adolescents ages 12 to 17 are the most numerous users. In general, individuals with some college education are least likely to report inhalant use than those with less than a college education.

While inhalant abuse is common in both rural and urban settings, it is also a problem in suburban settings. In many of the early studies, disproportionate attention focused on urban racial and cultural factors that were believed to be keys to explaining the overinvolvement of racial and ethnic minority youths in inhalant abuse. Later studies challenged this perspective and have focused instead on adverse socioeconomic conditions, particularly economically depressed urban and rural communities, and inadequate family support systems that are common to inhalant abusers in all communities. Even these studies are methodologically limited and episodic; thus they do not provide irrefutable inhalant patterns and trends.

Inhalants. We should keep in mind the fact that while inhalant abuse has been loosely defined as the deliberate inhalation of a wide range of solvents, nitrates, aerosols and gases, researchers generally characterize inhalant use patterns by the modes of use rather by the substances consumed. More specifically, inhalants generally include vapors, gases, and solvents that are ingested to induce mood shifts and mind altering psychoactive effects. These substances include a broad range of products readily available as household, industrial and medical products. That is why it is more difficult to classify inhalants than it is to classify opioids, barbiturates and amphetamines.

Solvents include a multitude of products such as gasoline, transmission fluids, paint thinners, airplane glues, cements and other substances that vaporize when exposed to room temperature. Aerosols include propellants that spray themselves, e.g., hairsprays, cooking oil sprays, deodorants, fabric protectors and, of course, spray paints. Amyl and butyl nitrates include smooth muscle relaxants and agents used to dilate the blood vessels. Cyclohexyl nitrate is one of the key ingredients in room deodorizers. Unlike other substances used as inhalants, these substances stimulate and enhance sexual performance. Nitrates such as amyls and butyl nitrate are more likely to be used by young adults.

Inhalants are sniffed or snorted; huffed, bagged or inhaled by filling balloons; or sprayed directly into the nostrils or throat (Beauvais, 1992; Crites & Rouse, 1988; Sharp & Carroll, 1978). These substances are readily and quickly absorbed through the lungs and distributed to the brain and the central nervous system. In a short amount of time, a user feels the intoxicating effects, but the duration is very short. Lightheadedness, euphoria, dizziness and other alcohol-like effects can be followed by hallucinations, delusions, slurred speech and uncoordinated movements, and occasionally, stupor. Some users become belligerent or apathetic and have impaired movement and vision. Concomitant with successive repeated inhalant use is a possibility of a loss of sensation, a loss of consciousness or a loss of life.

As noted earlier, while many people experiment with inhalants, most of them cease their use, and only a few of them become regular users and possibly chronic users. Chronic users talk about the need to use an inhalant, and they often experience mild withdrawal symptoms when they have not used it. Except for nitrates, most volatile inhalant substances produce pleasurable effects because they act as depressants on the central nervous system (NIDA, 1999; Rosenburg, 1990). Nitrates product effects that act as anesthetic agents; that is, they numb the senses. It is important to remember that the pleasurable effects of inhalants are short-lived and require successive use and dosages to recapture the effects.

Inhalant Users. For novice users, inhalants are one of the few illicit substances where "instructions" and "instructors" are not necessary. Beginners can easily administer inhalants to themselves, using objects that are easily accessible to them at home. Generally, inhalants are among the first illicit drugs that young children experiment with because they are readily available, inexpensive to buy, and have various pleasurable side effects. While generally associated with Hispanic, African American and Native American users in their respective *barrios*, inner-cities and reservations, these patterns of use are common across all ethnic groups in all geographic settings, and they are rapidly spreading throughout the U.S.

Given a "typical" user's personal characteristics, such as a member of a dysfunctional family and resident in an economically ravaged community, inhalant abusers are generally viewed as difficult to treat and monitor. Research studies and policies designed to alleviate or lessen inhalant abuse are usually local and seldom do they involve long-term, national actions. Even after receiving state or local inhalant alerts, most community policymakers' and agency practitioners' attention are seldom shifted from the more "pressing" drug abuse problems–marijuana, LSD, speed, PCP, heroin, cocaine, crack, crank, and, now, ecstasy.

Clearly, inhalant abusers can select from a potpourri of substances (Barrett et al., 1990; Oetting et al., 1988; Oetting & Webb, 1992). Yet, despite abundance of inhalants, local preferences develop and users go out of their way to obtain their choice (Fredlund et al., 1990; Wallisch, 1998). In truth, they are discerning consumers (Maxwell & Liu, 1995), and that sometimes culminates in face-to-face group snorting or sniffing activities (Beauvais, 1992). These networks do not necessarily overlap and they reflect preferences that in many ways are not obvious to noninhalant users. Even though inhalants are gateway drugs, their use is typically seen and treated as déclassé. Similar to crack heads and winos, inhalant users are low-class (Mata & Andrew, 1988).

Inhalant abusers are difficult to categorize. There is considerable agreement among researchers, however, that inhalant use comprises distinct patterns of behavior. But there is no consensus as to which qualities or properties of inhalants attract particular users or make the users distinct. Spotts and Shontz (1982) suggested looking at inhalants users' personality types and the other drugs they use in combination with inhalants, but little has been done in that area of research. Liu and Maxwell (1995) argue convincingly for researchers to give attention not just to the quantity of inhalants used but also the age of the users, the type of solvents used and their purposes, environmental settings and other contextual aspects of inhalant use. It is also important, they argue, to determine whether or not which specific substances, if any, are consistently used in conjunction with the specific inhalants. To date, most researchers still base their categories of inhalant abuse on quantity, opting not to clearly address variations of use over time or measures of quantity and frequency. When examining this problem, the wide range of solvents used among the various age groups and changes in these uses over time are all viable foci for research. Because of the myriad of combinations that can be made with these factors, it is unlikely that consensus criteria to describe inhalant abusers will evolve.

Albaugh and Albaugh's (1979) Cheyenne and Arapaho Indians study defined a sniffer as anyone who habitually uses or has a need for a feeling of intoxication through the use of a volatile solvent. Stybel et al. (1976) defined a sniffer as anyone who has inhaled hydrocarbon fumes or reported behavioral activity consistent with hydrocarbon inhalants. Other writers refer to sniffers as being either chronic or social users of inhalants. Cohen (1973) identified three types of inhalant abusers: (1) experimenters who try a solvent once or a few time and then discontinue the practice; (2) occasional or social users who use inhalants infrequently; and (3) chronic users ("heads") who use inhalants daily. De Barona and Simpson (1984) identified three kinds of inhalant users: (1) experimental; (2) recreational; and (3) chronic. These types were derived from a survey of 293 youths admitted to Texas drug prevention programs. Chronic inhalant users sniff on a regular basis.

Beauvais and Oetting (1987) suggested a three-fold grouping of users: (1) adults who are substance dependent; (2) adolescent poly-drug users; and (3) young inhalant users. Age, frequency of use, amount of use, dependence, and problems associated with status (legal, social, psychological and employment) are central to this typology. Users' networks or clusters of users frequently determine a groups' inhalant abuse patterns, substance preferences, and dependence problems. Unfortunately, few studies have replicated or expanded or refocused Beauvais and Oettings's research. Even though only a few studies have addressed the concerns and recommendations postulated by researchers in the 1970s and 1980s, the data that has been collected provide useful information concerning inhalant use and abuse. Moreover, there seems to be a consensus that a single inhalant use or multiple uses over a short period of time characterizes the inhalation of volatile solvents such as gases and aerosols (Beauvais, 1992). Agreeing with those distinctions, Sharp and Rosenberg (1996) expanded the category of solvent use to include nitrous oxide.

Although frequency of inhalant use provides several useful indicators of chronicity of use, there is little to suggest actual inhalant abuse transitions. Even less is known about users' decisions concerning which drug they will experiment with next or when and why they change to other substances. Moreover, comprehensive explanations of the consequences of chronic inhalant use based on frequency have yet to be made. Therefore classifications of inhalant users and abusers continue to be based on usage patterns or inhalant dependency cycles.

HEALTH CONSEQUENCES OF INHALANT ABUSE

Given the heterogeneity of substances inhaled, the full extent of health-related consequences have been difficult to determine because of the different pharmacological effects. Moreover, current methods of assessment may not be sensitive enough to detect injury over time. Also, tolerance occurs with some substances but not with others and some users' tolerance is rapid but for others it comes over a long period of time. Inhalation of substances such as nitrous oxide seem not to increase in tolerance either by regular use or increase in dosages; however, other health consequences do arise with even intermittent use. In any case, inhalant use and abuse pose dangers such as neural loss among chronic abusers, damage to the peripheral nervous system, asphyxia arrhythmias (cardiac arrest and circulatory shock), and intentional or unintentional injuries.

Nearly all substances inhaled produce intoxicating and reinforcing effects by the depressing of the central nervous system or they act as an anesthetic agent on the circulatory system by the dilating and relaxing of the blood vessels. A rapid high is very similar to alcohol intoxication, including effects such as lack of inhibitions, drowsiness, lightheadedness and, in some cases, agitation. Those effects can occur during or shortly after an inhalant is used. High dosages can cause confusion, delirium, a general loss of sensation, unconsciousness, and heart arrhythmias. Most inhalant users report headaches, dizziness, perspiration, nausea, vomiting and even fainting during early use.

In terms of the use of volatile substances during pregnancy, numerous studies have established that some inhalants affect unborn fetuses and pregnancy. Toluene and other hydrocarbons have been associated with retarded brain development, microencephaly, hyperactivity, psychological and language developmental delays, and the retardation of growth. Clinical animal studies of nitrate use show that it induces methemoglobinemia (Sharp et al., 1992). Clearly, more comprehensive studies in this area are needed and warranted. While inhalants can and do cause death, even among novice users, few deaths are caused directly by them. Garriotti (1990) concluded that the smallest number of deaths in 1989 were caused by inhalants. The actual order of violent deaths were suicide (28%), accidents (26%), homicides (23%), and inhalants (18%). Close examination by medical examiners lead to the conclusion the inhalant deaths involved the use of toluene, nitrous oxide, gasoline or freon. Here too, additional studies are warranted. I will now discuss selected social epidemiology aspects of inhalant abuse.

SOCIAL EPIDEMIOLOGICAL DIMENSIONS

In terms of social epidemiological dimensions, national and state surveys suggest that inhalants are among the earliest substances used by our nation's children and that this use normally peaks in the eighth grade (see Table 12.1). Although the gap between male and female users is closing (Farabee, 1995), monitoring the Future Surveys and the National Household Survey found that as boys and girls grow older, inhalant use is more prevalent among boys than girls. In short, among older users, regular and chronic inhalant use is more common among males than females but, as I stated earlier, the gap is lessening. Although both the MTF survey and the NHSDA report show declines over the past five years, inhalant abuse rates are higher than those reported since the late 1970s. In terms of new users, the rate for the first use of inhalants in ages 18 to 25 group rose from 3.7 percent to 10.7 percent per 1,000 between 1989 and 1997. The MTF survey also indicates that the percentage of students who have ever tried inhalants remains at higher levels but less than reported by the NHSDA. In terms of age, inhalant rates doubled for adolescents between the ages of 12 and 17, and nearly tripled for those between the ages of 18 and 25.

Monitoring The Future Surveys. MTF surveys chronicle recent (past 30 days) and lifetime substance use of inhalants such as paints, glues and spray paints by eighth, ninth, and tenth grade students. These data provide important trends about the early inhalant use of students, which decrease as they

Table 12.1
PERCENTAGE REPORTING INHALANT USE IN THEIR LIFETIME BY
AGE GROUP AND DEMOGRAPHIC CHARACTERISTICS: 1997

| *Demographic Characteristics* | *Age Group in Years* | | | | |
	12–17	*8–25*	*26–34*	*35+*	*Total*
Total	7.2	10.1	8.3	3.8	5.7
Gender					
Male	7.2	13.8	11.2	5.3	7.7
Female	7.3	6.4	5.4	2.5	3.9
Race/Ethnicity					
White, non-Hispanic	8.1	13.4	10.3	4.3	6.6
Black, non-Hispanic	2.8	0.7	2.3	1.4	1.6
Hispanic	6.2	5.0	3.8	2.6	3.8
Population Density					
Large metropolitan area	6.3	10.8	8.4	4.3	6.1
Small metropolitan area	8.5	10.7	9.1	4.3	6.3
Non-metropolitan area	6.9	8.2	6.7	2.3	4.1
Region					
Northeast	4.2	6.4	5.9	4.0	4.6
North Central	7.5	12.2	10.3	2.4	5.6
South	6.7	9.2	6.9	3.3	5.0
West	10.1	12.5	10.3	5.9	7.9
Adult Education					
Less than high school	N/A	9.5	6.7	3.6	5.0
High school graduate	N/A	9.3	6.7	3.2	4.7
Some college	N/A	11.7	11.4	5.1	7.6
College graduate	N/A	9.5	8.1	3.7	5.0
Current Employment					
Full-time	N/A	10.6	8.9	5.6	7.0
Part-time	N/A	12.9	8.8	2.5	6.7
Unemployed	N/A	6.0	7.0	4.7	5.5
Other	N/A	7.9	5.5	1.6	2.6

Source: National Household Survey.

grow older. In terms of lifetime use of inhalants, the younger students reported higher rates of experimenting with inhalant use than did the older students. In 1991, 17.6 percent of the eighth graders surveyed said they had used
inhalants at some point in their lives. The rate for this age group remained
fairly steady through the following year, 1992, and then it made a steady
climb upwards, topping out at 32.6 percent in 1995, but still remained at a
high level, with 19.7 percent of eighth graders reporting lifetime use of
inhalants.

Increasingly, the older the students become, the less likely they are to
report ever using inhalants. Ninth and tenth graders report less lifetime use
of inhalants than eighth graders. For example, in 1991, 15.7 percent of the
ninth graders and 17.6 percent of the tenth graders reported lifetime inhalant
use. Again, like the eighth graders, the ninth graders' reported a steady
increase in inhalant use until 1995, where the ninth graders use topped out
at 19.3 percent. After 1996, the reported lifetime use decreased each year to
17 percent in 1999. The tenth graders reported a significant drop in inhalant
use between 1991 and 1992. Again, mirroring the behavior of the younger
respondents, inhalant use increased slightly each year, reaching its peak in
1994 at 17.7 percent. The reported use went down steadily each of the following years until it reached an all-time low of 15.2 percent in 1998 and was
up slightly, to 15.4 percent the following year.

There appears to be a discrepancy in the data. In the eighth grade, students reported a high incidence of inhalant use, but two years later, when
those students were in the tenth grade, their incidence of lifetime inhalant use
declined. That is, 21.6 percent of eighth graders reported having used
inhalants in 1995, but only 16.1 percent of tenth graders reported lifetime
inhalant use in 1997. There are two possible explanations for this disparity.
The first is that students who use inhalants and other illicit substances are at
a higher risk of repeating grades or dropping out of school entirely. The
other explanation is that as students get older, they are reluctant to report
ever using inhalants. In any case, after the eighth grade there was an overall
decrease in reported lifetime inhalant use in all three age groups. We now
will turn our attention to data collected from the National Household Survey
on Drug Abuse and the State of Texas surveys.

NHSDA. The National Household Survey of Drug Abuse shows that the
rate of lifetime inhalant use actually increased among the groups surveyed
from 1997 to 1998. This was true in almost all of the sub-categories and held
true for the total reported lifetime use (5.7% in 1997 and 5.8% in 1998).
While this was a slight increase, it was more significant in several demographic groups, including Hispanics and African Americans. In 1997, 3.8
percent of Hispanics and 1.6 percent of African Americans reported some
lifetime use of inhalants. By 1998 those numbers had climbed to 4.1 percent

Table 12.2
PERCENTAGE REPORTING INHALANT USE IN THEIR LIFETIME BY
AGE GROUP AND DEMOGRAPHIC CHARACTERISTICS: 1998

Demographic Characteristics	Age Group in Years				
	12–17	*8–25*	*26–34*	*35+*	*Total*
Total	6.1	10.8	9.1	3.8	5.8
Gender					
Male	6.1	14.0	11.8	5.9	7.9
Female	6.0	7.6	6.4	2.0	3.7
Race/Ethnicity					
White, non-Hispanic	7.2	14.2	11.2	4.2	6.6
Black, non-Hispanic	2.1	2.2	2.1	2.2	2.2
Hispanic	5.6	5.9	5.5	2.4	4.2
Population Density					
Large metropolitan area	5.1	9.4	10.5	4.4	6.1
Small metropolitan area	6.5	14.0	8.3	3.7	6.2
Non-metropolitan area	7.4	7.1	7.0	2.8	4.4
Region					
Northeast	4.9	11.1	9.9	5.3	6.7
North Central	7.4	13.8	9.9	3.2	6.1
South	5.1	7.9	7.2	2.6	4.2
West	7.3	12.1	10.5	4.9	7.1
Adult Education					
Less than high school	N/A	10.4	8.9	2.0	4.3
High school graduate	N/A	8.7	9.2	3.1	5.0
Some college	N/A	12.8	9.9	4.2	7.0
College graduate	N/A	12.2	8.3	5.4	6.4
Current Employment					
Full-time	N/A	11.5	10.2	5.9	7.7
Part-time	N/A	12.7	9.9	3.1	6.6
Unemployed	N/A	14.7	6.1	7.4	9.2
Other	N/A	6.6	3.8	0.8	1.7

Source: National Household Survey.

and 2.2 percent, respectively. The survey showed that 12 to 17 year-old Hispanics reported less use in 1998 than in 1997 (5.6% versus 6.2%), while those 26 to 34 years old reported a significantly higher rate (5.5% in 1998 and 3.8% in 1997). However, this changed in 1998, with 6.1 percent of males 12 to 17 years of age reporting lifetime use and six percent of females reporting lifetime inhalant use. In general, males were twice as likely to report inhalant use in their lifetime than females. Respondents who resided in the Northeast region of the U.S. reported higher inhalant use in 1998 than in 1997 (6.7% versus 4.6%). College graduates also reported a higher lifetime use in 1998 than in 1997 (6.4% versus 5%). Likewise, unemployed respondents reported a dramatic increase in lifetime use in one: to 9.2 percent in 1998 from 5.5 percent in 1997.

Although overall inhalant use by females decreased slightly between 1997 and 1998 (3.9% and 3.7%), young females between the ages of 12 and 17 were still slightly more likely to report lifetime use than their male cohorts in 1997 (7.3% versus 7.25%). Another item of interest between the two surveys is the high percentage of respondents from large metropolitan areas where reported lifetime inhalant use was 6.1 percent in 1998. When considering population density, the overall reported lifetime use of inhalants was greater in large metropolitan areas than in small metropolitan areas, suburban areas and rural areas. Respondents who resided in large metropolitan areas were least likely to report "recent past use" in this survey. What this seems to indicate is that even though respondents from large areas experiment with inhalants more than those from less populous areas, they are less likely than people from the small urban and non-metropolitan areas to use inhalants chronically.

Texas Surveys. The Texas Commission on Alcohol and Drug Abuse (TCADA) administers a survey to public high school students every two years. During the last ten years, the survey was modified to include elementary school students as well as secondary students because TCADA became aware that many very young students were also using illegal substances and alcohol. The results from the surveys administered from 1992 to 1998 indicated that a startling number of students were experimenting with inhalants such as glues, gasoline and spray paint in order "to get high."

It should be noted that the 1992 survey was worded differently than the surveys that followed. In 1992, substances were listed individually. In 1994,

Chart 12.1
Youth Survey Inhalant Results: 1998-1992

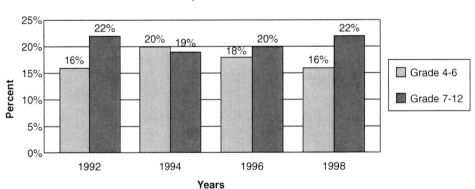

Source: TCADA

the words "to get high" followed each of the substances, e.g., paint thinner "to get high." It was thought that in 1992 some students may have erroneously admitted using an inhalant when they sniffed gasoline or glues unintentionally. This modification was made in order to clarify the intentions of the respondents. In 1992, 16 percent of students from grades four to six reported they had tried inhalants at some point in their lives. Also, 22 percent of students in grades seven to 12 reported lifetime use of inhalants. In 1994, 20 percent of students in grades four to six and 19 percent of those in grades seven to 12 admitted inhalant use. While the younger students reported less inhalant use in 1996 and 1998 (18% and 12% respectively), the older students' inhalant use increased steadily (from 19% in 1994 to 20% in 1996 and 22% in 1998).

Female students reported less lifetime inhalant use than males (23.4% of males and 20.7% of females) in 1998, up from 20.5 percent for males and 19.2 percent of females who reported use in 1996. What is important in this data is that both males and females reported increased amounts of inhalant use. The same survey compared inhalant use among students in grades seven to 12 who were at high-risk of dropping out of school (HRDOS) to those who were not. In 1998, 35 percent of HRDOS had used inhalants at some point in their lives and 7.4 percent had used them in the past month. What is most striking about these data is that they report inhalant use declining significantly with age. Over ten percent of the seventh graders surveyed reported inhalant use in the past month, but only 3.8 percent of the twelfth graders reported recent inhalant use. Likewise, 23.9 percent of seventh graders reported lifetime use compared to 15 percent of seniors. Also, almost one-fourth (23.9%) of the HRDOS seventh graders reported lifetime inhalant use and 15 percent of HRDOS seniors reported lifetime inhalant use. While 14.6 percent of all high-risk students reported inhalant use in the past month, students who were not at high-risk of dropping out reported considerably less past month inhalant use (7.4%).

In addition to the increase in inhalant use among young students in Texas, the survey also showed that the use of marijuana was increasing very rapidly. In 1994, 23.3 percent of Anglo students, 28.5 percent of African American students, and 28.9 percent of Hispanic students surveyed admitted lifetime marijuana use. In 1998, those numbers jumped to 33.9 percent, 33.2 percent and 37.8 percent, respectively. The Hispanic secondary students reported a much higher use of alcohol, inhalants and marijuana. And, while all three ethnic groups reported an increase in substance use, Hispanics' use increased faster than the other groups. Even though Hispanic students reported a lower incidence of alcohol use, they used more inhalants and marijuana than ever before (22.5% inhalant use in 1996 versus 25.2% in 1998; 34.8% marijuana use in 1996 versus 37.8% in 1998). When we look at past month use, we also

Table 12.3

PERCENTAGE OF TEXAS SECONDARY STUDENTS WHO HAD EVER USED
INHALANTS: 1994–1998

	1994	*1996*	*1998*
Total students	18.7%	19.8%	N/A
Gender			
Male 20.30%	20.50%	23.00%	
Female 17.20%	19.20%	21.00%	
Ethnicity			
Anglos 19.10%	20.80%	23.00%	
African-American	11.40%	11.30%	13.05%
Hispanics 22.20%	22.50%	25.00%	
Family Structure			
Live with both parents	17.30%	18.30%	21.00%
Other family structures	21.00%	22.30%	25.00%

Source: TCADA

Table 12.4

PREVALENCE AND RECENCY OF USE OF INHALANTS BY GRADE:
TEXAS SECONDARY STUDENTS NOT AT HIGH RISK OF DROPPING OUT–1998

	Ever Used	*Past Month*	*School Year*	*Not Past Year*	*Never Used*
Inhalants	**21.00%**	**7.40%**	**4.00%**	**9.30%**	**79.40%**
Grade 7	23.90%	10.70%	3.90%	9.20%	76.10%
Grade 8	24.80%	10.30%	4.80%	9.60%	75.30%
Grade 9	21.30%	7.40%	4.30%	9.60%	78.70%
Grade 10	19.00%	5.50%	4.00%	9.60%	81.00%
Grade 11	17.99%	4.50%	3.40%	9.10%	83.00%
Grade 12	15.00%	3.80%	2.90%	8.30%	85.00%

Source: TCADA

Table 12.5

PREVALENCE AND RECENCY OF USE OF INHALANTS BY GRADE:
TEXAS SECONDARY STUDENTS AT HIGH RISK OF DROPPING OUT–1998

	Ever Used	*Past Month*	*School Year*	*Not Past Year*	*Never Used*
Inhalants	**35.00%**	**14.60%**	**6.50%**	**14.00%**	**65.00%**
Grade 7	37.60%	19.00%	6.00%	12.60%	62.40%
Grade 8	40.80%	19.00%	8.60%	13.30%	59.20%
Grade 9	37.50%	16.40%	6.60%	14.60%	62.50%
Grade 10	31.80%	11.00%	6.40%	14.30%	68.20%
Grade 11	31.40%	11.60%	4.90%	14.80%	68.60%
Grade 12	29.00%	8.90%	5.80%	14.30%	17.00%

Source: TCADA

see an increase in inhalants use among the Hispanic population (6.1% in 1996 versus 10.1% in 1998).

Overall, HRDOS students reported higher inhalant use rates than non-HRDOS students and used inhalants at a younger age. It appears that Hispanic students may be at greater risk to use inhalants and other substances than other students, but in Texas all students seem to be experimenting and using drugs more extensively. In fact, TCADA found that overall inhalant use was up 5.8 percent from 1994 to 1998; the average age for initial use of inhalants was 14.4 years; for alcohol use it was 12.9 years; and for marijuana use it was 14.6 years. By 1998, that had all changed with students reporting the average age of first inhalant use to be 12.2 years, alcohol 13.3 years, and marijuana 13.5 years. What is significant here is that alcohol is no longer the first illicit substance many students experiment with. These data indicate that perhaps students are experimenting with inhalants while in elementary and middle schools and "graduating" to alcohol and marijuana at approximately the same time. Older students are reporting less inhalant use. Once students discover it to be a quick and easy high, they move to other substances.

RESEARCH AGENDA FOR THE TWENTY-FIRST CENTURY

As we have seen in this chapter, there is a clear need for sustained, systematic and comprehensive research to address inhalant use and abuse issues. As new substances emerge, both licit and illicit ones, there is an urgent need to determine the basis for their initiation and dependency. In addition, the differences in inhalant use by distinct age groups and prevalence of inhalant use among high-risk minority group youths and school dropouts are a few other things that merit more research. A review of the methods used to control inhalant abuse in the United States demonstrates several ways to address the issue. Currently, there are 38 U.S. jurisdictions that have legislation in place to deal with inhalant abuse. Prohibition against the use of toxic chemicals vary from state to state. A general list of prohibited substance inhalants are: vapor releasing substance toxic substances, toluene, materials containing toluene, nitrous oxide, whippet kits, aerosal sprays, model glue, butyl nitrite, butane lighters, anesthesia, chlorofluorocarbon, cement containing toluene, butane/canisters, and other abusable volatile chemicals. Twenty-three states have prohibitions against the abuse of inhalable compounds.

Fourteen states target the sale of inhalants to minors. Minnesota targets sales to minors and also has a general prohibition against the abuse of inhalable compounds. Massachusetts requires retailers to check the identification of inhalant purchasers. Minnesota and Texas require postings of warnings against inhalant abuse. Arizona, California, Georgia, Idaho, Iowa, Louisiana, New Mexico, Maryland and Massachusetts mete out fines and jail time for inhalant offenders. Connecticut, Nevada and Vermont only provide for fines. Although a majority of jurisdictions have criminal sanctions against the abuse of inhalants, only three states–New Mexico, Maine and New Hampshire–offer treatment as a part of their criminal justice systems. The nature of inhalant abuse and its social costs warrant the inclusion of treatment options in any proposed inhalant abuse legislation. All states could benefit from sharing their accumulated experiences in trying to curb inhalant abuse through legislation. Perhaps someone will draft model legislation to address inhalant use and abuse.

Apart from laws and other regulations that control inhalants abuse, there is a need for ongoing community-based field studies and surveys. Issues that evolve around inhalant abuse indicate that more attention be given to factors such as lack of family support, family violence, lack of positive role models, poor parental supervision, parental drug use, breakdown of the extended family system, and low communal attachments. Equally important is the need to focus attention on inhalant users and abusers associations with different peer groups as well as media and subcultural influences on the initiation, continuation, escalation and cessation of inhalant use among individuals at risk of using other drugs, particularly women and minority youth.

Most of the studies that focus on cultural values, attitudes toward inhalant use, acculturation-related stress or loss of cultural identification of minority group individuals are outdated. No less important is the need for studies to examine the role of youth rebelliousness, deviance and criminal activities pertaining to inhalant use. Because it is a worldwide problem, additional studies must address the existence of multinational subcultures of inhalant users and crosscultural etiologies (local, endemic or worldwide), worldwide drug availability and distribution networks, and international attitudes pertaining to the use of inhalants.

Clearly, studies that test psychological, developmental and psychopathological models would help us to understand factors that cause low self-esteem, depression, aggressive behavior and ineffective coping styles among inhalant abusers. Also, more must be learned about high-risk minority children who do not abuse drugs. These studies are necessary for future policy and practice efforts because they could lead to the early identification of people at-risk of inhalant use or identification of the motivating factors responsible for the cessation of inhalant use. Similar to studies that research crack and Ritalin use, some attention should be focused on the etiological relationship between inhalant-using youths and learning disabilities. These studies could focus on identifying early childhood behaviors and characteristics of high-risk inhalant abusers, such as attention deficit disorders, hyperactivity and learning deficits.

There is a great need for inhalant abuse intervention research that incorporates scientific approaches that target causes and the progression of chronic inhalant use. Cluster outreach models should be designed to focus on individual, family, peer networks and community (school, workplace, neighborhood) dimensions of inhalant abuse. The primary goals of these intervention research efforts could be to develop a scientifically sound knowledge base concerning the efficacy and effectiveness of specific inhalant abuse prevention policies and programs, and to develop and test innovative intervention strategies. Of all the areas of clinical and basic research, the treatment of inhalant abuse, especially solvent abuse, is one of the most inadequately studied aspects of inhalant abuse. Health service researchers should be given more funds to analyze the existing therapeutic approaches and to suggest new strategies to deal with inhalant abusers.

Central to these studies should be a focus on inhalant abuse treatment designed specifically for young children, older adolescents, and chemically dependent pregnant woman as well as individuals with co-occurring medical and/or mental disorders. Relatedly, youths involved in criminal activities and under the supervision of juvenile justice authorities should be high priority research populations. Emphasis could be placed on evaluating counseling, psychotherapy, family and group therapy, social skills training, acupuncture and medication as relevant approaches to the treatment of inhalant abusive youths.

Outreach strategies, home visitations and extensive case management also should be examined in terms of keeping inhalant-dependent persons of all ages in treatment and rehabilitation programs until they are discharged by agency staff following successful treatments. For policymakers and practitioners, there is a clear need for researchers to examine the form and extent to which professional, political, economic and administrative factors relate influence and impact the accessibility, accountability and effectiveness of therapeutic programs and support services.

Additionally, research should be directed towards developing helpful screening techniques, including biological (e.g., brainstem evoked responses) and other creative measures. Other studies should identify pre-existing neurobiological, psychosocial and environmental factors that significantly impact on treatment outcomes. In terms of clinical and laboratory methodologies, there is an uncontested need to develop improved methods of detecting and treating medical conditions associated with inhalant abuse. Social epidemiological and clinical studies ought to be developed to improve methods of detecting and differentiating types of inhalant use, especially long-term use.

Not less important is the need to clarify the role of psychiatric disorders as both a cause and a consequence of inhalant abuse. This would entail developing and testing neuropsychological interventions and related techniques that allow practitioners to differentiate the effects of inhalants from other drugs. In short, further research is needed to incorporate epidemiological, clinical and natural history approaches to evaluate the medical sequelae and neuropsychological/neuropsychiatric consequences of inhalant use. Several medical sequelae, including hearing loss, neurological degeneration, metabolic acidosis, and loss of cerebral functions, have been correlated with inhalant abuse.

As a growing number of substances in various products are being abused, animal studies of these substances need to be correlated with human studies. This is especially true for identifying various clinical syndromes that include: measures of acute and long-term irreversible neurological effects, clarification of the role of psychiatric disorders as both a cause and a consequence of inhalant abuse, and improved methods for evaluating the physiological effects of inhalants in human subjects. An unrelenting concern of this chapter is the need for carefully designed and correctly conducted investigations about inhalant abuse and its etiological, epidemiological, psychosocial, developmental and socioenvironmental dimensions. Measured responses and accountable programs require data heretofore unavailable or incomplete for sustainable comprehensive federal, state and local planning efforts. In summary, more must be done to stimulate basic social sciences and applied research in this area so that sustained, substantive and useful interventions can be utilized.

REFERENCES

Ackerly, W.C. & Gibson, G. (1964). Lighter fluid "sniffing." *American Journal of Psychiatry, 120*(11), 1056–1061, 1964.

Albaugh, B. & Albaugh, P. (1979). Alcoholism and substance sniffing among the Cheyenne and Arapaho Indians of Oklahoma. *International Journal of the Addictions, 14*(7), 1001–1007.

Anderson, H.R.& Macnair, R.G. (1985). Ramsey, J.D. Deaths from abuse of volatile substances: A national epidemiological study. *British Medical Journal, 290,* 304–307.

Barnes, G.E. (1979). Solvent abuse: A review. *International Journal of the Addictions, 14*(1), 1–26.

Barrett, M.E. & Joe, G.W. (1990). Simpson, D.D. *Acculturation Influences on Inhalants: A Four-year Followup of Mexican American Youth.* Fort Worth: Texas Christian University, Institute of Behavioral Research.

Bass, M. (1984). Abuse of inhalation anesthetics. *Journal of the American Medical*

Association, 25(5), 604.

Beauvais, F. (1992). Volatile solvent abuse: Trends and patterns. In C. Sharp, F. Beauvais & R. Spence (Eds.), *National Institute on Drug Abuse Research Monograph 129: Inhalant Abuse, A Volatile Research Agenda.* Rockville, MD: National Institute on Drug Abuse.

Beauvais, F. & Oetting, E.R. (1987). Toward a clear definition of inhalant use. In the *International Journal of the Addictions, 22*, 779–784.

Chadwick, O. Anderson, H. (1989) Neuropsychological consequences of volatile solvent abuse: A review. *Human Toxicology, 8*, 307–312.

Cohen, S. (1973). The volatile solvents. *Public Health Review, 2*, 185–214.

Compton, W., Cottler, L., Dinwiddie, S. et al., (1994). Inhalant use: Characteristics and predictions. *The American Journal on Addictions, 3*, 263–273.

Cunningham, S.R., Dalzell, G.W., McGirr, P. & Khan, M.M. (1987). Myocardial infarction and primary ventricular fibrillation after glue sniffing. *British Journal of Industrial Medicine, 294*, 739–740.

DeBarona, M.S. & Simpson, D.D. (1984). Inhalant users in drug abuse prevention programs. *American Journal of Drug & Alcohol Abuse, 10* (4), 503–518.

Dinwiddie, S.H. Zormuski, C.F. & Rubin, E.H. (1987). Psychiatric correlates of chronic solvent abuse. *Journal of Clinical Psychiatry, 48*, 334–337.

Farabee, D. (1995). *Substance Use Among Female Inmates Entering the Texas Department of Criminal Justice–Institutional Division: 1993.* Austin: Texas Commission on Alcohol and Drug Abuse.

Fejer, D. & Smart, R. (1973). The knowledge about drugs, attitudes towards them and drug use rates of high school students. *Journal of Drug Education, 2*(4), 377–388.

Fischman, C.M. & Oster, J.R. (1979). Toxic effects of toluene: a new cause of high anion gap metabolic acidosis. *Journal of the American Medical Association, 241*, 1713–1715.

Fredlund, E.V., Spencer, R.T., Maxwell, J.C. & Kavinsky, J.A. (1990). *Substance Abuse Among Youth Entering Texas Youth Commission Reception Facilities: Executive Summary.* Austin, TX: Texas Commission on Alcohol and Drug Abuse.

Garriotti, J.C. (1990). Death Among Inhalant Abusers. Paper presented at the Inhalant Abuse Research Symposium, Houston, Texas.

Goetz, C.G. (1985). Organic solvents. In C.G. Goetz (Ed.), *Neurotoxins in Clinical Practice* (65–90), Jamaica, NY: Spectrum.

Linden, C. (1990). Volatile substances of abuse. *Emergency Medicine Clinics of North America, 8*, 559–577.

Liu, L. & Maxwell, J. (1995). *1994 Texas School Survey of Substance Use Among Students: Grades 7–12,* Austin: Texas Commission on Alcohol and Drug Abuse.

Lockhart, W.H. & Lennox, M. The extent of solvent abuse in a regional secure unit sample. *Journal of Adolescence, 6*, 43–45.

Mata, A.G., Jr. & Andrew, S.R. Inhalant abuse in a small rural south Texas community: A social epidemiological overview. In R. Crider & B. Rouse (Eds.), *National Institute on Drug Abuse Research Monograph 85: Epidemiology of Inhalant Abuse: An Update.* Washington, DC: U.S. Government Printing Office.

Maxwell, J.C. (1994). *Substance Abuse Trends in Texas.* Rockville, MD: National

Institute on Drug Abuse.

National Institute on Drug Abuse. (1999). *National Household Survey on Drug Abuse: Main Findings, 1998.* Washington, DC: U.S. Department of Health and Human Services.

National Institute on Drug Abuse. (1996). *Monitoring the Future Study.* Washington, DC: U.S. Department of Health and Human Services.

Oetting, E.R., Edwards, R.W. & Beauvais, F. (1988). Social and psychological factors underlying inhalant abuse. In *National Institute on Drug Abuse Research Monograph 85: Epidemiology of Inhalant Abuse: An Update.* (172–203). Washington, DC: U.S. Government Printing Office.

Oetting, E.R. & Webb, J. (1992). Psychosocial Characteristics and their links with inhalants: A research agenda. In C. Sharp, F. Beauvais & R. Spence (Eds.), *National Institute on Drug Abuse Research Monograph 129: Inhalant Abuse, A Volatile Research Agenda.* Rockville, MD: National Institute on Drug Abuse.

Parker, S. (1989). Use and abuse of volatile substances in industry. *Human Toxicology, 8,* 271–275, 1989.

Pryor, G.T., Bingham, L.R. & Howd, R.A. (1978a). Behavioral toxicology in rats of a mixture of solvents containing substances subject to inhalation abuse by humans. *Toxicology & Applied Pharmacology, 45,* 252 (abstract), 1978a.

Pryor, G.T., Howd, R.A., Malik, R.J. et al. (1978b). *Biomedical Studies in the Effects of Abused Inhalant Mixtures.* Annual Report No. 2, Rockville, MD: National Institute on Drug Abuse.

Ron, M.A. (1986). Volatile substance abuse: A review of possible long term neurological, intellectual and psychiatric sequelae. *British Journal of Psychiatry, 148,* 235–246.

Rosenberg, N. & Sharp, C. (1992). Solvent toxicity: A neurological focus. In C. Sharp, F. Beauvais & R. Spence (Eds.) *National Institute on Drug Abuse Research Monograph 129: Inhalant Abuse. A Volatile Research Agenda* (pp. 117–172). Rockville, MD: National Institute on Drug Abuse.

Rosenberg, N.L. (1990). Neurotoxicity from Solvent Inhalant Abuse and Occupational Exposure to Solvents. Paper presented at the Inhalant Abuse Research Symposium, Houston, Texas. June.

Schutz, C. Chilcoat, H. & Anthony, J. (1994). The association between sniffing inhalants and injecting drugs. *Comprehensive Psychiatry, 35,* 99–105.

Sharp, C.W., Beauvais, F. & Spence, R.E. (Eds). (1992). *Inhalant Abuse: A Volatile Research Agenda, NIDA Research Monograph 129.* Rockville, MD: National Institute on Drug Abuse.

Sharp, C. & Rosenberg, N. (1996). Inhalant related disorders. In A. Tasman, J. Kay & J. Liebermana (Eds.) *In Psychiatry: Volume 1* (p. 835). Philadelphia: W.B. Saunders.

Spotts, J.V. & Shontz, F.C. (1982). Ego development, dragon fights, and chronic drug abusers. *International Journal of the Addictions, 17,* 945–976.

Streicher, H.Z., Gabow, P.A., Moss, A.H. et al., (1981). Syndromes of toluene sniffing in adults. *Annals of Internal Medicine, 94*(6), 758–762.

Stybel, L.J., Allen, P. & Lewis, F. (1976). Deliberate hydrocarbon inhalation among low socioeconomic adolescents not necessarily apprehended by the police. *International Journal of the Addictions, 11,* 345–361.

Swadi, H. (1996). Psychiatric symptoms in adolescents who abuse volatile substances. *Addiction Research, 4,* 1–9.

Taher, S.M., Anderson, R.J., McCartney, R. et al. (1974). Rental tabular acidosis associated with toluene "sniffing." *New England Journal of Medicine, 290,* 765–768.,

Wallisch, L. (1998). *1996 Texas Survey of Substance Use Among Adults.* Austin: Texas Commission on Alcohol and Drug Abuse.

Watson, J.M. (1979). Morbidity and mortality statistics on solvent abuse. *Medical Science & Law, 19*(4), 246–252.

PART V

NATIVE AMERICANS

Chapter 13

TRENDS IN DRUG ABUSE AMONG NATIVE AMERICANS

ELAINE ZAHND, SUE HOLTBY, AND DORIE KLEIN D. CRIM

In assessing the trends of alcohol and other drug use (AOD) among Native Americans,[1] common assumptions about nationwide widespread alcoholism is one of the first misunderstandings to be confronted. Tribes are extremely diverse, with a variety of histories, cultural and spiritual traditions, economic resources, as well as different AOD use patterns. Comparing the two states with the largest Native American populations, California and Oklahoma, offers a prime example of those differences. While Indians in Oklahoma are primarily members of large federally-recognized tribes, California's Native American population is highly urbanized, and is comprised of tribes from all over the United States. California is also home to a smaller rural population of indigenous tribes who live in isolated rancherias, tribal lands, and nearby towns (Goldberg-Ambrose & Champagne, 1996). Trying to describe typical patterns of Native American use on a national level proves difficult because of these tribal and demographic differences. Thus, while national statistics provide general insights on Native American AOD use patterns, they often mask tribal diversity, as has been the case with other ethnically aggregated data (May, 1996). Furthermore, the deeply ingrained historic stereotype of the "drunken Indian" does little to promote understanding of the actual realities facing Native Americans and their current AOD use patterns.

In reviewing overall patterns of AOD use among Native Americans nationwide, three broad socioeconomic, cultural and demographic trends form the basis for better understanding. First, Native Americans face the continued challenge of high poverty rates nationwide. Historically, they have been outside the economic mainstream, and their marginalization has resulted in widespread poverty and the attendant social problems. Native American health and socioeconomic indicators, while improving overall, continue to lag significantly behind those of the general population, with the lag growing for some indicators (Young, 1996). For example, annual mean income for Native Americans fell from 62 percent of Whites' in 1979 to 55 percent in 1989 (Gregory et al., 1996). Their households, compared to all households, are considerably poorer, and more likely to be female-headed (Indian Health Service, 1994; Sandefur & Liebler, 1996) than U.S. households in general. The second factor is the demographic composition of the Native American population. Their communities are fast-growing, young populations.

Youthful patterns of AOD experimentation, when combined with poverty and alienation, may lead to substance-related harms. At the same time, the desire for educational and economic opportunity and success are part of the community's vision of a better future for Native American youth. The third influential factor is a trend toward incorporating cultural, traditional and spiritual activities into alcohol and drug prevention and treatment and approaches. In many cases, these have taken the form of intertribal activities, especially in places like California, where programs often serve people of many different tribes (Zahnd et al., 1999). Balancing the desire for mainstream economic and educational success with the desire to hold onto their cultural and spiritual traditions provides both strength and conflict for many Native Americans as they struggle to succeed in "two separate worlds."

Within this overall context, this chapter describes recent trends in Native American alcohol and other drug use, and discusses some of the methodological issues inherent in conducting research with this population. The first sections summarize the literature on patterns of alcohol and drug use among American Indian adults, women and youth, respectively. These are followed by a description of that a specific focus on women. The final part of the chapter concludes with a discussion of protective factors and community strengths that may mitigate alcohol and drug-related problems.

Our knowledge of Native American alcohol problems is bounded by the limited research to date. Because Native Americans constitute less than 1 percent of the U.S. population, and they are increasingly dispersed geographically, obtaining reliable population estimates from reporting systems and research studies is difficult. For example, regularly conducted national surveys such as the National Health Interview Survey (NHIS), Behavioral Risk Factor Surveillance System (BRFSS), and the National Health and Nutrition Examination Survey I and II (NHANES), which ask about alcohol, drug and tobacco use, do not provide separate estimates for American Indian/Alaska Natives. They are included in the "other" category, effectively eliminating meaningful data. In some cases, researchers report Native

American data as raw numbers, percentages and confidence intervals, and discuss the findings with appropriate cautionary comments (Burhansstipanov & Satter, 2000).

The difficulty of obtaining robust samples of Native Americans is addressed in two ways. Some researchers combine data over several years to obtain large enough sample sizes for meaningful analysis, and thus provide trend use data (Denny & Holtzman, 1999; Greenfield & Smith, 1999). Other researchers focus on state, regional or local level samples because smaller scale surveys, involving tribal, reservation, agency-based, in-depth ethnographic or clinical samples are often the only effective ways to survey hard-to-reach populations. Most Indian-specific research has been carried out in the Indian Health Service Areas (IHS) of the Southwest, Northern Plains, and Oklahoma, as well as Alaska. It should be noted that the IHS does not provide full national coverage and is limited in actual service to about 62 percent of all American Indians (Snipp, 1996), disproportionately enrolled members of federally-recognized Western tribes.

Of eight Indian-specific surveys of drinking recently summarized by May (1996), the majority are now over ten years old and are of reservation populations. Little research has been carried out in cities, and even less in urban areas outside IHS centers. There have also been few studies in rural non-reservation regions, particularly among smaller and nonfederally-recognized tribes. Yet Indians' lives are increasingly mobile and heterogeneous; their experiences are no longer confined to life on the reservations and nearby cities. In addition, a large proportion of Indians marry outside their tribe or marry non-Indians. Researchers are just now beginning to examine drinking and drug use among Indians of mixed tribes or ethnicities (May & Gossage, 1999). And much of the early historical and anthropological source documents on Native Americans have been found to be of little use in tracking trends, given their stereotyped views of American Indian drinking (e.g., "firewater" myths, etc.) (May, 1996).

ADULT DRINKING AND DRUG USE PATTERNS

One of the primary sources of AOD that use data in the U.S. is the National Household Survey on Drug Abuse (NHSDA). The NHSDA combined data from 1991 to 1993 on Native Americans and found higher rates of both heavy drinking[2] and drug use[3] among Indians, when compared to the general U.S. population. Almost seven percent of American Indians reported past month heavy drinking compared to 5.3 percent of the general population. The contrast for past month drug use was even greater, with 11.3 percent of Indians reporting such use compared to 5.6 percent of the general

U.S. population. Native American heavy drinking rates ranked second among the nine ethnic groups surveyed, and their drug use ranked first (U.S. Substance Abuse and Mental Health Service Administration, 1991 to 1993). While the comparative figures give cause for concern, the data also shows that the majority of American Indians do not report either current heavy drinking or illicit drug use.

Chronic drinking patterns[4] were surveyed by combining 1993 to 1996 Behavioral Risk Factor Surveillance System (BRFSS) data as part of a health status report on Native Americans. The findings suggest that Indians self-report higher rates of chronic drinking (4.5%) than all U.S. races combined (2.8%), with approximately six times as many American Indian men as women reporting chronic drinking (8.0% vs. 1.3%). Similarly, Native American men and women are more likely to report cigarette smoking than men and women of all races (32.6% vs. 22.4%) (Denny & Holtzman, 1999).

Of particular concern when reviewing patterns of Native American alcohol use is the rate of binge drinking.[5] According to the BRFSS health status report cited above, both American Indian men and women were more likely to be binge drinkers than men and women of all races in the general U.S. population. Specifically, 28.1 percent of American Indian men reported such behavior compared to 21.3 percent of men of all races, while 9.6 percent of American Indian women reported past month binge drinking compared to 6.9 percent of women of all races (Denny & Holtzman, 1999). Recent research suggests that chronic heavy binge drinking may be more socially and even physiologically harmful than regular heavy drinking. This finding, if valid, has enormous implications for prevention. In numerous surveys of Native Americans, modal weekly frequency of drinking is low to moderate (e.g., one to two times), while number of drinks per occasion is high (e.g., well over five) (Klein et al., 1995; Zahnd & Klein, 1997). May (1996) summarizes American Indian surveys as finding "a tendency toward heavy binge drinking (more than five drinks per episode) and highly adverse results from drinking" (p. 240). In an Oklahoma household survey (Smith et al., 1995), of the women who reported drinking, 26 percent of the American Indians compared to 15 percent of the women overall had drunk five or more drinks during an occasion in the past month. For men, the comparable percentages were 38 percent of the American Indians and 30 percent of all men.

While Native Americans have, on average, higher rates of problem alcohol and drug use than the general population, it must be emphasized that heavy or binge drinking is by no means universally found in Indian country. First, studies have found sizable differences in regional and tribal drinking patterns, and tribal alcohol-related morbidity and mortality rates, which interact with gender and age effects (Christian et al., 1989). No elevated rates of alcohol-related problems have been found in some tribes in Oklahoma and the Southwest, whereas serious problems have been found among other tribes in those same areas, as well as tribes in the Northern Plains. Studies show that these same Northern Plains reservations have extremely high homicide rates, while many Southwestern reservations do not (Armstrong et al., 1996b). The other important factor is that even in tribes with high rates of drinking problems, there are sizable numbers of abstainers, including lifelong abstainers and former heavy drinkers.

NATIVE AMERICAN WOMEN'S DRUG USE PATTERNS

Results of a current pilot study on substance-related violence affecting low-income American Indian women in urban and rural nonreservation regions of California (N=110) suggest similar patterns of binge drinking. Women were surveyed at American Indian health and social service agencies, excluding AOD or domestic violence programs. A total of 43 in-state and out-of-state tribes were represented, and all respondents were queried about their AOD use patterns. While 19 percent of the women currently abstained from drinking, 18 percent reported drinking five or more drinks as their usual number of drinks[6] on recent drinking occasions, and 31 percent reported problem drinking as measured by the CAGE[7] or self-identification as having a drinking problem in the past 12 months (Zahnd et al., unpublished, 2000). Asked about the greatest number of drinks consumed in one day in the past 12 months, 15 percent reported 12 or more, 12 percent reported drinking between eight and 11 drinks, and 19 percent reported drinking between four and seven drinks. Eight percent had drank 24 or more drinks in one day during the past 12 months. In addition, over 35 percent reported being drunk more than six times in the past 12 months, and 15 percent of the sample reported having a problem with alcohol in the past 12 months (Zahnd et al., unpublished, 2000).

This study also found widespread drug use and self-reported drug problems among Native American women. Marijuana was the most commonly cited drug, with 25 percent reporting use in the past 12 months, and six percent reporting use in the past 30 days. Methamphetamine was the second most commonly reported drug; 17.3 percent of the sample reported past 12 month use, while four percent reported using it in the past 30 days. The third most commonly cited drug was cocaine or crack, with 14 percent of the sample using it in the past 12 months, and five percent in the past 30 days. Smaller numbers reported tranquilizer, inhalant or heroin use. Almost 25 percent of the sample said they should cut down on the their use, and 17 percent reported having a problem with drugs in the past 12 months (Zahnd et al., unpublished, 2000). This is the same as the proportion of women who said they have a drinking problem. A concurrent study of toxicology screening results for pregnant patients in Indian Health Service clinics found a 26 percent positive rate for alcohol or illicit drugs (Epstein & Mader, 1996). This replicated earlier surveys of these clinics, finding up to a third of pregnant patients reporting prenatal alcohol or drug use, and up to half tobacco use (CAIHS, 1994). In a study of the impact of warning labels on alcohol consumption among pregnant American Indian and African American drinkers, 21 percent of the American Indian women reported drinking during pregnancy, and half of those had drank three or more drinks on at least one occasion during the pregnancy (Kaskutas, 1992).

High AOD rates were also found in an earlier California-based study, which collected information on self-reported needs, problems and concerns of American Indian/Alaska Native women who were pregnant and/or parenting young children (Klein et al. 1995a; Zahnd & Klein, 1997). A total of 290 urban and rural respondents were sampled for that study, using tribal and community-specific clinics and other agencies. Women from over 90 tribes were included. A screening threshold for at-risk problem drinking or drug use was developed.[8] Of the 290 respondents, 171 (59%) screened into the subsample of at-risk users (Zahnd & Klein, 1997; Klein et al., 1995a). These at-risk women were then asked if they had ever consumed five or more drinks on one occasion during the past (or pre-conceptual) 12-month period; 78 percent (n=134) responded affirmatively. The majority of these (61%) in fact drank five or more drinks on one drinking occasion at least weekly. Most importantly, the median number of usual drinks reported per drinking occasion by the screened-in sample was 5.75 (Zahnd & Klein, 1997). Drug use was also queried. Among the 171 at-risk women, of all drugs used, marijuana was the most common, with 75 percent of the 171 reporting lifetime use, followed by methamphetamine (55%), hallucinogens (33%), crack cocaine (20%) and inhalants (10%). Over 10 percent had injected drugs in their lifetime. During the past or pre-conceptual three months, marijuana was again the most commonly used drug (51%), followed by methamphetamine (35%). Among the nonpregnant screened-in subsample (n=115), past-30-day marijuana use was reported by 46 percent, and methamphetamine by 28 percent (Zahnd & Klein, 1997).

In this study, rural women were as likely as urban women to report AOD use. More screened-in at-risk women in the rural region reported having five or more drinks on one occasion in the past/prior 12 months (87%) than did those in the urban region (69%). For drug use, rural women reported somewhat more frequent marijuana use during the previous three months (56%) than did urban women (46%), as well as more methamphetamine use (42% rural vs. 28% urban). More urban than rural women reported using other drugs, notably crack (9% urban vs. 1% rural) or powder cocaine (15% urban vs. 4% rural) (Zahnd & Klein, 1997). Providers' surveys in rural and semi-rural clinics serving pregnant or parenting American Indian women have estimated that about half of them were affected by family or intergenerational substance abuse (Stone, 1994) and similar percentages have had a partner with a drinking or other drug problem (Hussong et al., 1993).

The bimodal pattern of alcohol use described in the previous section may be even more pronounced among women than among men. For example, a household survey in Oklahoma (Smith et al., 1995) found that only 23 percent of Indian women and 40 percent of Indian men had drank in the previous month, compared to 28 percent of all women and 44 percent of all men statewide. On many reservations, studies show that a sizable proportion of Fetal Alcohol Syndrome children were siblings, suggesting a concentration of heavy prenatal maternal drinking (May et al., 1983).[9] A "maturing out" effect for older American Indian women and men (Kunitz & Levy, 1994; May, 1996; Mail & Johnson, 1993) has been noted to parallel "maturing out" patterns of heavy substance use in the general population.

RECENT FINDINGS ON NATIVE AMERICAN YOUTH DRUG USE PATTERNS

While reliable national surveys of substance use prevalence in the general population of American Indian adolescents are rare, the research cited in this section does provide reliable estimates of trends in Indian youth's alcohol and drug use. According to these studies, there has been some recent diminution in drug use among Native American in-school adolescents, as there has been for other in-school adolescents. However, Indian teenagers continue to have higher rates than teenagers of other ethnic groups. Surveys of national samples of Indian adolescents suggest a potentially dangerous binge drinking pattern among many (Mail & Johnson, 1993), and they indicate that many youth begin experimenting with alcohol, inhalants and other drugs at an early age (Beauvais, 1992; Beauvais et al., 1989). There continues to be a subgroup of adolescents, including many school dropouts, who heavily use drugs, including alcohol and the dangerous inhalants (glue, gasoline, etc.) as well as marijuana (Beauvais, 1996). This pattern is also true for California American Indian youth (Austin et al., 1993).

More comprehensive behavioral health surveys of American Indian and youth of other ethnicities have also found higher rates of co-occurring mental health problems among the Indian youth (Beals et al., 1997; Blum et al., 1992). Use of tobacco, in both chewed and smoked forms, is extraordinarily high among Native adolescents, exceeding 50 percent in some communities in California (Bruerd, 1990; Hodge et al., 1994). With respect to young women's use, some recent surveys of Native American adolescents have found overall prevalence of drinking by girls to approach that of boys (Mail & Johnson, 1993), and to exceed that of girls from any other ethnic group (Weibel-Orlando, 1986/1987).

SUBSTANCE-RELATED HARMS AMONG NATIVE AMERICANS

Alcohol-related problems appear to have a sizable impact on Indian morbidity and mortality (May, 1996; Young, 1996). The four leading causes of death for Native Americans ages 25 to 44 are, respectively, accidents (many related to alcohol), liver disease and cirrhosis (directly caused by alcohol), homicide, and suicide (many of the latter two related to alcohol) (Indian Health Service, 1994). Overall, the Indian Health Service calculated that 1989-1991 age-adjusted American Indian alcohol-caused mortality rates were 430 percent higher than for the total U.S. population (Indian Health Service, 1994). Healthy People 2000 and 2010 goals consequently set special objectives for American Indians for reductions in cirrhosis, Fetal Alcohol Syndrome, drug-related deaths, and alcohol-related vehicle crashes. In addition, there are special goals for decreases in other alcohol- and drug-related injury, including male partners' physical abuse of women, homicide, and accidents. While Indian male rates of alcohol-related morbidity and mortality substantially exceed female rates, Indian women's rates are nevertheless far higher than those of the general female population (Indian Health Service, 1994). Testimony to the U. S. House of Representatives in 1986 put cirrhosis as accounting for one out of five deaths of Native American women ages 35 to 44 (Moss, 1993). An analysis of 1970s-era cirrhosis deaths among American Indians found that half occurred among women (Mail & Johnson, 1993).

Similarly, a report to Congress by Indian Health Services on health needs in California, found that "tobacco and alcohol use are having a devastating impact on the health of California Indians," and that 40 percent of deaths are attributable to smoking and nearly that proportion to drinking (U.S. Department of Health, 1991, pp. 4, 59). The deaths directly attributable to alcohol include vehicle crashes, which disproportionately affect adolescents and young adults, and those from cirrhosis and other liver diseases, which can strike adults in their prime if they are long-time heavy drinkers.

Data also suggest potentially high rates of violence in American Indian communities, which are frequently alcohol-related. Homicide death rates for Indians in IHS areas exceed those of the total population in all age groups and in both genders. For example, for females ages 15 to 24, the rates per 100,000 for 1989–1991 were 8.3 for Indians and 6.3 for all females; for females ages 25 to 34, 12.8 and 7.2 respectively; for females 35 to 44, 10.1 and 4.8 (Indian Health Service, 1994). Considering both violent and alcohol-related official arrest data, Silverman summarizes comparative studies since World War II as generally showing disproportionate Indian rates compared to the total population. In 1990, Native American arrests per 100,000 were 6,256.8, compared to 4,483.7 for the total population (Silverman, 1996). Figures on prison inmates show that Native American women and men are overrepresented (Hutton et al., 1996; Lujan, 1995), particularly in large reservation states. For the larger reservations reporting on their own judicial systems, the most common misdemeanor offenses found in a 1996 survey are disorderly conduct, simple assault and battery, intoxication, and driving under the influence (Zion & Zion, 1996). Tribal judges report that most offenses "involve alcohol abuse and personal violence among families, relatives, and members of the community. Crime on Indian reservations often makes victims of people who are in continuing relationships with the perpetrators of given offenses" (Zion & Zion, 1996, p. 102).

A study using trend data from BRFSS found that 3.7 percent of men of all races reported driving under the influence at least once in the previous month, while 4.7 percent of American Indian men did. Regional variation in the Indian sample ranged from 3.0 percent in the Southwest to 6.7 percent in the Northern Plains (Denny & Holtzman, 1999). Alcohol and other drug use also appear to be a factors in violent victimization against American Indians. Another previously cited study using trend data suggests that perceived offender AOD use was a factor in 57 percent of the violent crimes perpetrated against American Indians (Greenfeld & Smith, 1999). Perpetrator AOD use was less likely to be reported in violent crimes committed against Whites (44%) or Blacks (35%). While the majority of violent crime reported did not involve either alcohol or drugs, perceived alcohol use by the aggressor was reported by 38 percent of Native American victims compared to 29 percent of Whites, 21 percent of Blacks, and 20 percent of Asians (Greenfeld & Smith, 1999).

Focusing on substance-related harms affecting Native American women, many reported in a previously cited California study having experienced negative consequences from their substance use. Unsurprisingly, 68 percent of a sample that had screened in for heavy or problem AOD use (N=171) reported experiencing an alcohol-related problem in general, or a specific negative consequence of drinking (e.g., arrest, abuse) (Zahnd & Klein, 1997; Klein et al., 1995). When asked about drugs, 44 percent acknowledged a substance-related consequence. For alcohol, the most commonly named consequence was being hurt, beaten or taken advantage of. The Indian women in the study reported more alcohol- than drug-related problems overall, including more alcohol- than drug-related arrests (Klein et al., 1995; Zahnd et al., in press; Zahnd & Klein, 1997). Violence also emerged as a major issue in this study. Large numbers of the at-risk users reported personal experiences of lifetime victimization. Asked if they had ever been attacked with a gun, knife or other weapon, 43% (n=74) responded affirmatively. Even more (64%; n=109) reported they had been attacked with the intent to seriously injure, without a weapon. Asked if anyone had ever made them engage in a sexual act through force or threat of force, 36% responded affirmatively.[10] In fact, almost half affirmed having sought police help or a restraining order for domestic violence. Large numbers also reported having been victimized prior to age 18, and the majority said they had "big problems growing up." These included physical and sexual abuse, family alcohol or drug use, and loss of or separation from parents.

At the community level, when asked whether fighting or violence was a problem among people they knew when people drank, 83% of the screened-in sample (n=141) responded affirmatively. When asked whether fighting or violence was a problem among people they knew when people used or dealt drugs, 78% (n=133) said yes (Klein et al., 1995a; Zahnd et al., in press; Zahnd & Klein, 1997). With respect to the influence of violence on women's own drinking patterns, in a Western study of American Indian clinic patients, 65 percent of the domestic violence counselees report having alcohol problems, compared to 39 percent of other sampled clinic patients (Norton & Manson, 1995). A study of female client records in IHS treatment centers notes that over three-fourths had experienced childhood physical or sexual abuse and adult domestic violence (Center for Reproductive Health Policy Research, 1995). Kunitz and Levy, in their longitudinal study of Navajo drinking, present case studies of female alcoholics with harsh and tragic histories of parental abandonment, paternal sexual abuse, rape, spousal battering, loss of children, sibling illness and death, injuries, and chronic sickness. These women understandably report drinking in order to feel better (Kunitz & Levy, 1994).

The association between drinking and violence is not limited to Native American women (Zahnd et al., 1997). Miller and colleagues have consistently found higher rates of victimization among substance-involved non-Indian women they have interviewed in treatment clinics, drinking-driver programs, criminal justice inmates, shelter residents, mental health clients, and household controls (Miller et al., 1989; Miller, 1990; Miller, 1996). In the majority of cases, male partners also engaged in heavy drinking. Furthermore, there is mounting evidence that women frequently drink and use drugs heavily as a means of self-medication following physical or sexual abuse, as noted above for Indian women (Kilpatrick, 1993; Miller, 1990; Miller et al., 1993; Widom, 1993).

Concerning American Indian women's strategies for managing alcohol-related problems, an ethnographic study from the 1970s describes Indian women's coping with male drinking in a rural Western community (Leland, 1978). The older women appeared to have accepted the men's weekend drinking, whereas younger women often engaged in informal social control over the men's excesses through networking with other women, and a few women regularly joined their men in drinking. These coping styles appeared to be similar for both the roughly one-third of the women who reported rarely drinking themselves, for the third who drank (sometimes heavily) on occasions, and for the third who drank both heavily and frequently. Research among older female Navajo drinkers documents many women who originally drank "to keep my husband company" (Kunitz & Levy, 1994). However, given the contemporary shifts in most women's lives, with greater independence and earlier onset of social drinking, fewer young women today may report these patterns. Overall, much of our knowledge on this topic to date comes primarily from fiction and autobiographical literature. While there has been a paucity of behavioral research, such phenomena are common historic and contemporary themes in Native American women's novels.

The bimodal pattern of problem drinking discussed earlier (i.e., significant proportions of both problem drinkers and abstainers in the population) does not mean an absence of negative effects for the abstainers and light drinkers. The toll exacted by heavy drinking and substance-related harms among Indian families, partners and friends is felt by substance users and nonusers alike (Kunitz & Levy, 1994; Leland, 1978). Even members of tribes without historical drinking problems are affected, given today's mobility, intertribal families, and intertribal socializing. This may be particularly true for women, whose nurturing role is central to family and community.

In terms of harm to Indian children and youth, studies of child abuse and neglect suggest that although neglect is more common than physical or sexual abuse among Native Americans (DeBruyn et al., 1992), as is true for the general population, sexual abuse among American Indians appears to be underreported (Lujan et al., 1989). For American Indians (as for other groups), high proportions of abuse are found to be substance-related. In one case-control records study in the Southwest, of those formally identified as child abuse or neglect cases, over three-fourths included alcohol-involved incidents, and similar proportions of the parents or guardians have alcohol or drug problems (DeBruyn et al., 1992). However, the researchers also reported substance abuse problems in over half of the control group families.

There are also physiological and psychopharmacological vulnerabilities commonly found in abusive families that are related to, and exacerbated by, heavy drinking. An example is Fetal Alcohol Syndrome. Most heavy prenatal drinkers are themselves the children of heavy-drinking parents (May et al., 1983), and the problems inherent in intergenerational alcoholism are compounded by developmental disabilities that create special vulnerability to abuse (DeBruyn et al., 1992; LaDue et al., 1992; Lujan et al., 1989). Another common element is family disruption: an estimated one-fourth of all Indian children have been sent away from home at some point, to foster homes, boarding schools, or out-of-tribe adoption (Bachman, 1992).

There is, however, reason for optimism. The statistical trends in alcohol-related morbidity and mortality among American Indians—like those of other Americans—have shown improvement in recent years (Young, 1993). American Indian rates remain elevated compared to the general population (Dumbauld et al., 1994; Institute for Health Policy Studies, 1992; U.S. Department of Health, 1991), but the trends are positive.

POSSIBLE CAUSES OF AOD PROBLEMS AMONG NATIVE AMERICANS

In attempting to identify possible distal causal factors of AOD-related problems, some scholars have argued that non-Indian-specific factors such as marginalization, racism and poverty are key (Robbins, 1979). AOD use patterns and problems are strongly, albeit complexly, correlated with socioeconomic status and ethnicity (Caetano & Herd, 1988; Wilsnack, 1996), as well as etiologically associated with such factors as anomie and powerlessness (Levinson, 1983; McClelland et al., 1972). Among Native Americans, the common pattern of heavy or binge drinking discussed earlier has been linked to a number of external factors: the prohibition of alcohol on many reservations which led to off-site drinking (Weibel-Orlando, 1986, 1987); Indians traditionally being unwelcome at local white-owned premises; and observation of white male drunken demeanor as the earliest encounters with alcohol use (Levy & Kunitz, 1974; MacAndrew & Edgerton, 1969; Mail & Johnson, 1993). Other researchers emphasize internal factors such as tribal social organization around hunting or agriculture that permitted periodic excesses (Levy & Kunitz, 1974; Young, 1993), and eventual association of these social occasions with cultural solidarity and resistance (Hodge, 1988; Weibel-Orlando, 1986, 1987). A visible and socially shared "drunken comportment" (MacAndrew & Edgerton, 1969) has been found in many of these intense, public drinking occasions, as observed by ethnographers (Marshall, 1983).

The particular form and effects of "internal colonialism" (Blauner, 1972) on Native Americans (e.g., forced reliance on government, jurisdictional disputes, dislocation) have been cited as the key to understanding the antecedents of substance-related problems such as social disorganization, culture conflict, and a particular subculture of violence (Bachman, 1991). A survey of Native American urban clinic patients in the Southwest found that alcohol abuse is associated with high stress levels, poverty, and cultural discontinuity (e.g., language) between reservation and city life (Joe & Miller, 1989). Psychologists have attributed self-destructive behaviors among American Indians to post-traumatic stress disorder resulting from conquest (Duran et al., 1994), and a survey of hospitalized veterans does find a higher prevalence of alcohol, drug and mental health disorders among the American Indian substance-dependent than non-Indian substance-dependent patients (Walker et al., 1994). It should be noted that post-traumatic stress disorder for women has been identified as a consequence of sexual and physical abuse among substance-involved women (Fullilove et al., 1994; Kilpatrick et al., 1989), but not necessarily among all abused women (Campbell et al., 1994).

Other scholars disagree with the emphasis on deficits. Green (1993) argues that more important in predicting problems today is the presence or absence of a strong ethnic identity as a resiliency factor. Some anthropologists (Levy & Kunitz, 1974) have focused on internal tribal cultural norms as causing certain styles of drunken behavior, including aggression. Research on ethnicity and alcohol problems among other groups has focused on the contributions of cultural traditionalism–generally seen as protective–and acculturation, which is often found to be a risk factor for alcohol problems, albeit in conjunction with other variables (Caetano, 1987). For Indians, the meanings and implications of traditionalism and acculturation are likely to differ from those drawn about immigrant populations. Other authors suggest developing less polarized ways of measuring the influences of traditionalism and acculturation (Joe & Miller, 1989; Oetting & Beauvais, 1989), and emphasize socioeconomic status as a potentially significant mediating variable. Green (1993) found, for example, that higher attachment to Native American traditions does not by itself predict lower rates of the problematic behaviors under discussion.

In examining the factors associated with alcohol and drug use among Native American youth, some research suggests that family circumstances are strongly influential, in addition to peer influences (Swaim et al., 1993). For example, "weekend partying" is often intergenerational (Bachman, 1992). Other explanations have pointed to genetics and other physiological characteristics, psychological and psychosocial development, culture, and socioeconomics (Beauvais & Segal, 1992). These widely-differing theories on the causes of AOD use among Indian youth are by no means always distinct or mutually exclusive. But from a psychosocial perspective, both family and peer relationships have been equally emphasized (Swaim et al., 1993).

Institutions that have been hypothesized to have major effects on young Indians' alcohol and drug use are reservations, schools, neighborhoods, religion or spirituality and, traditionalism (Zahnd et al., 1999). From a cultural perspective, it has been argued that promotion of the ability to thrive in both the Indian and mainstream worlds (referred to as bicultural competence) is of crucial importance to preventing substance abuse among Native Americans (LaFramboise & Rowe, 1983; Schinke et al., 1988).

CONCLUSION

It is difficult to obtain population-based statistics on Native American drinking and drug use patterns and associated harms because Indians comprise only one percent of the U.S. population, and they are no longer concentrated on reservations. In fact, less than one quarter of Indians now live on reservations. The majority live in large urban centers where they are geographically dispersed, making representative sampling extremely expensive. Sampling limitations notwithstanding, there are a number of reliable data sources that do allow us to assess trends in Native American drinking, drug use and related problems. These sources are based on national data that have been aggregated over several years, and smaller studies that focus on specific Native American communities.

Results indicate that, overall, American Indians continue to have higher rates of heavy or problem drinking and associated morbidity and mortality than the general population. In addition, most prevalence estimates indicate a bimodal drinking pattern among Indians; that is, significant proportions of both abstainers and problem drinkers. Among drinkers, binge drinking is common, and rates of interpersonal violence among Indians are well above the national norm. American Indian youth exhibit drinking trends that parallel those of adults, as do their trends in alcohol-related accidents. In addition, suicide and homicide are higher among young Indians than among other ethnic groups of the same age, although definitive links to alcohol use have not been reported in the literature.

In presenting trends in alcohol and drug use among Native Americans, it is important to note rates of use and problems vary markedly within the Indian population. Some regions and tribes have been affected by alcohol to a much greater extent that others. While self-report prevalence statistics and morbidity and mortality data show a *continuing* problem of alcohol abuse among segments of the Native American population, and to a lesser extent drug-related problems, there is reason for optimism. Alcohol and drug abuse prevention and treatment programs have become institutionalized in many Indian communities, and are increasingly incorporating Native American spiritual and lifestyle traditions into recovery modes. Some concentrate on the traditions of particular tribes, while others, particularly in California, have developed intertribal approaches to healing and revitalizing American Indian families and communities.

In assessing protective factors and community strengths, the rich cultural diversity of America's Indian tribes is at the forefront. Cultural strength is reflected in the tremendous variation in individual, familial, and community activities that emerge from a multitude of tribal traditions and practices. There are often strong extended family ties in Native American communities, which are deep sources of support (Center for Reproductive Health Policy Research, 1995). These ties constitute potential protective factors for many individuals, as well as encourage prevention and intervention strategies. Many Native American prevention and treatment activities today emphasize strengthening cultural cohesion as part of recovery. For example, the "Red Road" to sobriety incorporates spirituality in its approach (Rush, n.d.), and the "Sacred Circle" and "Sacred Hoop" emphasize social commitment as a means of achieving lifestyle changes. Abstinence from substance use, and nonviolence have been identified as traditional American Indian values, as in the well-known Alkali Lake experiment (Guillory et al., 1988). In short, the importance of a culturally specific approach to addressing Native American substance use cannot be overemphasized.

NOTES

1. The terms "American Indian," "American Indian/Alaska Native," or "Indian" are all commonly used by members of the Native American community, and thus will be used interchangeable with Native Americans in this chapter.
2. Heavy drinking was defined as five or more drinks per day on five or more days during the past thirty days.
3. Illicit drug use was defined as the nonmedical use of marijuana, cocaine, opiates, inhalants, hallucinogens or psychotherapeutics at least once during the past 30 days.
4. Chronic drinking was defined as the consumption of 60 or more alcoholic beverages in the past month.
5. Binge drinking is defined as the consumption of five or more alcoholic beverages on at least one occasion in the past month.
6. The percentage of women who responded affirmatively reported having five or more drinks "nearly all the time" or "more than half the time" on their usual drinking occasions in the past 12 months.
7. The CAGE is a validated quick assessment tool that measures problem use of alcohol. The four questions ask if the respondent felt she ought to cut down on her drinking, if the respondent was *annoyed* by people criticizing her drinking, if she ever felt *guilty* about her drinking, and if she ever had a drink first thing in the morning to get rid of a hangover *(eyeopener)*.

8. The screening threshold is described in detail in the author's 1995 publication (Klein et al., 1995b).
9. The prevalence of female abstention, with a resulting concentration of drinkers, has also been found among African-American women (Herd, 1988).
10. It should be noted that women were asked to include attacks and threats by family and intimates as well as strangers.

REFERENCES

Armstrong, T.L., Guilfoyle, M.H. & Melton, A. Pecos. (1996). Native American delinquency: An overview of prevalence, causes and correlates. In M.O. Nielson & R.A. Silverman (Eds.), *Native Americans: Crime and Justice* (pp. 75–88). Boulder, CO: Westview Press.

Austin, G. E. Oetting, E.R. & Beauvais, F. (1993). *Recent Research on Substance Abuse among American Indian Youth.* Los Alamitos, CA: Southwest Regional Educational Laboratory.

Bachman, R. (1991). An analysis of American Indian homicide: A test of social disorganization and economic deprivation at the reservation county level. *Journal of Research in Crime & Delinquency, 28*(4), 456–471.

Bachman, R. (1992). *Death and Violence on the Reservation: Homicide, Family Violence, and Suicide in American Indian Populations.* New York: Auburn House.

Beals, J., Piasecki, J., Nelson, S., Jones, M., Keane, E., Dauphinais, P., Red Shirt, R., Sack, W. & Manson, S. (1997). Psychiatric disorder among American Indian adolescents: Prevalence in Northern Plains youth. *Journal of American Academy of Child & Adolescent Psychiatry, 36*(9), 1252–1259.

Beauvais, F. (1992). Indian adolescent drug and alcohol use: Recent patterns and consequences. *American Indian and Alaska Native Mental Health Research Journal, 5*(1), 1–78.

Beauvais, F. & Segal, S. (1992). Integrated model for prevention and treatment of drug abuse among American Indian youth. *Journal of Addictive Diseases, 11*(3), 63–80.

Beauvais, F. (1996). Trends in drug use among American Indian students and dropouts, 1975–1994. *American Journal of Public Health, 86*(11), 1594–1598.

Beauvais, F., Oetting, E.R., Wolf, W. & Edwards, R.W. (1989). American Indian youth and drugs, 1975–1987: A continuing problem. *American Journal of Public Health 79*(5), 634–636.

Blauner, R. (1972). *Racial Oppression in America.* Chicago: University of Chicago Press.

Blum, W.R., Harris, L., Bergeisen, L. & Resnick, M.D. (1992). American Indian–Alaska Native youth health. *Journal of the American Medical Association, 267*, 1637–1644.

Bruerd, B. (1990). Smokeless tobacco use among Native American school children. *Public Health Reports, 105*(2), 196–201.

Burhannsstipanov, L. & Satter, D. (2000). Office of Management and Budget racial categories and implications for American Indians and Alaska Natives. *American*

Journal of Public Health, 90(11), 1720–1723.

Caetano, R. (1987). Acculturation and drinking patterns among U.S. Hispanics. *British Journal of Addiction, 82*, 289–299.

Caetano, R. & Herd, D. (1988). Drinking in different social contexts among white, black, and Hispanic men. *Yale Journal of Biology & Medicine 61*, 243–358.

California Area Indian Health Services Office (CAIHS). (1994). *Brief Summary: Prevalence of Alcohol and Drug Use During Pregnancy among American Indians served by Indian Health Programs in California.* Sacramento: California Area Office, Indian Health Service, Public Health Service.

Campbell, J.C., Miller, P., Cardwell, M.M. & Belknap R.A. (1994). Relationship status of battered women over time. *Journal of Family Violence, 9*(2), 99–111.

Center for Reproductive Health Policy Research. (1995). *Evaluating the Effectiveness of Alcohol and Substance Abuse Services for American Indian/Alaska Native Women.* Final Report submitted to Indian Health Service. San Francisco, CA: Institute for Health Policy Studies, University of California San Francisco.

Christian, C.M., Dufour, M. & Bertolucci, D. (1989). Differential alcohol-related mortality among American Indian tribes in Oklahoma, 1968–1978. *Social Science & Medicine, 28*(3), 275–284.

DeBruyn, L.M., Lujan, C.C. & May, P.A. (1992). A comparative study of abused and neglected American Indian children in the Southwest. *Social Science & Medicine, 35*(3),

Denny, C.H. & Holtzman, D. 1999. *Health Behaviors of American Indians and Alaska Natives: Findings from the Behavioral Risk Factor Surveillance System, 1993–1996.* Atlanta, GA: Centers for Disease Control and Prevention.

Dumbauld, S., McCullough, J.A. & Sutocky, J.W. (1994). *Analysis of Health Indicators for California's Minority Populations.* Sacramento: California Department of Health Services.

Duran, E., Guillory, B. & Turgley, P. (1994). Domestic violence in Native American communities: The effects of intergenerational post-traumatic stress. Unpublished paper.

Epstein, M. & Mader, S. (1996). *Tobacco, Alcohol and Other Drugs Used During Pregnancy among American Indians in California 1995.* Sacramento: California Area Office, Indian Health Service, Public Health Service.

Fullilove, M.T., Fullilove, R.E., Smith, R.E., Winkler, M., Michael, K., Panzer, P.G. & Wallace, R. (1994). Violence, trauma and post-traumatic stress disorder among women drug users. *Journal of Traumatic Stress, 6*(4), 533–543.

Goldberg-Ambrose, C. & Champagne, D. (1996). *A Century of Dishonor: Federal Inequities and California Tribes.* Report to the Advisory Council on California Indian Policy. Los Angeles: University of California Los Angeles, American Indian Studies Center.

Green, D.E. (1993). The contextual nature of American Indian criminality. *American Indian Culture & Research Journal, 17*(2), 99–119.

Greenfeld, L.A. & Smith, S. (1999). *American Indians and Crime.* Washington, DC: Bureau of Justice Statistics, U.S. Department of Justice.

Gregory, R.G., Abello, A.C. & Johnson, J. (1996). The individual economic well-being of Native American men and women during the 1980s: A decade of moving backwards. In G.D. Sandefur, Rindfuss, R.R., & Cohen, B. (Eds.), *Changing Numbers: Changing Needs: American Indian Demography and Public Health* (pp. 133–171). Washington DC: National Academy Press.

Guillory, B., Willie, E. & Duran, E. (1988). Analysis of a community organizing case study: Alkali Lake. *Journal of Rural Community Psychology, 9*(1), 27–35.

Hodge, F. (1988). Attributes of Heavy-Drinking Behavior Among American Indians at Three Reservation sites. Paper Presented at the Kettil Bruun Society Alcohol Epidemiology Symposium, Berkeley, CA.

Hodge, F.S., Cummings, S.R., Frederick, L. & Kipnis, P. (1994). *Prevalence of Smoking/Smokeless Tobacco Use in 18 Northern California American Indian Health Clinics.* Berkeley, CA: Center for American Indian Research and Education, Western Consortium for Public Health.

Hussong, R.G., Bird, K. & Murphy, C.V. (1993). *Substance Use Among American Indian Women of Child Bearing Age.* Auburn CA: Chapa De Indian Health Program.

Hutton, C., Pommersheim, F. & Feimer, S. (1996). I fought the law and the law won. In M.O. Nielson & Silverman, R.A. (Eds.), *Native Americans, Crime and Justice* (pp. 209–220). Boulder, CO: Westview, Press.

Indian Health Service. (1994). *Trends in Indian Health.* Washington, DC: Department of Health and Human Services, Public Health Service.

Institute for Health Policy Studies. (1992). *American Indians in California: Health Status and Access to Health Care.* Washington, DC: Indian Health Service, Public Health Service.

Joe, J.R. & Miller, D.L.. (1989). Barriers and survival: A study of an urban Indian health clinic. *American Indian Culture and Research Journal, 13*(3), 4233–4256.

Kaskutas, L.A. (2000). Understanding drinking during pregnancy among urban American Indians and African Americans: Health messages, risk beliefs, and how we measure consumption. *Alcoholism: Clinical and Experimental Research, 24*(8). 1241–1250.

Kilpatrick, D.G. (1993). Violence and Women's Substance Abuse. Paper Presented to the National Conference on Drug Abuse Research and Practice, National Institute on Drug Abuse, July.

Kilpatrick, D.G., Saunders, B.E., Amick-McMullan, A., Best, C.L., Veronen, L.J. & Resnick, H.S. (1989). Victim and crime factors associated with the development of crime-related post-traumatic stress disorder. *Behavioral Therapy, 20*, 199–214.

Klein, B., Zahnd, E., Kolody, B., Holtby, S., Midanik, L. (1995). *Final Report of the Pregnant and Parenting American Indian Study.* Berkeley, CA: Western Consortium for Public Health and San Diego State University Foundation. Submitted to California Department of Alcohol and Drug Programs.

Kunitz, S.J. & Levy, J.E. (1994). *Drinking careers: A Twenty-five Year Study of Three Navajo Populations.* New Haven: Yale University Press.

LaDue, R.A., Streissguth, A.P. & Randels, S.P. (1992). Clinical considerations pertaining to adolescents and adults with Fetal Alcohol Syndrome. In T.B. Sonderegger (Ed.), *Perinatal Substance Abuse: Research Findings and Clinical Implications* (pp. 104–131). Baltimore: Johns Hopkins University Press.

LaFramboise, T.D. & Rowe, W. (1983). Skills training for bicultural competence: Rationale, and application. *Journal of Counseling Psychology, 30*, 589–595.

Leland, J. (1978). Women and alcohol in an Indian settlement. *Medical Anthropology, 2*(4), 85–119.

Levinson, D. (1983). Alcohol use and aggression in American subcultures. In R. Room & G. Collins (Eds.), *Alcohol and Disinhibition: Nature and Meaning of the Link* (pp. 306–321). National Institute on Alcohol Abuse and Alcoholism Research Monograph 12. Washington DC: US Government Printing Office.

Levy, J.E. and Kunitz, S.J. (1974). *Indian Drinking: Navajo Practices and Anglo-American Theories.* New York: Wiley.

Lujan, C. C. (1995). Women warriors: American Indian women, crime and alcohol. *Women & Criminal Justice, 7*(1), 9–33.

Lujan, C., DeBruyn, L.M., May, P.A. & Bird, M.E. (1989). Profile of abused and neglected American Indian children in the southwest. *Child Abuse & Neglect, 13*, 449–61.

MacAndrew, C. & Edgerton, R.B. (1969). *Drunken Comportment: A Social Explanation.* Chicago: Aldine.

Mail, P. & Johnson, S. (1993). Boozing, sniffing and toking: An overview of the past, present and future of substance use by American Indians. *Journal of the National Center for American Indian & Alaska Native Mental Health Research, 5*, 1–33.

Marshall, M. (1983). "Four hundred rabbits": An anthropological view of ethanol as a disinhibitor. In R. Room & G. Collins (Eds.), *Alcohol and Disinhibition: Nature and Meaning of the Link* (pp. 186–204). National Institute on Alcohol Abuse and Alcoholism Research Monograph 12. Washington DC: U.S. Government Printing Office.

May, P.A., Hymbaugh, K.J., Aase, J.M. & Samet, J.M. (1983). Epidemiology of fetal alcohol syndrome among American Indians of the Southwest. *Social Biology 30*, 374–387.

May, P.A. (1996). Overview of alcohol abuse epidemiology for American Indian populations. In G.D. Sandefur, R.R. Rundfuss & B. Cohen (Eds.), *Changing Numbers, Changing Needs: American Indian Demography and Public Health* (pp. 235–261). Washington DC: National Academy Press.

May P.A. & Gossage, J.P. (1999). New Data on the Epidemiology of Adult Drinking and Substance Use Among American Indians of the Northern States: Male and Female Data on Prevalence, Patterns, and Consequences. Paper Presented at the Conference on Comorbidity among American Indians, Albuquerque, New Mexico.

McClelland, DC, Davis, W.N., Kalin, R. & Wanner, E. (1972). *The Drinking Man.* New York: Free Press.

Miller, B.A. (1990). The interrelationships between alcohol and drugs and family violence. In M. De La Rosa, E.Y. Lampert, & B.Gropper (Eds.), *Drugs and Violence: Causes, Correlates and Consequences* (pp. 177–207). National Institute on Drug Abuse Research Monograph 103. Washington DC: U.S. Government Printing Office.

Miller, B.A. (1993). Investigating links between childhood victimization and alcohol problems. In S.E. Martin (Ed.), *Alcohol and Interpersonal Violence: Fostering*

Multidisciplinary Perspective (pp. 315–322). National Institute on Alcohol Abuse and Alcoholism Research Monograph 24. Washington DC: U.S. Government Printing Office.

Miller, B.A., Downs, M.R., & Testa, M. (1993). Interrelationships between victimization experiences and women's alcohol use. *Journal of Studies on Alcohol Supplement, 11*, 109–117.

Moss, K. (1993). Charting a new course: Finding alcohol treatment for Native American women. Paper written for the Drug Policy Foundation, Seventh Annual Conference.

Norton, I.M. & Manson, S.M. (1995). A silent minority: Battered American Indian women. *Journal of Family Violence, 10*(3), 307–317.

Oetting, E.R. & Beavais, F. (1989). Epidemiology and correlates of alcohol use among Indian adolescents living on reservations. In D. Spiegler, D. Tate, A. Aitken & C. Christian (Eds.), *Alcohol Use Among U.S. Ethnic Minorities* (pp. 239–262). National Institute on Alcohol Abuse and Alcoholism Research Monograph 18. Washington DC: U.S. Government Printing Office.

Robbins, R. (1979). Alcohol and the identity struggle: Some effects of economic change on interpersonal relations. In M. Marshall (Ed.), *Beliefs, Behaviors and Alcoholic Beverages: A Cross-cultural Survey* (pp. 158–190). Ann Arbor: University of Michigan Press.

Rush, A.G. n.d. Recovery and prevention in Native American communities. Resource Paper. Sacramento: California Department of Alcohol and Drug Programs.

Sandefur, G. D. & Liebler, C.A. (1996). The demography of American Indian families. In G.D. Sandefur, R.R. Rindfuss, & B. Cohen (Eds.), *Changing Numbers: Changing Needs: American Indian Demography and Public Health* (pp. 196–218). Washington DC: National Academy Press.

Schinke, S.P, Orlandi, M.A., Botvin, G.J., Gilchrist, L.D., Trimble, J.E. & Locklear, V.S. (1988). Preventing substance abuse among American-Indian adolescents: A bicultural competence skills approach. *Journal of Counseling Psychology, 35*(1), 87–90.

Silverman, R. A. (1996). Patterns of Native American crime. In M.O. Nielson & R.A. Silverman (Eds.), *Native Americans, Crime and Justice* (pp. 58–74). Boulder, CO: Westview Press.

Smith, D.W., Hann, N.E., Hays, C.W. & Young, L. (1995). Native American Supplement Oklahoma Behavioral Risk Factor Survey. Paper Presented to American Public Health Association, October.

Snipp, C. M. (1996). The Size and distribution of the American Indian Population: Fertility, mortality, residence and migration. In G.D. Sandefur, R.R. Rindfuss, & B. Cohen (Eds.), *Changing Numbers: Changing Needs: American Indian Demography and Public Health* (pp. 17–52). Washington DC: National Academy Press.

Stone, K. (1994). Maternal Child Health High Risk Infant Project, American Indian Health Services, Trinidad, CA. Unpublished communication.

Swaim, R.C., Oetting, E.R., Thurman, P.J., Beauvais, F. & Edwards, R.W. (1993). American Indian adolescent drug use and socialization characteristics: A cross-cultural comparison. *Journal of Cross-Cultural Psychology, 24* (1), 53–70.

United States Department of Health and Human Services. (1991). *Report to Congress on the Indian Health Service with Regard to Health Status and Health Care Needs of American Indians in California.* Washington DC: Indian Health Service

United States Department of Health and Human Services. (1991–1993). *National Household Survey on Drug Abuse.* Substance Abuse and Mental Health Services Administration.

Walker, R. D., Howard, M.O., Anderson, B. & Lambert, M.D. (1994). Substance dependent American Indian veterans: A national evaluation. *Public Health Reports, 109* (2), 235–243.

Weibel-Orlando, J.C. (1986–1987). Drinking patterns of urban and rural American Indians. *Alcohol, Health & Research World, 11*(2), 9–13.

Wilsnack, S.C. (1996). Patterns and trends in women's drinking: Recent findings and some implications for prevention. In J.M. Howard, S.E. Martin, P.D. Mail, M.E. Hilton & E.D. Taylor (Eds.), *Women and Alcohol: Issues for Prevention Research* (pp. 19–64). National Institute on Alcohol Abuse and Alcoholism Research Monograph 32. Washington DC: U.S. Government Printing Office.

Young, T.J. (1993). Alcoholism prevention among Native-American youth. *Child Psychiatry & Human Development, 24* (1), 41–47.

Young, T. K. (1996). Recent health trends in the Native American population. In G.D. Sandefur, R.R. Rindfuss, & B. Cohen (Eds.), *Changing Numbers: Changing Needs: American Indian Demography and Public Health* (pp. 53–78). Washington DC: National Academy Press.

Zahnd E. & Klein, D. (1997). The needs of pregnant and parenting American Indian women at risk for problem alcohol or drug use. *Journal of American Indian Culture & Research, 21*(3), 119–144.

Zahnd, E., D. Klein & Needell. B. (1997). Substance use and issues of violence among low-income pregnant women: The California Perinatal Needs Assessment. *Journal of Drug Issues, 27* (3), 563–584.

Zahnd, E., D. Klein, R. Clark & Brown, A. (1999). *Alcohol and Drug Prevention Education for American Indian Youth in California.* Sacramento: California Department of Alcohol and Drug Programs.

Zahnd, E., Klein, D., Holtby, S., & Bachman, R. (2000). Special Issues and Problems Impacting Native Communities: *Alcohol-Related Violence Among American Indians. In P. Mail, (Ed.), Alcohol Use Among American Indians and Alaska Natives: Multiple Perspectives on a Complex Problem,* National Institute on Alcohol Abuse and Alcoholism Research Monograph, in press.

Zahnd, E. Holtby, S., Klein, D., McGrath, C., & Lordi, N. (2001). American Indian Women: Preventing Violence and Drinking Preliminary Findings. Berkeley, CA: National Institute on Alcohol Abuse and Alcoholism and Office for Research on Women's Health. Paper Presented to the Preventing Violence and Drinking Advisory Group.

Zion, J. & Zion, E.B.. (1996). "Hazho's Sokee"–stay together nicely: Domestic violence under Navajo common law. In M.O. Nielson & R.A. Silverman (Eds.), *Native Americans, crime and justice* (pp. 96–112). Boulder CO: Westview Press.

Chapter 14

SUBSTANCE ABUSE TREATMENT FOR NATIVE AMERICANS

DEBORAH JONES-SAUMTY

Much has been written on the extent and impact of substance abuse (including alcohol, tobacco and other drugs) among Native Americans (Burns, 1995; Mail & Johnson, 1993; May, 1982, 1989; U.S. Department of Health & Human Services, 1994; Westermeyer, 1997). These studies have often served to perpetuate the myths associated with "drunken Indians" and provided more negative than positive information about Indian people and their communities. It is unfortunate that establishing the prevalence and discussing the effects of such a pervasive problem as substance abuse among the Native occupants of America has served to obscure its complexity and variation, while reinforcing old myths and stereotypes (May, 1982).

While it is true that many of the most serious health problems among Native people in the United States may be directly related to substance abuse (Young, 1994), it is also true that substance abuse among Native people may have its roots in the cultural conflict, social disintegration and imposed "acculturation" suffered by Native tribes over the past 200 to 300 years.

Recently there has been more attention devoted to the numerous concomitant factors of substance abuse among Native Americans, including physical, psychological, sociocultural, cognitive, neurological and neuropsychological (Cheadle et al., 1994; Dingman, 1996; Roski et al., 1997; Gutierres et al., 1994; Nixon et al., 2000; Robin et al., 1998; Taylor, 2000; Trimble, 1995; Westermeyer et al., 1993). Further, there has been an emerging movement toward cultural-sensitive and cultural-specific treatments for Native Americans clients. It is these efforts to understand and work with the strengths of Indian communities and to assist them in dealing with their own problems that will be the focus of this chapter.

SUBSTANCE ABUSE TREATMENT

Substance abuse treatment is growing more widespread and changing rapidly. Managed care has exerted a tremendous influence in all areas. Indeed, the treatment system for substance abuse in the United States is quite complex. In order to be responsive to the changing needs of the treatment population, a treatment system must necessarily include a variety of settings, models, techniques and providers.

A recent survey of substance abuse treatment facilities, conducted by the Substance Abuse and Mental Health Services Administration (SAMHSA, 1999), showed that in 1999 more than half (54%) of all treatment facilities in the United States had managed care contracts (compared to 32% in 1995). A total of 15,239 treatment facilities (95% of all eligible facilities) participated in the survey. Most (60%) treatment programs were located in private non-profit facilities. The study also found that outpatient treatment was the most widely available type of care (82%), followed by residential treatment (25%), partial hospitalization programs (19%), and outpatient detoxification (13%). Approximately two-thirds of all treatment facilities offered substance abuse prevention programs. Nearly half (45%) of all treatment facilities provided programs for dually diagnosed clients and they also served persons in the criminal justice system (47%). About 34 percent offered programs for adolescents, and 22 percent of the treatment facilities offered programs for persons with HIV/AIDS, as well as programs for pregnant or postpartum women. Special programs for clients with DUI or DWI arrests were offered by 38 percent of all treatment facilities.

The delivery of substance abuse treatment services can differ greatly according to treatment philosophy, treatment setting (inpatient, residential, outpatient, etc.) and treatment modality. As one can see from the SAMHSA survey, there are many types of treatment programs specializing in treating a wide variety of clients and substance-related disorders. The delivery of culturally sensitive treatment services to Native Americans clients can add yet another level of complexity to an already overburdened system.

When a Native American client has a substance abuse problem, it is at this point that most managed care agencies and service providers turn to the Indian Health Service (IHS), the primary federal resource for substance abuse treatment in American Indian communities. While this is true as an overall principle, the Indian Health Service is not an "entitlement" program such as Medicare or Medicaid. The capacity of the Indian Health Service to meet the health care needs (including substance abuse treatment) of American Indian people is based on the amount of funds appropriated by Congress on an annual basis. In simple terms, the Indian Health Service is often unable to meet all of the health care needs of Indian people because of a lack of available funds (Cunningham, 1993).

In response to the federal government's shortfalls in funding Indian health services, individual tribes have exercised their rights to self-governance by contracting with the Indian Health Service to provide health care services specifically tailored for their own tribal members. This allows tribal health care programs to administer their own health care financing through formula funding from the Indian Health Service. They can also get third-party reimbursement from private insurance, Medicare or Medicaid coverage (Indian Health Care Improvement Act, PL 100-173). Indeed, many tribes allocate additional funds from tribal enterprises such as gaming, land management, petroleum resources, and other business profits, to go directly toward health care financing for tribal members and their families.

Thus, we have seen the emergence of many tribally controlled health clinics and substance abuse treatment programs established with the express purpose of creating more culturally relevant treatment services. The cultures of tribal communities are rich in traditions that influence many components of daily life, including modes of dress, preferences for foods, gender roles, art, literature, music and language. The challenge in developing and delivering culturally sensitive treatment services is explicit in the sheer variety of Indian cultures as well as the evolution of Indian traditions through historical events and trauma.

The U.S. Bureau of Indian Affairs recognizes 478 Indian tribes within the continental United States of America. There are an additional 50 to 52 tribes in the U.S. with no official status. Among these contemporary tribes, there are 142 Native languages still spoken (Heinrich et al., 1990). Thus, it seems clear that cultural sensitivity in treatment programming is a tremendous challenge that must be carefully devised—slowly and with much consideration. Many tribes have undertaken the creation of substance abuse treatment programs that build in the strengths of their own tribal practices and traditions. An additional strength of these programs has been the staffing that includes tribal members trained as substance abuse counselors, psychologists, physicians, nurses and other service providers. Clearly, by placing these tribal treatment programs within Native American communities, the stage has been set for culturally sensitive treatment services.

Unfortunately, there are few studies in the scientific literature reporting on the developmental processes, treatment outcomes, or quality of service delivery in these unique and specialized substance abuse treatment programs. The available studies of substance abuse treatment for Indian communities have numerous limitations, including being largely based on alcohol treatment, lacking adequate descriptive data on service providers and treatment approaches, having small numbers of participants (mostly male), being poorly designed with a lack of random sampling or comparison/control groups, providing little or no longitudinal data, and focusing mainly on reservation-based tribes (Flores, 1986; Gutierres et al., 1994; Shore & von Fumetti, 1972; Westermeyer et al., 1993; Westermeyer & Neider, 1994).

In a 10-year follow-up study of 45 Native American alcoholics, Westermeyer and Peake (1983) found that 62 percent of the patients (42 of the original 45) located for a follow-up interview still had problems with alcohol, in spite of repeated attempts at treatment. Only 17 percent had been abstinent from alcohol for two years or more, and 21 percent had died. Further findings indicated that recovery from alcoholism was not related to severity of alcoholism. The authors suggest that low employment rates at the time of original admission to treatment, poor job skills, the absence of stable family environments, and the predominance of violence in the drinking environment may have contributed to the poor treatment outcome for those American Indian clients.

A more recent study of 522 nonreservation residing Native Americans in treatment for substance abuse provides some of the first available data that attempts to overcome some of the limitations of previously collected data sets (Nixon et al., 2000). This preliminary study points to the similarity of ethnic minority subgroups across a wide range of alcohol use variables, and the study describes the use patterns of other substances and the consequences of substance abuse. Specifically, the Native American group (473 males, 49 females) included representatives from eleven different nonreservation tribes from inpatient substance abuse treatment facilities. The results of the study revealed that Native American clients were significantly younger and had fewer years of formal education than randomly selected, matched comparison groups of African Americans (AA) and European Americans (EA).

Approximately 85 percent of the Native Americans self-reported as having a "problem" with alcohol, compared to 81 percent of the European Americans, and 60 percent of African Americans. Similarly, just over 70 percent of Native American Indians reported a family history of alcohol problems, compared to 65 percent of European Americans, and 60 percent of African Americans. With regard to the use of drugs, both Native Americans and European Americans reported marijuana use most frequently, while African Americans reported that they used cocaine and other stimulants most frequently. Finally, the age of their first use of alcohol was considerably younger for Native Americans (11.21 years) than for the comparison groups (EA=12.06 years, AA=14.08 years) (Nixon et al., 2000).

Another area of study in the drug treatment literature focuses on the characteristics of Native American substance abusers. In a series of studies, Westermeyer and his colleagues (1993; 1994), examined issues of age and psychiatric diagnosis; family history of substance abuse; and prior treatment for substance abuse. These studies suggest that Native Americans experience greater negative consequences relative to their use and abuse of alcohol and other drugs. In a sample of 100 Native American substance abuse clients (71% males), the primary differential variable for predicting the presence of a secondary psychiatric diagnosis was age. The study identified three profiles for Native American substance abusers: (1) younger patients presented with substance abuse and a secondary psychiatric disorder; (2) middle-aged patients presented with only a substance abuse disorder; and (3) the oldest group of patients presented with substance abuse and an organic mental disorder (Westermeyer et al., 1993). Another study in which this same sample was compared to a non-Indian control group found that the American Indian patients were more likely to have a first-degree relative with a substance use disorder, more likely to have received prior inpatient care for substance use disorders, and more likely to have been admitted to a hospital for detoxification (Westermeyer & Neider, 1994).

Gutierres et al. (1994) looked at the characteristics of a sample of 58 Native American Indian clients (28 females, 30 males) in a residential treatment facility in Phoenix. The substance abusers in this sample represented 15 different tribes and averaged about 28 years of age. A majority of the subjects (82.7%) lived on a reservation (72% female, 96.2% male). More than three-fourths (81%) of the Native American clients completed residential treatment. The authors attribute this result to the participation of clients in "culturally sensitive residential treatment programs" and the accommodation of allowing children to accompany their mothers into treatment. While the degree of acculturation in Native American clients did not predict treatment completion, the high treatment completion rate suggests that the flexibility of the program in allowing clients to choose traditional or standard forms of therapy provided a range of alternatives sufficient to meet the needs of individuals acculturated in white society and more traditional Native clients.

The findings of the study reveal similarities as well as differences in male and female Native American clients in treatment for substance abuse. While there was no gender difference in treatment completion, females experienced more family dysfunction (i.e., family history of substance abuse, and emotional/physical/sexual abuse), and reported fewer years of formal education (55.6% had less than 12 years). More than one-fourth (25.9%) of females were divorced, and only one-third (34.6%) of the females were raised by biological parents. With regard to the use and abuse of substances, all Native American male respondents reported using alcohol and marijuana, while all Native American Indian female respondents used alcohol and 77.8 percent reported using marijuana. These groups were remarkably similar in terms of the age of their first use of alcohol (12.7 years for females vs. 13.1 years for males), age of first use of other drugs (15.5 years for females vs. 15.0

years for males), years of alcohol use (13.0 years for females vs. 12.7 years for male), and years of other drug use (11.4 years for females vs. 10.4 years for males).

Factors related to treatment completion in this sample of Native Americans in a residential substance abuse treatment facility were an important part of the study. Treatment completion occurred when subjects remained in the program for the required 45 to 60 days. Divorced subjects were found to be less likely to complete treatment, as well as those subjects who had spent a significant amount of time in foster care. Also, subjects who reported the use of cocaine and depressants (i.e., tranquilizers) were less likely to complete treatment (Gutierres et al., 1994).

TREATMENT PROGRAM COMPONENTS

Substance abuse treatment programs for American Indian clients must necessarily include members of their family and other close persons, their cultural tribal traditions and practices (including spirituality), and an understanding of their role as a member of a community. While it is important for treatment programs to offer a comprehensive array of services, to thoroughly describe their philosophy of treatment and to profile the background and training of their service providers, there are other contextual elements that are equally important when treating American Indian clients, e.g., the location of the treatment facility, the therapeutic context of the services, and interagency cooperation.

First, let us discuss the setting of a treatment program. The most recent data from the U.S. Census Bureau indicate that many Indian people are urban dwellers who reside away from reservations and tribal home areas (U.S. Bureau of the Census, 2001). Indeed, some of the largest concentrations of Native Americans are found in large cities such as New York, Los Angeles, San Francisco and Phoenix. While this migration toward urban areas may be primarily traced to economic conditions, some Native Americans remain in urban areas as a result of the U.S. government's relocation programs in the 1950s. Therefore, a further consideration for the location and setting of a treatment program must be the diversity of tribal groups in large urban areas. With this knowledge in mind, a treatment program must involve a strong cultural component with the flexibility to offer a wide variety of activities according to the tribal representation of clients. For example, a program might have language classes and and sweat lodges during one quarter, and art and history classes or drumming and singing lessons in another quarter. The key is flexibility, respect and a variety of cultural activities that will meet the needs of contemporary Native American clients in treatment: "The diversity of background of American Indians in drug treatment suggests that there is no one type of intervention program that will reach all individuals at risk" (Gutierres et al., 1994).

The therapeutic context of substance abuse treatment can be a very important predictor in both the response to treatment as well as the overall treatment outcome. It is here that health care agencies, Indian tribes, and other programs have the opportunity to frame a treatment program within the cultural context of their Native American clients. These programs incorporate into their activities the unique sociocultural characteristics of their Native American clients. In formulating a treatment program responsive to the needs of Native clients, it is important to establish a collaborative relationship with indigenous authorities (community, tribal and spiritual leaders, traditional healers) and to encourage and support clients' participation in spiritual ceremonies, social events and other traditional activities. This type of treatment atmosphere is customized for Native Americans clients and can only be accomplished when the clients are genuinely involved in the treatment planning process to insure clear goals for treatment and firm program guidelines.

Similarly, treatment programs and treatment service providers must cooperate in providing an extended clinical path for Native American clients that involves multiple providers, and multiple opportunities for therapy, personal growth and rehabilitation. Some of these multiple pathways for treatment may include family counseling, psychotherapy, relapse prevention, vocational rehabilitation, psychotropic medication, care and counseling for patients with HIV/AIDS, physical fitness and nutrition, parenting classes, child development, life skills training, and aftercare services. Case management should be a strong component in any treatment program, but it is especially important in agencies that work with urban Indian clients, who may have very little social support, and with rural and reservation-based Indian clients, who may return to families and friends and continue to drink and use drugs.

TREATMENT ISSUES

Numerous studies have looked at the various historical and sociocultural issues related to substance abuse among Native Americans (LaFromboise & Rowe, 1983; Mariano et al., 1989; Schinke et al., 1988; Schinke et al., 1990; Swaim et al., 1993; Thurman et al., 1990). Other researchers have discussed the multigenerational effects of alcohol and other drug use on the physical and mental health of Native American (French, 1989; Gutierres et al., 1994; Jones-Saumty et al., 1983; May, 1982). Thus, a great deal of research has been devoted to identifying and understanding potential treatment issues for Native Americans substance abuse clients.

In this section we will deal with three of the most important substance abuse treatment issues currently facing Native Americans: (1) traumatic impact of historical events; (2) physical and psychological disorders co-occurring with substance abuse; and (3) cultural sensitivity and cultural competency in diagnosis, assessment, and treatment.

One of the most important treatment issues that must be considered is the tremendous impact that historical events have had on Native American peoples of all tribes. As evidence of the notoriety of this issue is an article that recently appeared in the *American Psychologist*, the journal of the American Psychological Association (Belcourt-Dittloff & Stewart, 2000). The authors addressed the role of perceived racism manifest as broken treaties, boarding schools for Indian children, and the forced removal of tribes from their homelands. They hypothesize that historical racism may be a contributory stressor affecting biopsychosocial functioning of Native American clients, similar to the historical experiences of African Americans. Further, they discuss the impact of historical trauma and intergenerational grief on the therapeutic setting: "In terms of historical racism, the atrocities and mistreatment, such as broken treaties and attempted genocide, have fostered in many American Indians a great deal of mistrust for both the government and many non-American-Indian people" (p. 1166). Because trust is the key to building a therapeutic relationship, this legacy of mistrust could certainly have a negative effect on the relationship with the therapist as well as expectations for therapeutic outcome.

In another study, Brave et al. (1998) discussed the concept of historical racism as a natural consequence of the fact that Native Americans have long experienced racism and oppression as a result of colonization and its accompanying genocidal practices. For all Indian people, the product of such an immense loss of life, land and culture has been a legacy of chronic trauma and unresolved grief. In another study, Beauvais and LaBoueff (1985) concluded that substance use results from cynicism and despair created by dependency fostered by paternalistic federal policies toward American Indian communities.

The effects of such tremendous losses as well as the unresolved grief, despair and persistent trauma are readily apparent in the poverty and hopelessness seen in many Indian communities. The physical and mental health of Native Americans have been shown to be plagued by high rates of heart disease, liver disease, diabetes and accidental injuries, as well as disproportionately high rates of suicide, homicide, domestic violence, child abuse and alcoholism (Young, 1994). Therefore, it is imperative that treatment programs and service providers be aware of the historical trauma and related grief for American Indian clients and that they be willing to work with clients and their families to minimize those effects and to halt the progress of historical racism.

The second treatment issue to be discussed in this section will be the co-occurrence of physical and/or psychological disorders with substance abuse in Native American clients. While it is beyond the scope of this chapter to determine whether or not the substance abuse occurred in response to one of these other problems or vice versa, it is particularly important to call to the reader's attention the complexity of this issue for both treatment programs as well as treatment providers. The high relapse rate for substance abuse may be indirectly related to the lack of attention many treatment programs give to co-occurring disorders amongst Native Americans.

Little work has been done in the area of co-occurring disorders and substance abuse within Native American treatment populations. However, the ten leading causes of death among Natives appear to have either a direct or indirect relationship to substance abuse: (1) cardiovascular disease, (2) cancers, (3) accidents, (4) diabetes, (5) liver disease and cirrhosis, (6) cerebrovascular disease, (7) pneumonia, (8) suicide, (9) homicide, and (10) chronic obstructive pulmonary disease (Indian Health Service, 1996).

The prevalence of co-occurring disorders may vary widely across tribal groups. Some tribes have been devastated by alcoholism and it effects on its people's physical health, including heart disease, cancer, diabetes and liver disease. Other tribes seem to be particularly affected by products of substance abuse, such as vehicular accidents, violence, suicide and homicide; while still other tribes suffer from the indirect effects of substance abuse in terms of increased rates of divorce, domestic violence, child abuse, poverty and unemployment. The responsibility for being aware of these conditions cannot be minimized. People who design therapeutic components and treatment activities for urban and rural health care facilities should take into account the physical conditions of their Native American clientele. Similarly, tribal treatment programs must operate with appropriate and ample knowledge of the health status and health care needs of the tribal members and their families.

Another aspect of disorders co-occurring with substance abuse is the rate of psychopathology. Indeed, results from two large studies have concluded that the "prevalence of comorbid psychiatric illness and substance abuse disorders is high" in the general U.S. population (Beeder & Millman, 1997). Data from the Epidemiologic Catchment Area (ECA) study suggests that more than half of individuals who abuse drugs other than alcohol have additional psychiatric illness, with cocaine abusers demonstrating 76 percent comorbid illnesses (Helzer & Pryzbeck, 1988). Another psychiatric perspective indicates that approximately 29 percent of all persons in the United

States who are diagnosed with mental illness also have a lifetime history of either drug abuse or dependence. Even higher rates of psychopathology were noted for those patients diagnosed with alcoholism (34.5%) (Lehman et al., 1994).

Clinical studies revealed that 77 percent of patients in a sample of 321 alcoholics had psychological disorder (DSM III axis I or II) in addition to alcoholism at some time in their lives. Major depression was the most common diagnosis in females, and antisocial personality disorder was the most common diagnosis in males (Hesselbrock et al., 1985). Other clinical studies indicate poorer treatment outcome for substance abuse patients with coexisting psychiatric diagnoses (Rounsaville et al., 1987).

We have already discussed the work of Westermeyer and his colleagues who found that among Native American substance abusers, age of the client was the primary differential variable for predicting the presence of secondary psychiatric diagnosis (Westermeyer et al., 1993). Unfortunately, as noted earlier, this is an area of research that is very sparse and requires much more study and considerations than we are able to offer at this time. Suffice it to say that physical and psychological co-occurring disorders remain a very important issue in the treatment of substance abuse for Native American communities.

The third and final treatment issues are cultural sensitivity in program design and cultural competency of substance abuse treatment staff. It is crucial that clinicians working with (or intending to work with) Native American clients become culturally competent in order to minimize the effects of historical trauma and racism, previously discussed in this section. It is an unfortunate fact that many well-meaning treatment programs have simply hired Native Americans as service providers with the assumption that this makes their program "culturally competent." This is a naïve and insensitive approach to the complex and serious issues confronting all American Indians and Alaska Natives.

Hillary Weaver (1997) outlined three components of cultural competency for clinicians who treat Native American clients: (1) knowledge of the client's cultural context, including history and world view; (2) awareness of the care provider's assumptions, values and biases pertaining to Native Americans; and (3) appropriate intervention strategies and skills. These are valuable guidelines for service providers in any substance abuse treatment program.

Another approach to understanding cultural competence is Berry's (1980) work focusing on the equivalences of cultures. He refers to three types of equivalence between cultures: conceptual, functional and metric. *Conceptual equivalence* recognizes that every culture has developed ways of looking at the world that makes sense to its people. An example might be the existence of substance abuse in the Indian community. While its presence is difficult to ignore, many Native Americans are at a loss to explain the concept of substance abuse and its impact on their community because substance abuse has no equivalent with their view of the world.

Functional equivalence recognizes that the purpose or significance of an apparently similar behavior may differ across cultures. That is to say, a behavior may be functionally equivalent (essentially the same behavior) yet have a different meaning. An example might be a non-Indian who experiences shame and guilt when drinking in the presence of family members, while an Indian person often shares the experience of drinking as a social activity with family members. Indeed, refusal to drink with family members may be seen as rejection in many Native American cultures.

Finally, *metric equivalence* means that items, scales and tests that measure constructs often operate differently across cultures, or the relationship between variables is not the same across cultures. An example might be the words used to describe behaviors on an attitude scale that may be interpreted differently, such as "I drink to feel better." To a test developer, the inherent relationship between drinking and feeling better might be scored in the direction of deviance. A Native American might perceive this statement as positive affirmation for drinking, but be scored by the researcher as a "deviant." The key here is for clinicians to be aware that their own cultural context may differ greatly from their Native American clients' cultural context, even if the clinicians themselves, are Native Americans as well. True cultural competency that will require considerable efforts and significant amounts of time be spent in extended discussions between clinicians and clients to share their cultural perspective. It is imperative that treatment agencies acknowledge the need for cultural competency and provide their staff time and resources to build their treatment activities and professional development accordingly.

SUMMARY AND RECOMMENDATIONS

In this chapter we have focused on some of the pervasive problems that evolve around substance abuse among Native Americans in the United States. We have discussed the status of health among Native peoples, reviewed the available research on substance abuse treatment offered to them, and identified three salient issues in substance abuse treatment for Native Americans: (1) historical trauma and intergenerational grief; (2) physical and psychological disorders co-occurring with substance abuse; and (3) cultural sensitivity and cultural competency in substance abuse treatment.

As a Native American psychologist, I continue to struggle with these treatment issues for the clients I work with and for the Indian people in the communities I serve. While all of these issues are important, the need for cultural competency in treatment programs seems to be the most pressing as our nation begins a new century. The pathway to cultural competency in substance abuse treatment for Native Americans will involve dealing with the other issues identified in this chapter, especially historical trauma and co-occurring disorders. The time and efforts necessary to become cultural competent must be given by all providers, administrators and programs in the field of substance abuse treatment.

REFERENCES

Bauvais, F. & Laboueff, S. (1985). Drug and alcohol abuse intervention in American Indian communities. *International Journal of the Addictions, 20*, 139–171.

Beeder, A.B. & Millman, R.B. (1997). Patients with psychopathology. In J.H. Lowinson, P. Ruiz, R.B. Millman & J.G. Langrod (Eds.), *Substance Abuse: A Comprehensive Textbook* (pp. 551–563). Baltimore: Williams & Wilkins.

Belcourt-Dittloff, A. &. Stewart, J. (2000). Historical racism: Implications for Native Americans. *American Psychologist, 55*, 1166–1167.

Berry, J. (1980). Introduction to methodology. In H. Triandis & J. Berry (Eds.), *Handbook of Cross-cultural Psychology.* Volume 2. Methodology (pp. 1–28). Boston: Allyn & Bacon.

Brave Heart, M.Y.H. & DeBruyn, L.M. (1998). The American Indian holocaust: Healing historical unresolved grief. *American Indian & Alaska Native Mental Health Research, 8*, 56–78.

Burns, T.R. (1995). How does I.H.S. relate administratively to the high alcoholism mortality rate? *American Indian & Alaska Native Mental Health Research, 6*, 31–45.

Cheadle, A., Pearson, E., Wagner, E., Diehr, B.M. & Koepsell, T. (1994). Relationship between socioeconomic status, health status, and lifestyle practices of American Indians: Evidence from a Plains reservation population. *Public Health Reports, 109*, 405–413.

Cunningham, P.J. (1993). Access to care in the Indian Health Service. *Health Affairs,* (Fall), 224–233.

Dingman, S.M. (1996). Differences between Caucasians and American Indians on the cognitive laterality battery. *Neuropsychologia, 34*, 647–660.

Flores, P.J. (1986). Alcoholism treatment and the relationship of Native American cultural values to recovery. *International Journal of the Addictions, 20*, 1707–1726.

French, L.A. (1989). Native American alcoholism: A transcultural counseling perspective. *Counseling Psychology Quarterly, 2*, 153–166.

Gutierres, S.E., Russo, N.F. & Urbanski, L. (1994). Sociocultural and psychological factors in American Indian drug use: Implications for treatment. *International Journal of the Addictions, 29*, 1761–1786.

Heinrich, R.K., Corbine, J.L. & Thomas, K.R. (1990). Counseling Native Americans. *Journal of Counseling & Development, 69*, 128–133.

Helzer, J.E. & Pryzbeck, T.R. (1988). The co-occurrence of alcoholism with other psychiatric disorders of the general population and its impact in treatment. *Journal of Studies on Alcohol, 49*, 219–224.

Hesselbrock, M.N., Meyer, R.E. & Keener, J.J. (1985). Psychopathology in hospitalized alcoholics. *Archives of General Psychiatry, 42*, 1050–1055.

Indian Health Service (1996). *Trends in Indian Health.* Rockville, MD: U.S. DHHS.

Jones-Saumty, D., Hochhaus, L., Dru, R. & Zeiner, A.R. (1983). Psychological factors of familial alcoholism in American Indians and Caucasians. *Journal of Clinical Psychology, 39*, 783–790.

LaFromboise, T. & Rowe, W. (1983). Skills training for bicultural competence: Rationale and application. *Journal of Counseling Psychology, 30*, 589–595.

Lehman, A.F., Myers, C.P., Corty, E.C. & Thompson, J.W. (1994). Prevalence and patterns of "dual diagnosis" among psychiatric inpatients. *Comprehensive Psychiatry, 35*, 106–112.

Mail, P.D. & Johnson, S. (1993). Boozing, sniffing and toking: An overview of the past, present and future of substance abuse by American Indians. *American Indian & Alaska Native Mental Health Research, 5*, 1–33.

Mariano, A.J., Donovan, D.M., Walker, P.S., Mariano, M.J. & Walker, R.D. (1989). Drinking-related locus of control and the drinking status of urban Native Americans. *Journal of Studies on Alcohol, 50*, 331–338.

May, P.A. (1982). Substance abuse and American Indians: Prevalence and susceptibility. *International Journal of the Addictions, 17*, 1185–1209.

May, P.A. (1989). Alcohol abuse and alcoholism among American Indians: An overview. In T.D. Watts & R. Wright, Jr. (Eds.), *Alcoholism in minority populations* (pp. 95–119). Springfield, IL: Charles C Thomas.

Nixon, S.J., Phillips, M. & Tivis, R. (2000). Characteristics of American Indian clients seeking inpatient treatment for substance abuse. *Journal of Studies on Alcohol, 61*(4), 541–547.

Robin, R.W., Long, J.C., Rasmussen, J.K., Albaugh, B. & Goldman, D. (1998). Relationship of binge drinking to alcohol dependence, other psychiatric disorders, and behavioral problems in an American Indian tribe. *Alcoholism: Clinical & Experimental Research, 22*, 518–523.

Roski, J., Perry, C.L., McGovern, P.G., Veblen-Mortenson, S. & Farbakhsh, K. (1997). Psychosocial factors associated with alcohol use among adolescent American Indians and whites. *Journal of Child & Adolescent Substance Abuse, 7*, 1–18.

Rounsaville, B.J., Dolinsky, Z.S., Babor, R.F. & Meyer, R.E. (1987). Psychopathology as a predictor of treatment outcome in alcoholics. *Archives of General Psychiatry, 44*, 505–513.

SAMHSA: Substance Abuse & Mental Health Services Administration, (1999). Annual survey of substance abuse treatment facilities. Washington, DC: U.S. Department of Health & Human Services.

Schinke, S.P., Orlandi, M.A., Botvin, G.J., Gilchrist, L.D., Trimble, J.E. & Locklear, L.D. (1988). Preventing substance abuse among American Indian adolescents: A bicultural competence skills approach. *Journal of Counseling Psychology, 33*, 87–90.

Schinke, S.P., Orlandi, M.A., Schilling, R.F., Botvin, G.J., Gilchrist, L.D. & Landers,

C. (1990). Tobacco use by American Indian and Alaska Native people: Risks, psychosocial factors and preventive intervention. *Journal of Drug Education, 35,* 1–12.

Shore, J. & Von Fumetti, B. (1972). Three alcohol programs for American Indians. *American Journal of Psychiatry, 11,* 134–139.

Swaim, R.C., Oetting, E.R., Thurman, P.J., Beauvais, F., & Edwards, R.W. (1993). American Indian adolescent drug use and socialization characteristics: A cross-cultural comparison. *Journal of Cross-Cultural Psychology, 24,* 53–70.

Taylor, M.J. (2000). The influence of self-efficacy on alcohol use among American Indians. *Cultural Diversity & Ethnic Minority Psychology, 6,* 152–167.

Thurman, P.J., Jones-Saumty, D. & Parsons, O.A. (1990). Locus of control and drinking behavior in American Indian alcoholics and non-alcoholics. *American Indian & Alaska Native Mental Health Research, 4,* 31–39.

Trimble, J.E. (1995). Toward an understanding of ethnicity and ethnic identity, and their relationship with drug use research. In G.J. Botvin, S. Schinke & M.A. Orlandi (Eds.), *Drug Abuse Prevention with Multiethnic Youth* (pp. 3–27). Thousand Oaks, CA: Sage.

U.S. Bureau of the Census, (2001). *U.S. Census: American Indian and Alaska Native Statistics.* Washington, DC: U.S. Bureau of the Census Web Site.

U.S. Department of Health & Human Services. (1994). *Eighth Special Report to The U.S. Congress on Alcohol and Health.* (DHHS publication–ADM–94–3699). Rockville, MD: National Institutes of Health.

Weaver, H. (1997). The challenges of research in Native American communities: Incorporating principles of cultural competence. *Journal of Social Service Research, 23,* 32–39.

Westermeyer, J. (1997). Native Americans, Asians, and new immigrants. In J.H. Lowinson, P. Ruiz, R.B. Millman & J.G. Langrod (Eds.), *Substance Abuse: A Comprehensive Textbook* (pp. 712–715). Baltimore: Williams & Wilkins.

Westermeyer, J. & Neider, J. (1994). Substance disorder among 100 American Indian vs. 200 other patients. *Alcoholism: Clinical & Experimental Research, 18,* 692–694.

Westermeyer, J. & Peake, E. (1983). A ten-year follow-up of alcoholic Native Americans in Minnesota. *American Journal of Psychiatry, 140,* 189–194.

Westermeyer, J., Neider, J. & Westermeyer, M. (1993). Substance use and other psychiatric disorders among 100 American Indian patients. *Culture, Medicine, & Psychiatry, 16,* 519–529.

Young, T.K. (1994). *The Health of Native Americans.* New York: Oxford University Press.

Chapter 15

A MODEL FOR FETAL ALCOHOL SYNDROME PREVENTION IN NATIVE AMERICAN POPULATION

Grace Xueqin Ma, Jamil Toubbeh, Janette Cline, and Anita Chisholm

Alcohol is an inextricable and largely inescapable part of American culture (Nockels, 1995). It is one of the oldest substances used by man. Its promotion and use have been, and still are, pervasive in Western societies. People drink for a variety of reasons; many suffer its adverse effects. Although alcohol consumption in the U.S. population is common, its effect on female adolescents has received limited attention. A growing body of research indicates that females may be at higher risk of developing alcohol-related problems at lower levels of consumption than males. These problems are closely associated with reproductive dysfunctions, rapid development of alcohol-dependence, and victimization (NIAAA, 1990).

Alcohol remains the most commonly abused substance among adolescents. Windle (1990), citing the National Adolescent Student Health Survey, reports that 75 percent of eighth graders and 87.3 percent of tenth graders have used alcohol. The National Institute on Drug Abuse's Pregnancy and Health Survey estimates that alcohol exposure occurs in 20 percent of pregnancies annually in the U.S. Fetal alcohol syndrome (FAS) is the direct result of alcohol use during pregnancy, especially during the first and second trimesters. Babies with FAS have lower birth weights, facial abnormalities (flat bridge of the nose, small and widely-spread eyes, and sloping foreheads), and mental retardation. These babies may also exhibit behavioral abnormalities that include hyperactivity, attention deficits, impulsiveness, learning disabilities, reduced habituation, feeding difficulties, developmental, speech and hearing delays, and a range of coordination deficits. Many of these abnormalities are considered permanent (Steissguth et al., 1986).

284

The incidence of FAS in the general population is 1.9 per 1,000 live births (Abel & Sokol, 1987). Among women who are alcohol-dependent, estimates of FAS frequency are 29 per 1,000 live births (Rosett et al., 1983). Today, FAS is the leading cause of mental retardation in the U.S. (Abel & Sokol, 1987).

According to the Centers for Disease Control and Prevention, incidence of FAS per 10,000 births for different ethnic groups is as follows: Asians 0.3; Hispanics 0.8; Whites 0.9; African Americans 6.0; and Native Americans 29.9 (Chavez et al., 1989). Torres (995) estimates that FAS rate among some Native American groups is six times the national average (Torres, 1995). For instance, in one Native American high-risk group of mothers who had one birth associated with alcohol-related problems, 25 percent had given birth to FAS babies (May et al., 1983). The Indian Health Service (IHS, 1996) has identified substance abuse as the most prominent health problem among Native Americans. The agency has estimated that drinking problems are experienced by as many as 50 percent of the population of some reservations.

Although highly variable among different Native American communities, alcohol abuse has been identified as a factor in one of the five leading causes of death for Native Americans. Mortality rates associated with crashes and alcoholism are 5.5 and 3.8 times higher, respectively, among Native Americans than among the general population (NIAAA, 1994). Alcohol abuse is often reported in association with vehicular accidents, cirrhosis, suicide, homicide, and family problems. Where high rates of alcoholism are reported, 75 percent of all accidents are alcohol-related (NIAAA, 1994).

Among Native American adolescents in particular, there is widespread and heavy consumption of alcohol, generally at higher rates than among non-Indians, and with fewer gender differences (Oetting & Beauvais, 1993). Several factors appear to contribute to the overall high rates of alcohol use among these adolescents. In addition to peer group encouragement, Native American adolescents face cultural dislocation, lack of clear-cut sanctions against alcohol use in their own milieu, lower rate of perceived harm resulting from its use, poor self-esteem, and poor economic conditions—a few of the determinants of potential high-risk behavior.

OBJECTIVES OF THE FAS PREVENTION PROGRAM

The objectives of this FAS prevention program were to develop substance abuse prevention products, as well as materials and tools, with a special emphasis on communication strategies to address prevention and/or reduction of the incidence of FAS among Native American adolescents. The objectives required that products, materials and tools be culturally sensitive, developmentally appropriate, accurate, and responsive to the needs of the target population.

The health communication process model (USDHHS, 1989) was used as a theoretical foundation for this prevention program design. The model consists of six components in the health communication process. These include: (1) planning and strategy selection, (2) selecting communication channels and materials, (3) developing materials, (4) implementation, (5) assessing effectiveness, and (6) feedback to refine the program. Prevention research could easily be integrated within this framework, which has been successfully applied to numerous programs of the National Cancer Institute, the National Institute on Alcohol Abuse and Alcoholism, and the Center for Substance Abuse Prevention.

Consistent with this conceptual model, phase one of the project was a needs assessment based on interviews with prevention professionals. The purpose was: (1) explore the types of prevention media that are appropriate to Native American adolescents, sixth through eighth graders; (2) evaluate existing programs and materials relating to FAS prevention for relevancy and cultural competency in Native American communities; and (3) facilitate the production of culturally relevant and competent prevention materials that would have a tangible, positive impact on Native American adolescents. These activities constituted the first two components of the model, namely, planning and strategy selection, and communication channels and materials selection.

The overall purpose of the professional needs assessment was to provide recommendations that would facilitate the development of appropriate FAS prevention materials for the target population. This assessment was employed because the research team believed that estimates of general need, service demand and service problems are based, in part, on the collection and analysis of professional or expert knowledge and experience in relevant disciplines. The approach, particularly in the behavioral sciences, is a critical component of any needs assessment research.

Phase two of this project focused on the development of FAS prevention materials based on the recommendations derived from the professional assessment survey. In phase three, a pilot study was conducted among the target populations to assess knowledge and attitudes' change in FAS prevention.

In line with the project phases, the data is presented in three segments, as Phase 1, Professional Needs Assessment; Phase 2, Development of FAS Prevention Program; Phase 3, Evaluation. Phases 2 and 3 comprise the remaining components of the health communication process model alluded to earlier. Discussion and conclusion sections with specific recommendations follow.

Phase 1: Professional Needs Assessment Method

Participants. Forty-nine prevention professionals were randomly selected from a total list of 180 professionals in six states with large Native American populations. The states included: Oklahoma, New Mexico, Arizona, California, Montana and Alaska. The 180 professionals represented the major prevention programs, within the states in schools and communities, including Native American schools and communities.

Criteria employed for this sample selection were: (1) expertise in the areas of substance abuse and FAS prevention; and (2) experience in working with Native American adolescents in schools or communities. Professional participants in the final sample were known prevention specialists and gatekeepers representing school counselors, directors of prevention programs, health educators, and Indian education specialists.

Instrument and Procedure. The professional needs assessment survey instrument was developed by a team of prevention professionals, health educators, and researchers, several of whom were substance abuse prevention specialists who have worked with Native American adolescents. The instrument was pilot-tested by nine prevention professionals with similar backgrounds to those participants in the final sample. The team reviewed, analyzed and revised the instrument based on the results of the pilot study, and ensuring that the overall instrument was culturally sensitive and is in line with the research objectives. Eight research questions were developed to determine the needs and appropriate FAS prevention strategies for sixth through eighth grade Native American adolescents. They were:

- What are the key issues and risk factors facing the student population in your school or community?
- Are there materials/programs available at your school to teach students FAS prevention? If yes, have these programs/materials been used regularly? At what grade level?
- Which age group do you think need more attention in FAS prevention (4th–5th, 6th–8th, 9th–12th)?
- What communication media are useful to you in disseminating prevention information and making impact on the target populations?
- Do you believe a videotape that focuses on preventing FAS could be beneficial to students at sixth through eighth grade levels? Why?
- If you were to develop a video on FAS, would it be most in a coed class or a gender-specific class?
- What kind(s) of information would be most effective in attracting the sixth through eighth grade students' attention concerning the issue of FAS?
- What Native American cultural elements would capture students' atten-

tion (sixth through eighth)?

An in-depth telephone survey was administered to these professionals to obtain opinions and recommendations on FAS prevention among Native American adolescents. Each interview lasted approximately 30 minutes. The interviews, carried out over a period of 30 days, were administered by trained members of the research team. Each interview was preceded by a statement delineating project objectives and the responsibilities of the interviewed party. Participants in the survey were assured of anonymity and confidentiality. The data obtained were analyzed by means of SPSS Windows 95 statistical software package.

RESULTS

Nearly a third of the respondents identified family problems as the most serious risk factor for early adolescents. Families often harbor members who may be alcohol- or drug-dependent, or who may be tolerant of alcohol or drug abuse. Low family income, limited parent education and gang involvement, in that order, ranked second. Other risk factors included teen pregnancies and unprotected sex among adolescents, boredom and loneliness, lack of guidance, and absence of discipline at home, or parental role modeling. Table 15.1 presents an overview of the responses and the ranking order of risk factors to which early adolescents are subjected in their local schools and communities.

Existing Resources. When asked what materials and programs were available in their schools and communities to teach sixth through eighth grade students about FAS prevention, 70 percent of the respondents reported that these were unavailable in their schools and communities. Thirty percent indicated limited availability, addressing primarily upper grades

Table 15.1
RISK FACTORS FACING THE TARGET POPULATION

	Mean Score*
Family problems	4.4
Use of alcohol and other drugs	3.2
Low family income	3.0
Limited education of parents	2.2
Gang involvement	2.2

*Mean score with 1 being least serious, 5 most serious.

(9th–12th). Respondents noted some available "generic" prevention materials were obtained from the Center for Substance Abuse Prevention, Indian Health Service clinics, and State Health departments.

Age Group and FAS Prevention. In response to perceptions of the needs for FAS prevention across various grade levels or age groups, the majority of respondents (74%) felt that sixth through eighth graders should be given more attention. Reasons cited:

- *high risk behaviors*–The age group identified (6th through 8th grades) is vulnerable to high-risk behaviors;
- *decision-making*–Children in this age group are in the beginning stages of making decisions regarding high-risk behaviors such as alcohol and drug use and sexual activity;
- *early intervention*–The importance of reaching children before high school.
- *receptiveness*–The age group is more open to learning.

Communication Media and Prevention. Thirty-three percent of the respondents identified videotapes as the most viable method of disseminating prevention information to the target age group. Computer, written materials, and curriculum ranked fairly high. T-shirts and posters ranked last. Other media mentioned in the survey included television, storytelling, educational workshops on FAS prevention, and animation or some hands-on materials such as bumper stickers. Table 15.2 presents an overview of the responses of the entire sample and shows the mean score ranking order for each communication medium and its usefulness in developing and disseminating FAS prevention materials to 6th through 8th grade Native American adolescents.

Video as an Effective Prevention Tool. A large majority (90%) of the respondents felt that videotapes focusing on prevention of FAS would be

Table 15.2
COMMUNICATION MEDIA PREFERENCES AND FAS PREVENTION

	*Mean Score**
Videotape	4.72
Computer	4.04
Written materials	3.24
Curriculum	2.90
T-shirt	2.76
Poster	2.70

*Mean score with 1 being least useful, 5 most useful.

most beneficial to sixth through eighth graders. According to these respondents, a videotape would:

- *increase awareness and understanding* of FAS and that these issues are relevant to adolescents;
- *provide a visual mode of learning* which can be more effective than verbal delivery methods alone;
- *provide an avenue to reflect cultural aspects* of Indian people.

Gender and FAS Prevention. Sixty-one percent of the respondents indicated that a videotape on FAS prevention would be most useful in coed classes. Thirty-nine percent stated that videotapes would be most useful when directed at a gender-specific class. When respondents were asked why they favored coed classes, the dominant theme was the shared responsibilities between males and females with regard to FAS prevention. Those who favored gender-specific presentation noted that the subject may inhibit participation and learning. They also mentioned that community norms dictate their preferences for gender-specific presentations.

FAS Prevention Content and Format. Participants were asked to provide responses to content as well as presentation format in FAS prevention for sixth through eighth grade students. Responses were as follow:

- *Content*–Should address basics and be provided in language appropriate to the grade levels. The focus of the message should be on awareness of FAS and its prevention; linking behaviors with consequences; addressing the issue of peer pressure; and emphasizing responsibility and ability to control personal behaviors (e.g., decision-making skills).
- *Presentation format*–Animated characters, storytelling and small group presentations were recommended as effective methods for the age groups. Others included the presentation of subtle visuals of FAS babies, integration of music when possible, and use of peers, i.e., Native American adolescents to discuss issues of relevance.

Native American Culture and Prevention. When asked what powerful elements of Native American cultures would capture the attention of adolescents when linked with FAS, respondents recommended the incorporation of some traditional beliefs and activities into prevention curricula. Respondents suggested that traditional beliefs should address the value of life and reverence for nature, respect, honor and kinship, pride in Indian status, family values, and involvement of elders, while traditional activities should emphasize the involvement of song and dance, storytelling, sweats and gatherings.

Phase 2: Development of FAS Prevention Program

Format Design. Phase 2 of the project focused on the development of a culturally appropriate, age-specific multimedia FAS prevention package. Recommendations emanating from the professional needs assessment formed the basis of decisions regarding the types of media utilized for dissemination of prevention messages, as well as other relevant information. For example, the needs assessment called for use of videos, computer-assisted technology, and written materials, respectively, as the most preferred means of knowledge transfer. In line with this finding, a videotape was produced to accompany a curriculum guide featuring 19 lessons each with specific goals and learning objectives. Each lesson also consisted of lecture, research projects, experiential learning activities and class discussion. The videotape, titled *Faces Yet to Come*, was used in conjunction with a curriculum guide to provide a comprehensive educational format that combined visual, auditory, and experiential learning to reinforce student understanding of central ideas.

Additional written materials, including a project flyer and program brochure, were also created to provide succinct, easy to understand information regarding generic concepts of FAS, and concepts that are relevant to Native American adolescents.

A project World Wide Web page was further developed in response to professional prevention specialists' recommendations. This project web site provided access to descriptions of project materials, ordering information, and links to other web pages focusing on Native American issues and prevention initiatives.

Content Design. The professional needs assessment indicated consistent recommendations on the content of prevention materials. The need to present prevention messages that link actions to consequences, and emphasizing responsibility and address peer pressure, was underscored. These elements were integrated with the prevention materials to enhance their effectiveness. Additionally, and in line with professional recommendations, prevention materials emphasized the importance of healthy choices and decision-making with regard to the use of alcohol that linked sexual activities to pregnancy. These materials stressed the shared responsibility for FAS prevention between males and females.

The presentation in videos of subtle visuals of FAS victims, along with pictures of animals which have been utilized in FAS research, was used as a tool that was deemed less harsh than the presentation of the severe distortions that result from fetal damage in humans–more appropriate approach with this age group.

Finally, certain Native American cultural elements were integrated into the prevention materials, such as the value of life, reverence for nature, seventh generation concepts (responsible for healthy future generations of Indian Nations). Emphasis on respect, honor, and kinship was also placed on pride in one's Indian status.

Phase 3: Evaluation

Evaluation comprised the third phase of the prevention project. The evaluation was to determine whether the prevention materials met the intended purpose of the objectives, test the data presented in the professional needs assessment, reveal unanticipated problems, and, ultimately, assess the effectiveness of the materials to determine any knowledge change in FAS prevention in the target population.

The evaluation was conducted at two middle school sites. These sites were selected based on the large enrollment of Native American students. Ninety (90) sixth through eighth grade students were randomly selected from these two school sites and 85 participated in both pre- and post-tests.

The evaluation instrument was developed by the research team to measure students' reported knowledge change in FAS prevention, including risk factors, side effects associated with alcohol consumption during pregnancy, decision-making on health, and responsibilities for prevention. Prior to use, the instrument was pilot-tested and changes were made to enhance clarity and ease of administration.

Participation in the evaluation process was voluntary and completion of the questionnaire was deemed implied consent to participate. Students were asked to complete the questionnaire immediately before and two weeks after the program.

The analysis showed significant knowledge increase in FAS prevention. Participants' reactions to the prevention program were favorable. The responses of the preliminary evaluation are summarized below.

Table 15.3
KNOWLEDGE AND ATTITUDE CHANGE IN FAS PREVENTION

	Pre test %	Post test %	Change %
Knowledge			
alcohol affects body, emotions, and behaviors	88.2	95.2	7.0
pregnant women drinking alcohol hurst the baby	78.2	97.2	19.0
alcohol in breast milk affects the baby after birth	53.0	81.2	28.2
FAS cause mental retardation and other disorders	66.1	89.3	23.2
Native American 7th generation concepts are clear	48.2	96.4	48.2
Attitude			
both male and female responsible for FAS prevention	83.9	89.3	5.4
FAS can be prevented	66.1	96.4	30.3
even best friends ask me to drink, I would not use it	76.8	89.3	12.5
making healthy choices is part of FAS prevention	67.0	75.0	8.0

Although both knowledge and attitudes of FAS prevention denoted a change in the positive direction, knowledge change seemed greater than that of attitudes. Overall, information provided in Phase 2 and Phase 3 was consistent with the recommendations drawn from Phase 1, indicating generalizability of the findings.

DISCUSSION

Prevention specialists representing various disciplines and work environments appear to converge on some principles and approaches to counter trends among young adolescents to engage in high-risk activities, particularly those that lead to addiction or FAS. This survey revealed two important facts about current prevention efforts nationally and, particularly, in Native American communities. First, the lack of adequate and appropriate prevention resources and programs on alcohol use and its relationship to FAS for early adolescents; and second, the dearth of programs that address the needs of early adolescents at high risk of involvement in decision-making and behavior that can lead to addiction or FAS. These observations support in part, the findings of the Oklahoma State Department of Health (1996).

In a report, titled *Oklahoma Teen Pregnancy Fact Sheet*, the percentage of births to unmarried teens had climbed from 29 percent in 1975 to 63 percent in 1994. Many pregnancies occur in the age group 13–14. Because of the relationship between alcohol use among young teens and sexuality, the absence of resources and programs that target this age group has contributed largely to a higher incidence of FAS. Nearly 20 percent of pregnancies in the U.S. show alcohol exposure. Among Native Americans, exposure to alcohol is much higher. This is reflected in the high incidence of FAS–29.9/10,000 for Native Americans versus 0.9 for Whites, 0.8 for Hispanic, and 6.0 for African Americans (Chavez et al., 1989). Clearly, there is a need for more effective prevention programs aimed at the most vulnerable age groups.

The large majority of prevention specialists agree that prevention activities should be initiated as early as possible, targeting, first, the age groups in grades sixth through eighth, and continuing through high school. Content and presentation format should vary with each age group. Videotapes comprise a powerful medium of communication, while others, such as written materials, posters, T-shirts, and verbal presentations, adapted to specific age groups, should be incorporated into the overall prevention approach. The role of music, especially rap, as a facilitator in transmitting the prevention message cannot be underestimated.

CONCLUSION

Although FAS is a devastating life-time disability, it is the most preventable of all disabilities. At the core of its prevention is education. This three-phased project assessed needs as perceived by prevention professionals, then designed and evaluated a prevention program based on these needs, demonstrated the feasibility of establishing and implementing viable FAS prevention programs in schools that serve Native American adolescents, particularly those at highest risk of engaging in behaviors that result in FAS pregnancies. The age group comprising sixth through eighth graders was deemed to be the target group where the prevention effort can lead to higher success than other groups.

The products of this project, namely, good quality and culturally relevant prevention curricula and tools, aimed at imparting knowledge and changing attitudes, do not guarantee health behavior change. Timely reinforcement is essential particularly in a rapidly changing environment and a market that is clearly consumer oriented and whose media type is geared toward the younger age groups. Most importantly, prevention aimed only at females of childbearing age falls far short of ameliorating the problem, even though FAS falls in the domain of the female. Visible educational approaches cannot exclude contributing factors such as parental role modeling, youth leadership, guidance of other influential individuals and the community at large. Pregnancies that result in FAS births are products of shared actions, hence responsibilities.

REFERENCES

Abel, E.L. & Sokol, R. (1987). Fetal alcohol syndrome is now the leading cause of mental retardation. *Lancet, 2,* 1222.

Beauvais, F. & LaBoueff, S. (1985). Drug and alcohol abuse intervention in American Indian communities. *International Journal of the Addictions, 20*(1), 39–171.

Chavez, F.G., Cordero, J.F., & Becerra, J.D. (1989). Leading major congenital malformations among minority groups in the United States, 1981–1986. *Journal of the American Medical Association, 261*(2), 205–209.

Indian Health Service (1996). *1996 Trends in Indian Health.* Rockville, MD: Indian Health Service.

May, P.A., Hymbaugh, K.J., Aase, J.M. & Samet, J.M. (1983). Epidemiology of fetal alcohol syndrome among American Indians of the Southwest. *Social Biology, 30,* 374–387.

National Institute of Alcohol Abuse and Alcoholism (1994). *Alcohol Alert,* No. 23 PH 347, January.

Nockels, M. (1995). Fetal alcohol syndrome: Why drinking and pregnancy don't mix. *The Medical Reporter.* June 22, 1–4.

Oetting, E.R. & Beauvais, F. (1993). Recent research on substance abuse among American Indian youth. *Prevention Research Update #11.* Los Alamitos, CA: Southwest Regional Educational Laboratory.

Oklahoma State Department of Health. (1996). *Oklahoma Teen Pregnancy Fact Sheet.* OK: Child Guidance Services.

Resett, H.L., Weiner, L. & Edelin, K.C. (1983). Treatment expertise with pregnant problem drinkers. *JAMA, 248,* 2029–2033.

Steissguth, A.P., Aase, J.M., Clarren, S.L., Randels, S.P., LaDue, R.A. & Smith, D.F. (1986). Fetal alcohol syndrome in adolescents and adults. *Journal of American Medical Association, 265,* 1961–1967.

Torres, C. (1995). Another broken promise. Budget cuts and Native American health. *Perspective.* December, 1995.

U.S. Department of Health and Human Services (USDHSS). (1989). *Making Health Communication Programs Work: A Planner's Guide* (NIH Publication No. 89–1493). Washington, DC: U.S. Government Printing Office.

Windle, M. (1990). Alcohol use and abuse: Some findings from the National Adolescent Student Health Survey. *Alcohol Health & Research World, 15,* 5–10.

PART VI

CULTURALLY APPROPRIATE APPROACHES
FOR SUBSTANCE ABUSE ISSUES

Chapter 16

TIPS AND TECHNIQUES FOR SUBSTANCE ABUSE SERVICE PROVIDERS

GEORGE HENDERSON AND GRACE XUEQIN MA

This final chapter does not attempt to provide a how-to-do-it approach with clearly outlined steps to follow. Lists are presented, but they are used primarily to summarize various thoughts. Helping relationships often do not allow a rigid structure; therefore, this chapter presents a "be-it-yourself" approach because health care professionals need an attitude of *being for others* instead of doing for them. From this perspective, it is more important for the care provider to be *aware* rather than to be an expert. To be aware and to care about the worlds, values and lifestyles of clients are significant aspects of the processes staff members utilize when promoting positive intrapersonal, interpersonal and intergroup relationships. Although a considerable amount of statistics are presented in this book, it is important for the reader never to lose sight of the *individual* who has a substance abuse problem. As Jung (1957) said:

> It is not the universal and regular that characterize the individual, but rather the unique. He is not to be understood as a recurrent unit but as something unique and singular. . . . At the same time, man, as member of a species, can and must be described as a statistical unit; otherwise nothing general could be said about him. . . . This results in a universally valid anthropology or psychology . . . with an abstract picture of man as an average unit from which all individual features have been removed. But it is precisely these features which are of paramount importance for understanding man. . . . The individual, however, as an irrational datum, is the true and authentic carrier of reality, the concrete man as opposed to the unreal ideal or normal man to whom the scientific statements refer. (pp. 16–20)

Scattered throughout the text are explicit and implicit statements about the roles of professionals in health care. Some of the skills involved are listening, being empathetic, recognizing the client's as well as one's own self-interest and needs, being flexible, having a sense of correct timing, utilizing the client's resources, and giving relevant information.

A DELICATE BALANCE

Substance abuse is a social, mental and physiological condition. Much of the job of health care providers is to assist or accompany clients as they deal with discrimination, rejection, and low social status. Sometimes these problems are overt, but most often they are covert. Specific goals of such helping include:

1. Reaffirming to clients the fact that they are people first and people with addictions second.
2. Assisting clients to understand the physiological facts and also the social issues involved in their substance abuse.
3. Encouraging clients to deal with their own feelings that center on being substance abusers.
4. Aiding clients to emotionally and intellectually accept their addiction emotionally and intellectually without devaluing themselves.

Clients who abuse substances are people, not things to be manipulated. Sometimes they are fragile people–frightened, confused and defensive. And they are always "abusive" people. Care providers should not be impatient with or insensitive to their clients' hurts, fears and hostility. Throughout this book we allude to empathy, congruence and unconditional positive regard. Like teachers, health care providers should be guides, not gods. Most helpers acknowledge their own humanity, but too often they forget that individuals who abuse substances are, as Menninger (1942) pointed out, people: "The world is made up of people, but the people of the world forget this. It is hard to believe that, like ourselves, other people are born of women, reared by parents, teased by brothers, . . . consoled by wives, . . . flattered by grandchildren, and buried by parsons and priests with the blessings of the church and the tears of those left behind" (p. 114).

The words inscribed on a plaque hanging in the office of a professional helper are instructive: "I feel so much better, less helpless and guilty since I found out I was not chosen to be God." All humans fail from time to time. This is not the worst that can happen to care providers, if they admit their failures and, where appropriate, refer clients they cannot help to someone who can. Throughout this process, neither the identity of the helper nor that of the client must be destroyed.

To incorporate another person is to swallow him up, to overwhelm him; and thus to treat him ultimately as less than a whole person. To identify with another person is to lose oneself, to submerge one's own identity in that of the other, to be overwhelmed, and hence to treat oneself ultimately as less than a whole person. To pass judgement . . . is to place oneself in an attitude of superiority; to agree offhandandly is to place oneself in an attitude of inferiority. . . . The personality can cease to exist in two ways–either by destroying the other, or being absorbed by the other–and maturity in interpersonal relationships demands that neither oneself nor the other shall disappear, but that each shall contribute to the affirmation and realization of the other's personality. (Storr, 1961, pp. 41, 43)

It is of crucial importance that practitioners involved in helping substance abusers avoid labeling, stereotyping and rationalizing away the unique persons who defy reduction and simplification. Behavioral sciences theories certainly have their place and are presented throughout this book as invaluable heuristic tools for helpers to use. Even so, health care providers must be willing to discard these theoretical devices when they do not fit the situation or when they cease to provide understanding of individuals or groups of substance abusers. Harding (1965) was correct: "We cannot change anyone else; we can change only ourselves, and then usually only when the elements that are in need of reform have become conscious through their reflection in someone else" (p. 75).

As a rule, health care providers must be in touch with and have grasp of what is going on within their own selves before they can help their clients to make appropriate choices. Whether they are involved in a helping relationship as professionals, paraprofessionals or friends and confidants, it is inevitable that at some point in the relationship the problem of making choices will arise. Helping relationships in which choosing to cease from using addictive substances is continually delayed or postponed by the client and avoided by the "helper" should be seriously questioned.

There is a delicate balance between helping and doing. Clients who abuse substances must be allowed to do all that they can for themselves with the assistance of care providers. The work of the professional or paraprofessional includes helping clients to fill a need, receive a service, and otherwise solve or resolve substance-related problems. The core material of the helping relationship is interaction of the basic attitudes and emotions of both the care providers and their clients. All clients need to be treated as individuals, to be allowed to express their feelings, to receive empathetic responses, to be allowed to make choices and decisions, and, within the legal parameters of confidentiality, to have their secrets kept.

In order to help their clients, health care personnel must be willing to learn from them, to discover not only their weaknesses but also their strengths. First, they must learn what a client knows and would like to know. Second, they must be astute observers of role behaviors. This means analyzing the actions and reactions between people; sorting out their attitudes, values and beliefs; and understanding the emotions underlying human behaviors. Roles are never static, not even the role of "drug addict." Thus, most health care providers walk a thin line, which they fall off from time to time. They must care about their clients, but not too much or they will lose their objectivity. The task is formidable: Clients must be given the best chance of social adjustment and the least chance of disillusionment. This, of course, is the perennial problem of humanely managing emotions and realistically maximizing clients' abilities to cease being dependent on drugs. Clearly, considerable human relations skills are needed to perform these delicate tasks. In this imperfect world, substance users and abusers expect much from the individuals to whom they entrust their aspirations and lives.

CONTEXTS OF HELPING

It is of utmost importance to know what the client is feeling. Physicians usually can relieve the physiological symptoms of substance abuse, but other health care providers are needed to relieve the psychological pain. Family members and friends can sometimes help in this process. Succinctly, effective helping occurs within the contexts of environment, culture, social roles and power.

Environment. It is necessary only to look around in order to see how the physical environment affects the quality of the helper-helpee interaction, considering the differences between inner-city slums and affluent suburbs, mountains and seashores, chemically polluted and nonpolluted communities. Environments are equivalent to nonverbal statements about health care: They cause clients and their helpers to feel fearful or relaxed, cheerful or sad, open or closed.

Culture. Culture preference is a major problem in most helper-helpee interactions. Members of different cultures live in different worlds. Inability to understand and communicate with culturally different persons renders would-be helpers therapeutically impotent. It is culture, more than substance abuse, that stands between care providers and clients.

Social Roles. Shakespeare said it quite well in *As you Like It:* "All the world's a stage. And all men and women merely players. They have their exits and their entrances, and one man in his time plays many parts." Some practitioners forget that "professional" is a role and not themselves. Conversely, "substance abuser" is a role and not the essence of the individuals so labeled. Inflexible role players are unable to change when solutions require role adaptation.

Power. It is clear that most care providers have a degree of power over their clients. Practitioners who are authoritarian and dominating tend to be less helpful than their colleagues who are democratic and encourage client initiatives. Part of the helpers' dilemma is that they must be sufficiently detached from clients to exercise sound judgment and at the same time have enough concern to provide sensitive, empathetic care. It is possible for professional helpers to suppress on a conscious level emotional responses while counseling and assisting clients, but this detachment does not remove the stress and concern hidden in the unconscious domain of their minds. The pathological process of detachment that tends to produce mature helpers also tends to produce cynical clinicians.

THE FIRST STEPS

The first step in establishing rapport with clients is to help them relax. To do so, care providers must be relaxed. If they are worried about being physically or verbally attacked, they will not relax. Generally, clients are also anxious about their initial contact with health care professionals. For most low-income clients the presence of professionals produces feelings of great discomfort. Even their decision to withdraw involves anxiety. During these stressful periods, health plans or conversations related to them may only serve to panic clients. Staff members must learn to slow the pace and talk about less-threatening subjects. A few minutes of informal conversation can often reduce stress.

Some culturally different clients approach care providers in ways that are outright defensive. Most individuals using defense mechanisms usually do not have faculty personalities. Instead, it is their use and abuse of substances that are faculty. Protection of the ego is normal, and disproportionate use of defenses indicates a lack of security. Rationalizations, reaction formation, regression and other defense behaviors are ways most clients try to maintain their psychological balance. Clients who imagine that they are objects of a care provider's rejection develop rigid, persistent and chronic ego-protection devices. Continued feelings of rejection will result in behaviors inappropriate to reality. An example is the Asian American client who imagined that all of the White staff members disliked him. To protect himself, he withdrew from voluntary contact with them. One concerned outreach worker asked him "Why do you avoid me?" He answered "Because you don't like me. You smile at all the White [clients] but you never smile at me." Issues that center on race or ethnic identity frequently cause clients and professional helpers to overreact.

Staff members are frequently disappointed when their clients respond to their efforts by being unfriendly. Sometimes these helpers vindictively conclude that their clients are inferior people; they even see faults that do not exist. There is a bit of irony in situations where historically rejected clients (low-income ethnic minorities) reject their rejectors (middle-income White staff members). Unfortunately, few White staff members appreciate this irony. It is understandable and regrettable that staff members who have not been adequately prepared to work with culturally different people develop negative attitudes toward such persons. Fortunately, practitioners who fear ethnic minorities usually seek employment in predominantly White suburban communities that have grossly exaggerated "few problems."

Some health care providers see the helping process as one in which they make intricate diagnosis of clients and then use a wide variety of helping methods and techniques on them. Still other professionals define clients as being sick and themselves as being well. These are not really helping relationships. On the contrary, they are controlling relationships. When clients become objects rather than subjects, they are no longer the persons who act but instead becomes the persons acted on.

Helping clients who abuse substances to tell what they feel requires more than a receptive listener, and it is more than collecting predetermined data. Care providers who believe that the predetermined interview schedule is the only effective method of eliciting pertinent information about clients should learn from the experiences of social workers. Perlman (1957) wrote:

> It has long said in casework, reiterated against the sometime practice of subjecting the client to a barrage of ready-made questions, that the client "should be allowed to tell his story in his own way." Particularly at the beginning this is true, because the client may feel an urgency to do just that, to pour out what *he* sees and thinks and feels because it is his problem and because he has lived with it and mulled it within himself for days or perhaps months. Moreover, it is "his own way" that gives both caseworker and client not just the objective facts of the problem, but the grasp of its significance. To the client who is ready and able to "give out" with what troubles him, the caseworker's nods and murmurs of understanding—any of those nonverbal ways by which we indicate response—may be all the client needs in his first experience of telling and being heard out. (p. 142)

Not all clients can easily talk about their substance abusive behaviors. Practitioner comments such as "I imagine that this is not easy for you to talk about" and "Go on, I'm listening" may be enough encouragement for some reticent clients. Others will need direct questions to help them focus their conversation. Accurate information is not the result of passive listening; it is the by-product of interpretive talking and active listening. Effective listening is demanding; most people have to work hard at listening to hear what others are trying to say. And it is especially difficult for some care providers to listen to clients' lies, excuses and hostility.

Few people know exactly how they feel about their substance abuse until they have communicated sufficient data to another person. To tell someone what and how they feel is in itself a relief for many clients, but telling is not enough. Problem resolution must follow if the helping relationship is to be complete. This is likely to occur when the client's questions pertaining to his or her problems are amply discussed. The words of Tournier (1957) sum up the process of helping clients who abuse substances to communicate: "Through information I can understand a case, only through communication shall I be able to understand a person" (p. 25).

The dynamics of problem solving are threefold. First, the facts that surround the substance abuse and dependency must be understood. Facts frequently consist of objective reality and subjective reactions to it. Second, the facts must be thought through. They must be probed into, reorganized, and turned over in order for the client to grasp as much of the total configuration as possible. Third, a plan must be devised that will result in some type of adjustment.

Fact-finding is more complex than many authors suggest. Seldom are professional helpers taught to elicit information from people of color—how to talk to them, how to listen to them, and how to provide them helpful feedback. However, this does not mean that there are only a few professionals who can communicate effectively with ethnic minority substance abusers. There are many who do so, but most of them are self-taught. Something as important as effectively communicating with anyone who uses and abuses substances should not be left to intuition or chance. It should be a part of all health-related college curricula and in-service agency training programs.

Numerous studies have concluded that a large number of persons who use and abuse substances receive insufficient information about their health conditions. For example, many ethnic minorities terminate agency relationships without ever having understood what their care providers decided were their needs, why certain procedures were followed, what, if anything, their failures consisted of and what the reasons for them were. The rights of clients include the right to courteous, prompt and the best treatment. They also include the right to know what is wrong, why it is wrong, and what can be done about it. A case could be built that this ignorance is a by-product of the helping mystique. That is, professional and lay helpers typically are perceived as being men and women whose training and predilections place them in a special service category. To put it even more bluntly, there is a tendency for clients to be in awe of agency personnel who try to help them. This intangible dimension of the helping process is merely one reason for helper-client communication failures. Attention must be given to other reasons for communication breakdowns.

Some clients make no effort to communicate accurate information about their situation. In other instances, agency personnel fail to request needed information, particularly that which would give them basic understanding of the substance abusers' cultural normals. Thus, communication is a two-way process in which, both health care providers and their clients distort messages. And some participants forget or misinterpret information that has been clearly communicated to them. Furthermore, affirming the hypothesis that people who understand their substance abusive behaviors adjust more quickly than those who do not is sparse. From this narrow perspective one could conclude that clients' understanding of their substance abusive behaviors is unimportant. However, if a central agency goal is to educate or inform clients, then it is important for clients to understand what is happening to them. In the end, the quality of the information health care providers are able to give clients is directly proportional to the quality of information they solicit from them. Additional ways to facilitate the communication process include the following tips:

1. Respect the family. In most instances, the family can be a valuable resource. Many of the decisions made by substance abusers are family matters because one way or another most family members are impacted by the behavior of the substance abuser.
2. Try to understand the client's customs.
3. Analyze your feelings about various kinds of substance users and abusers.
4. Avoid patronizing or condescending approaches to clients.
5. When giving information, do not merely ask if clients understand what you have said. Ask them to tell you what they think you have said.

The presence of clients from multicultural and multiethnic backgrounds is a source of potential problems. And these problems often center on language and cultural differences. Much of this communication disconnect grows out of *ethnocentrism*, the belief that one's own ethnic group is superior to others. When health care providers act out their ethnocentrism on the job, their clients who are negatively affected

CROSS-CULTURAL HELPING

Tradition-oriented people of color who seek health care outside their own ethnic groups usually do so because neither they nor their family members or friends can help them. Ideally, health care providers will offer assistance that will minimize cultural conflicts. In general, care providers who are different from their patients or clients in terms of culture have more difficulty initially giving empathy, congruence, respect and acceptance. To be more specific, practitioners who understand the social and psychological backgrounds of their clients are better able to help them than their colleagues who lack this knowledge. Indeed, caring and congruency exhibited by White outreach workers, for example, obviates the hostile feelings of their ethnic minority clients. The act of giving care to another human being is a rare opportunity to cross cultural divides.

Contrary to popular notion, little empirical evidence supports the assumption that race or ethnic group *per se* is related to the level of understanding between health care providers and their ethnic minority clients. Generalizations about race and cross-cultural helping should be made with great care. At best, the literature on the subject is inconclusive. Several studies suggest that cultural barriers make the development of successful cross-cultural helping highly improbable. Other studies conclude that well-trained, empathetic staff members can establish effective relationships with clients from other racial or ethnic backgrounds. It is this latter perspective that we advocate.

Health care providers who do not know the various social class dimensions of ethnic minorities also are unlikely to know that despite common language, color and historical backgrounds, all members of a particular minority group are not alike. It is presumptuous and counterproductive to talk about *the* Blacks or *the* Indians or *the* Latinos as if members of these or other groups have only one set of behavior characteristics. This book has focused on ethnic group characteristics, but the reader is reminded that social class differences often are more determinant of clients' behaviors than their ethnic group background. That is why middle-class clients moreso than lower-class clients readily adjust to health care agencies routines.

Careful thought should be given to care providers who ostensibly have everything in their favor when working with clients from their own ethnic group. Several factors frequently mitigate against them being effective. First and most important, most college-trained minority group practitioners are Anglo-Saxon in terms of their professional behaviors and personal values. They are, in short, carbon copies of their White colleagues. Of course, many minority group care providers are able to maintain their ethnic identities with a minimum loss in credibility in the eyes of their White colleagues and minority clients. However, some minority helpers appear condescending to their minority clients, who describe them as being "snobby" or "snooty."

In other instances, ethnic minority staff members feel quite marginal–estranged from their White colleagues and no longer comfortable with members of their own ethnic group. These individuals appear cold and detached to both minority and majority clients. Another problem is the possibility that clients of color will displace to minority group staff members their hostility for White persons.

A related issue seldom explored in depth is the lack of empathy and sensitivity some care providers have for clients other than those of their own ethnic group. Native American staff members, for example, sometimes display hostility towards African Americans, and Mexican Americans reject Chinese Americans.

White health care agency personnel, who constitute the overwhelming majority of professional helpers, are beginning to come to grips with their own bigotry and that of their colleagues. Ideally, such introspection will lead to an honest appraisal of their hostile feelings and, ultimately, reconciliation with persons from other ethnic groups. *Proactive helpers* rather than reactive ones are needed if the vicious circle of bigotry is to be broken.

Although the preceding chapters addressed specific issues, it seems appropriate here to reiterate that it is important for care providers to remember that bilingualism and biculturalism present a special kind of challenge. For example, Spanish-speaking Americans are the largest number of bilingual-bicultural patients in American hospitals and clinics, and "language, culture and ethnicity play the most important role in the formation of the self-concept, and in the development of cognitive coping skills. The three concepts are analytically different, yet they are interrelated" (Stomayer, 1997, p. 195). Also important is the fact that most bilingual-bicultural substance abusers have not assimilated into the American melting pot because they prefer not to assimilate.

Notwithstanding cultural differences, the helping relationship has qualities that are the same whether it is between social worker and client, outreach worker and community resident or teacher and student. The psychological equilibrium that underlies occupational roles reside at a much deeper, more fundamental level than a list of behaviors learned in cultural diversity seminars. Effective help at an emotional level is initiated not so much by techniques or special knowledge of different cultures but rather by the positive attitude of the helper. It is also important to note that experienced helpers without college degrees may have a better conception of what constitutes a helping relationship than their colleagues who have mastered the theoretical concepts but have few practical experiences applying them.

While written for professionals who provide counseling/therapy for females, the principles adopted in 1979 by the American Psychological Association's Division of Counseling Psychology are relevant to all care providers who work with ethnic minorities who use and abuse substances. We have paraphrased the principles for practitioners whose clients are ethnic minority substance abusers:

    1. Care providers must be knowledgeable about ethnic minorities and factors that influence their substance use and abuse, particularly those

that pertain to historical, psychological and social issues.

2. Care providers must be aware that certain assumptions and precepts of theories relevant to their practice may apply differently to ethnic minorities. Specifically, professional helpers must be aware of the theories that limit or curtail rehabilitation of ethnic minorities who abuse substances.

3. After formal training, care providers must continue throughout their professional careers to explore and learn of issues related to ethnic minorities.

4. Care providers must recognize and be aware of various forms of oppression and how these interact with racism and substance use and abuse.

5. Care providers must be knowledgeable and aware of verbal and non-verbal process variables (particularly with regard to power in the helping relationship) as these affect ethnic minorities who are substance abusers, so that the helper-client interactions are not adversely affected. The need for shared responsibility between clients and care providers must be acknowledged and implemented.

6. Care providers must be capable of utilizing skills that are facilitative to ethnic minorities in general who use substances and ethnic minorities in particular who abuse them.

7. Care providers must ascribe to no preconceived limitations on the direction or nature of the life goals of ethnic minorities who use and abuse substances.

8. Care providers must be sensitive to circumstances in which it may be more desirable for an ethnic minority client to be seen by a staff member who is an ethnic minority or a person who has had experiences with substances he or she is abusing.

9. Care providers must use nonracist and nondemeaning language in substance abuse counseling/therapy, supervision, teaching and publications.

10. Care providers must not engage in sexual activity with their clients.

11. Care providers must be aware of and continually review their own values and biases and the effect of these on their clients.

12. Care providers must be aware of how their personal functioning may influence their effectiveness in working with ethnic minorities and persons who use and abuse substances. They must monitor their functioning through consultation, supervision or therapy so that it does not adversely affect their work.

13. Care providers must support the elimination of racism within their agency and among their colleagues.

Professional helpers must go beyond giving lip service to valuing cultural differences. They must take an active stance in protecting those differences. Advocacy is a proactive process of empathy and listening rather than telling. It also involves supporting the positive goals identified by clients and knowing when to collaborate with other care providers. In the end, ethnic similarities are not adequate substitutes for people who are (1) linguistically compatible with ethnic patients, (2) empathetic and (3) well trained. This means that the initial edge minority practitioners may have with minority clients will be lost if they cannot get beyond ethnic history and identity. These considerations should not, however, be interpreted as sastisfying the need for college programs and community agencies to recruit and train considerably more ethnic minority personnel.

UTILIZATION OF AVAILABLE RESOURCES

A major problem in getting services to people who abuse substances is an agency's geographical location and resources utilization patterns. There are too few agencies or associations or foundations charged with the responsibility of sponsoring research about substance abuse and fostering services for substance abusers. In addition, there are too few substance abuse-oriented organizations that offer interrelated or complementary services. It is this small maze of organizations through which people who abuse substances or their advocates have to go for treatment. Further, there are several substance abuse prevention organizations with similar names but dissimilar services and that adds to the consumers' confusion.

Another major problem many substance abusers have is not knowing what community resources are available. It may seem strange that most substance abusers are not familiar with the services pertaining to them. It must be remembered that, historically, they have been *told* where to go rather than being encouraged to make this decision for themselves. Fortunately, substance abuse prevention agencies as a generalizable group no longer are subscribing to the idea that "If a client needs a service someone will tell them where to get it." A growing number of service providers are helping clients to become much more astute at seeking and receiving information. And a growing number of private care providers are aware that the federal government and most states have information and services that their clients must be aware of.

Any community substance abuse program undertaken to improve opportunities for ethnic minorities and reduce their substance abuse must reward socially acceptable behaviors. Also, based on individual needs, there must be a wide variety of programs. For example, personality disturbances can be ameliorated in agencies that provide individual treatment; family conflicts are best handled with marriage and family therapists; educational deficiencies are problems for schools to abate. Each agency is part of a gestalt in which the whole is greater than the individual parts. Therefore, it is important for substance abusers to see and understand the total number of community resources available to help them. Finally, the more effective programs are those in which the people served are actors and not merely objects acted upon.

Programs designed primarily for the institutionalization and containment of persons with substance abuse problems are inferior to those which have carefully designed individual growth activities and continuous counseling. Any agency or program that is capable of helping clients to succeed or fail on their own abilities is vastly superior to those in which they must passively await the capricious or paternalistic and materialistic decisions of their care providers. The following minimum activities are basic to the curtailment of substance abuse:

1. Existing effective substance abuse-oriented agencies should be expanded, and new opportunities for substance abusers should be created. This may require adjusting agency programs to meet new needs.
2. Basic health orientations should be provided community-wide to prepare and to familiarize potential clients with existing opportunities and to prepare them for future ones.
3. Counseling programs should be expanded to raise the educational and occupational aspirations of substance abusers whose addictions evolve around school and job failures.
4. Provisions for rewarding approved client behaviors should be built into agency services. Such rewards could include verbal praise, more difficult rehabilitation tasks, certificates, vouchers, and timely terminations.
5. Periodic surveys should be made in order to evaluate the effectiveness of existing services and point out gaps in total services. It is imperative that stratified samplings of the substance abuse population be used in such surveys.

Cohesive agency staff members are the primary source of security for clients. Because staff members serve as the foremost determiners of their clients' self-esteem during drug rehabilitation, feelings of worth depend on the clients' self-perceived social status within an agency. It should not be surprising that clients who believe they are members of low-status or underprivileged groups tend toward feelings of self-hatred and worthlessness. Ohlsen (1970) listed several characteristics of an effective agency. The most important characteristic is that the staff members cooperate to achieve common goals. This means that they:

1. Know why the agency exists.
2. Have created an atmosphere in which their work can be done.

3. Have developed guidelines for making decisions.
4. Have established conditions under which each staff member can make his or her unique contributions.
5. Have two-way communication among its members.
6. Have helped each other to learn how to give and receive help.
7. Have learned to cope with conflict.
8. Have learned to analyze their organization functioning processes and improve them.
9. Provide a safe place in which to periodically express their ideas and receive honest reactions from others.

Because sensitivity to their own feelings is a prerequisite to effective helping, it may be beneficial for substance abuse agency personnel to undergo some type of multicultural sensitivity training. Numerous studies provide extensive evidence for the idea that care providers trained in such programs are more successful than those who are not trained. If the research studies reviewed in the earlier chapters of this book are correct in their assertion that helping can be accomplished only on the terms of the healthier person in the relationship, it becomes necessary to have some criteria for determining who is best able to assist culturally different clients. Health care providers who have not "gotten themselves together" in terms of race or ethnic relations are not able to optimally assist minority group clients. Many researchers and practitioners have stressed the importance of the interpersonal relations between care providers and their clients. The development of clients' health adjustment may be facilitated or retarded because of the care provider's own state of health. Also, care providers must sincerely accept their clients.

Lowell wrote, "Sincerity is impossible unless it pervades the whole character." To be genuine in a helping relationship requires care providers to be aware of their own inner feelings. If these inner feelings are consistent with the expressed behaviors, it can be said that the care providers are genuine and congruent. It is this quality of realness and honesty that allows staff members to keep a steady focus on reality. To some neophyte staff member it may seem that self reality is too brutal for them. Granted, the truth is not always painless; as an old saying goes, "The truth shall make ye free, but first it shall make ye miserable." It is also important to note that being open and honest is not a license to be brutal. A helpful, as opposed to a destructive, self analysis is very much like the difference between a fatal dose and a therapeutic dose of a pain killer; it is only a matter of degree. In the process of attempting to be transparently real, it is wise for staff members to evaluate their failures, their reasons for being less than honest. To protect themselves from the truth about their own health is to make a very serous judgment. It is to say that they are incapable of facing their relationship problems.

In the next section, Shae (2001), a teacher in an alternative school in

Oklahoma, described how she uses concepts found in Bolman and Deal's book, *Leading with the Soul*, to foster classroom success and thereby minimize the substance abuse risk for her students–children and their parents. There is much relevance in her approach for practitioners who work exclusively with substance abusers.

TEACHING WITH SOUL

When I finished reading *Leading with the Soul*, I was trying to pick a leadership gift that I used in the classroom. The more I thought about it, the more I realized that after 18 years of teaching, I am using all four gifts. First, I needed to make sure I understood what the gifts were, decide my own connection with them, and then understand how I apply them.

I understand that the search for the spirit or the soul is not merely a journey to finding emotional balance. It is a search for meaning. More than attitude, it is a way of life and a matter of perception. This allows me to create a positive interpersonal connection with other people. When I have this connection, my life is enriched. How could it not be? By using the four gifts of leadership, I give my students and others I meet a living example of love, caring, compassion and understanding. I allow my friends and family members to grow with me and around me, not under me.

To discover how these four gifts are used in my classroom, I gave my program an autopsy. When I looked at the structure of a class, the first gift I saw was *authorship*. I saw it in the area of academics. This occurs when my students talk and look at sequential tasks and skills. The children learn through assessments what skills they have. As they work through these skills, it is very important for me to give credit when it is due: positive reinforcement for positive accomplishments is important. When teachers take notice of their students' progress and improvement, it gives them pride in what they have accomplished. Authorship/acknowledgement is a good beginning for improving one's self-esteem. Often these children have had great difficulty with learning because of emotional and behavioral difficulties. By using the gift of authorship, I create a relationship that allows for a second gift: *love.*

Love is an emotion that some of my children freely give and receive. These children and their parents show empathy and compassion for other children and their difficulties. There are some children however who don't fall onto this category. They are critical of themselves and of others. They show little or no compassion or understanding for anyone. This is especially true for some of the parents I teach. Their world appears to be narrow and shallow. To show love towards these children and their parents can be difficult. There is often a wall of mistrust and deep feelings of anger. Whether children or parents, their feelings seldom have anything to do with me or the position I hold within the school district. The mistrust and anger are usually issues left unresolved from their past. One of the first ways I show the parents love is to listen to their stories and refrain from passing judgment. After listening, we share experiences. We talk about problems with our children, our jobs, and our personal lives. We talk about how certain situations are difficult, how we have choices to make, and how those choices affect us. I let them know that I am not perfect, and with humor I remind them—and me—that kids do not come with instructions.

We also discuss what is important to them. Sometimes it's academic success and grades. Other times they want their children to focus on social skills and anger management. To make the relationship work, I must ask questions and listen to their answers. I do not want to attempt a guess. When I first started teaching, I tried to place my personal issues on them. Quickly, I learned this wouldn't work. In problem-solving with parents and children there must be give and take and, more often than not, compromises. If I follow this game plan—asking questions and seeking answers, listening without judgment—this interpersonal working relationship can be very positive. Approximately 50 percent of my parents and students are with me for three years or more. You can imagine how close we become. After we have spent all of this time together, lived through trials and errors, shared hugs and tears, the love that started the relationship is truly reciprocal.

By offering love and compassion and finding that it is accepted, trust comes into play. With trust comes the third leadership gift: of *power*. During group discussions, my students have the opportunity to talk about many topics, ranging from social interactions, drugs, anger management and personal safety. We discuss feelings—how to handle them and how to protect ourselves from others. These topics are necessary because often my students feel threatened and confused. They misread their environment and are reactive rather than proactive. Through these discussions, I offer them empowerment: the power to make their choices and understand what consequences, good or bad, may transpire.

When they learn to trust their environment (the classroom), my students seem to feel secure in making their own choices. They will continue to make mistakes and their emotions will be ongoing battles. But through my love and trust, they soon realize they actually have power and control. There is a flip side to this, however. I must also teach them to know what issues and in what areas they do not have power and control. I tell the children that they can't change a parent's divorce or a parent's absence in their lives; and brothers and sisters might continue to pick on and tease them. They learn that they are only responsible for their own actions. The way they respond to the academics and the affective groups provides a basis for the last gift: *significance.*

In our daily discussions of group goals, we discuss joys and concerns. We give significance to the choices they make in their daily lives. This includes choices made in school, home and the community. We accept progress and failure. Together, we celebrate each other's successes and acknowledge our failures. They may clap and cheer when a classmate accomplishes a difficult task, such as an academic skill mastered, a positive interaction with a peer or conflict resolved with another person. There are many significant moments in their lives. It may be the first time or the tenth time an accomplishment is made. When others notice their progress or give compassion for a failure, it provides significance to their lives.

Authorship, power and significance in my classroom are enhanced through a behavior reinforcement program. My students choose a weekly goal and decide in their group how they are going to accomplish it. They set up a plan of action and discuss possible outcomes. They empower each other to make these decisions and feel independent and responsible for solving their own problems. Their goals may be academic or behavioral. Either way, a wonderful growth process takes place.

It doesn't matter which gift of leadership I offer first to the children. Sometimes they are ready to accept it and sometimes they are not, similar to the way Steve and Maria acted when discussing love. Steve made a comment about Maria giving him love since the first time they meet. When he made the comment she was not ready to accept it, they referred to it as "a matter of timing." I try to acknowledge when I have offered a leadership gift to a child or a parent and it's either the wrong gift or poor timing. In those instances, I get a look of confusion and they either walk away or become verbal about something else. I try to go with the flow. That is, if they are not ready for a particular discussion or topic, I let it go and try again another day.

If I am intuitive, the children and adults I work with will tell me where I need to start with them and what I need to do. Sometimes I start with authorship, other times I start with love and understanding. Each individual has his or her own personal needs. Their lives, perceptions and cognitive abilities are key factors to where I start. Other variables include neurological or biochemical problems. Each child and parent enters the classroom on his or her own terms, regardless of their personal history, psychological or physiological difficulties.

As for choosing one of these gifts as my foremost strength, I would have to say it is love. Whether it's from my personality, my heart or my religious faith, I do strongly believe in unconditional love. The friendship and compassion we share with each other is endless. Just because this may be my strength doesn't mean it is easy for me to do. Teaching and sharing these gifts can be difficult. I continue to try to do the right things. In my day-to-day interactions with children and adults, I try to make a significant impact. I can give them emotional gifts for their journey or I can give them grief. I prefer to give them gifts.

EPILOGUE

Four subtle attitudinal characteristics are necessary for optimum health provider-client interactions to occur: (1) Practitioners must manifest *empathetic understanding* of their clients; (2) Practitioners must manifest *unconditional positive regard* toward their clients; (3) Practitioners must be *genuine* or *congruent*; that is, their words match their feelings; and (4) the practitioner's responses must match the clients' statements in intensity of affective expression. Of course, these four conditions must be communicated to clients. In an effort to conceptualize this process, Rogers (1961) formulated what he called a "process equation" of a successful helping relationship: genuineness plus empathy plus unconditional positive regard for the client equals successful interaction $(G + E + UPR = Success)$.

It is a staff member's basic beliefs and values rather than his or her grand schemes, methods or techniques that are the real determiners of a client's agency adjustment. Specifically related to helping ethnic minorities, the major task of the staff is to provide experiences in which realistic choices are possible. Ideally, through positive interactions the fears and anxieties that restrain clients from being honest can to some extent be resolved, and they can make a commitment to a healthy course of action and learn how to make their decision a reality. Of course, there will be instances when clients do not achieve their goals, i.e., when the goals are too difficult, when clients lack the motivation to change or when they are conditioned to fail. If skillfully handled, however, ideally these instances are not perceived by the clients as permanent failures. Rather, they are identified as situations in which they have to learn how to cope with barriers to specific rehabilitation goals.

It is important to note that ethnic minority clients may need more (or a different kind of) attention than White clients. That be an overgeneralization, since each client should be looked at individually in order to determine his or her needs. Even so, it is imperative that health care providers be cognizant of barriers created by ethnic or social class differences. If Hispanic clients are hesitant to trust non-Hispanic staff members, for example, it may be because they do not trust members of that particular ethnic group, or it may be because the staff members' nonverbal messages to them are "stay away." If done tactfully, care providers can get these issues out in the open with a minimum of defensiveness. It may be that the clients are not aware of their own nontrusting behaviors, or the staff members may actually be projecting their own nontrusting attitude onto the clients. That is why it is best to acquire and keep these feelings, perceptions and thoughts out in the open so that trust can be built. This does not mean that the care provider-client relationship will there after always nice and sweet.

Most nonwhite clients' problems are rooted in their social environments. Certainly family therapy is an alternative. Another alternative is social action designed to change health care organizations. One of the reasons why many care providers are continually frustrated is because the problems they are called on to solve are themselves the products of other institutional or community organizations. If staff members really want to be helpful, some of them will have to be active in community change. The most significant changes they can make, however, involve their own attitudes and behaviors.

A client's rehabilitation frequently depends not on his or her adjustment to a particular health care facility but instead on being placed in another one. This kind of environmental change is not without a theoretical foundation; it is modeled after milieu therapy, preventative and community or social psychiatry. We can take as our illustration the model of milieu therapy, in which the hospital environment serves as a therapeutic instrument, and patterns of human relationships are consciously attuned to the treatment or developmental needs of the residents. When this model is applied to people of colors, it becomes clear that more often than not (because community health resources are not attuned to their needs), they do not get the institutional treatment they need. There are at least seven steps agency staffs can and must take if all clients are to be aided and allowed to become fully functioning persons:

1. Regard each client as a vital part of the health care process.
2. View all clients positively, because whatever diminishes a client's self–humiliation, degradation, or failure–has no place in substance abuse agencies.
3. Provide for cultural and individual differences.
4. Apply the criterion of self-determination to every health care experience.
5. Learn how things are seen by the clients.
6. Allow ample opportunities for clients to explore issues pertaining to their substance use and their health care environment.
7. Help clients to be independent of substances through achieving feelings of satisfaction in nonabusing ways.

One of the most important aspects of helping in health care settings is that some clients do not seem to want to be helped. At least they do not appear to want to be helped by health care providers. Many clients who ask for help are afraid that it will not be given. There are numerous ways of asking for help. For example, missing appointments may be a plea for help. Consequently, staff members must be aware of these subtle pleas and be prepared to enter into a growth-producing rather than punitive relationship with clients, even though the odds may be heavily weighted against a client being able to cease his or her substance abuse.

As noted earlier, the challenge to the health care professional is to demonstrate that competence and empathy are not traits unique to members of a particular ethnic group. For example, competent, sensitive White therapists can, when judged by their deeds, be considered as black as any of the African American clients with whom they work. Blackness is more than a condition of the skin: it is thinking and behaving in ways acceptable to Black Americans. Black clients grudgingly admit that these White staff members have "soul." Similarly, competent Black care providers have been able to demonstrate to White clients that some Black Americans have "culture."

There is an underlying assumption in the health professions that trained persons can make a significant contribution to the lives of others if their training has instilled a commitment to effectively using themselves in the helping process. The primary technique or instrument in the helping relationship is the ability of staff members to become instruments to be used by their clients to achieve health needs that must be met (at least from the clients' perception) and to achieve some measure of self-fulfillment in doing so. From the practitioners' point of view, this goal of self-fulfillment means that clients will become more realistic and not cease being substance abusers. And the drama goes on and on. Perhaps the following observations will place our book within a meaningful behavioral context:

1. Care providers cannot solve their clients' substance abuse problems, but they may be able to help them solve their own problems.
2. Every client's problem has more than one possible solution.
3. The easiest, least creative, response to cross-culture conflict is to pretend that it does not exist.
4. Every client behaves according to unwritten ethnic group customs and traditions.
5. Powerful factors in clients' decision-making include family precedents and cultural or religious norms.
6. Humor can help practitioners and clients over rough spots; they must be able to laugh at themselves and with other people.
7. Previous cross-cultural experiences are valuable assets if they used a general guide. However, if viewed as offered the correct answer to every cross-cultural problem, experience (as well as the other information in this book) will be a liability.
8. All care providers will make mistakes in cross-cultural interactions, but they should learn from their mistakes and not repeat them.

Nationally, there is a new spirit of change in substance abuse agencies. Administratively, changes are being championed by a new breed of senior administrators, those who dare to innovate, risk public ridicule, and deviate from tradition in order to solve cross-cultural drug rehabilitation problems. Status quo conformists and technocratic midgets are on the way out. Therefore, the concept of rigid structures and inept practitioners is slowly giving ground to a picture of human services personnel who have a passion for their jobs and will to do what is best for their clients.

REFERENCES

Bolman, L.G. & Deal, T.E. (2001). *Leading With Soul: An Uncommon Journey of Spirit.* San Francisco: Jossey-Bass.

Harding, M.E. (1965). *The "I" and the "Not-I."* Princeton, NJ: Princeton University Press.

Jung, C.G. (1957). *The Undisclosed Self.* New York: Mentor.

Menninger, K. (1942). *Love against hate.* New York: Harcourt, Brace & World.

Perlman, H.H. (1957). *Social Casework: A Problem-solving Process.* Chicago: University of Chicago Press.

Satomayor, M. (1977). Language, culture and ethnicity in developing self-concepts. *Social Casework, 58,* 198.

Storr, A. (1961). *The Integrity of the Personality.* New York: Atheneum.

Shave, C, (2001). Unpublished paper presented in HR5113 at the University of Oklahoma, July 19.

Tournier, P. (1957). *The Meaning of Persons.* New York: Harper & Row.

AUTHOR INDEX

SUBJECT INDEX

A

academic performance, 63

access to health care, 30, 31, 48, 193

access to tobacco, 67

accidents
  alcohol related, 256, 285
  automobile, 7, 11, 73
  inhalant use, 232

acculturation
  in Asian Americans, 145
  in Hispanic Americans, 197–199
  in Mien people, 159
  in Native Americans, 261, 270, 274

Acculturation Rating Scale for Mexican-
    Americans, 202

acculturative stress, 14

acknowledgement, 313

acquisition stage, 62

action stage, 62–63

activities to curtail drug abuse, 311

acupuncture treatment, 160

addiction. *see* drug addiction

addiction clinic, role of, 165

adjunct therapy sessions, 135

adolescents
  African American and drug use, 60–61,
      88
  African American and familial factors,
      64–66
  African American and personal factors,
      61–64
  African Americans and social factors,
      66–69
  American Indian alcohol abuse, 284,
      285
  American Indian drug use, 255–256

Columbian, 195
risk factors, 288

adult outpatient treatment, 137

advertisements, effects of, 62, 74, 196

aerosols, 228

African American Extended Family
    Program, 31–32

African Americans
  adolescents and drug use, 60–61
  adolescents and familial factors, 64–66
  adolescents and personal factors, 61–64
  adolescents and social factors, 66–69
  and alcohol use, 22, 73–74, 140
  attitudes about treatment, 130–131
  church-based interventions. *see* church-
      based interventions
  clinical setting interventions. *see* clinical
      setting interventions
  communities and churches, 90
  community-based interventions. *see* com-
      munity-based programs
  and family, 64–66, 132–133
  health problems of, 14
  misperceptions, 76–78
  population of, 5
  prescription drug use, 73–76
  prevention and cessation strategies,
      78–80
  psychotherapy for, 138–139
  self-quitting articles, 104–114
  smoking cessation articles, 91–98
  statistics of drug use, 59
  and tobacco use, 14, 74, 87–89
  treatment issues, 131–135
  treatment programs for, 31–33

agonist medications, 157

AIDS, 73, 76, 197